LIBRARY OF HEBREW BIBLE/ OLD TESTAMENT STUDIES

482

Formerly Journal for the Study of the Old Testament Supplement Series

T&T CLARK • LIBRARY OF BIBLICAL STUDIES

EZEKIEL: A COMMENTARY

Paul M. Joyce

t&t clark

NEW YORK • LONDON

For Alison, Sinéad and Olivia

11/09

T & T Clark International, 80 Maiden Lane, New York, NY 10038

T & T Clark International, The Tower Building, 11 York Road, London SE1 7NX

T & T Clark International is a Continuum imprint.

Paperback cover: Marc Chagall, *Vision d'Ezéchiel*, gravure 104, *La Bible, II*, Edition Tériade, Paris 1931-56 (détail)

Library of Congress Cataloging-in-Publication Data
Joyce, Paul (Paul M.)
Ezekiel : a commentary / Paul M. Joyce.
p. cm. -- (The library of Hebrew Bible/Old Testament studies ; 482)
Includes bibliographical references and index.
ISBN-13: 978-0-567-02685-9 (hardcover : alk. paper)
ISBN-10: 0-567-02685-X (hardcover : alk. paper)
ISBN-13: 978-0-567-48361-4 (paperback)
1. Bible. O.T. Ezekiel--Commentaries. I. Title. II. Series.

BS1545.53.J69 2008
224'.407--dc22

2007034752

06 07 08 09 10 10 9 8 7 6 5 4 3 2 1

CONTENTS

PREFACE

A word is in order about the nature of this commentary and its relation to others. There is no intention in this volume to address every critical issue in the book of Ezekiel, still less to rehearse everything of significance that has been written about each of them. These tasks are admirably handled, in their very different ways, by Zimmerli and Block. My purpose is to make a distinctive contribution to the interpretation and understanding of the book of Ezekiel, particularly in terms of its theology, grounded in both historical research and literary sensitivity. I have provided an extensive introduction so that issues may be introduced thematically. Also, I have written at proportionately greater length on many earlier chapters of the book so as to discuss on their first appearance features and motifs characteristic of the whole. The intention is to draw out the theology of the book of Ezekiel (in so far as possible) in its own terms, using the tools of textual, historical and literary criticism. This then leaves the work of constructive appropriation of the text to others, whether of Jewish, Christian or other background. Hopefully this commentary can make a contribution to that important task by way of foundations. While based on the Hebrew and the Greek, the commentary is presented with reference to the New Revised Standard Version of the Bible in English (hereafter referred to as NRSV).

All Ezekiel scholars are indebted to the two great Ezekiel commentators of our era, Zimmerli and Greenberg. Zimmerli alas I never met: he was to have been the honoured guest at the 1985 Ezekiel Colloquium in Leuven, but he died in 1983. Greenberg, however, was present at that gathering and moreover welcomed me both to his Jerusalem office and subsequently to his home on Purim, where we talked of Esther as well as Ezekiel. I had extensive contact with two very different doyens of exilic studies, now both deceased, Peter Ackroyd and Robert Carroll. I am grateful for conversations and friendships with colleagues within the "Theological Perspectives on the Book of Ezekiel" section of the Society of Biblical Literature, which I currently have the privilege of chairing.

While responsibility for any shortcomings in the present volume is mine alone, thanks are due to these and to many others, notably John Barton, who originally inspired my love of biblical studies, John Rogerson, a valued mentor for many years, and Ronald Clements, who first encouraged me to write a commentary on Ezekiel. I am indebted also to James Barr, Ernest Nicholson, Hugh Williamson, Christopher Rowland, John Day, George Brooke, John Sawyer, John Eaton, Johan Lust, Gerard Norton, David Lamb, Michael Goulder, Ida Glaser, Renée Hirschon, Christopher Jones and Charmian Beer. I am grateful to

Andrew Mein and Claudia Camp, the editors of the Library of Hebrew Bible / Old Testament Studies, to Burke Gerstenschlager and Gabriella Page-Fort of Continuum and to Duncan Burns, my indefatigable copy-editor.

As with my previous Ezekiel book, the influence of my wife Alison, both personal and intellectual, has been crucial over the years. Like that volume, this commentary is dedicated to her, joined now by our daughters Sinéad and Olivia.

Paul M. Joyce
Oxford and Birmingham
2007

Preface to Paperback Edition

I am glad of the opportunity provided by the publication of a paperback edition to update the bibliography and to correct a few typographical errors and infelicities.

PMJ, May 2009

ABBREVIATIONS

ABD	*The Anchor Bible Dictionary*. Edited by D. N. Freedman. 6 vols. New York: Doubleday, 1992
AnBib	Analecta Biblica
ANET	*Ancient Near Eastern Texts Relating to the Old Testament*. Edited by J. B. Pritchard. 3d ed. with supplement. Princeton: Princeton University Press, 1969
ASORMS	American Schools of Oriental Research Monograph Series
ASTI	*Annual of the Swedish Theological Institute*
ATANT	Abhandlungen zur Theologie des Alten und Neuen Testaments
ATD	Das Alte Testament Deutsch
AV	Authorized Version
BA	*Biblical Archaeology*
BDB	F. Brown, S. R. Driver and C. A. Briggs, *Hebrew and English Lexicon of the Old Testament*. Oxford: Clarendon, 1907
BEATAJ	Beiträge zur Erforschung des Alten Testaments und des Antiken Judentums
BETL	Bibliotheca Ephemeridum Theologicarum Lovaniensium
BhEvTh	Beihefte zur evangelischen Theologie
BHS	*Biblia Hebraica Stuttgartensia*. Edited by K. Elliger and W. Rudolph. Stuttgart: Deutsche Bibelstiftung, 1977
Bib	*Biblica*
BibInt	*Biblical Interpretation*
BibOr	Biblica et orientalia
BJRL	*Bulletin of the John Rylands Library*
BKAT	Biblischer Kommentar, Altes Testament
BN	*Biblische Notizen*
BSac	*Bibliotheca sacra*
BTB	*Biblical Theology Bulletin*
BTrans	*The Bible Translator*
BWANT	Beiträge zur Wissenschaft vom Alten und Neuen Testament
BZ	*Biblische Zeitschrift*
BZAW	Beihefte zur Zeitschrift für die alttestamentliche Wissenschaft
CBC	Cambridge Bible Commentary
CBQ	*Catholic Biblical Quarterly*
ConBOT	Coniectanea biblica: Old Testament Series
CQR	*Church Quarterly Review*
DJD	Discoveries in the Judaean Desert
Eng. Tr.	English Translation
ET	*Expository Times*
ETL	*Ephemerides Theologicae Lovanienses*
ETR	*Etudes théologiques et religieuses*

FB	Forschung zur Bibel
FOTL	The Forms of the Old Testament Literature
FRLANT	Forschungen zur Religion und Literatur des Alten und Neuen Testament
HAR	*Harvard Annual Review*
HAT	Handbuch zum Alten Testament
HCOT	Historical Commentary on the Old Testament
Heb.	Hebrew
HKAT	Handkommentar zum Alten Testament
HSM	Harvard Semitic Monographs
HSS	*Harvard Semitic Studies*
HTR	*Harvard Theological Review*
HUCA	*Hebrew Union College Annual*
IB	*The Interpreter's Bible*. Edited by G. A. Buttrick et al. 12 vols. New York: Abingdon, 1951–57
ICC	International Critical Commentary
IEJ	*Israel Exploration Journal*
JAOS	*Journal of the American Oriental Society*
JBL	*Journal of Biblical Literature*
JBQ	*Jewish Bible Quarterly*
JETS	*Journal of the Evangelical Theological Society*
JNES	*Journal of Near Eastern Studies*
JNSL	*Journal of Northwest Semitic Languages*
JSOT	*Journal for the Study of the Old Testament*
JSOTSup	Journal for the Study of the Old Testament: Supplement Series
JSPSup	Journal for the Study of the Pseudepigrapha: Supplement Series
JSS	*Journal of Semitic Studies*
JTS	*Journal of Theological Studies*
KAT	Kommentar zum Alten Testament
KeH	*Kurzgefasstes exegetisches Handbuch zum Alten Testament*
KHAT	Kurzer Hand-Commentar zum Alten Testament
LHBOTS	Library of Hebrew Bible/OldTestament Studies
MT	Masoretic Text
NAC	New American Commentary
NCB	New Century Bible
n.d.	No date
NEB	New English Bible
NGTT	*Nederduitse gereformeerde teologiese tydskrif*
NIB	New Interpreter's Bible
NICOT	New International Commentary on the Old Testament
NJPS	New Jewish Publication Society Version
NRSV	New Revised Standard Version
NS	New Series
OBO	Orbis Biblicus et Orientalis
OBT	Overtures to Biblical Theology
OTE	Old Testament Essays
OTL	Old Testament Library
OTM	Oxford Theological Monographs
OTP	*The Old Testament Pseudepigrapha*. Edited by J. H. Charlesworth. 2 vols. New York: Doubleday, 1983

OtSt	Oudtestamentische Studiën
PEQ	*Palestine Exploration Quarterly*
RB	*Revue Biblique*
RevQ	*Revue de Qumran*
RHPR	*Revue d'histoire et de philosophie religieuses*
RSV	Revised Standard Version
RTL	*Revue théologique de Louvain*
SBB	Stuttgarter biblische Beiträge
SBL	Society of Biblical Literature
SBLDS	Society of Biblical Literature Dissertation Series
SBLMS	Society of Biblical Literature Monograph Series
SBLRBS	Society of Biblical Literature Resources for Biblical Study
SBLSCS	Society of Biblical Literature Septuagint and Cognate Studies
SBT	Studies in Biblical Theology
SJOT	*Scandinavian Journal of the Old Testament*
TBT	*The Bible Today*
TRE	*Theologische Realenzyklopädie*
ThB	*Theologische Bücherei*
ThLZ	*Theologische Literaturzeitung*
ThQ	*Theologische Quartalschrift*
ThR	*Theologische Rundschau*
ThZ	*Theologische Zeitschrift*
TOTC	Tyndale Old Testament Commentaries
UBL	Ugaritisch-biblische Literatur
UCOP	University of Cambridge Oriental Publications
UF	*Ugarit-Forschungen*
VT	*Vetus Testamentum*
VTSup	Supplements to Vetus Testamentum
WBC	Word Biblical Commentary
WMANT	Wissenschaftliche Monographien zum Alten und Neuen Testament
WUNT	*Wissenschaftliche Untersuchungen zum Neuen Testament*
ZAH	*Zeitschrift für Althebraistik*
ZAW	*Zeitschrift für die alttestamentliche Wissenschaft*
ZDMG	*Zeitschrift der deutschen morgenländischen Gesellschaft*
ZThK	*Zeitschrift für Theologie und Kirche*

INTRODUCTION

Time and Place

Our own time and place as readers profoundly affect our experience of and interpretation of a biblical text, but the time and place of Ezekiel's original ministry remain vital issues. When and where something happened is often the key to why it may have happened. The Hebrew prophets addressed specific situations and those who continued to hand on their words and to supplement them were themselves conditioned by their own (inevitably rather different) contexts. These factors have long been recognized, but they have been given fresh emphasis by an increased acknowledgement of the importance of the social dimension of prophecy in ancient Israel (e.g. Wilson 1980). The ministry of the prophet Ezekiel and the tradition to which his work gave rise cannot be understood except against the background of the particular circumstances to which they were a response.

Time: The Exilic Age as the Period of Ezekiel's Ministry

The book of Ezekiel presents the prophet's ministry as being conducted from the year 593 B.C.E. onwards (Ezek 1:2). The events of the first two decades of the sixth century brought upon Judah a catastrophe of unprecedented scale. In 597 and again in 587 Judah suffered crushing defeats at the hands of the Babylonians, and a significant proportion of the population was transported a thousand miles to Mesopotamia. It might seem at first that conditions for the exiles were not as bad as might have been feared. Unlike in the deportation of inhabitants of the northern kingdom of Israel by the Assyrians in the eighth century, the Judahite exiles were not scattered but were placed in ghetto-like settlements in Babylonia, such as Tel-abib (Ezek 3:15). They seem to have enjoyed freedom of association: the elders are depicted gathering to the house of Ezekiel (8:1; 14:1; 20:1). The "letter to the exiles" in Jer 29 certainly indicates an expectation that the exiled community will enjoy the liberty to "build houses and live in them; plant gardens and eat what they produce; take wives and have sons and daughters" (Jer 29:5–6). And yet, even if conditions were in some respects tolerable, we must take with full seriousness the anguish and bitterness against Babylon reflected in Ps 137:9: "Happy shall they be who take your little ones and dash them against the rock!" Though the physical events of destruction and exile were certainly devastating, the real nub of the disaster lies in its psychological and emotional impact, the traumatic depths of which Smith-Christopher (2002) vividly presents. And it is especially the theological dimension of this trauma that is crucial for understanding the book of Ezekiel. For within just a few years

Judah was robbed of all the main elements in her theological system: land, chosen people status, city, temple and monarchy. The events of defeat and exile at the hands of the Babylonians and the theological questions that they posed are the essential key to understanding Ezekiel and his tradition.

Such a setting cannot be taken for granted, however, for not all scholars have regarded the events of the early sixth century as determinative for the book. In 1930, C. C. Torrey denied the existence of an historical Ezekiel altogether; he argued that the book is a third-century redaction of a pseudepigraphal work purporting to have been written in the reign of the seventh-century king Manasseh. A later editor moved the scene from Jerusalem to Babylonia, a setting found only in "a series of brief and easily recognized interpolations" (Torrey 1930:44). In support of such a late date of composition and editing, Torrey found references to Persia and to Alexander the Great (seen as the model for "Gog" in chs. 38–39; cf. also Browne 1952) and discerned numerous Aramaisms. Others advanced theories that were in certain respects similar (e.g. Smith 1931; Messel 1945). The work of these scholars illustrates the danger of over-imaginative theorizing that goes well beyond what is demanded by, or can be sustained by, the evidence of the biblical text. Even so, more recently, not dissimilar hypotheses have been put forward by J. Becker (1982) and U. Feist (1995), and a revival of scepticism about the historicity of the exile has been part of the more general trend to a "minimalist" approach to the history of Israel favoured by some of late, as reflected in a number of the essays in an important collection edited by Grabbe (1998).

There are in fact many factors that lend credibility to the sixth-century setting. The historical circumstances portrayed broadly reflect what is known of the sixth century from extra-biblical sources such as the *Babylonian Chronicle* (cf. Grayson 1975). The issues addressed by the book fit with the period and appear to reflect the situation of national loss associated with it. Moreover, by the end of the sixth century, reality will have taken over from aspiration in many respects (with regard, for example, to temple or monarchy), and many expectations will have been falsified by historical developments (cf. Clements 1986, 1996a). The work coheres with other biblical evidence for the sixth century and its theological trends, including the reassessment of issues of divine action and human or national responsibility, evidenced for example in Jer 31, Deut 30 and Ps 51. The links with other biblical traditions suggest that the location of the book of Ezekiel in the sixth century is very plausible, for example on the one hand indebtedness to eighth-century prophecy and on the other the presence of elements of nascent apocalyptic. Furthermore, with regard to the language of the book, the studies by Hurvitz (1982) and Rooker (1990) show persuasively that the language is best described as belonging to the "transition" between Classical Biblical Hebrew and Late Biblical Hebrew, which would fit the sixth century. Cumulatively, the case for staying with the sixth-century setting that the book claims for itself is overwhelming. Several important volumes on the exilic age (notably Albertz 2001; Lipschits 2005) have recently complemented classic earlier studies (such as Ackroyd 1968) and serve to reinforce the case for a sixth-century setting in great detail.

Before leaving the theme of the exile, we may note that some of the essays in the important collection edited by Grabbe (1998) and also in another collection on exile edited by Scott (1997) have—sometimes in the context of historical scepticism—offered profound insights about the function of "exile" as a motif. For example, Carroll (1997b) and Davies (1998) help us see that "exile" is not merely a descriptive term, but is also an ideological one, referring not merely to an event or a fact but to an interpretation, an articulation of identity and self-definition. These are issues that episodes of human dislocation and diaspora in Armenia, the former Yugoslavia and so many other parts of the world in modern times have shown tragically to be very much alive (cf. Cohen 1997).

Place: Babylonia as the Location of Ezekiel's Ministry

I have stressed that the early sixth century provides the context for Ezekiel's activity in temporal terms; but what of geography? Where did he exercise his ministry? The book of Ezekiel presents the prophet's ministry as being conducted in Babylonia (Ezek 1:1–3). In 33:21 we read, "In the twelfth year of our exile…someone who had escaped from Jerusalem came to me and said, 'The city has fallen'." The book clearly portrays Ezekiel as one of the exiles of 597 who was in Babylonia when Jerusalem fell in 587. There is no reference to his preaching anywhere other than in Babylonia. Accordingly, the great majority of commentators believe that Ezekiel's ministry took place entirely in Babylonia; he is the great prophet to the exiles, as Jeremiah is the great prophet to the community in Judah (e.g. Zimmerli 1979a; Greenberg 1983a).

However, certain features of the book led some scholars, notably Herntrich (1933), to question this view and to suggest that Ezekiel's ministry may have been not in Babylonia but in Jerusalem. The detailed description of the abominations in the Jerusalem temple in ch. 8 was one such feature stressed by Herntrich. Another was the presence of passages that might be thought to make more sense if spoken in Jerusalem, notably the oracle in ch. 12 concerning "the prince in Jerusalem and all the house of Israel in it" (12:10). This speaks of Ezekiel performing a sign (digging his way out through a wall carrying an exile's baggage), which is said to symbolize the coming exile of the prince and those in Jerusalem (vv. 10–11). Herntrich claimed that this would be a much more effective sign if performed in the sight of those it concerned directly in Judah rather than before those already in exile in Babylonia. On the basis of this and similar evidence, he argued that Ezekiel exercised the whole of his ministry in Jerusalem. Herntrich followed certain other scholars (Torrey 1930; Smith 1931) in suggesting that at some point redactors had carried out a systematic revision of the book of Ezekiel, giving it a fictional Babylonian setting; this view later found some support from Garscha (1974:294–303). Perhaps more influential than the position of Herntrich, however, has been that particularly associated with Bertholet (1936). This represents a compromise between the traditional view, that Ezekiel's ministry took place entirely in Babylonia, and the view of Herntrich, that the prophet remained in Jerusalem throughout. Bertholet suggested that Ezekiel had in fact two ministries, one beginning in 593 not in Babylonia but in Jerusalem, and a second in Babylonia following the fall of Jerusalem in 587; in this way Bertholet hoped to do justice to the evidence for both locations. Oesterley and Robinson, working at much the same time as Bertholet, suggested that Ezekiel was active in Jerusalem until 597, and thereafter in Babylonia (Oesterley and Robinson 1934). Other scholars have adopted similar compromises (e.g. Irwin 1943; Steinmann 1953), and there have also been more complex theories, such as that of Pfeiffer (1948:536), who envisaged the prophet moving back and forth a number of times between the two locations.

These discussions arise from genuine difficulties, noted long ago in the rabbinic tradition (e.g. by Rashi). It is, however, by no means clear that the problems raised by the traditional view are sufficiently serious to justify the alternative theories of Herntrich, Bertholet and those who have followed them. The detailed description of the abominations in the Jerusalem temple found in ch. 8 could quite easily have been produced in Babylonia by a man who had, it seems, been a priest in Jerusalem before his deportation (1:3). The book clearly states that it was "in visions of God" that Ezekiel was taken to Jerusalem (8:3; cf. 40:2). There is no justification for regarding these references as evidence of physical journeys to Jerusalem from Babylonia or as indirect evidence of a ministry in Jerusalem. As Ackroyd wrote of ch. 9 (within the same visionary context as ch. 8): "The exiles in Babylonia, who are the prophet's primary audience, are the disobedient to whom it must be said that the judgement upon Jerusalem is the judgement upon themselves" (Ackroyd 1968:109). As for ch. 12, Zimmerli argued persuasively that even this chapter does not demand a Jerusalem setting: "Ezekiel speaks in exile about the fate of those who remain in Jerusalem, who are threatened by the divine judgement which the exiles, whose hope depends on the continued existence of Jerusalem, refuse to see" (Zimmerli 1979a:269). Thus Zimmerli regards ch. 12 as primarily directed to the exiles, even though it speaks of the fate of the community in Judah. It may be appropriate here to draw a comparison with the oracles against foreign nations that are a feature of the book of Ezekiel as of many other prophetic books. Taylor wrote that "No one has yet insisted that Ezekiel's oracles to the foreign nations should have been delivered on Ammonite territory or in Tyre or Egypt" (Taylor 1969:23–24). Brownlee did in fact subsequently argue for this implausible option (Brownlee 1983; 1986:xxiii–xxxiii), but Taylor's point remains a persuasive one. It may be admitted that, taken independently, the material in chs. 8 and 12 might be read as indicating a Jerusalem setting for at least part of Ezekiel's work. However, the book places the whole of the prophet's ministry in Babylonia, and the difficulties that are raised by this are not sufficient to demand that it be abandoned. There are, moreover, no convincing positive grounds for the hypothesis that redactors have imposed a fictional exilic setting. It seems reasonable to conclude, then, that Ezekiel's ministry was indeed located entirely in Babylonia.

Unity, Authorship and Redaction

There is considerable debate among scholars as to how much of the book of Ezekiel is actually from the prophet himself and concerning the provenance and date of any secondary material. Such questions are not new. We read in the Babylonian Talmud (*b. B. Bat.* 14b–15a): "The Men of the Great Assembly wrote Ezekiel, the Twelve, Daniel and the Scroll of Esther." Rashi (1040–1105) supposed that the reason Ezekiel did not write his own book was that he lived outside the land of Israel. In modern times, however, the problem of the authorship of Ezekiel was acknowledged only gradually. The distinctive orderly format of the book led most scholars, even up to the early twentieth century, to think that this book was, for the most part, free of the problems that had already been recognized in the other major prophetic books. Smend wrote, "The whole book is...the logical development of a series of ideas in accordance with a well thought-out, and in part quite schematic, plan. We cannot remove any part without disturbing the whole structure" (Smend 1880:xxi). Modern scholars acknowledged at an early date that sections of Isaiah and Jeremiah might be from hands other than those of the two prophets. However, matters seemed rather different with regard to the book of Ezekiel. Gunkel felt able to describe Ezekiel as "the first prophet who wrote a book" (Gunkel 1906:90) and G. B. Gray could write that "No other book of the Old Testament is distinguished by such decisive marks of unity of authorship and integrity as this" (Gray 1913:198).

However, this scholarly consensus was not to remain unchallenged. There had already been hints of an alternative approach in the works of Kraetzschmar (1900) and J. Herrmann (1908), but it was Hölscher who in 1924 first articulated a more critical view of the unity of the book of Ezekiel (Hölscher 1924). He proposed that only one seventh of the book actually came from the prophet; the bulk he attributed to a Zadokite redactor in Jerusalem in the early fifth century. Hölscher's work marked an important turning-point in the history of Ezekiel scholarship. The unity and integrity of the book could never again be taken for granted. A decade or so after Hölscher's crucial contribution, Cooke wrote that "It is no longer possible to treat the Book as the product of a single mind and a single age" (Cooke 1936:v). Hölscher had opened the way for others to embark on the difficult task of attempting to distinguish between those parts of the book that may with some certainty be traced back to the prophet himself and those that may be regarded as secondary additions.

Criteria of Authorship

The seven major criteria upon which theories about the unity and authorship of the book of Ezekiel have generally been based may be distinguished in the following way:

Poetry and Prose

The first is the distinction between poetry and prose. Hölscher's approach was based primarily upon the theory that poetry or verse was more likely to go back to the prophet himself, prose material being the work of later hands. He sought to rescue Ezekiel the Poet from the book that bore his name. Thus, for example, the whole of chs. 6 and 7 were rejected as secondary prose. Hölscher was here influenced by the work of Duhm, who had argued that poetry was the natural mode of expression in the ecstatic state in which the prophets proclaimed their messages (Duhm 1892, 1901). Applying this theory rigorously to the book of Ezekiel, Hölscher reduced the number of verses attributed to the prophet from the 1273 of the traditional view (i.e. the whole book) to a mere 170.

How helpful is the distinction between poetry and prose as a criterion in determining which parts of a book are primary? Poetic form may indeed in certain cases be an indication of earlier date; for example, many believe that in the book of Jeremiah the poetic oracles are more likely to go back to the prophet himself than is the prose material. However, Jeremiah also illustrates that this criterion can never be applied in a mechanical way, for it seems likely that many of the secondary prose passages have some basis in words of Jeremiah himself, albeit adapted to different situations. In the case of Ezekiel the application of this criterion is more problematic. There are indeed some cases where prose material is probably correctly identified as secondary; for example, 27:12–25a, which may have been adapted from a trade document. In general, though, we do not find in the prose material of the book a particularly distinctive style or theology that may easily be contrasted with that of the poetic passages. Cooke believed that the points of contact between the poetry and the prose were sufficient to "suggest a common source" (Cooke 1936:xxvi; cf. Kessler 1926). Although he was inclined to underestimate the difficulties involved in the question of unity, these words are an important corrective to Hölscher's excessively rigorous application of his criterion. Chapters 17 and 19 of Ezekiel afford a good example of the continuities between the poetry and the prose of the book. Both contain allegorical treatments of the historical and political background to the prophet's ministry and yet the literary form is rather different in each case, ch. 17 being essentially in prose, ch. 19 in poetry (recognizing that the distinction is difficult to maintain). These two chapters contain, broadly speaking, the same kind of material; the particular content of ch. 19 has led to the adoption of the *qînâ* ("lament") metre, but this poetic format does not in itself give ch. 19 a stronger claim than ch. 17 to be regarded as primary material. Hölscher's analysis failed to do justice to such real continuities between poetry and prose and attempted to provide too simplistic an answer to the question of authorship.

Repetition

A second criterion relates to the repetition that is a feature of much of the book. For example, in 36:1–15, the introductory formula "Thus says the Lord GOD" occurs no less than seven times (vv. 2, 3, 4, 5, 6, 7, 13), and similar concluding formulae occur twice (vv. 14, 15). The most common formula of all in the book, occurring over seventy times in its various forms, is the phrase "that you may know that I am the LORD" (e.g. Ezek 35:4, 9, 12, 15). It has often been suggested that such repetition is the result of secondary additions and glosses. This view has been taken by Bertholet (1936), Pfeiffer (1948), May (1956) and, in an especially extreme form, by Vogt (1959). Some have stressed the importance of the Greek Septuagint (LXX) of the book of Ezekiel, claiming that it reflects a more faithful and less encumbered text than the longer and more repetitive Hebrew Masoretic Text (MT). This was argued in thc nineteenth century by Hitzig (1847) and Cornill (1886), and in the twentieth by Jahn (1905) and Wevers (1969). For example, when considering 20:43, Wevers judges the words *ʾašer ʿaśîṯem* ("that you have committed") to be a late addition to the MT unattested by the LXX.

A number of the repetitions in Ezekiel may indeed be the result of scribal errors or deliberate glosses. For example, the repetition in 16:6 of the words *wāʾōmar lāḵ bᵉḏāmayiḵ ḥᵃyî* ("As you lay in your blood, I said to you, 'Live!'") is widely regarded as a case of accidental dittography. A judicious consideration of such possibilities is to be found in the work of Fohrer (1951), and Zimmerli's commentary exemplifies a careful weighing of the evidence of the LXX in these cases (e.g. 1979a:279, on 12:22). We should resist, however, the over-confident reconstruction of a concise and unrepetitive "original" text that Wevers offers, based as it is on the presupposition that "The true oracle in its original form was concise, even bordering on the cryptic" (Wevers 1969:35). While there is probably some truth in this description, it cannot be made to support a dogmatic rule. Indeed a number of scholars have seriously criticized the validity of repetition as a criterion of authorship. Carley (1975:54) and Boadt (1978:489–90) argued that repetition and redundancy might well characterize the prophet's own style and cannot of themselves be taken as indicators of a later hand. The problem of discerning whether a particular feature is a characteristic of Ezekiel himself or of some subsequent stage in the tradition is one that occurs with many of these criteria.

Textual Criticism

Reference has already been made to textual criticism. This has indeed been particularly important for some in the exploration of the redactional process, as for example in the work of Lust in relation to Ezek 36. When discussing P. 967, the earliest and best witness to LXX Ezekiel, Lust (e.g. 1981a) changes what has been seen as a text-critical problem, internal to the LXX, into a more literary-critical issue, arguing that the Hebrew text of Ezekiel originally had the same "omissions" and even the same sequence as P. 967. He contends that 36:23c–38 was an insertion in the Hebrew, a possibility entertained also by Zimmerli (1983:242–48). (See further the "Text and Versions" section, below.)

Priestly Case Law and Language

A further criterion relates to the occurrence of language that seems to have affinities to that of priestly case law; for example, the use of the phrase *ṣaddîq hûʾ* ("such a one is righteous") in 18:9 and the phrase *mōṯ yûmāṯ* ("He shall surely die") in 18:13. The major passages in question are 3:17–21; 14:1–20; 18:1–20; 22:1–16 and 33:1–20. This material, in whole or in part, is regarded as secondary by Hölscher (1924), May (1956), Schulz (1969) and Garscha (1974). These scholars all regard the occurrence in Ezekiel of language that seems to be related to priestly case law as a distinctive mark of the activity of redactors.

The book of Ezekiel certainly contains much material with strong affinities to priestly language and vocabulary. However, it is also evident that Ezekiel himself was a priest (1:3), and it is reasonable to regard at least some of the priestly features of the book as directly related to this fact. This is not to say that all priestly language must derive from the prophet; such features are certainly found in sections that seem, on other grounds, to include some secondary material (e.g. chs. 40–48). In fact, priestly language characterizes the book as a whole. It appears to be typical of the form of expression of the prophet himself, as Reventlow (1962) stressed, and yet it seems to be characteristic also of secondary strata. Priestly language is one of many features shared by Ezekiel and the tradition he shaped; in short, it is of no independent significance as a criterion of authorship.

Deuteronomistic Affinities

There is a certain amount of material in Ezekiel that exhibits similarities to the deuteronomistic literature. For example, 6:13 features subject matter and vocabulary typical of that tradition: "when their slain lie among their idols around their altars, on every high hill, on all the mountain tops, under every green tree, and under every leafy oak." Some scholars have argued that such material is not to be attributed to the prophet himself: S. Herrmann noted the deuteronomistic colouring of chs. 34–37 in particular, pointing, for example, to the recurrent formula, "You shall be my people, and I will be your God" (36:28; 37:27; cf. 34:30–31) and also to the use of the word *lēḇ* ("heart") in 36:26. He attributed this material to a deuteronomistic school active in Palestine during the later part of the exilic period (Herrmann 1965:241). This approach was pursued in further detail by Liwak, who claimed to discern in Ezekiel a range of deuteronomistic insertions of varying length (Liwak 1976).

That there are at least some deuteronomistic elements in the book seems undeniable. Even Zimmerli, who tended to minimize these, had to recognize such affinities in 6:13 (Zimmerli 1979a:46). And yet it is difficult to tell in what way these are related to the words of Ezekiel, since they are often closely juxtaposed to features that are more obviously characteristic of the prophet himself, as we shall see when discussing the promise of a "new heart" and a "new spirit" in 36:26–27. There is no reason to believe that Ezekiel himself would have been immune to the influence of deuteronomistic theology and style either in his native Jerusalem or in Babylonian exile. Redactors may well be responsible for a proportion of the deuteronomistic features in the book, but it cannot be demonstrated that all must be explained in this way. We must conclude, then, that deuteronomistic language is, like priestly language, of no independent significance as a criterion of authorship.

Grammar and Motif

Another criterion that has been employed in the debate is that of consistency of grammar and motif. For example, Wevers argues that since the judgement oracle in 6:3–7 begins "I, I myself will…" it should be in the first person throughout and that words that do not conform to this expectation must be accretions to the original text. Here, Wevers bases his argument on consistency of grammar; elsewhere, he focuses on consistency of motif. In ch. 17, Nebuchadrezzar is portrayed as a great eagle in v. 3 and as an east wind in v. 10; Wevers concludes that the latter must be an accretion (1969:32, 33–34).

How legitimate are such arguments? First, it is of course reasonable to expect of an author a certain degree of consistency; what appear to be outright contradictions within biblical material, such as in Gen 37, are rightly regarded as at least raising the question of multiple authorship. However, in Ezekiel it is difficult to employ the criterion of consistency with any confidence. There are some cases where it may be of help; for example, it is possible that ch. 16 contains secondary material, since the literary image of the foundling Jerusalem becomes complicated and confused in the latter part of the chapter. However, apparent inconsistency need not necessarily indicate secondary elaboration. In 34:15, YHWH himself is spoken of as shepherd of the sheep, whereas it is his servant David who appears as shepherd in v. 23. This shift could be taken as evidence of redaction, but it could equally be read as the use of a characteristic motif by a single author. Wevers' argument from consistency has much in common with his attempt to trim the text of Ezekiel to a concise "original" by excising repetitions. On the whole, one should resist the tendency to impose excessively stringent demands of consistency upon texts that are often metaphorical or poetic in nature.

Theological Content

Argument from consistency can take another form, namely that based on theological content. A number of the chapters in Ezekiel that are predominantly concerned with judgement conclude on an optimistic note (11:14–21; 16:59–63; 17:22–24; 20:40–44). These passages are often regarded as secondary additions, largely because they disrupt the consistency of theological outlook of the judgemental chapters in which they occur. It is, of course, reasonable to expect some degree of theological consistency. However, it should not be assumed that themes of judgement and promise could not be juxtaposed in the earliest stratum. (I shall later advance a case for the early dating of 11:14–21.) Some have seen a hopeful tone itself as a sign of secondary material. Whereas the primary provenance of most of the judgemental material in the book often goes unchallenged, it is in relation to hopeful passages in Ezekiel that such questions loom largest for many scholars. Herrmann (1965), for example, judged the hopeful material as a whole to be secondary, but hope is integrally related to judgement in Ezekiel's theology, both themes being rooted in the prophet's conviction of the holiness of YHWH. One should not regard hope as, in itself, necessarily constituting evidence of secondary provenance, even if specific doubts must be acknowledged in particular cases (such as 17:22–24).

The view that a scholar holds concerning questions of unity and authorship in the book of Ezekiel and their understanding of the theology of the prophet are usually closely related—indeed, circularity of argument is an ever-present danger. We may contrast the positions of two particular scholars here: I have already noted that Herrmann believed that none of the material in the present book of Ezekiel that speaks of the deliverance of Israel derives from the prophet himself; Ezekiel is exclusively a prophet of judgement (Herrmann 1965:290). Raitt, on the other hand, regarded much of the hopeful material in the book as primary and interpreted the shift from judgement to deliverance as a characteristic feature of the theology of Ezekiel himself (Raitt 1977:108–10). The danger of built-in assumptions dictating results is all too evident, especially where theology is involved. As with the discussion of any prophetic book, an important safeguard is to draw upon a broad range of evidence, employing wherever possible different criteria side by side (e.g. there are literary as well as theological arguments for regarding the latter part of ch. 16 as secondary).

The Homogeneity of the Ezekiel Tradition

In addition to illustrating the caution that is always demanded by such discussions, the above survey has in fact highlighted a distinctive feature of the book of Ezekiel: the nature of the book is such that it is particularly resistant to any straightforward division between primary and secondary material. This is surely not because the whole book is from the prophet Ezekiel—there are, as we have seen, indications to the contrary—but rather because of the marked homogeneity of the Ezekiel tradition, in which secondary material bears an unusually close "family resemblance" to primary. In this respect Ezekiel differs significantly from the other two major prophetic books. In Isaiah, for example, chs. 24–27, 40–55 and 56–66 stand apart in a distinctive way, both stylistically and theologically. In Jeremiah, the prose sermons have a characteristic style and theology that seems to distinguish them from the primary material in the book. In Ezekiel, however, even the section within which scholars have most commonly discerned secondary material, namely chs. 40–48, exhibits throughout numerous elements of continuity with what are likely to be primary strata of the book. Chapters 1–39 are characterized by a degree of homogeneity that makes the separation of primary and secondary material unusually difficult.

Some examples will help illustrate the homogeneity of the Ezekiel tradition. In Ezekiel there is often difficulty in discerning whether a distinctive feature is a characteristic of the prophet Ezekiel himself or of some subsequent stage in the tradition. For example, are repetitions the result of accretions or do they represent an important feature of Ezekiel's own style? Such questions do not permit a straightforward solution; answers may often be of the "both/and" variety. We may well here be dealing with genuine features of the words of the prophet Ezekiel that have nevertheless been heightened in the course of redaction, and so have become more characteristic of the finished book than of the primary material. Another example of this is provided by the priestly affinities of much of the material: there seems little reason to doubt the witness of the book that Ezekiel was himself a priest and one would therefore expect his own style to reflect this; on the other hand, such features may well have been heightened in the course of transmission.

There are cases where the classical style of the developed Ezekiel tradition is found in concluding summary sections, which round out the theology of Ezekiel with a symmetry and completeness that the prophet himself may never have achieved. Good examples are 28:25–26 and 39:21–29. It may be significant that these sections contain the only two examples in the book (28:26b; 39:22) of Israel knowing that "I am YHWH" when YHWH punishes the nations (the subject of the verb in 28:26b is ambiguous). An analogy may help here. In a city or village of historical and architectural importance, the local authorities may decree that all new building should be at least coherent with the old, indeed it may be stipulated that the very same building materials be used, whether granite or Cotswold stone. Modern additions may reflect many new needs and technological developments, but an unmistakable "family resemblance" unites the architecture. In some cases one can never be absolutely sure how much goes right back to the earliest times; indeed, sometimes a "classic" status may be achieved by something which is in reality a relatively late, stylized version. So with the book of Ezekiel, there is much evidence to suggest a tenacious continuity of tradition, with regard both to content and to style (see further Joyce 1995a).

Consensus Achieved and Lost

There emerged something of a consensus position by the 1960s, according to which much material in Ezekiel was judged to be from the prophet but the book was acknowledged to be the product of a long tradition. Such a view was represented by, for example, Fohrer (1955) and Eichrodt (1970), and—above all—by Zimmerli (1979a, 1983), whose work will long remain a major landmark in Ezekiel studies. Zimmerli developed the theory of an Ezekiel "school" and posited a long process of accretion and redaction. He saw each of the book's complex oracles as composed of a core from the prophet plus later additions. He described this process of expansion as *Fortschreibung*, "extrapolation," and this was credited to his "school of Ezekiel" (e.g. Zimmerli 1980). For Zimmerli, the "school" hypothesis served to explain the marked homogeneity of the Ezekiel tradition. For all the additions and elaborations, the process is essentially one of continuity, for in Zimmerli's view the complex redactional history nevertheless "preserves for us on the whole the peculiar characteristics of the prophet"

(Zimmerli 1965:515). And so we could describe this mid-twentieth century critical consensus as in many respects a conservative one.

The critical study of Ezekiel has tended to polarize in two rather divergent directions in more recent years, each reflecting in a different way the distinctively homogeneous nature of the Ezekiel tradition. One trend is represented by the attempt to establish a refined stratification of the book, reconstructing its redactional history in minute detail. The work of Garscha affords a good example of this approach, and its appearance in 1974 was symptomatic of the breakdown of the critical consensus, interestingly exactly fifty years after Hölscher's work of 1924 opened up the question for the first time. Garscha attributed only about 30 verses of the entire book to Ezekiel himself. He believed that the basic structure of the book and its uniformity of style were the result of the work of a redactor active either in about 485 or 460 and went on to discern several further layers, the book only being completed in about 200 B.C.E. In contrast to the tendency of many earlier scholars to see the integration of the prophetic and the priestly as one of the distinctive features of Ezekiel himself, Garscha made a sharp distinction between the prophetic and the priestly, assigning the priestly material to a secondary stratum. The grounds for Garscha's stratification must, however, be questioned. It is the alleged lack of stylistic and structural uniformity in the book that leads him to doubt its unity in the first place. He then concedes that some uniformity is nevertheless to be recognized, and this he ascribes primarily to the work of the redactor whom he dates to the first half of the fifth century. And yet Garscha does not demonstrate that these elements of uniformity must be traced to a secondary stratum. Any such hypothesis should be resisted until it can be shown that stylistic and structural uniformity cannot be from the primary level. When a particular distinctive feature is discerned, there is to be recognized at least a *prima facie* case for regarding it as a mark of the prophet himself, in the absence of clear evidence to the contrary.

Garscha is by no means the only scholar to discern many layers within the text. Comparable theses have been advanced by Schulz (1969), Simian (1974), Hossfeld (1977), Bettenzoli (1979), and more recently Pohlmann (1996; 2001). The degree of complexity varies, but their analyses, like that of Garscha, multiply hypotheses unnecessarily and assert more than the evidence can possibly sustain. One can see why scepticism about the diachronic task (which attempts to trace the development of the book through time) has grown in many quarters. Those who adopt the stratifying approach are often over-confident about assigning material to periods of which we know relatively little (such as the fifth century B.C.E.) and all too cavalier about dismissing dates that appear in the text. Moreover, these stratifications tend to become subjective: Garscha attributes the priestly language of the book to a stratum different from that which he regards as responsible for the characteristic style of the Ezekiel tradition, in spite of the fact that there are good grounds for regarding priestly language as an integral feature of that style. Moreover, both Garscha and Schulz speak of a "Deutero-Ezekiel," and yet each assigns different materials to the redactor upon whom he bestows the name (Garscha 1974:303–5; Schulz 1969:163–87). As Muilenburg pointed out, the variety of the conclusions arrived at by the more radical scholars of Ezekiel is itself sufficient to counsel greater caution with regard to such attempts at stratification (Muilenburg 1962a:569).

What of the other pole of recent Ezekiel studies? A very different approach is to be found in the work of those scholars who prefer to analyse the text in its present form rather than posit a hypothetical history of its development. The words "synchronic" or "holistic" are variously applied to such studies. This position is by no means necessarily a flight to naïve conservatism; its proponents are generally skilled in the use of historical-critical methods but believe them no longer adequate to the task, and instead resort to other critical methods, sometimes including structural analysis and rhetorical criticism.

We may take as an example of this trend the work of Greenberg, for whom traditional rabbinical reading conventions constitute a major influence. For Greenberg, each of the book's long oracles and visions is treated as a unit having multiple parts within an overall coherent structure. He writes: "There is only one way that gives any hope of eliciting the innate conventions and literary formations of a piece of ancient literature, and that is by listening to it patiently and humbly" (Greenberg 1983a:21). He deduces that the book is "the product of art and intelligent design… A consistent trend of thought expressed in a distinctive style has emerged, giving the impression of an individual mind of powerful and passionate proclivities" (Greenberg 1983a:26). There is an interesting irony here, related to the phenomenon of homogeneity described earlier: the very feature of Ezekiel that led others to stratify the text ever more finely has led Greenberg to abandon the quest for layers altogether. Indeed, it is what we have called the "family resemblance" between primary and allegedly secondary material in Ezekiel that leads Greenberg to espouse his "holistic" interpretation. Boadt (1978) and Nobile (1982) adopt approaches that are in certain respects similar, as do Niditch (1986), Matties (1990), Galambush (1992) and Renz (1999a).

Greenberg's scepticism concerning alleged secondary elaboration provides a valuable corrective to speculations like those of Garscha. However, such a position all too easily slides from a healthy agnosticism about editorial layers into an implicit assumption of authorship by the prophet himself; this is equally unjustified and fails to take seriously the evidence of redactional activity that is to be discerned. The analogy with the other major prophetic books, Isaiah and Jeremiah, suggests that it is likely that the book of Ezekiel too developed through a complex process of redaction, even though the evidence is in this case less apparent. It was suggested earlier that holistic reading by no means necessarily represents a flight to naïve conservatism. However, the conservative tendency is evident. Greenberg writes: "The persuasion grows on one as piece after piece falls into the established patterns and ideas that a coherent world of vision is emerging, contemporary with the sixth-century prophet and decisively shaped by him, if not the very words of the prophet himself" (Greenberg 1983a:27). This leads Greenberg inexorably towards the belief that the "individual mind" that he discerns is that of Ezekiel. This assumption is never fully explored or defended directly; instead it is cumulatively implied with the help of some seductive rhetoric, tempting to those who think it would be nice if Ezekiel wrote the whole book after all.

Neither an elaborate stratification nor a holistic interpretation fully recognizes the particular complexity and difficulty of the questions of unity and authorship in the book of Ezekiel. The former goes too far, offering detailed answers where none is legitimately to be sought; the latter does not go far enough and fails to address important questions concerning the historical development or "depth dimension" of the text. And yet both approaches reflect the distinctive homogeneity that we have seen to characterize the Ezekiel tradition: Garscha's stratifications have to be so minutely detailed precisely because there is no clear-cut distinction between the style and theology of Ezekiel and of those who followed him; but it is this same "family resemblance" between primary and secondary material that allows Greenberg to imply that it all comes from the prophet himself.

We must endeavour where possible, then, to discriminate between primary material and secondary elaboration, but we must undertake this task in the realization that "assured results" will be rare. As Terence Collins puts it: "The book Ezekiel is characterized at one and the same time by both literary unity and literary complexity" (Collins 1993:91). The diachronic task is difficult but that does not mean that it is impossible, or that it is invalid. The fact that consensus is rarely achieved makes one all the more aware of the partial nature of our evidence and of the subjective nature of our judgements. But this calls for a sober and modest recognition of constraints, not a pessimistic retreat from or casual abandonment of such a task. Although the completed book reflects a long and complex history, it probably reflects much of the prophet Ezekiel and his teaching; and yet one must beware the easy assumption and (for some) attractive idea that one is dealing with the very words of the prophet. One may often have to be content with a proper agnosticism about this. With Clements, I think it likely that the book of Ezekiel was essentially complete by the end of the sixth century B.C.E. (Clements 1986). This is the more probable in that by the end of that century reality will have taken over from aspiration in many respects (with regard, for example, to temple or monarchy), and many expectations will have been falsified by historical developments. We can, then, with a measure of confidence speak of the sixth-century witness of the book of Ezekiel, and also regard that witness as profoundly influenced, both in content and in style, by Ezekiel himself.

THEOLOGICAL THEMES

Ezekiel's Theology of Judgement

The first twenty-four chapters of the book of Ezekiel contain one of the most sustained and vehement declarations of judgement to be found anywhere in the prophetic literature of the Hebrew Bible. These chapters speak of "disaster after disaster" (7:5), in language that is violent and at times crude: "My anger shall spend itself, and I will vent my fury on them and satisfy myself; and they shall know that I, the LORD, have spoken in my jealousy, when I spend my fury on them" (5:13). The wrath of YHWH expresses itself in judgement by fire, sword, wind, famine, wild beasts and pestilence (5:2, 16–17). So violent is the language used that it is hard not to regard this section of the book as containing a cruel and vindictive message, calling down upon the people the most dreadful calamities imaginable. It is as though Ezekiel wishes these things upon his own people. However, this must be read in the light of catastrophic events that had already come upon Israel, events that demanded theological interpretation. Ezekiel—already deported—offers a key to understanding the disaster that has engulfed the nation.

The context of the ministry of Ezekiel in early sixth-century Mesopotamia (see the "Time and Place" section, above) is a situation beset with profound theological questions posed by the Babylonian crisis. Judah had lost her land, and with it, it seemed, her status as the chosen people of YHWH. She had been stripped of her city, her temple, and of not one but two kings. With all these elements of identity removed, it is hardly surprising that profound theological questions were raised. The fate of the community formed a central and indispensable part of Israel's faith in her God. Had YHWH himself been defeated by the Babylonian gods? It does seem that some thought of imperial conquest in terms of the vanquishing of local gods by the imperial gods, and we have evidence that a number of Judahites in the early sixth century in fact embraced the worship of gods other than YHWH (Ezek 8; cf. Jer 44:18). Some managed to hold on to the belief that YHWH was powerful and indeed was responsible for what was happening to them; and yet, for many of these, profound questions were raised about the justice of a god who could permit such things (cf. Ezek 18:29, "Yet the house of Israel says, 'The way of the Lord is unfair'"). To quote John Austin Baker: "some drew the straightforward conclusion that their god was less powerful than the foreign gods; others decided that he was unjust. In both cases the result was that the nerve of their religion was cut, and that they lapsed into either paganism or despair" (Baker 1970:30).

Too many discussions of the events of defeat and deportation by the Babylonians rush on to speak of the lessons that Israel learned from these experiences, and to show how growth came out of suffering; in so doing they fail to take the depth of the disaster with full seriousness (e.g. Whitley 1957 and Winton Thomas 1961). This catastrophe might well have proved to be the end of Israel as a religious community. That it did not owed everything to a small group of theologians who boldly attempted to account for the disaster within the framework of faith in YHWH. In Judah, the prophet Jeremiah and also, it seems, the authors of the Deuteronomistic History struggled to give a Yahwistic account of events. Among the exiled community, this task apparently fell initially to just one person, namely Ezekiel.

Ezekiel, in this respect like Jeremiah, articulated the theological meaning of the national crisis: the present disaster was YHWH's powerful and just act, punishing his own people for their sins. The punishment fits the crime, an entirely appropriate response to the heinous sins of Israel, wherein YHWH's justice is vindicated. This may not seem a very edifying or even a theologically acceptable message to many modern readers; it depends upon the idea that Israel's God manipulates world events and uses war as an instrument to punish sin. But it is important to remember that Ezekiel is not a leisured work of systematic theology but rather an example of crisis literature written in an extreme situation. Ezekiel's theological message of judgement offered at least a glimmer of theological light to a people who had lost all; it made possible an initial assimilation of the traumatic disaster, which could eventually become the basis of subsequent more positive lessons.

Any adequate Yahwistic response would have to vindicate both the power and the justice of the God of Israel. This was, of course, not the first time that such a task had been faced by the prophets of Israel. A century and a half before, the Assyrian empire had posed a dire threat to the Hebrew kingdoms; indeed, the northern kingdom of Israel fell around 721 B.C.E. and Judah nearly suffered the same fate around 700. During that period, four great prophetic figures attempted to give a theological explanation for this historical disaster. Amos and Hosea working in the north and Isaiah and Micah in the south advanced the view that, far from representing the routing of YHWH by Assyrian gods (cf. 2 Kgs 19:10–13), these events were the powerful and just act of YHWH who was angry with the sins of his people. Isaiah spoke of Assyria as a "rod" raised up by YHWH to beat his recalcitrant people (cf. Isa 10:5: "Ah, Assyria, the rod of my anger—the club in their hands is my fury!"). It is difficult to overstate the importance of this episode in "sharpening the tools" for the prophetic response to the Babylonian crisis at the start of the sixth century. Ezekiel and his Yahwistic contemporaries were confronted by a scenario remarkably similar to that which had faced the eighth-century prophets—only this time Jerusalem was not spared. Whereas in the Assyrian crisis the adequacy of the prophetic response was not tested to breaking point, since Judah survived intact (albeit under the shadow of imperial domination), the Babylonian crisis appeared to falsify all the promises of old. Thus the eighth-century prophets had provided invaluable resources—but could the same theological rationale for historical disaster bear all the weight that was now to be placed upon it?

The first twenty-four chapters of the book of Ezekiel assert in an unqualified way the responsibility of Israel for the fate that has befallen the nation. Given that everything that constituted the identity of Israel had been lost this time, it is hardly surprising that the theological explanation for this is given in the most thoroughgoing of terms. Ezekiel asserts that the events do not constitute meaningless chaos, but rather the just punishment of a sinful people by their powerful God. "For the land is full of bloody crimes; the city is full of violence. I will bring the worst of the nations to take possession of their houses" (Ezek 7:23–24)—this was indeed a hard message, but it at least offered theological meaning to a generation that was experiencing the loss of all that defined its identity. Moreover, Ezekiel's theology of judgement has broader theological implications. There is room for only one God who runs the affairs of the world as a whole. Implicit here are the nascent claims of monotheism as well as universalism, themes that would be articulated more explicitly in Isa 40–55 later in the exile.

The much-debated ch. 18 is devoted to making it clear that the present generation is punished for its own sins and not for the sins of previous generations. Ezekiel is consistent about this elsewhere too. For Ezekiel, the past is only ever *illustrative* of the nation's propensity to sin, as in 20:30, "Therefore say to the house of Israel, 'Thus says the Lord GOD: "Will you defile yourselves after the manner of your ancestors and go astray after their detestable things?,"'" and 16:44, "See, everyone who uses proverbs will use this proverb about you, 'Like mother, like daughter'." Ezekiel is here distinctively different from a number of roughly contemporary theological witnesses. For example, towards the culmination of the Deuteronomistic History, 2 Kgs 23:26 reads: "Still the LORD did not turn from the fierceness of his great wrath, by which his anger was kindled against Judah, because of all the provocations with which Manasseh had provoked him." Lamentations 5:7 declares, "Our ancestors sinned; they are no more, and we bear their iniquities," and Jer 31:29, "In those days they shall no longer say: 'The parents have eaten sour grapes, and the children's teeth are set on edge.' But all shall die for their own sins; the teeth of everyone who eats sour grapes shall be set on edge." It is vital to recognize that the couching of this last text (superficially so similar to Ezek 18:2–4) as a hope for the future acknowledges that the present situation is unfair; as a result, the Jeremiah text and the Ezekiel text mean very different things.

While Ezekiel may be seen as the most radical of these witnesses in affirming the absolute responsibility of the present generation for its own fate, the "price" of this stance is an apparent failure to acknowledge the intergenerational effects of sin. The "sour grapes" saying so vigorously rejected in 18:2 was probably an established proverb, perhaps associated with the wisdom tradition (Morgan 1981:109–10; Darr 2004). Like all such material, it had no doubt been handed on because it was seen as encapsulating a truth about life, in this case that children are affected by their parents' actions. It would be a mistake to read into Ezekiel's rejection of the saying a blanket denial of this traditional insight. Rather, his purpose is a very precise one: to liberate his audience from the morale-sapping effects of passing the buck to others for the situation in which they found themselves.

Ezekiel and Repentance?

So dominant in Ezekiel is the emphasis on the thoroughgoing and all-engulfing nature of the disaster that is even now coming upon the nation that it can be difficult to work out what place the prospect of repentance might have within the context of the prophet's theology of judgement. Given the strong emphasis on the defeat and exile being punishment for national sin (there are numerous references to Israel being treated precisely as she deserves, for example, 7:27: "According to their way I will do to them, and according to their own judgements I will judge them") and the repeated motif of "no pity" (5:11; 7:4, 9; 8:18; 9:5, 10), it might be thought that repentance might offer an escape from the disaster or, if not that, then that repentance might prove the key to a new future beyond the disaster.

In most passages of judgement all talk of repentance is eclipsed (e.g. ch. 9; 14:12–23). There are just two explicit references to repentance in Ezekiel, at 14:6 ("Therefore say to the house of Israel, 'Thus says the Lord GOD: "Repent and turn away from your idols; and turn away your faces from all your abominations"'") and 18:30 ("Therefore I will judge you, O house of Israel, all of you according to your ways, says the Lord GOD. Repent and turn from all your transgressions; otherwise iniquity will be your ruin"). The context of the latter reference is of further interest. Verse 31 reads, "Cast away from you all the transgressions that you have committed against me, and get yourselves a new heart and a new spirit! Why will you die, O house of Israel?" and v. 32, "For I have no pleasure in the death of anyone, says the Lord GOD. Turn, then, and live." The notion of "turning" is important and we should note the following further positive references, in addition to those in 14:6 and 18:30, 32: Ezek 18:21, 23, 27; and 33:11, 14, 19. In these two contexts, it is stated that "if the wicked turn away from all their sins that they have committed and keep all my statutes and do what is lawful and right, they shall surely live; they shall not die" (18:21).

In the light of all this, it is perhaps not surprising that some scholars have emphasized the place of repentance in Ezekiel, for example Stalker (1968:161–62), Mosis (1975), Matties (1990:109) and McKeating (1993:85). But what are we to make of Ezekiel's language? Wherever a call to repentance is found in Ezekiel it is in a context where it is quite clear that the judgement is unavoidable and indeed already happening. And so the call to repentance cannot offer a means of averting the judgement. Rather, it seems to serve in part at least as a rhetorical device, underlining the responsibility of Israel for the now inevitable (indeed present) disaster. Israel has had every warning and is wholly to blame for the crisis that is even now engulfing the nation. Discussion of these issues has sometimes been obscured by the fact that, not surprisingly, readers of Scripture, both Jewish and Christian, have over the centuries heightened the profile of the call to repentance in prophetic texts such as Ezekiel, in order to sustain their religious value. If we try to lay aside such concerns, it becomes clear that even apparently straightforward appeals may not be quite what they seem, but may rather express what the people would have needed to do to avert disaster, had they not already shown themselves unwilling or incapable. A. Vanlier Hunter wrote helpfully on this matter: "Perhaps we have not perceived the full and terrible impact of classical judgement prophecy until we realize that a subtle part of the judgement lay in the temporary inefficacy of repentance to which the people were nevertheless called" (Hunter 1982:280). Several scholars over recent years have rightly highlighted the place of theodicy in the message of the prophets (cf. Schmidt 1973; Barton 1987), emphasizing that the prophets were more concerned to explain and justify the judgement of God than to persuade people to act in ways that might avert it.

Not even Ezekiel's motif of the "watchman" (Heb. *ṣōpeh*; NRSV: "sentinel") is as straightforward as it might seem. This material is found in 3:16–21 and 33:1–9 (with the language picked up also in the remainder of ch. 33): "Mortal, I have made you a sentinel for the house of Israel; whenever you hear a word from my mouth, you shall give them warning from me. If I say to the wicked, 'You shall surely die,' and you give them no warning, or speak to warn the wicked from their wicked way, in order to save their life, those wicked persons shall die for their iniquity; but their blood I will require at your hand" (3:17–18); and at the end of the first passage the positive case: "If, however, you warn the righteous not to sin, and they do not sin, they shall surely live, because they took warning; and you will have saved your life" (3:21). The second passage is very similar: "If the sentinel sees the sword coming and does not blow the trumpet, so that the people are not warned, and the sword comes and takes any of them, they are taken away in their iniquity, but their blood I will require at the sentinel's hand" (33:6). Superficially both passages appear to refer to an open call to repentance. The metaphor seems to be that of the lookout in the fields who calls out (or blows the trumpet), so that the warning can be acted upon, to fight off thieves or wild animals. However, what is actually said through the watchman? It is "You shall surely die" (3:18; 33:8). This is not the call of a watchman but rather a term from the context of law, indeed nothing other than the formal declaration of the sentence of death. Wilson argues that the prophetic task here is not to call the people to repentance, but "to deliver to the accused a legal decision which Yahweh has already given" (Wilson 1972:96). This mixture of metaphors is revealing. This watchman material, which appears first in the context of the prophet's call, is above all about the weighty and terrible responsibility placed upon the prophet. It is striking that the positive case is only mentioned briefly and in a subordinate way (at 3:21 and at 33:5b, "if they had taken warning, they would have saved their lives"). But it is 33:5a that summarizes the actual situation of the nation in a nutshell: "They heard the sound of the trumpet and did not take warning; their blood shall be upon themselves."

Ezekiel in fact nowhere envisages that repentance might now avert the disaster. And yet the language of repentance is by no means absent, as I have acknowledged. It may indeed be in part ironic ("would that you had…"), but some further account needs to be given of its presence. Within the context of the book of Ezekiel as a whole the calls may also be seen as anticipating a time when YHWH will grant a new beginning. Ezekiel's God will not in the end allow the sin of Israel to be the last word. Beyond the disaster the prophet looks to a new God-given beginning for his people in which "life" will consist in the fullness of relationship with God in contrast to the "death" of estrangement from him. Ezekiel 18:30–31 ("Get yourselves a new heart and a new spirit!") anticipates the promise of Ezek 36:26–27 ("A new heart I will give you, and a new spirit I will put within you"), much as Deut 6:4–5 ("Hear, O Israel: The LORD is our God, the LORD alone. You shall love the LORD your God with all your heart, and with all your soul, and with all your might") finds fulfilment in Deut 30:6 ("Moreover, the LORD your God will circumcise your heart and the heart of your descendants, so that you will love the LORD your God with all your heart and with all your soul, in order that you may live").

Also, more immediately, the calls to repentance represent a concern that the exiles should conduct their lives in accordance with God's will. Consistent with the radical God-centredness of Ezekiel, there is here a recurrent concern to emphasize the righteousness of YHWH. This is well expressed by Wilson, who writes that "even Ezekiel, who proclaimed that Jerusalem's future doom could not be avoided under any conditions, urged the Israelites already suffering the judgement of exile to keep themselves righteous (Ezekiel 18)" (Wilson 1998:216). Matties writes: "The assumption is often made that the call to repentance must have the intention of averting impending disaster. That dichotomy is unnecessary. It is possible to announce judgement without thinking that repentance will avert judgement. Similarly, a call to repentance need not imply the guarantee of salvation" (Matties 1990:108).

Mein is particularly helpful in reflecting on what a realistic call to repentance in the exilic context might mean. He argues that ch. 18 "in the specific examples used…reflects the new lifestyles of the exiles, and the possibilities open to them" (Mein 2001a:212). Whereas Ezekiel's critique elsewhere is addressed to the Jerusalem leaders' management of the royal cult (e.g. ch. 8) and their conduct of foreign policy (e.g. chs. 17 and 19), the moral horizon is here much more limited. Moreover, restoration is not in view, for Ezek 18 fails to relate fully to the institutional and communal life of a restored Israel. Chapter 14 too is relevant here: "It is highly significant that the two most unequivocal calls for repentance come in chapters 14 and 18 which…can be seen as most directly reflecting the present situation of the exiles" (Mein 2001a:212). "Thus it seems possible that for Ezekiel repentance is a concept which functions at the level of the domestic day-to-day life of the exiles more than at the national-political level…it may be that the call to repentance in Ezekiel itself forms part of the evidence for the more limited, domestic scope of the exiles' moral world" (Mein 2001a:213).

Ezekiel and Individual Responsibility?

There has been a long tradition of interpretation that has insisted that a distinctive feature of Ezekiel's theology of judgement is its emphasis on individual responsibility, that is, the moral independence of contemporary individuals. This has sometimes been seen as representing a landmark in Israel's religious development (e.g. Davidson 1904:282–86; Causse 1937:201; Lindblom 1962:387). However, this must be contested, particularly on the ground that Ezekiel's overriding concern is consistently to explain a disaster that is national and thereby collective. It is important to distinguish the issue of individual responsibility, in the sense of the moral independence of contemporary individuals, from the question of the moral independence of generations, though these two have often been confused in discussion of Ezekiel. Consideration of the nature of Israel's responsibility as presented in Ezekiel has focused especially on chs. 9, 14 and 18. These all assert unequivocally that the events of defeat and exile are YHWH's just punishment of Israel's sins, and in this respect they may be said to be typical of chs. 1–24 as a whole, dominated by the theme of the absolute responsibility of Israel for the punishment that is engulfing the nation.

The expression of this responsibility is throughout a good deal less individualistic than has often been suggested. Individualistic motifs feature in both ch. 9 (where a mark is to be put on the foreheads of those who sigh and groan over the abominations that are committed) and 14:12–23 (where it is implied that Noah, Daniel or Job would save at least their own lives by their righteousness if they were present), but these motifs are subordinate to a more collective primary theme, namely the imminent onset of the thorough judgement of the nation. The purpose of the mark on the forehead in ch. 9 is to make it quite clear that those who are to perish do so according to absolute justice. There seems to be no direct interest in the possibility that there may be some righteous to be spared. When the prophet asks "Ah Lord GOD! will you destroy all who remain of Israel as you pour out your wrath upon Jerusalem?" (9:8), the answer appears to be in the affirmative: "The guilt of the house of Israel and Judah is exceedingly great." And when the man clothed in linen returns at the end of the chapter we are not told whether he had found any righteous. As for Noah, Daniel and Job, these are legendary paragons of virtue; even they would not save their own children, so wicked is this nation. But of course they are not present at this dark time. Indeed, the final verses of the chapter take it for granted that any chance survivors will be undeserving ones, whose sins will only serve to confirm the overall justice of the national judgement. Moreover, while 14:1–11 employs the admittedly individualistic concept of excommunication, it seems to envisage the "cutting off" of the idolatrous nation as a whole, rather than merely the punishment of individual idolaters.

But it is ch. 18 of which most has been made, with its discussion of the "sour grapes" proverb. Ezekiel responds to a people who claim that they are suffering for the sins of their ancestors. This chapter has been seen as a charter for individual responsibility. However, it is vital to see that the context of the whole discussion is one in which Ezekiel and his audience have already been exiled. The situation is one of a national calamity, which has to be explained. Ezekiel presents three hypothetical figures in vv. 1–20, a righteous man, his wicked son, and his righteous grandson. These cases are presented as individual ones because Ezekiel is employing the priestly case law format. Each individual here in fact stands for a generation, with the crucial case being the youngest, righteous generation. Ezekiel insists that if this last generation really were innocent, it would not be punished. In this subtle chapter we then see Ezekiel's audience protesting in v. 19 that the son *should* suffer for his father's sin. They have a vested interest in defending a theory that would vindicate their innocence in spite of their suffering. But Ezekiel cleverly manoeuvres them towards acknowledging that they are in fact sinful and that the justice of God is vindicated. The second half of the chapter turns to discuss what happens when the wicked turn from their sins or indeed when the righteous go to the bad. Ezekiel argues that the past is forgotten. Some, for example Raitt (1977:49), have seen vv. 21–32 as making an individualistic offer. But as with vv. 1–20, so this section too uses the examples of individuals to serve an argument about the community (addressed significantly as the "house of Israel"). The language of the liturgy of entrance into the sanctuary is reapplied to the discussion of a crisis that is inevitably communal and national. The "watchman" (or "sentinel") material of chs. 3 and 33 too (discussed earlier in connection with the theme of repentance) must be read in the light of what is in fact always the context of Ezekiel's discourse, namely the overriding concern with the fate of the nation in an inevitably corporate catastrophe.

So, not even these passages support the view that Ezekiel is the great exponent of individual responsibility some have portrayed. Moreover, the overwhelmingly corporate nature of the chapters dealing with judgement is echoed in the hopeful material in the book, where we find that renewal is consistently presented as a corporate experience. The promise of a "new heart" and a "new spirit" (36:26–27; cf. 11:19) is addressed to the "house of Israel" (36:22, 32). The "dry bones" of ch. 37 are said to be "the whole house of Israel" (37:11), and the promise of new life there is addressed by YHWH to "my people" (37:12, 13). Ezekiel 37:15–28 looks forward to the reunification of Judah and Israel; v. 22 emphasizes that they shall no longer be two nations but "one nation" under "one king," while v. 24 speaks of the promised king as "one shepherd" over the people (cf. 34:23). The final verses of ch. 37 (vv. 26–28) envisage the restored community gathered around the sanctuary, a theme that is explored at length in the last nine chapters of the book (chs. 40–48; cf. 20:40–44).

Furthermore, the common view that the contribution of Ezekiel marked a crucial stage in the evolution of individualism in Israel not only misrepresents the evidence concerning Ezekiel but also attempts to impose an excessively simple pattern upon language about collective and individual responsibility in the Hebrew Bible as a whole. If one sets Ezekiel within a broader context (Joyce 1989; Kaminsky 1995), one finds that the complexities that characterize the understanding of responsibility in the book of Ezekiel become less puzzling; indeed, they may be seen as typical of the Hebrew Bible as a whole. The variation between more individualistic elements and more collective elements may be seen as typical of the diversity that marked language relating to responsibility in all periods. The absence from Ezekiel of any sense that individualistic elements are being advanced as innovations is readily understandable in the light of the fact that notions of individual responsibility seem to have played a part in thought about responsibility in Israel from early times (in both legal practice, as in Deut 24:16, and narratives traditions, such as Gen 18).

Nonetheless, it would be a mistake to *underestimate* the place of individualistic themes in Ezekiel's statement of Israel's responsibility. The individualistic dimension of the motif of the marking of the forehead in ch. 9 or the sparing of paragons of virtue in ch. 14 (or again of the judging "between sheep and sheep, between rams and goats" in 34:17–22) should indeed be taken seriously, even though, as we have noted, Ezekiel is unoriginal in all this. Discussion has been helpfully nuanced over recent years by several important contributions. Mein's notion of a moral "re-scaling" in the exilic context sheds light on the issue of Ezekiel's so-called individualism as well as on the theme of repentance discussed earlier: "Only moral actions on a more individual, domestic scale are possible…on the more domestic scale of relations between individuals and families, repentance remains an option" (Mein 2001a:214). Kaminsky argues persuasively for making more of the individualistic language of ch. 18 as evidence for a real concern with the individual: "The primary focus may in fact be communal, but that does not preclude a strong concern for the individual. Just as the general context qualifies the individualistic language and indicates that it is being used in the service of a communal sermon, the individualistic language qualifies the communal elements in certain ways" (Kaminsky 1995:171). He continues: "such individualistic language may not indicate an attempt to assert the total moral autonomy of each individual, but it seems very likely that Ezekiel employs it as an attempt to arouse the individuals who compose the larger nation to accept responsibility for the current state of the nation" (Kaminsky 1995:171–72).

That Ezekiel deals with these matters on an "occasional" rather than a systematic basis is nowhere better illustrated than in some remarkable words found towards the end of the major section constituted by chs. 1–24: "Say to the land of Israel, 'Thus says the LORD, "I am coming against you, and will draw my sword out of its sheath, and will cut off from you both righteous and wicked. Because I will cut off from you both righteous and wicked, therefore my sword shall go out of its sheath against all flesh from south to north"'" (Ezek 21:3, 4 [Heb. vv. 8, 9]) This would seem to confirm the interpretation supported here that Ezekiel is not concerned with individual responsibility. These words have scant regard for any with a mark on the forehead, little respect even for any Noahs, Daniels or Jobs. They clearly pose a problem for any scholar wishing to present Ezekiel as a great individualist; thus, for example, Irwin claimed that the passage quoted from ch. 21 must come from early in the prophet's ministry, before he had reached the full maturity of his individualistic view (Irwin 1943:331–32). But such special pleading is unnecessary, for Ezekiel's concerns are in no way systematic.

The Future does not Depend on Repentance

Given the bleakness of chs. 1–24, it is remarkable that Ezekiel comes to speak of a new future. This is only possible on the basis of the radical judgement he has announced. Ezekiel never says that a new future might depend on better behaviour on Israel's part. There is indeed to be a future but it is undeserved and depends solely on YHWH. As there was a call to righteousness that would nevertheless in no way avail to avert disaster, similarly among those enjoying deliverance there is abundant evidence of the sinful and undeserving nature of those involved. We see this in the recurrent motif of self-loathing on the part of survivors, whether accidentally spared or the recipients of God's undeserved deliverance. Self-loathing is found at 6:9; 20:43 and 36:31. The related motif of shame is found at 16:52, 54, 61, 63 and 36:32 (cf. 7:18; 43:10–11; 44:13). In several cases survivors illustrate the deserved and just nature of the punishment that has taken place: 12:16 and 14:22–23 (cf. 6:8–10; 7:16). (On the theme of shame in Ezekiel, see Odell 1992; Lapsley 2000a:130–56; 2000b; Stiebert 2000, 2002a:129–62; Smith-Christopher 2002:105–23.) These motifs certainly serve to underline the vital fact that in Ezekiel the new future is never earned by righteousness; repentance is never the ground for a new beginning. When a new future is promised it is for God's own reasons; right behaviour follows only afterwards, as a consequence (as in 36:22–32).

Not all have recognized this. Zimmerli dated ch. 18 to the period after the fall of Jerusalem in 587 because, he argued, a call to repentance then is more appropriate (Zimmerli 1979a:377). This overlooks the fact that repentance plays no part in the new beginnings in Ezekiel. Lapsley writes of the exiles, "perhaps there is hope for them if they are of the right disposition" (Lapsley 2000a:76). This is misleading in so far as there is any suggestion here of a link with a future beyond exile; the conditional "if" has no place in Ezekiel in terms of national restoration. Matties sees ch. 18 as "an exhortation to the people to qualify for the return, which will include both temple and land in the presence of Yahweh" (Matties 1990:186). But there is in fact in Ezekiel no question of the people having to qualify for the return, which will depend solely on YHWH's own purposes.

Helpful light is shed by Mein's emphasis on the shift from activity to passivity in the exilic situation:

> The people themselves take no action to bring about the revival of their fortunes, but are rather YHWH's pawns. There may be some connection between this movement from responsibility to passivity and the actual social circumstances of the exiles, who have gone from being people of some importance, with a wide range of moral possibilities open to them, to people for whom the relationships of individuals, family and business form the whole of their moral perspective. (Mein 2001a:215)

Both the righteousness that would not avert disaster and the sin that does not prevent deliverance highlight that all depends on God's continuity of providential activity. "Grace" is absolutely characteristic of Ezekiel. Although the word *ḥēn*, often translated "grace," is not used, there is much in Ezekiel that shares affinities with what the Christian tradition has spoken of in terms of "grace." And far from this being an anachronistic imposition of New Testament ideas, it is Christianity that is the borrower here. Exilic theological developments are fundamental to New Testament and especially Pauline theology (cf. Young and Ford 1987:60–84).

Radical Theocentricity

In the use of a range of formulae and motifs in Ezekiel we find evidence of a distinctive emphasis on the absolute centrality of YHWH and his self-manifestation, a radical theocentricity that is of an order difficult to parallel anywhere in the Hebrew Bible. In a trio of seminal studies, Zimmerli established this in magisterial fashion (Zimmerli 1953, 1954a, 1957a, collected in English in Zimmerli 1982a).

The so-called Recognition Formula or Proof-Saying is the most characteristic expression of the radical theocentricity (God-centredness) of this prophet and of the tradition that he shaped: "and you (or they) shall know that I am YHWH" (NRSV: "the LORD"). The formula occurs in Ezekiel some fifty-four times in its basic form and over twenty more times with minor variations (Joyce 1989:91). The basic pattern consists of a statement that YHWH will punish (or deliver) Israel (or the nations), followed by the words "and you (or they) shall know that I am YHWH." Generally the group for whom knowledge of YHWH is anticipated is the same as that which is said to be the object of YHWH's punishment or deliverance. However, this is not always the case; in fact, a wide range of permutations is to be found, the consistent factor being that the formula is always associated with the account of an action of YHWH. What of the background of the formula? There are two parts of the Hebrew Bible where similar expressions occur, namely the books of Kings (e.g. 1 Kgs 20:13, 28) and the book of Exodus (e.g. Exod 7:17). The widespread view is that it had its origin in oracles against the nations (Zimmerli 1957a; Fohrer 1970:104). By a paradoxical inversion of an established form, the use of the formula has, at some point, been broadened to include oracles against Israel. The actions of YHWH are, it appears, deliberately directed toward the end that it may be known that "I am YHWH." This somewhat cryptic message is normally presented without elaboration. This gives the formula a certain aura of mystery, which serves to highlight the theocentricity of Ezekiel's presentation. Moreover, the concern that it should be known that "I am YHWH" is at times so pressing that the specific recipients of this revelation fade into relative obscurity and it becomes unclear precisely who is being addressed—in such cases we are forcefully reminded that the focus is upon the God who is known rather than upon those by whom he is known. As Childs argued, the specificity of Ezekiel's situation and his audience is often blurred in what may be seen as the beginnings of the canonical process toward the final form of Scripture (Childs 1979:161–62). It is no surprise that this should be particularly evident in the book of Ezekiel, for this is a prophet who is all but eclipsed by God.

A second important formula in this connection is the phrase "in the sight of the nations" or "in their sight." Closely related are the expressions "among the nations" and "among them." Characteristically they are used of YHWH himself as witnessed by the nations; some texts speak of the profanation of YHWH's name in the sight of the nations (20:9, 14, 22), while others look forward to his self-vindication in their sight (36:23). References to the nations are very bare and give no indication of any positive interest in their response for its own sake. The concern is not with the nations knowing or witnessing YHWH so much as with YHWH being known and witnessed. As with the "I am YHWH" formula, so here too we find abundant evidence of the radical theocentricity of Ezekiel. The overriding concern is that YHWH should be known as he is: "so I will display my greatness and my holiness and make myself known in the eyes of many nations. Then they shall know that I am the LORD" (38:23).

A third formula is "For the sake of my name." Why does YHWH act to save his people? Is it in order to punish the nations that he delivers Israel? Judgement on the nations plays a significant part in Ezekiel, but at no point does it appear to constitute in itself the primary motive of YHWH's actions (indeed, the oracles against the nations in Ezekiel seem more about teaching lessons to Israel). Is it, then, because Israel deserves favour that YHWH delivers the nation? On the contrary, "Thus says the Lord GOD: 'It is not for your sake, O house of Israel, that I am about to act'" (36:22). Admittedly, it is said that Israel will be cleansed (36:25), given a "new heart" and a "new spirit" (36:26), and made to walk according to YHWH's statutes (36:27), but all of this is a promise for the future, part and parcel of the gift of restoration, and certainly not a condition upon which it depends. It is in Ezekiel that the conviction that divine favour is undeserved is articulated more consistently than anywhere else in the Hebrew Bible: "'It is not for your sake that I will act,' says the Lord GOD, 'let that be known to you. Be ashamed and dismayed for your ways, O house of Israel'" (36:32). Is it, then, out of love for Israel that YHWH acts to deliver the nation? Even in ch. 16, which relates the story of the foundling girl, all the phrases used appear to be either legal or sexual; we do not find here much evidence of warmth of affection (Shields 1998a); moreover, the reference is to the original election of Israel, from which she subsequently fell away, rather than to a promise of restoration. In ch. 23, the allegory of Oholah and Oholibah, the language of affection is absent too, and in ch. 24, in which the destruction of the sanctuary at Jerusalem is compared to Ezekiel's loss of his wife (24:16), at no point is the sanctuary spoken of as loved by YHWH himself. Neither the word *ʾāhēḇ* ("love") nor the word *ḥeseḏ* ("steadfast love, kindness"), or related forms, is ever used in Ezekiel in connection with YHWH. We shall not, it seems, find in the love of YHWH the basic reason for his restoration of Israel.

The primary motivation of the dramatic initiative of restoration is summed up rather in our third formula, that which speaks of YHWH acting for the sake of his "name" (Heb. *šēm*). Ezekiel 36:22 provides a typical example: "It is not for your sake, O house of Israel, that I am about to act, but for the sake of my holy name, which you have profaned among the nations to which you came." There are fourteen references to the divine "name" in Ezekiel. On five occasions reference is made to YHWH "acting" for the sake of his name (20:9, 14, 22, 44; 36:22). He is also said to "have concern for" his name (36:21), to "sanctify" his name (36:23), to "make known" his name (39:7), and to "be jealous for" his name (39:25). It is of particular importance that the verb with which the divine "name" most frequently appears is *ḥālal*, "to profane." Profanation of the "name" is mentioned on no less than nine occasions (20:9, 14, 22, 39; 36:20, 21, 22, 23; 39:7). A high proportion of the cases of the word in Ezekiel occur in two significant passages. The first of these is ch. 20, which presents a survey of Israel's long history of sin, as an illustration of the wayward inclinations of this nation. Three times it is said that YHWH had resolved to punish his people as they deserved, but on each occasion he withheld his hand (20:9, 14, 22). YHWH's restraint is explained in all three cases (with only minor variations) in the words, "But I acted for the sake of my name, so that it should not be profaned in the sight of the nations, in whose sight I had brought them out." The other passage, 36:20–32, looks forward to YHWH's imminent deliverance of Israel; we read that when the people of Israel were exiled among the nations, they profaned YHWH's "holy name," for it was said of them, "These are the people of the LORD, and yet they had to go out of his land" (36:20). As a result, YHWH had concern for his "holy name," declaring, "It is not for your sake, O house of Israel, that I am about to act, but for the sake of my holy name" (36:22). Both of these passages, then, speak of the profanation of the "name" of YHWH and state that it is for the sake of this "name" that YHWH acts to spare an undeserving Israel. In both it would seem that the primary purpose of YHWH's activity is the vindication of his reputation; what aspect of his reputation is particularly in mind? The profanation of the divine "name" appears to consist essentially in the casting of doubt upon YHWH's power and effectiveness. The words that the nations utter in 36:20, "These are the people of the LORD, and yet they had to go out of his land," amount to a charge that YHWH was too weak to prevent other nations (aided presumably by their gods) from exiling his people. The nations express similar opinions elsewhere in Ezekiel too, as in 25:8 and 35:10. That it is essentially the power of YHWH that is questioned by the nations is confirmed by the fact that it is the restoration of Israel that will ultimately vindicate his "name" in their eyes. The nations have misinterpreted Israel's defeat as a sign of YHWH's weakness. He must now (even at the cost of waiving the rigour of his judgement) act to correct this misconception and vindicate his reputation as a powerful god. It would not be inaccurate to say that in Ezekiel YHWH in this way acts out of "divine self-interest."

The fourth and last feature of the language of Ezekiel that gives clear expression to his God-centred emphasis is the theme of divine holiness (Heb.

root *qdš*). The "name" of YHWH often appears in the fuller form "holy name" (e.g. 36:22), while in 36:23 YHWH is spoken of as "vindicating the holiness of" (NRSV: "sanctifying") his "great name." It appears, then, that there is in Ezekiel a close association between the divine "name" and words to do with holiness. In addition to the nine occasions when the noun *qōdeš*, "holiness," is used with "name," the verb *qdš* is frequently employed in closely related contexts. We find in the use of this verb in Ezekiel a strongly theocentric focus. This is underlined by the fact that the subject is normally YHWH himself (the verb generally having a reflexive sense: "I will vindicate my holiness," "I will sanctify myself"). The emphasis on the holiness of YHWH in Ezekiel is not without parallel elsewhere. There are particularly close affinities between Ezekiel and the Holiness Code (Lev 17–26), as was demonstrated by Reventlow (1961). It seems likely that Ezekiel's use of the root *qdš* owes something also to previous prophetic usage, notably that of Isaiah of Jerusalem, as was argued by Bettenzoli (1979). Nevertheless, as Muilenburg wrote, "Ezekiel's awareness of the divine holiness is more awesome, more sublime and majestic, more cosmic and 'tremendous' than that of his prophetic predecessors" (Muilenburg 1962b:622). The motif of divine holiness in Ezekiel gains particular force from the fact that it forms part of a network of interrelated themes. To a remarkable degree, language pertaining to the holiness of YHWH occurs together with and shares the emphases of the other formulae here reviewed. It should be noted also that the phrase "in the sight of the nations," or a related formula, is almost always to be found where the verb *qdš* is used in Ezekiel. Moreover, every such case occurs in conjunction with the "I am YHWH" formula (or a variation upon it). Furthermore, in those passages in which the verb *qdš* is used, the theme of the vindication of YHWH's power is usually prominent (as in 28:22; 36:23; 38:23).

It is in such a context that we read of the gift of a "new heart" and a "new spirit" (36:26–27; cf. 11:19), the primary purpose of which is to preclude the otherwise inevitable danger of YHWH having to punish his people again, with the renewed risk of the profanation of his "name" that would bring. Israel's response is so important that YHWH himself promises to make it possible. This paradoxical conception raises the question of how far the responsibility of Israel remains intact. Echoes of the theme of Israel's responsibility do remain, even in ch. 36: Israel is to "be careful to observe my ordinances" (36:27) and is to loathe herself for her iniquities and her abominable deeds (36:31). Ultimately, however, since obedience is guaranteed, it would seem that the responsibility of Israel has been subsumed in the overriding initiative of YHWH. At times, even the presentation of judgement in Ezekiel is so God-centred that Israel's responsibility seems to be undercut. This is seen in the reference to the punishment of the prophet whom YHWH himself has deceived (14:9–10) and in the bizarre verse that speaks of YHWH giving to his sinful people "statutes that were not good and ordinances by which they could not live" (20:25). Even such things as these can, it seems, be traced to this paradoxical God—"so that they might know that I am the LORD" (20:26). This trend is all the more marked in the material relating to deliverance. If in 20:25–26 YHWH enables sin that he might be known, in 36:26–27 he enables obedience for the sake of his "name." Ultimately, YHWH acts because he is YHWH and must be known to be YHWH.

The Departure of YHWH and his Return

The book of Ezekiel opens with the great vision of ch. 1, where the divine throne itself is witnessed in far-off Babylonia. YHWH is with his people in exile, no longer tied to the land of Israel. Chapter 1 here anticipates the departure of YHWH from the temple that will be recounted in chs. 10–11. That departure has a dual function, well expressed by Kutsko: "The absence of God from the temple (the removal of the divine *kāḇôḏ*) is both theodicy and theophany; it allows the presence of God to be associated with Israel in exile" (Kutsko 2000a:99). This affirmation of YHWH's presence with the exiles is one of the distinctive contributions of Ezekiel. We read in 11:16 that YHWH will himself become a *miqdāš mᵉʿaṭ* to his people; he himself is to be their sanctuary "in some measure" (Joyce 1996) in the countries where they have gone. It is, however, as though the price of this presence with his dispersed people is that YHWH has abandoned his temple. But in the final section of the book comes the grand return of the deity to his shrine (ch. 43), echoing many ancient Near Eastern models. The return of YHWH to his sanctuary is one of many satisfying symmetries that the book of Ezekiel features, and is in keeping with the particularly orderly nature of this book. Yet is it not also a disappointment that Ezek 43 brings back the deity and shuts him up again in his temple? Is this a timid retrenchment, an undoing of the profound contribution of the book whereby the limitations of place had been transcended? By no means. The throne vision of ch. 1, and indeed the *miqdāš mᵉʿaṭ* of 11:16: none of this is undone, but rather all needs to be borne in mind when the glory of YHWH returns from the east and fills the temple. This return does not erase the aforementioned motifs. The presence of God with his people wherever they are is not a temporary provision. Rather, the affirmation of 43:7 that "This is the place of my throne and the place of the soles of my feet" stands within the context of that overarching theology of the freedom of God. Moreover, the theme of the closed east gate of 44:2 does not run counter to this. The point there is that the gate is hallowed because YHWH has passed through it to return to the place of his special abode. It is not suggested that God is now shut up in his house. Having abandoned his sanctuary for a time, YHWH now commits himself to dwell in his sanctuary permanently. But this remains, within the grand architecture of the book of Ezekiel, in tension with the affirmation of his presence with his people in their dispersion. This is a rich theology, with a finely balanced dialectic between the presence of YHWH with his people wherever they are and his honouring of the particular location of the revelation of his holiness. The deity has indeed returned to his special place, where he will dwell among the people of Israel forever. But his freedom and mobility have also been established forever. It was noted earlier that Ezekiel's theology of judgement had broader theological implications, the portrayal of YHWH as the God who runs the affairs of the whole world carrying with it the nascent claims of theological universalism. Now, in the assurance that YHWH will be with his people wherever they are, we see another face of Ezekiel's universalism.

There is a further dimension to be considered, that which could be expressed, at least in picture terms, as the vertical plane or the heavenly dimension. For it is important that for Ezekiel, as for the priestly tradition within which he stood, the divine *kāḇôḏ*, "glory," that dwells on earth is an expression of his immanent presence that does not exhaust his being. More needs to be said about the theme of transcendence, in connection with how we are to understand Ezekiel's temple as presented in the book's last great vision (chs. 40–48). Ezekiel's temple has been understood in many different ways. Some have interpreted it as based in part on a preserved description or even blueprint of the first, Solomonic temple; others have read it as first and foremost a plan for a restoration temple; and others again have seen it as primarily an eschatological temple. In the long run, this material would certainly be read both in the context of an actual restoration after return from exile and also in terms of eschatological hope, but what was the earliest situation? The view that these chapters are to be seen as reflecting a visionary ascent to the heavenly temple, championed especially by Tuell (1996), deserves more attention than it has received. Indeed, there are grounds for believing that Ezek 40–42 was based in the first instance on a vision of the heavenly temple seen by Ezekiel himself during the exile (a view presented in detail in Joyce 2007). It is this theology of transcendence that undergirds Ezekiel's theology of universalism in its various aspects. Ezekiel features not only a dialectic between the presence of Israel's God with his people wherever they are and his honouring of the particular place of the special revelation of his holiness, but also a nuanced balance between the immanence of the deity and his overarching transcendence.

Ezekiel and Earlier Traditions

Ezekiel is indebted to tradition in a rich variety of ways. The theological agenda he addresses is defined by a range of traditions that appear to have broken down and to be in crisis: "the land" divinely promised to the patriarchs; Israel's status as a special people, chosen by YHWH; the city of Jerusalem; the temple; the monarchy. What does Ezekiel know of traditions that feature elsewhere in the Hebrew Bible? It is important to keep an open mind about when these are to be dated relative to Ezekiel, but we may begin by briefly reviewing these traditions in biblical order.

In various ways creation themes appear in the book. The prophet is addressed throughout as "Son of Man" (Heb. *ben-ʾādām*; NRSV: "Mortal"), and this evokes the first chapters of Genesis. The moral renewal of the nation in ch. 36 involves endowing with "a new spirit" and "my spirit," which echoes Gen 2:7 (notwithstanding the use of different terminology), as does the "dry bones" passage of ch. 37, with its twofold pattern of gathering and inspiring. More generally, the restored land is presented in idealistic natural terms in these chapters, like a new creation or a new Eden (notably Ezek 36:35: "And they will say, 'This land that was desolate has become like the garden of Eden'"). That the restoration material in Ezekiel should draw upon creation rather than conquest traditions is not surprising, for it is typical of Ezekiel that Israel plays no active role. The river of Ezek 47 evokes not only the rivers of Gen 2:10–14 but also ancient Canaanite tradition, and the book may be indebted to other creation themes much older than Genesis: the mythological traditions of the primal human being in the case of Ezek 28 and of the cosmic mountain in that of ch. 40.

As for flood traditions, a rainbow features in Ezek 1:28: "Like the bow in a cloud on a rainy day, such was the appearance of the splendour all around" (cf. Gen 9:13). But whether this is an allusion to the tradition of Genesis (a sign of divine favour) or just to the colours of the natural phenomenon is difficult to say. Judgement images in chs. 1–24 recall the Flood (notably 13:13: "Therefore thus says the Lord GOD: 'In my wrath I will make a stormy wind break out, and in my anger there shall be a deluge of rain, and hailstones in wrath to destroy it'"). Noah appears in ch. 14, alongside the other traditional figures of Daniel and Job (14:14, 20).

Patriarchal references are rare in the pre-exilic prophets, but their reappearance in exilic-era literature is noteworthy (e.g. Isa 40–55 and the so-called Priestly source). Ezekiel features a number of mentions of the patriarchs. That patriarch language reappears in the exilic age is not surprising, since the people had lost the land and looked to the traditions that claimed that it had been promised to their ancestors. Ezekiel 33:24 contains the one Ezekiel reference to Abraham, and interestingly it appears on the lips of sinners: "Mortal, the inhabitants of these waste places in the land of Israel keep saying, 'Abraham was only one man, yet he got possession of the land; but we are many; the land is surely given us to possess'" (cf. Isa 51:2, where similar sentiments are expressed as a legitimate hope by the anonymous prophet). Along similar lines, Ezek 28:25 and 37:25 speak of the restored people settling on the land given to Jacob. There are two other Jacob references: in 20:5 Israel is referred to as the offspring of the house of Jacob, while in 39:25 Jacob is used as a synonym for the whole house of Israel. Within the hopeful material of the book, references to ancestors (Heb. *ʾāḇôṯ*) are again to the patriarchs as recipients of the promise of land (20:42; 36:28; 37:25; 47:14). In contrast to this, within the judgemental material, references to ancestors (Heb. *ʾāḇôṯ*) denote sinful forefathers (2:3; 20:4, 24, 27, 36). Ezekiel makes it clear (consistent with ch. 18) that it is not because of the sins of these ancestors that Ezekiel's generation is condemned, but because they act similarly: "Therefore say to the house of Israel, 'Thus says the Lord GOD: "Will you defile yourselves after the manner of your ancestors and go astray after their detestable things?"'" (20:30)

Like patriarch language, Exodus themes return in the exilic age, not surprisingly since the people have lost all that YHWH's saving acts had led to. Exodus terminology is found in Isa 40–55 and in Jeremiah (e.g. Jer 23:7–8), and this is a feature of Ezekiel too, especially ch. 20, for example v. 34: "I will bring you out from the peoples and gather you out of the countries where you are scattered, with a mighty hand and an outstretched arm, and with wrath poured out" (cf. Zimmerli 1960). Lust highlights the affinities between Exod 6:2–8 and Ezekiel (Lust 1996), not least with regard to covenant language. The declaration "I am YHWH" both in this passage and elsewhere in Exodus (e.g. Exod 7:17) may well be the primary basis of Ezekiel's "Recognition Formula," as argued by Fohrer (1961:310). Ezekiel is presented in various ways as a second Moses (McKeating 1994; Levitt Kohn 2002b), and the Sinai affinities of the mountain of ch. 40 have also been noted (Levenson 1976).

The word "Zion" is never used in Ezekiel, but related city and temple motifs, as mediated especially by priestly tradition, are important (Renz 1999b). Monarchy is severely critiqued, because of its role in the downfall of the nation. David is mentioned only in the context of future hope (Ezek 34:23–24; 37:24–25), in ways that include significant downgrading of monarchic aspirations (Joyce 1998). One might well not expect the wisdom tradition to be of particular importance in Ezekiel, since wisdom is a relatively secular tradition, whereas Ezekiel is a markedly priestly book. But there are some points of contact. More than many prophetic books, Ezekiel features proverbs (e.g. 12:22; 18:2; cf. Darr 2004). The proverbs in 15:2 and 16:44 are set in the wider context of an allegory, a form with affinities to wisdom. Like Isaiah and Jeremiah, Ezekiel attacks self-sufficient wisdom (e.g. 28:3, addressed to the prince of Tyre: "You are indeed wiser than Daniel…"). Chapter 14 refers to three paragons of righteousness, two of whom, Daniel and Job, have particular affinities with the wisdom tradition (14:14, 20). That the profile of wisdom is not higher in Ezekiel may cohere with the ultimate marginalization of matters royal, and—on a larger scale—the eclipsing of human aspiration, in the context of the book's radical theocentricity. But that there are nonetheless some links with wisdom is not altogether surprising, for Ezekiel was exiled with the king and other members of the elite, and, in any case, as the centuries passed, wisdom and its influence became increasingly pervasive in Israel.

We should distinguish between general awareness of traditions, of the kind reviewed so far, and the more specific question of literary relations. (On the literary relations of Ezekiel, see Burrows 1925, Freedy 1969, and Zimmerli 1979a:41–52.) We must heed the warning of Fohrer concerning the need for caution in suggesting literary affinities, since many features may have been general currency. This is particularly important given the partial and selective nature of our sources (Fohrer 1952:135). One needs to discriminate between a range of possibilities: literary dependence; oral dependence; joint access to a shared tradition, written or oral; broader, more diffuse affinities and even coincidental independent developments, albeit within a shared cultural setting. Then there is the possibility of the redaction of Ezekiel by hands associated with other books of the Hebrew Bible, and conversely the influence of the book of Ezekiel on the redaction of other books. Clearly there is much in this area that cannot be known with confidence. Moreover, where influence seems likely we need to be open-minded about the direction in which it might go.

In Ezekiel we encounter a man who is both priest and prophet (cf. Sweeney 2001). Let us consider each, as ways into Ezekiel's tradition history and literary relations. Ezekiel was a priest before he was a prophet, and the priestly tradition is determinative for him and his book. Levitt Kohn's study of ninety-seven terms leads to the conclusion that Ezekiel appropriates priestly terminology but also feels comfortable situating it in new contexts (Levitt Kohn 2002a). Language with affinities to priestly case law is characteristic of the book; for example, the use of the phrase *ṣaddîq hûʾ* ("Such a one is righteous") in 18:9 and the phrase *môṯ yûmāṯ* ("He shall surely die") in 18:13. The major passages in question are 3:17–21; 14:1–20; 18:1–20; 22:1–16 and 33:1–20. Some have regarded such priestly affinities as relevant to issues of redaction (see the "Unity, Authorship, and Redaction" section, above); but because these features can readily be linked with the priest Ezekiel himself, it is unreliable to regard priestly affinities as distinctive of secondary strata.

On the nature of the relationship with the so-called Priestly source, Wellhausen and others thought "P" later than Ezekiel, although Ezekiel was heir to the same broad stream of tradition (Wellhausen 1883). An alternative scholarly tradition, largely but not exclusively Israeli, takes a different view. Hurvitz, using sophisticated linguistic methodology, compared the language of P with that of the book of Ezekiel to demonstrate that P is older (Hurvitz 1982; Haran 1979; cf. Rooker 1990). A related special case concerns the so-called Holiness Code or H, found in Lev 17–26. Ezekiel shares many similarities in ideas and expression with H (Reventlow 1962). There are, for example, close affinities between Ezek 6 and Lev 26. It may suffice to "explain much of the commonality of outlook and interest between the Book of Ezekiel and the authors of the Holiness Code and the Priestly Document as due to the dependence on the Jerusalem cult tradition that all three works shared" (Clements 1982:128). But there are other options. Some modern scholars, especially in earlier times, argued that Ezekiel was the author or editor of H (Graf 1866; Herrmann 1924:xix). But this gives insufficient weight to the differences, and so most have thought of H and Ezekiel as distinct and have posited influence one way or the other. Wellhausen (1883:395–402) argued that H is later than Ezekiel, and this position has been very influential. However, Klostermann contended that Ezekiel knew and used H in almost its present form, and others have taken a comparable view (Klostermann 1893; cf. Hurvitz 1982; Joosten 1996). And there are more complex positions. For example, Zimmerli contended that Ezekiel knew legislation of the exact type as is found in H, and adapted it to his needs, and yet he dates the final form of H much later than Ezekiel, Ezekiel having influenced the subsequent redactional history of H (Zimmerli 1954b). It is likely that we have to deal with some such complexity, but we cannot with confidence go further than the modest claim of Clements that "What we have in the two literary works of the Book of Ezekiel and the Holiness Code are compositions that have undoubtedly exercised a mutual influence upon each other" (Clements 1982:130).

"The word of the LORD came to the priest Ezekiel son of Buzi" (1:3). Ezekiel the priest now becomes also Ezekiel the prophet. Ezekiel's relationship with the prophetic traditions is a matter of special interest. His book is placed as one of the major prophetic books in both Jewish and Christian canons, and he is generally reckoned among the "classical" prophets by biblical scholars (though the use of this term of Ezekiel highlights its limited value). And yet in some respects, though relatively late compared with Isaiah and the other eighth-century prophets, he seems a primitive figure (e.g. 3:15: "I came to the exiles at Tel-abib, who lived by the river Chebar. And I sat there among them, stunned, for seven days"). Carley explored his links with so-called pre-classical prophecy and helpfully showed that these often explain his strangeness better than do theories of his mental instability (Carley 1975:69–81). Spirit language, associated especially with so-called pre-classical prophecy, has an important place in Ezekiel (Robson 2006). But Ezekiel walks very much also in continuity with the great eighth-century prophets. In his theology of divine judgement in history Ezekiel stands on their shoulders: YHWH uses a foreign nation to punish the sins of his own people (cf. Isa 10:5: "Ah, Assyria, the rod of my anger—the club in their hands is my fury!"). And there are many more specific debts of Ezekiel to these prophets. For example, Amos' talk of an "end" (8:2: "The end has come upon my people Israel; I will never again pass them by") seems to be taken up in Ezekiel (7:2, 6: "An end! The end has come upon the four corners of the land... An end has come, the end has come. It has awakened against you; see, it comes!). The portrayal of women to personify sinful nations (Ezek 16 and 23) owes much to Hosea, and Ezekiel's use of metal smelting as an image for judgement (22:17–22) seems indebted to Isa 1:22–25.

Ezekiel has a distinctive and complex relationship with his contemporary Jeremiah, whose ministry was exercised in Judah (Miller 1955; Vieweger 1993; Leene 2000, 2001). Within Ezekiel we see a rebirth of images from Jeremiah. From among many cases a few may be cited by way of example: swallowing a scroll (Jer 15:16; Ezek 3:1–3); YHWH fortifying the prophet against resistance (Jer 1:18–19; Ezek 3:8–9); a watchman or "sentinel" (Jer 6:17; Ezek 3:17); traditional paragons of virtue (Jer 15:1; Ezek 14:14, 20); bad and good shepherds (Jer 23; Ezek 34); and dry bones (Jer 8:1–2; Ezek 37). These and other cases raise the question of how to explain such similarities. It is tempting to assume that Ezekiel is the borrower, since it seems clear that Jeremiah was active as a prophet for some long time before him. Many similarities may well be explained that way, and this could involve actual dependence on written material or merely oral influence. But the issue is more complicated. Seitz writes: "The final form of the Book of Jeremiah reflects significant redactional intervention carried out under the influence of Ezekiel traditions" (Seitz 1989:295), and Collins comments: "In terms of the production of the books there is no doubt that Ezekiel in fact preceded Jeremiah, which has a very lengthy and complicated redactional history behind it" (Collins 1993:8). On a specific case, Gosse (2004a) argues that Ezek 18 and 20 influenced the conception of the "new covenant" in Jer 31:31–34. The probability is, then, that there has been mutual influence between Jeremiah and Ezekiel. We shall return to further consideration of this matter shortly.

Next we need to reflect on the place of deuteronomistic language within Ezekiel. There is a certain amount of material in Ezekiel that exhibits similarities to deuteronomistic literature. For example, Ezek 6:13 features subject matter and vocabulary typical of that tradition: "when their slain lie among their idols around their altars, on every high hill, on all the mountain tops, under every green tree, and under every leafy oak"; as does 18:6: "if he does not eat upon the mountains or lift up his eyes to the idols of the house of Israel"; and again 20:28: "For when I had brought them into the land that I swore to give them, then wherever they saw any high hill or any leafy tree, there they offered their sacrifices and presented the provocation of their offering; there they sent up their pleasing odours, and there they poured out their drink offerings." Levitt Kohn's (2002a) analysis of twenty-one terms leads her to the conclusion that there is considerable evidence of deuteronomistic influence on Ezekiel. Even Zimmerli, who tended to minimize the place of deuteronomistic elements in Ezekiel, had to recognize such affinities in Ezek 6:13 (Zimmerli 1979a:46). And for him (unlike Fohrer) the primary background for Ezekiel's central "Recognition Formula" is found in the Deuteronomistic History, for example 1 Kgs 20:13, 28 (Zimmerli 1957a:154).

Some have regarded deuteronomistic affinities as relevant to issues of redaction, with Herrmann (1965) and Liwak (1976) arguing for extensive deuteronomistic revision of Ezekiel (see the "Unity, Authorship, and Redaction" section, above); but because these features can be linked with Ezekiel himself it is unnecessary to regard deuteronomistic affinities as distinctive of secondary strata. There is no reason to believe that Ezekiel himself would have been untouched by the influence of deuteronomistic theology and style either in his native Jerusalem or in Babylonian exile. Redactors may well be responsible for a proportion of the deuteronomistic features in the book, but it cannot be demonstrated that all must be explained in this way.

Ezekiel takes for granted that there is to be only one central sanctuary. Could this reflect an indebtedness to the Josianic reforms usually associated with the deuteronomistic movement (2 Kgs 22–23; cf. Deut 12)? Mein observes that "the centrality of the Jerusalem sanctuary is an immovable datum of the religion" in the context of priestly as well as deuteronomistic theology (Mein 2001a:115). This being so, we should not overestimate the need for dependence on deuteronomistic influence here. And indeed more generally the deuteronomistic element in Ezekiel is relatively muted, and certainly less important than the priestly background. As with the issue of Jeremiah and Ezekiel, there are some challenging theories about the direction of any influence between deuteronomistic material and Ezekiel. Braulik (2001) argues that Deut 19–25 is a very late addition to Deuteronomy, drawing upon both Ezekiel and the Holiness Code; interestingly, he claims that Deut 24:16 depends upon Ezek 18.

Levitt Kohn (2002a) has offered an interesting thesis about the presence of both priestly and deuteronomistic language and concepts alongside each other in Ezekiel. She argues that Ezekiel appears to fuse P and D material, creating a synthesis all his own and yet similar to that effected by the Redactor of the Torah. Ezekiel thus anticipates the production of the Torah in its final form. However, there are problems with this. Levitt Kohn overstates the extent to which Ezekiel offers a unified national theology, moving beyond the exclusivity proposed by both P and D. Her picture of Ezekiel as synthesizer and reconciler stands at odds with the evidence that he was an intense and distinctive figure, influenced by various traditions (as we have seen) but far from being a "lowest common denominator" person. A better expression of the interrelation of priestly and deuteronomistic elements in Ezekiel would be to say that he is first and foremost a priest, but one not altogether immune from the deuteronomistic influences that eddied around him both in Jerusalem and in Babylonia.

Two theologically significant sections of Ezekiel raise important issues of literary relations and a closer look at these will serve to bring the present discussion towards a conclusion by illustrating some of the complexities of these matters in relation to Ezekiel. I refer to Ezek 11:19–20 ("I will give them one heart, and put a new spirit within them; I will remove the heart of stone from their flesh and give them a heart of flesh, so that they may follow my statutes and keep my ordinances and obey them. Then they shall be my people, and I will be their God") and 36:26–27 ("A new heart I will give you, and a new spirit I will put within you; and I will remove from your body the heart of stone and give you a heart of flesh. I will put my spirit within you, and make you follow my statutes and be careful to observe my ordinances"). Miller (1955) showed that the number of significant points of contact between Jeremiah and Ezekiel is greater where the material concerns future hope and restoration from exile. And indeed a number of passages in the book of Jeremiah exhibit significant similarities to the verses of Ezekiel we have just reviewed. Of these, the three most striking are Jer 24:7; 31:31–34; and 32:38–40. Von Rad regarded these parallels as so significant that he wrote: "One feels that Ezekiel must somehow have had Jeremiah's prophecies in front of him" (von Rad 1962–65:2.235).

We cannot, however, overlook the fact that these three passages in Jeremiah that bear the closest resemblance to Ezek 11:19–20 and 36:26–27 are among those Jeremianic prose passages in which deuteronomistic influence seems most apparent. What deuteronomistic features may be discerned in the two Ezekiel contexts? Much of the wording of Ezek 11:14–21 is close to Deuteronomy: the reference to the "scattering" of Israel in 11:16 recalls Deut 4:27, while the "gathering" promised in the following verse is reminiscent of Deut 30:3–5; moreover, the description of obedience in Ezek 11:20 closely resembles the language of Deut 26:16–19. In Ezek 36 too we find marked affinities with Deuteronomy; for example, the description of the renewal of nature in vv. 29–30 employs a number of words particularly characteristic of Deuteronomy (e.g. *dāg̱ān*, "grain"). There are two respects in which our texts are most significantly paralleled by Deuteronomy and the wider deuteronomistic literature. These are, indeed, two of the features shared with the Jeremiah texts we reviewed earlier. They are the "covenant" formula, "You shall be my people, and I will be your God" (Deut 26:17–18; 29:13 [Heb. v. 12]), and the motif of the "heart" (*lēḇ*; *lēḇāḇ*) as the place of moral response to YHWH (Deut 6:4–6; 30:2, 14). In Deut 30:6 we find the remarkable statement that YHWH will circumcise the "heart" of Israel, so that his people will be able to fulfil the command (of Deut 6:4–5) to love YHWH with all their "heart." This promise, so like the Ezekiel passages, takes us beyond the moral exhortation and challenge that characterize the bulk of Deuteronomy (note especially Deut 10:16: "Circumcise therefore the foreskin of your heart, and be no longer stubborn") to a recognition of Israel's need for YHWH to enable the response that he demands. It is probable that Deut 30 comes from the exilic period; we may perhaps discern here a deuteronomistic theology "come of age" under the shock of Babylonian conquest and deportation, events that appeared to demonstrate the inability of Israel to live up to the demands of YHWH. Such a development is reflected also at those points in the Deuteronomistic History where the "heart" is mentioned in connection with YHWH granting a new ability to do his will (e.g. 1 Sam 10:9: "When he turned his back to leave Samuel, God gave him another heart"; cf. 1 Kgs 8:58). The moral renewal of Israel promised in Ezekiel is so similar to this material that it is probable that Ezek 11 and 36 reflect deuteronomistic influence.

But were these deuteronomistic features mediated entirely by Jeremianic material or were they absorbed more directly? The likelihood is that Ezekiel both had direct access to such influence and that it was reinforced through his debt to Jeremiah. Moreover, the picture also needs to be broadened, for it would be a mistake to view the development of a theology of "grace" during the exilic period as an exclusively deuteronomistic phenomenon. Such themes are too widely evidenced for that to be the case. Among psalms that are likely to be exilic, we may note especially Ps 51: "Create in me a clean heart, O God, and put a new and right spirit within me" (Ps 51:10 [Heb. v. 12]; cf. Ps 79:8–9). Comparable hopes are a feature of Isa 40–55 (cf. Isa 43:25; 44:3; 48:9–11). Furthermore, the priestly elements of the Pentateuch are particularly marked by unconditional promises (e.g. Gen 9:8–17). It is doubtful whether all of these can be accounted for on the hypothesis of a complex web of dependence, whether oral or written. Rather, it is probable that here are independent responses to the same situation, albeit made in the light of much shared history and tradition. The experience of defeat and exile was indeed a traumatic one for Israel as a whole, demanding a radical re-evaluation of theological assumptions. Many came to feel that if there were to be a future it would have to depend entirely upon YHWH rather than upon the merits of Israel.

Two important features constitute the distinctive contribution of Ezekiel himself to the expression of the hopes of 11:19–20 and 36:26–27. First, the passages are both marked by the radical theocentricity that characterizes Ezekiel. Second and more specifically, both feature the word "spirit" (Heb. *rûaḥ*). It is conspicuously rare both in Deuteronomy (where it occurs just twice, at 2:30 and 34:9) and in Jeremiah (just once, at 51:11); by contrast, it occurs frequently in Ezekiel (41 times, excluding references to "wind"). How are we to account for the presence in Ezek 11:19–20 and 36:26–27 of features that seem to be distinctive of Ezekiel alongside those that appear to reflect deuteronomistic influence? We may conjecture that while still in Jerusalem prior to deportation in 597, Ezekiel imbibed at least some of the concerns and style of the deuteronomistic movement. These elements were reinforced both through an awareness of the Jeremiah tradition and through the influence of Deuteronomists active in Babylonian exile. The form of expression of the promise of renewal in Ezekiel thus came to owe much to the deuteronomistic movement (which may have continued to exercise an influence upon the redactional tradition after Ezekiel's time). Nevertheless, Ezekiel has also left his personal stamp on the expression of the promise, not only in his use of "spirit" language, but also in the radical theocentricity of his presentation.

Finally, we note that Ezekiel is remarkably bold in the way he draws upon past tradition. In spite of sharing a good deal with the deuteronomistic tradition and with Jeremiah, we see Ezekiel as distinctive not only in his use of "spirit" language but also in his insistence (ch. 18) that it is the present generation alone whose sins are being punished (in contrast to 2 Kgs 23:26 and Jer 31:29). Other examples of his independence in relation to traditions abound. Chapter 16 is scathing in its critique of the Zion tradition (v. 3: "Your origin and your birth were in the land of the Canaanites; your father was an Amorite, and your mother a Hittite"), as elsewhere Ezekiel is radical in his downgrading of monarchy; king and messiah are marginalized, as indeed is the national history that the kings had shaped (Joyce 1998). Another case, striking in view of Ezekiel's closeness to the priestly tradition, is found in his differences from Pentateuchal legislation in chs. 40–48 (compare, for example, Ezek 46:6 with Num 28:11; and see further the "Place in the Canon" section, below). But we see Ezekiel's radical freedom in the handling of tradition most clearly evidenced in ch. 20. In Ezekiel alone in the Hebrew Bible Israel sins even in Egypt, before the Exodus (v. 8; cf. 23:3, 8). And finally, remarkably, God gives "statutes that were not good and ordinances by which they could not live" (v. 25). In all of this Ezekiel works with an independent sense of authority and confidence rooted in his God-centred faith.

Structure

A distinctive feature of the book of Ezekiel is the extent to which it is arranged in a systematic and thematic fashion. It is in many ways the most orderly of the prophetic books—the contrast with the book of Jeremiah in this regard is particularly striking. It is difficult to know, however, how to weigh this orderliness. For a long time this was seen as evidence of original authorship by the prophet himself. Then it became typical to see it as the work of later editors. But neither extreme is correct. As with the theology and the style of Ezekiel, we are probably dealing here with a genuine feature of the work of the prophet Ezekiel that has nevertheless been heightened in the course of redaction and become more characteristic of the finished book than of the primary material.

The major sections of the book are as follows: chs. 1–3, presenting the prophetic call of Ezekiel; chs. 4–24, concerning YHWH's judgement upon Judah and Jerusalem; chs. 25–32, containing oracles against foreign nations; ch. 33 constituting the turning-point of the book; chs. 34–37, focusing upon hopes for the restoration of Judah; chs. 38–39 dealing with the episode of Gog of Magog; and chs. 40–48, presenting an extended vision of the temple (see the "Outline Analysis of Ezekiel," below, for more detail).

There is a rabbinic notion that the book of Ezekiel comprised two halves, the second more hopeful than the first (cf. *b. B. Bat.* 14b). Some have seen this as the key to Josephus' comment on Ezekiel where he tantalizingly states that Ezekiel "left behind two books" (*Ant.* 10.5.1 [79]). The extent to which judgement and hope are thus separated in this book is indeed striking. There are just four short passages of positive promise within the long section constituted by chs. 4–24, namely 11:14–21; 16:59–63; 17:22–24; 20:40–44. A strong case can be made for the originality of 11:14–21, both in the sense of it coming from the prophet himself and in the sense of it deriving from the period before 587. But it is likely that the other three passages represent redactional additions of a hopeful nature.

Chapter 1 serves as a prelude or overture to the entire book; themes of the work as a whole are here broached, foregrounded and given priority. Chapter 33, in which the news reaches the prophet that Jerusalem and its temple have fallen, functions as a turning-point or fulcrum within the book, after which the key shifts from minor to major, the theme from judgement to hope. Chapters 3 and 33 form "book-ends" around the first "half" of the ministry, with ch. 33 recapitulating various themes of the preceding chapters before the second "half" of the ministry (and the book) begins. The book has some significant groupings of material. For example, 1:1–3; 8:1–3 and 40:1–2 share many features, and the three major visions that they introduce are like great landmarks within the book. Chapters 16, 20 and 23 present three histories of the nation and its sin, and interspersed with these are the vivid allegorical judgements of chs. 15, 17 and 19. There are various elements of *inclusio* in the book, for example 1:28 ("This was the appearance of the likeness of the glory of the LORD") and 48:35 ("And the name of the city from that time on shall be, 'The LORD is There'"); chs. 3 and 33, with their themes of the prophet as "sentinel" (NRSV: "watchman") and of his dumbness; chs. 6 and 36, announcing judgement and later blessing upon the "mountains of Israel"; and, most important of all, the movement of the glory of YHWH, which departs from the temple in chs. 10–11 and returns in ch. 43. All in all, this is a book of impressive literary architecture.

A particularly distinctive feature of the book of Ezekiel is its dating schema. There are fourteen dates (not including 3:16, "at the end of seven days"), almost all in chronological sequence. The characteristic dating formula gives year, month and day (in that order). This schema confirms the impression of systematic order, and a debate similar to that described above has gone on about whether it derives from the prophet, from editors, or (most likely) from both. The dates are given in terms of the exile of King Jehoiachin (and, it seems, Ezekiel himself) in 597, running in sequence from 1:2 (the "fifth year," that is 593) to 40:1 (the "twenty-fifth year," that is, 573). This is the last of the sequence of dates in Ezekiel, although apparently later dates are found in 29:17 ("the twenty-seventh year," which would be 571) and 1:1 (the "thirtieth year"—a much debated crux, but this would be 568 if the reference were to the thirtieth year of the exile of Jehoiachin). These references, however interpreted, leave us a few years short of the release of Jehoiachin from prison, mentioned in 2 Kgs 25:27 (the "thirty-seventh year," that is, 561). Reference to the month is missing in three cases, 1:2; 26:1 and 32:17 (though the Greek text has a month, "the first," in 32:17), while 40:1 has "at the beginning of the year" instead of a month reference—the reference here is probably to the spring new year (cf. 45:21, which places Passover in the "first month").

It is interesting to note that the dating schema incorporates the section of oracles on the nations, rather than leaving it out. (Indeed, the Egypt cycle, in chs. 29–32, contains no less than six dates.) This coheres with the fact that these oracles are integral to the book, probably largely primary in authorship and are addressed indirectly to Israel. Davis notes that "The fact that Jerusalem's fate is linked to the fates of her enemies is underscored by the dating of the oracles of the nations; most of them cluster in the months immediately before and after Jerusalem's fall in 587" (Davis 1999:227). The Tyre and Egypt sections appear in the "wrong" order (at least on the basis of the dates in 26:1, the "eleventh year," and 29:1, the "tenth year"). Ezekiel 29:17 (the "twenty-seventh" year, that is 571) refers to the fact that Tyre, though subjugated, had not in fact fallen to the Babylonians (cf. 26:7), and looks like a correction of the earlier oracle, whether from Ezekiel himself, as Greenberg (1997:618) argues, or his redactors.

(In relation to the chronological framework, see further Parker and Dubberstein 1956; Freedy and Redford 1970; Kutsch 1985.)

Text and Versions

There is no shortage of textual problems in Ezekiel, and this is in part due to the remarkable content of the book. Cooke attributed the many uncertainties in the text "partly to the usual accidents of transmission, but even more to the extra-ordinary nature of the events described… [T]he very state of the text, with all its corruptions and inaccuracies, bears witness to the eager handling of those who studied it" (1936:xxvii).

The Masoretic Text (MT) of the Hebrew Bible was established in the fifth to eighth centuries C.E., though its consonantal text was probably complete before the end of the first century C.E. However, the earliest complete text of the MT that survives is the Leningrad Codex of 1008 C.E., and this is the base text for the standard critical edition, *Biblia Hebraica Stuttgartensia* (*BHS*), and its successor, the fifth edition of *Biblia Hebraica* (the so-called Quinta edition). Older but incomplete is the Cairo Codex, dating from 895 C.E.; this codex includes the Prophets and is available in a modern critical edition (for Ezekiel, see Perez Castro 1988). Reference should also be made here to the tenth-century Aleppo Codex, the base text for the Hebrew University Bible Project, the Ezekiel volume of which is now available (Goshen-Gottstein and Talmon 2004). Although there are many minor cases where later Hebrew manuscripts deviate from these and other early texts, they normally represent later errors, rather than independent ancient readings (Goshen-Gottstein 1967:253).

Some scholars defend the MT of Ezekiel in almost all cases, Greenberg being the most influential example over recent years (see especially Greenberg 1983a, 1997). Others have come to a different conclusion. Cooke (1936:xl) wrote: "In the Hebrew Bible perhaps no book, except 1 and 2 Samuel, has suffered more injury to its text than Ezekiel." It is clear that the MT cannot always be followed, for evidence suggests that at points corruption of the original Hebrew has occurred (e.g. see the commentary on 3:12, below). Sometimes whole sections seem significantly affected (e.g. chs. 7, 21 and 28:11–19). In such cases a reconstruction of the original Hebrew can be sought, though one should not automatically assume that the text is corrupt simply because its meaning now appears obscure. It is important to remember that our knowledge of ancient Hebrew remains limited, not least when dealing with a book that contains over 130 words that do not occur anywhere else in the Hebrew Bible. Emendation of the MT should normally be proposed only where textual evidence can be adduced. In the present commentary it should be assumed that the MT is followed, except where otherwise indicated.

Textual critics apply their skills to the Hebrew text in all its complexity, according to criteria that are constantly being developed, standard guides to which are provided by Tov (2001) and Würthwein (1995). But it is not only Hebrew that is to be assessed. The "ancient versions" are the translations of the Hebrew into other ancient languages, and these too can yield important evidence. Cornill's 1886 commentary gives a still valuable presentation of the characteristics of these versions of Ezekiel. Scholars generally make a distinction (not always easy to maintain absolutely) between the "primary" versions, that is, translations from the Hebrew itself, and "daughter" versions, which are themselves based on translations. Supreme among the primary versions is the Greek Septuagint (LXX), which has an important place in the study of the text of Ezekiel. This translation of Ezekiel from the Hebrew was probably made in the early second century B.C.E. (Harl, Dorival and Munnich 1994:111), much earlier than the final establishment of the MT in fifth to eighth centuries C.E. The Göttingen LXX is the first genuinely critical edition; the Ezekiel volume was produced by Ziegler (revised edition 1977). The LXX seems to be based on a Hebrew original (or *Vorlage*) that often differed from the text we know in the MT. It is theoretically possible that the LXX translators were working with a Hebrew original substantially the same as the MT, and that deviations are mostly due to the errors or deliberate changes introduced by the LXX translators. There are no doubt particular cases where this is so; for example, Zimmerli (1979a:421) found in the LXX of Ezek 21:3 (Heb. v. 8) "a classical example of a correction for dogmatic reasons." It is generally thought improbable, however, that such factors can account for the bulk of the deviations of LXX Ezekiel from the MT, not least because this Greek translation of Ezekiel is usually fairly literal (Ziegler 1953). There are good grounds for concluding that the LXX may at times have preserved a superior reading, or at least a clue as to the reconstruction of an improved reading of the Hebrew.

Some scholars have gone further, claiming that LXX Ezekiel reflects a more faithful and less encumbered text than the usually longer and more repetitive MT. This was argued as long ago as 1847 by Hitzig and by many since, including Wevers (1969), who relied heavily on the LXX, arguing that the repetitive Hebrew text of Ezekiel should often be trimmed in accordance with the LXX (concision being regarded here as a criterion of originality). A particular case of a modern scholar who gives decisive weight to the evidence of the LXX is Lust, who is responsible for the Ezekiel text for the Quinta edition of the Hebrew Bible. The first section of Lust's edited conference volume *Ezekiel and his Book* (1986d) contains many significant essays by him and others on the textual criticism of Ezekiel.

Yet not all are content to give the evidence of the LXX such authority. Carley (1975) and Boadt (1978) have plausibly shown that repetition and redundancy may be characteristic features of the prophet Ezekiel's own Hebrew. They argue that Hitzig and Wevers generally failed to take adequate account of the possibility of deliberate or indeed accidental shortening of a longer Hebrew text by the Greek translators. Boadt (1992:716) suggests the possibility that "the LXX has abbreviated long, difficult and perhaps boring passages to make them sharper and clearer for a Greek audience outside of Palestine." We have already noted that Greenberg is a stout defender of the MT. While he concedes that the MT "contains a good deal of variant readings (conflated passages) and explanatory increments not present in the Hebrew *Vorlage* of the Greek translators," he goes on to suggest that the prophet may have been his own first editor (Greenberg 1997:396). What Greenberg is proposing here is that Ezekiel himself may have left a version of the Hebrew (the ancestor of the MT) that was more developed than the Hebrew text that later came into the hands of the Greek translators. Cooke devoted much attention to considering the relative superiority of the MT and the LXX in numerous particular examples, arguing that the evidence must "be weighed in each case and considered on its merits, without a bias in favour of one side or the other" (1936:xli–xlvii). There is much to commend such a position, which steers a judicious course between the stances represented by the more recent commentaries of Wevers (strongly favouring the LXX) and Greenberg (vigorously defending the MT). It should be acknowledged though that, while Cooke's balanced approach is attractive, it runs the risk of creating a hybrid text that never actually existed as a whole and ultimately respects neither the MT nor the LXX. An influential trend in recent textual criticism has instead attempted to present the distinctive histories of the main texts (especially the MT and the LXX) as carefully as possible, recognizing the integrity of each.

Notwithstanding scholarly disagreements, the LXX is clearly important for the study of Ezekiel, and so it is appropriate to note some particular features of LXX Ezekiel. The earliest surviving Greek text of Ezekiel is P. 967, also known as the Chester Beatty–Scheide Papyrus 967, the significance of which has increasingly been recognized in the light of new evidence (Ziegler 1945/48, 1977; Lust 1981a; Barthélemy 1992:cxxv–cxxvi). It probably originated in the first half of the third century C.E. (Würthwein 1995:71–72, 194–95). There is much debate about the homogeneity and unity of LXX Ezekiel. Some scholars have argued that there was more than one translator; for example, McGregor (1985) defended a threefold division of the LXX text (chs. 1–25, 26–39, 40–48) and there have been variations on this view. On the other hand, Ziegler (1953) considered LXX Ezekiel to be essentially homogeneous. A major issue in assessing the homogeneity and unity of LXX Ezekiel concerns the variation of the Greek where the Hebrew has the double divine name (*ᵓᵃḏōnāy yhwh*, e.g. 2:4). Many LXX manuscripts vary internally in their rendering of the divine name, but it is significant that the earliest text, P. 967, is largely consistent in its use of the single word *kurios*. This has important implications. The first bears on the situation in Hebrew: many have doubted that the double divine name was an original feature of the Hebrew, precisely on account of its apparently inconsistent translation in the LXX. Commentators including Fohrer (1955:15) saw it as a late insertion in the Hebrew, while Cooke explained it as the result of a process of gradual accretion connected with the developing post-exilic practice of pronouncing *ᵓᵃḏōnāy* instead of the special name of Israel's God: "*Adonai Jahveh* may be a sort of scribal direction to pronounce *Adonai* where *Jahveh* stands in the text"

(Cooke 1936:33). But the largely consistent practice of the earliest Greek text on this point (using the single word *kurios*) leads Lust (1968) and others to defend the originality of the double name in the Hebrew. On balance, it is likely that the double name usage is original to the Hebrew, and that the single word *kurios* was the original LXX practice, with a later, albeit uneven, tendency in the Greek to assimilate to the Hebrew's double divine name. Furthermore, the consistency of the P. 967 usage in this regard makes it less likely that several translators shared in the preparation of the earliest LXX Ezekiel (though debate continues; cf. Lust 1986a:12; 1987a:221).

Questions are also raised about particular passages in LXX Ezekiel. For example, the LXX of ch. 16 has long been the subject of dispute: Thackeray (1921:38) considered it to be a supplement, while Turner (1956:21) regarded it as a composite text incorporating older strata. More generally, there is evidence that the earliest Greek text lacked altogether certain passages that are represented in the MT, for example, 7:6–9; 12:26–28; 13:7 and 36:23c–38 (see especially Lust 1986a:12–15). Particular attention has been devoted to the last of these cases. A distinct but closely-related phenomenon is the sequence of chapters in this earliest Greek text. Chapter 37 appears later in P. 967 than it does in the MT. Thus 36:1–23b is followed directly by chs. 38–39; then comes ch. 37, followed by chs. 40–48.

While P. 967 should be acknowledged as the earliest and best text of LXX Ezekiel, it is unclear what implications this might have for the Hebrew. It is one thing to attempt to recover the most original text of the LXX; it is another to identify its Hebrew *Vorlage*. Lust (e.g. 1981a) changes what has generally been seen as a text-critical problem, internal to the LXX, into a literary-critical issue, arguing that the Hebrew text of Ezekiel originally had the same omissions and even the same sequence as P. 967. He contends that 36:23c–38 was an insertion in the Hebrew, a possibility entertained also by Zimmerli (1983:242–48). Lust judges 36:23c–38 to be a late bridge between 36:1–23b and a newly transposed ch. 37. This is consistent with his general approach to the so-called longer "minuses" in LXX Ezekiel (i.e. those cases where the Greek is significantly shorter than the Hebrew): he observes that "Longer minuses are not likely to be attributed to a translator using literal translation techniques" (Lust 1986a:15).

These issues must be taken seriously, and Lust may well be correct in some particular cases. However, it is by no means clear that his overall thesis is justified. Not surprisingly, Greenberg reacts strongly against any attempt to deny the originality of MT 36:23c–38, writing that this "impoverishes, when it does not actually deform, the text" (Greenberg 1997:396; cf. 738–40). But there is truth in Lust's accusation that Greenberg is "convinced…of the autosufficience of the MT" (Lust 1986a:13), so Greenberg's stance in this particular case might well have been predicted. More significant critiques of the position represented by Lust are found elsewhere. Long ago Filson argued that the arrangement of P. 967 and its omissions could satisfactorily be explained on the grounds of accidental damage to the text at some early stage (Filson 1943). This line was also followed by Wevers (1969:273), in spite of his positive attitude to

LXX Ezekiel, and a similar argument was advanced by Spottorno (1982). Moreover, it is striking that no extant Hebrew text (including the Masada manuscript of Ezek 35:11–38:14 [Talmon 1999]) features either the omissions or the sequence of P. 967. Furthermore, much can be said in defence of the integrity of the Hebrew on literary and theological grounds: the account of the vindication of the divine "name" is far from complete at 36:23b and the *inclusio* formed by 36:22 and 36:32 is striking. Nonetheless, there is no getting away from the fact that there seem to have been two early divergent textual traditions, Hebrew and Greek. Each must be acknowledged as important without rejecting the significance of the other.

Until recent times, our oldest Hebrew texts of Ezekiel were medieval copies of ancient manuscripts, but the discovery of the Dead Sea Scrolls at Qumran in the mid-twentieth century yielded evidence approximately a millennium older. A major Ezekiel scroll was found in Cave 11, but, frustratingly, it was petrified and could not be unrolled, though some fragments were recovered from the surface (Brownlee 1963; principal edition, Herbert 1998). There are a number of references and allusions in Qumran material to the subject matter of the book of Ezekiel, but relatively little evidence bearing directly upon its text has appeared (for details, see Lust 1986c:90–93; Fitzmyer 1990:232–33; Brooke 1992:318–21). For example, Cave 4 has yielded a range of fragments from three Ezekiel manuscripts (Lust 1986c:93–99; Sinclair 1989; subsequently published in a principal edition, Sanderson 1997). Moreover, 4QFlorilegium seems to include a reference to Ezek 37:23 (Brooke 1985:116–18). Some minor Ezekiel materials were found in Caves 1 and 3. With regard to related material discovered elsewhere, the Damascus Covenant document from the Cairo Genizah explicitly quotes Ezek 9:4 and 44:15. Yadin found portions of an Ezekiel scroll at Masada, and he described them as "virtually identical with the traditional biblical texts" (Yadin 1966:187–89); this material, which contains 35:11–38:14, was subsequently published in a principal edition (Talmon 1999; cf. Talmon 1997). It was thought by some scholars that the Dead Sea finds had elevated the text-critical value of LXX Ezekiel over against the MT. For example, McGregor (1985:15–16) wrote: "Certain readings exhibited by Hebrew mss. from Qumran seemed to agree with the LXX against the MT, and hence indicated that a number of the LXX's differences with the MT might stem from a different *Vorlage* rather than from the idiosyncrasies of the translators." This debate continues, and weighing of the data is complex, but most scholars now see the Qumran and related finds as generally close to the MT. Indeed, this is true even of Lust; important here for him is the evidence of the Cave 4 fragments; for example, he says of 4QEz^{b} that "In general, the text is identical with the MT and does not support the corrections inspired by the LXX" (Lust 1986c:96). Overall, we can say that Qumran encourages some confidence in the MT of Ezekiel, affirming the antiquity of the text it represents.

The contribution of the other versions, especially the Aramaic Targum, the Syriac Peshitta and Jerome's Latin Vulgate, is often important but generally less so than the LXX. The Targum is the Aramaic paraphrase of the Hebrew text;

Targum Jonathan on the Latter Prophets was established as an authoritative text in Babylonia in around the fifth century C.E. (The critical edition is Sperber 1962; an English translation, with commentary, is found in Levey 1987.) The Peshitta is the Syriac translation of the Hebrew. Some scholars argue for a close affinity with the Aramaic Targums and highlight the Jewish milieu, while others emphasize the Christian background; there is a complex history of influence by and interrelation with the LXX (Weitzman 1999:68–86, 206–62). The critical edition of the Peshitta is that of the Leiden Project (Mulder 1985; cf. Mulder 1986). Turning to the Latin language, the so-called "Old Latin" was a translation from the LXX. It is generally a good witness to the earliest text of the LXX; in Ezekiel, it is often close to P. 967, as notably in Old Latin Codex Wirceburgensis (Bogaert 1978). Jerome's Vulgate, produced in the late fourth to early fifth centuries C.E., purports to be a translation directly from the Hebrew, but is much influenced by the LXX and later Greek versions. The Ezekiel volume of the "San Girolamo" critical edition of the Vulgate appeared in 1978.

Recent years have seen the appearance of some literary approaches emphasizing the "final form" of Ezekiel (e.g. Nobile 1982). Studies of this kind tend to marginalize issues of textual criticism. Considerable insight can be gained from these various "final form" readings, but the painstaking task of seeking the earliest text remains important. This is not to imply that certainty is attainable; while it is tempting to regard textual criticism as an objective enterprise, yielding assured results, the quest for an original, "pure" form of the text must ultimately be regarded as an abstract ideal. The Qumran finds have stimulated valuable reflection on what might be meant by the "text" of a biblical book (Tov 1982). Moreover, for all his tenacious attention to detail, Lust is admirably frank in acknowledging the provisional nature of textual criticism (Lust 1986a:8, 16–19; 1986b:53–54). It may often be that we do not have access to the original text, but the alternative can itself be exciting enough. For as we sift the complex range of textual variants, we may indeed eavesdrop on the conversations of interpreters in ancient times, as they wrestle with the remarkable tradition which is that of Ezekiel.

Place in the Canon

The incorporation of the book of Ezekiel into the Hebrew canon was by no means uncontroversial. Ezekiel was at various times in danger of being "withdrawn" (*gnz*, a technical term, for which a better translation might be "stored away"). Precisely what this means has been the subject of discussion. It could be that withdrawal is to be understood in a liturgical sense, referring to a decision not to use material in communal worship. It is surprising that doubts were raised about the book of Ezekiel, given its repeated claim to be divinely inspired prophecy, its striking religious content (including the radically God-centred emphasis) and features that imply an early date (such as the dating schema emphasizing exilic provenance).

The book of Ezekiel was regarded as problematic for three reasons. First, it contains explicit sexual language and this proved controversial in some quarters. For example, in the Mishnah (*m. Meg*. 4:10) Rabbi Eliezer is reported as saying that ch. 16, with its presentation of Jerusalem as a young girl, is not to be used as a reading from the Prophets. But two other problems received more attention in rabbinic discussion. Jerome reports in his *Epistle 53 to Paulinus* that, according to Jewish tradition, the beginning and the end of Ezekiel are to be read only by those aged thirty and over. The two problems concerned the boldness of the opening vision of the mobile divine throne (spoken of in later tradition as a chariot) and certain alleged deviations from the Torah in the final chapters of the book. Let us consider these in turn.

Among the rules in the Mishnah that restrict the public reading of certain portions of Scripture, we read that "They may not use the chapter of the Chariot as a reading from the Prophets, though Rabbi Judah permits it" (*m. Meg*. 4:10). Elsewhere the Mishnah states that the same passage may not be expounded even before one person alone, unless he is a sage that understands of his own knowledge (*m. Ḥag*. 2:1). The opening chapter of Ezekiel was clearly regarded as a "dangerous" passage. The Babylonian Talmud (*b. Ḥag*. 13a) recounts the cautionary tale of a child who was reading the book of Ezekiel at his teacher's house. We are told that the child "apprehended what *ḥašmal* [NRSV: "amber"; cf. Ezek. 1:4, 27] was, whereupon a fire went forth from *ḥašmal* and consumed him. So they sought to suppress the book of Ezekiel." This text also states: "Rabbi Johanan said to Rabbi Eleazar: 'Come, I will instruct you in the "Work of the Chariot".' He replied 'I am not old enough'."

The other issue concerns alleged deviations from Torah found in the final long section of Ezekiel, chs. 40–48. According to a famous story recounted in the Babylonian Talmud (*b. Šabb.* 13b), Ezekiel was in danger of being "withdrawn," but Hananiah ben Hezekiah, a sage of the first century C.E., sat in an upper chamber for as long as it took him to explain Ezekiel in ways consistent with the Torah. We learn more details elsewhere in the Babylonian Talmud. A problem is posed by the fact that Ezek 46:6 says that on the day of the new moon a young bull shall be offered, and six lambs and a ram, whereas Num 28:11 commands that, as well as a ram, *two* young bulls and *seven* lambs be offered. The Talmud reconciles these two texts by saying that if two bulls cannot be found, just one must be brought and, similarly, that if seven lambs are not to be found, six must be brought (*b. Menaḥ.* 45a). The other problematic Ezekiel texts mentioned in this section of the Babylonian Talmud are 44:31; 45:18, 20 and 46:7. It is interesting to note that, whereas inconsistency within the historical narratives of the Hebrew Bible could be tolerated (e.g. between Kings and Chronicles), divergence in matters of regulation was more problematic.

Such were the problems that worried the rabbis. But it would be a mistake to regard the central issue as being whether Ezekiel was worthy of inclusion within the canon of Scripture. On the contrary, rather than this book being judged second-rate or deficient, it was its very power and mystery that proved problematic. The book was regarded as dangerous (as illustrated graphically in the story of the child's death) precisely on account of its holiness. Since the text was the bearer of awesome mysteries it had to be treated with extraordinary respect. We can best view matters in the following way: whereas the Torah can generally be read without restriction, Ezekiel is deemed too powerful for that. Far from being deficient in its claims for canonical inclusion, Ezekiel could thus, in some respects, be said to have a higher status than even the Torah itself. As for the question of inconsistency with the Torah, it is important to see that this is an "inner-canonical" issue. Had it not been for an already established sense that the book of Ezekiel was inspired Scripture, inconsistencies between Ezekiel and the Torah would not have troubled the rabbis. Such divergences might well constitute a danger to the uneducated and therefore justify restriction of access, but the issue can be stated more positively: these very inconsistencies constitute "a signal that the text contains deeper meanings which are best left to the learned" (Barton 1986:72). With regard to two of the passages where (according to the Babylonian Talmud, *b. Menaḥ.* 45a) Ezekiel appears to contradict the Torah (44:31 and 45:18), rabbinic authorities are cited in favour of deferring resolution of the problem until the promised return of Elijah (cf. Mal 4:5–6). This may at first sight appear to be no more than an easy way out of a problem, yet on closer inspection this strategy proves to be a sophisticated hermeneutical tactic, acknowledging an excess of meaning in the text that draws us beyond our present understanding.

The closure of the canon of the Hebrew Bible has been the subject of particularly lively debate over recent decades. Leiman (1976) and Beckwith (1985) date this closure very early; Beckwith in particular argues that the process was complete long before the famous Council of Jamnia (Jabneh) in 90 C.E., indeed before the lifetime of Jesus (the latter point a matter of theological importance for Beckwith). On the other hand, Sundberg (1964) and Barton (1986, 1997) contend that the process was more protracted. To support the early canonical status of Ezekiel, Beckwith assembles evidence (in texts ranging from Ecclesiasticus to 1 Clement and the Mishnah) of Ezekiel being acknowledged as authoritative. There can be no doubt that the book of Ezekiel was highly regarded from early times (and it may well be significant in this connection that the book secured a place among the Prophets, rather than being placed in the third category of the Hebrew Canon, the Writings, in which are found all the other books about which there was significant dispute). Nevertheless, while Beckwith successfully demonstrates that the book of Ezekiel was highly regarded from early times, this does not in itself prove that the canon was formally closed from such an early point. Indeed, the very notion that while some books (including Ezekiel) were inside a canonical circle others were definitely excluded may well reflect the preoccupations of later centuries.

Ezekiel normally appears in the Hebrew Bible as the third of the major prophetic books, after Isaiah and Jeremiah, and is followed directly by the twelve Minor Prophets. Interestingly, however, rabbinic evidence testifies to some deviation from this standard order: the Babylonian Talmud (*b. B. Bat.* 14b–15a) places the Major Prophets in the order Jeremiah, Ezekiel, Isaiah (in spite of the acknowledged historical order of the prophets themselves), on the basis of their thematic content. Specifically, this text argues that the Former Prophets (Joshua–2 Kings) end on a note of destruction; Jeremiah continues this theme; Ezekiel begins with destruction but moves on to consolation; and, finally, Isaiah focuses on consolation. These books, read in this sequence, may be seen as communicating an important theological message about the way God's judgement is followed by his mercy, and it is striking to note the pivotal role given to Ezekiel in such a pattern. The presentation of the prophetic books in the English Bibles used by Christians (derived in this respect from the Greek Septuagint, followed by the Latin Vulgate) differs from the standard Hebrew pattern. Isaiah does precede Jeremiah, but the book of Lamentations, traditionally associated with Jeremiah, is placed before Ezekiel, while the book of Daniel (widely understood within Christian tradition as a prophetic work) separates Ezekiel from the twelve Minor Prophets. Whereas the Prophets occur in the middle of the Hebrew Bible, between the Torah and the Writings, they are found at the end of the Christian Old Testament; this too reflects Christian theological perspectives that regard the Prophets as prefiguring and preparing the way for the Christian gospel.

AFTER EZEKIEL: EZEKIEL IN TRADITION

The story of the reception of Ezekiel's own work begins long before the completion of the book. I have noted that the text bears many marks of interpretation and elaboration. It seems that the disciples of the prophet and their descendants, perhaps even a "school" of Ezekiel (as Zimmerli argued), were responsible for this process of elaboration.

The book of Ezekiel exercised a significant influence on the later writings of the Hebrew Bible. For example, Tuell has demonstrated the influence of Ezekiel on the content and more especially the form of Haggai and Zech 1–8 (Tuell 2000c), while Fishbane has explored the relationship between Ezek 44:1–14 and Isa 56:1–8 (Fishbane 1985:138, 142). Even more striking is the mark Ezekiel has made within Daniel (e.g. Dan 7; 10), Joel (esp. Joel 2–3) and Deutero-Zechariah (e.g. Zech 14). More generally, the book of Ezekiel had a pervasive effect on the development of apocalyptic, both within and beyond the canon (Dürr 1923; Rowland 1982; Dimant 1992). Some discussion of the social context of apocalyptic has suggested that it arose in marginal circles opposed to central priestly authority (Plöger 1968; Hanson 1979); however, as a book exhibiting both priestly and apocalyptic features, Ezekiel fits badly within such a polarized model, and indeed discussion of the evidence of Ezekiel (especially chs. 38–39) has played a significant role in the challenging of this so-called Plöger–Hanson hypothesis (Cook 1995a).

Ezekiel's name, which is used rarely even in his own book (1:3 and 24:24), is never mentioned elsewhere in the Hebrew Bible, but Ezekiel does feature in the Apocrypha, specifically in Ecclesiasticus (Sirach), which makes explicit reference to the prophet within the context of a survey of great figures in Jewish tradition (Sir 49:8: "It was Ezekiel who saw the vision of glory, which God showed him above the chariot of the cherubim"). The following verse can be construed to say that Ezekiel mentioned Job, which would presumably be an allusion to Ezek 14:14, 20.

In frequency of citation, Ezekiel generally fares less well in post-biblical tradition than either Isaiah or Jeremiah. One exception is *4 Macc* 18:10–18 (c. first century C.E.); this passage includes Ezekiel among "the law and the prophets," referring to the words of Ezek 37:3, "Can these bones live?" At much the same time, Philo was writing his *De Specialibus Legibus*, which features seven quotations from Ezekiel; among these, when paraphrasing the ceremonial commandments, Philo (*Spec*. 1.84) seems closer to Ezek 44:17–18 than to Lev 16:4. Josephus comments on Ezekiel among other classical prophets in his

Antiquities (Begg 1988); as already noted, he tantalizingly states that Ezekiel "left behind two books" (*Ant.* 10.5.1 [79]). Some have interpreted this in the light of the rabbinic notion that the book of Ezekiel comprised two halves, the second more hopeful than the first (cf. *b. B. Bat.* 14b). Alternatively, the reference could be to the so-called *Apocryphon of Ezekiel* (see Mueller and Robinson 1983; Mueller 1992, 1994). Though extant only in fragments and mostly in quotations in Greek from the Christian Fathers, this seems to stand in some relation to the biblical Ezekiel. It may have been a work in its own right or it could have its origin as a midrash on the canonical book; three of the five extant fragments bear some similarity to Ezekiel. While some scholars are sceptical about the five extant fragments necessarily being from one work (e.g. Cook 1996:534), Mueller (1994) has influentially argued that they are indeed from a single source, which was Jewish (rather than Christian) and written in Hebrew. He proposes a dating of around the first century B.C.E. to the first century C.E. Repentance and judgement are recurrent themes in the *Apocryphon*, with eschatological overtones. The title is drawn from Epiphanius' introduction to the longest and best-known fragment, which he attributes to Ezekiel's "own apocryphon" (*Panarion* 64.70). This features a parable about two men, one lame and the other blind, who are punished for robbing a king's garden. Stone, Wright and Satran (2000) have provided an excellent resource for the study of these and other apocryphal Ezekiel materials.

In passing, it should be explained that the *Exagoge* of "Ezekiel the Tragedian" (c. second century B.C.E.) is a drama that recounts the story of the Exodus from Egypt. It includes a non-biblical scene in which Moses has a vision of God enthroned on Sinai; there is some affinity with the vision of Ezek 1, but the name of the author could be merely coincidental (cf. Robertson 1985; van der Horst 1992b; Lanfranchi 2006).

The evidence of the Dead Sea Scrolls (on which see also the "Text and Versions" section, above) suggests that the priestly oriented eschatological prophecy of Ezekiel had a considerable impact at Qumran (Wacholder 1992). Prominent among the Ezekiel material that exercised a particular influence are the opening throne vision and the related material in ch. 10, the condemnation of the nation in chs. 16 and 23, the dry bones of ch. 37, and the final temple vision of chs. 40–48. Brooke has speculated that, given the recurrence of certain passages in the relatively small body of Qumran Ezekiel materials, it may be that there were "excerpted texts," that gathered these and similar Ezekiel materials for community use (Brooke 1992:318–21). While there are no extant running pesharim devoted to providing interpretations of Ezekiel (in the manner of the Habakkuk Commentary), indirect references abound. Particularly worthy of mention is 4Q Second Ezekiel, otherwise known as "Pseudo-Ezekiel" (c. mid-first century B.C.E.; found in fragments 4Q383–391, most importantly 4Q385). This is an example of so-called rewritten Bible, and is an apocryphal work modelled on the book of Ezekiel (Strugnell and Dimant 1988; Dimant 1992:49–50; Brooke 1998:286–90; Brady 2005). It is available in a principal edition (Dimant 2001). Pseudo-Ezekiel amplifies such material as Ezek 1, 10 and 37 (Dimant and Strugnell 1990; Kister and Qimron 1991–92). There is evidence that the work was known to early Christian writers, specifically the author of the letter of *Barnabas* (Kister 1990) and the author of the *Apocalypse of Peter* (Bauckham 1992). Moreover, Pseudo-Ezekiel is striking in the way it draws together material from Ezekiel and Isaiah in a manner similar to some use of Scripture in the New Testament, for example, Rev 4 (Brooke 1992:324–25). Bauckham (1996) argues that Pseudo-Ezekiel is in fact the same work as the aforementioned *Apocryphon of Ezekiel* known from fragments in the Christian Fathers, but most scholars doubt such an identification (e.g. Dimant 1992:49; Cook 1996:534; Brooke 1998:287).

There are allusions to many Ezekiel motifs within the sectarian literature of Qumran; to a large extent this reflects the apocalyptic nature of that community. For example, according to the Damascus Document the community of the new covenant arose 390 years after the destruction of Jerusalem (CD 1:6–10; cf. Ezek 4:5). The document also quotes, with some significant minor differences, Ezek 9:4 and 44:15 (CD 3:21–4:2; 19:11–12; cf. Lust 1986c:92–93). The start of the War Scroll refers to the "wilderness of the peoples" (cf. Ezek 20:35), and the same document features the name "Gog" (cf. Ezek 38–39) (Vermes 1997:127, 163, 175). The pervasive self-designation of the Qumran covenanters as "sons of Zadok" seems dependent on Ezek 44. Several non-sectarian compositions, found at Qumran but lacking the specific characteristics distinctive of the Qumran community, such as the Temple Scroll (11QTemple) and the work called *The New Jerusalem*, make use of Ezek 40–48 in particular (Dimant 1992:45–48). That these works do not seem to have originated in the community itself serves only to highlight the breadth of the influence of Ezekiel at this time.

The work known as the *Lives of the Prophets* includes a section on Ezekiel, in which a legend about the death of the prophet is recorded: "He died in the land of the Chaldeans during the captivity… The ruler of the people Israel killed him there as he was being reproved by him concerning the worship of idols" (Stone, Wright and Satran 2000:69–94). The notion that Ezekiel experienced opposition in Babylonia could perhaps echo the biblical reference to the binding of Ezekiel (Ezek 3:25: "As for you, mortal, cords shall be placed on you, and you shall be bound with them, so that you cannot go out among the people"; cf. Zimmerli 1979a:158–59). Hare suggests that the New Testament Letter to the Hebrews (Heb 11:37: "They were stoned to death, they were sawn in two, they were killed by the sword") may refer respectively to Jeremiah, Isaiah and (least certainly) Ezekiel (Hare 1985:383; cf. Wright 1997). Scholars are divided about the date of the *Lives of the Prophets*; most would place it around the first century C.E. (Hare 1985, 1992; Schwemer 1995, 1996), but Satran (1995) has argued that it derives from the Byzantine period. (On Ezekiel outside the Bible, see further Aberbach 1971 and Wright 1998.)

Of special importance in the reception history of Ezekiel is the tradition of Merkabah mysticism, an influential if controversial phenomenon within post-biblical Judaism, associated particularly with Johanan ben Zakkai (Scholem 1960; Gruenwald 1980; Halperin 1988). Such mysticism focused on the inaugural vision of Ezekiel. The word *merkāḇâ* ("chariot") is not found in Ezekiel, which speaks rather of a moving "throne" (*kissēʾ*), but the word is used in Sir 49:8. Meditation on Ezek 1 sometimes led to the experience of ecstasy, and this became the classic case of a biblical passage being regarded as the bearer of esoteric mysteries about the nature and even the appearance of God himself. The so-called "Riders of the Chariot" engaged in "soul ascents" to the palaces of heaven, where they saw God and his holy angels. Allusions to such mysticism are found in a range of rabbinic texts; these include, in the Babylonian Talmud, *b. Ḥag.* 14b, in the Palestinian Talmud, *y. Ḥag.* 77a, in the Tosefta, *t. Ḥag.* 2.1, and in the Mekilta de R. Simeon ben Yohai, *Mishpatim* 21.1. At Qumran around the first century B.C.E., the *Songs of the Sabbath Sacrifice* represent a particularly early example of such mysticism, clearly dependent on Ezekiel (especially chs 1, 10 and 40–48) (Newsom 1985; Vermes 1997:321–30). The text is available in a principal edition (Eshel 1998). It is striking that Ezekiel is connected to both the Merkabah tradition and, as we noted earlier, incipient apocalyptic. In fact, Rowland (1982) sees Merkabah mysticism as related very closely to apocalyptic (interpreted more in terms of cosmology than of eschatology) and indeed presents Ezek 1 as the tap root of the apocalyptic tradition. Some recent work in the history of Jewish mysticism has strengthened the case for seeing Ezekiel as central to the development of the mystical tradition (Wolfson 1994; Elior 2004).

The dangers relating to Merkabah mysticism were a concern in certain circles; this was one of the features associated with Ezekiel that led some in ancient times to regard the book as problematic (see the "Place in the Canon" section, above). Nevertheless, Ezekiel is frequently quoted, with standard formulae for citing Scripture (including "as it is written") in the Mishnah (e.g. *m. Yoma* 8.9 cites Ezek 36:25; *m. Mid.* 2.5 cites Ezek 46:21–22). The Ezekiel Targum (Sperber 1962; Levey 1987) evidences parallels between Ezekiel's reaction to the destruction of the temple in 587 B.C.E. and responses to the destruction of 70 C.E. In this respect, the Targum exemplifies the genius of Judaism in using traditional resources in wrestling with recurrent catastrophe (Mintz 1984). The development of the hope of resurrection within post-exilic Judaism owes something to Ezekiel's expression of the hope of national restoration in the striking vision of the valley of dry bones (Ezek 37). In Judaism, as in Christianity, there is a strong trend towards literal rather than metaphorical interpretation of the passage (Day 1996; cf. Greenberg 1997:749–51). The portrayal of this passage in the Dura-Europos synagogue wall paintings in Mesopotamia (c. third century C.E.) is representative of the ongoing role of Ezekiel in Judaism (Kraeling 1956; see further Stone, Wright and Satran 2000:101–12). The Jewish tradition of exegesis of Ezekiel has been rich, numbering among its major medieval contributors Kara, Rashi, Eliezer of Beaugency and Kimḥi (cf. Galambush 1999a:373) and among those in the modern period David and Jehiel Altschuler and Malbim. Continuity with this tradition is one of the distinctive features of the work of Greenberg (1997:411).

As a biblical prophet, Ezekiel enjoys a place of honour within Islam. However, Ezekiel (Arabic *Hizqil*) is, like Isaiah and Jeremiah, never mentioned by name in the Qur'an. Both the dry bones of Ezek 37 and the Gog of Magog material of chs. 38–39 are alluded to, but not explicitly linked with *Hizqil.* A few late Islamic sources identify an obscure Qur'anic personality with *Hizqil.* There are two references in the Qur'an (21:85–86 and 38:48) to a figure called *Dhu al-Kifl* ("One endowed with responsibility" or perhaps "One doubly endowed"). The link is tenuous, and one explanation is that it may rest on a supposed connection with Ezekiel's onerous responsibility as a watchman (Ezek 3:16–21; 33:1–9; NRSV: "sentinel"). Of related interest is an Islamic shrine to *Hizqil* (equated with *Dhu al-Kifl*) at al-Kifl in Iraq, venerated historically also by Jews. Sometimes Islamic tradition associates the figure of *Hizqil* with the period of the Judges, and may at points confuse him with Samuel. (On Ezekiel within Islamic tradition, see further Schussman 1998.)

If we turn to the place of Ezekiel in Christianity, though by no means one of the most frequently cited Old Testament books (and never mentioned by name), Ezekiel has left its mark on the New Testament. The image of the Good Shepherd (John 10) owes much to Ezek 34 (Manning 2004). More than once the resurrection language of the New Testament seems to allude to Ezek 37 (e.g. Matt 27:52; Rev 11:11; cf. Grassi 1964–65). The book of Revelation reflects the symbolism of Ezekiel at numerous points (e.g. the four living creatures in Rev 4 and Gog and Magog in Rev 20:7–10; cf. Vanhoye 1962; Ruiz 1989; Kowalski 2004; Sänger 2006). Goulder (1980–81) characteristically argued that much of the book of Revelation is shaped by liturgical reading of Ezekiel. Second Corinthians is indebted to Ezekiel at various places (e.g. 2 Cor 3:3; 6:16–17). The depth of Paul's dependence on Ezekiel is acknowledged by Young and Ford (1987:74–76) and by Hays (1989:128–31). Less widely recognized is the extent to which more generally the emergence of a theology of "grace" among the exilic prophets provides crucial background to Paul's interpretation of the Christian gospel. Some have read 2 Cor 12:2–4 as suggesting a link with Merkabah mysticism, indeed Bowker (1971) argued that Paul's conversion experience on the Damascus road took place in the context of such a vision.

Van der Horst (1992a) provides a fascinating treatment of the interpretation of the "statutes that were not good" of 20:25 in ancient Judaism and early Christianity, arguing that, in spite of the differences between these two traditions, the same lack of historical consciousness conditioned their responses to this notoriously difficult text. For the Christians, the "statutes that were not good" always referred to the commandments of the Torah itself or their interpretation, whereas for the Jews (sometimes perhaps reacting to Christian interpretations) they never referred to the Torah but only to rabbinic rules or pagan laws.

Ezekiel plays a recurrent if unobtrusive role in both Patristic and Scholastic literature, as Neuss (1911, 1912) demonstrated at length. (For a general survey of the reception history of Ezekiel in Early Christianity, see Dassmann 1988:1151–83; cf. Galambush 1999a.) Some of the great figures in Christian tradition have given close attention to the book. Within the Patristic era, Origen and Gregory the Great devoted homilies to it. Origen's massive and influential commentary survives only in fragments, but major commentaries by both Jerome and Theodoret are extant. An interesting case is provided by Jerome's handling of Ezek 44:2: "This gate shall remain shut; it shall not be opened, and no one shall enter by it; for the LORD, the God of Israel, has entered by it; therefore it shall remain shut." This verse is used as scriptural authority for the doctrine of the virgin birth, a reading facilitated in various ways by Jerome's Latin rendition (J. F. A. Sawyer, unpublished paper on "Ezekiel in the History of Christianity"). The Christian Fathers generally made much of Ezek 37 as a proclamation of the final resurrection of the dead. This features prominently in early church art (Neuss 1912), but, surprisingly, Ezek 37 rapidly disappears in Western art, and does not feature, for example, in the great twelfth-century cycle of wall paintings based on Ezekiel in the Doppelkirche Church at Schwarzrheindorf, near Bonn (Verbeek 1953; Königs 2000; Odell 2005:42). Distinguished among medieval expositors of Ezekiel were the so-called Victorines, especially Hugh (1096–1141) and Andrew (1110–1175) of St Victor, Paris. They were noted for their insistence on the literal sense of the Bible, and Andrew in particular drew systematically upon Jewish interpretation (Patton 1998a), features that characterized also the work of Nicholas of Lyra (c. 1270–1349) (Patton 1998b).

In later times, the prophet's radical theocentricity was much admired by John Calvin (1509–1564). His sermons on Ezekiel, delivered between 1552 and 1554 in the church of "La Madeleine" in Geneva, offer intriguing material on his exposition of the visions, including those on the restoration of Israel, Gog and Magog and also the great temple vision. They constitute a striking specimen of literal historical exegesis with a christological perspective (De Boer 2004). Calvin produced a commentary on chs. 1–20. This consists of revised transcripts of his last lectures, delivered in 1563–64 and first appearing in print in the year after his death (Parker 1986:29). Calvin's account of the inaugural vision becomes a statement of his doctrine of providence (Calvin 1994:41), and he finds support in Ezekiel for his doctrine of total depravity, as is seen in his comments on Ezek 11:19–20 (Calvin 1994:271). John Donne (1572–1631), poet and Dean of St Paul's, London, declared: "Amongst the four great ones, our prophet Ezekiel is the greatest…the extraordinary greatness of Ezekiel, is in his extraordinary depth, and mysteriousness" (Sermon 105; Potter and Simpson 1953–62). The ancient Jewish tradition of mystical speculation on Ezekiel spread to Christian circles, for example in J. Reuchlin's work *De arte cabalistica* (Reuchlin 1517). Another example of contact between Jewish and Christian scholars is found in the influence of rabbinic authorities on the Ezekiel translations of the English and Dutch Authorized Versions (Lloyd Jones 1968–69; Verdegaal 1986).

In the modern period, there are clear examples of the way the perspectives of readers have a marked influence on interpretation, and occasionally distort the text. For example, Ezekiel gained favour among some critics on account of his supposed individualism; such ideas survived well into the twentieth century (e.g. Causse 1937:201). Or again, Protestant prejudice about priests has sometimes been found. Kennett closed a chapter on Ezekiel with the words: "He was the father of Judaism, but of a Judaism in which the Gospel could not germinate… Of Ezekiel's teaching the almost inevitable outcome was Caiaphas, while Jeremiah marked out the way which led to Jesus Christ" (Kennett 1928:58). Ezekiel has often come off badly in modern times in comparison with prophets such as Jeremiah or Hosea (e.g. Robinson 1948). Ezekiel is not generally perceived as a congenial character, with whom readers can readily identify and onto whom they can project their sentiments and their spiritual aspirations. Some modern interpreters have attempted to render Ezekiel's theology more sympathetic, playing down the extent to which Ezekiel's God is merely concerned for his reputation and emphasizing the place of compassion and forgiveness (e.g. Carley 1975:59; Tiemeyer 2006a:259–60), but this has been at the expense of accuracy.

One interesting feature of the quest for the historical Ezekiel in the nineteenth and twentieth centuries (reflecting a preoccupation of the times) was the attempt to diagnose Ezekiel's condition in terms of a psychological illness that might explain his bizarre behaviour (Klostermann 1877; Broome 1946). More recently Halperin (1993) revived this approach, offering a thoroughgoing reductionistic Freudian reading (cf. Joyce 1995b). More nuanced psychological readings have been offered since by Smith-Christopher (1999; 2002:83–89), Garber (2004), Jobling (2004), Schmitt (2004) and Stiebert (2005). Feminist criticism, reading familiar passages with new eyes, has provided an impetus for a reassessment of the place of women and the feminine in Ezekiel. Chapters 16 and 23 in particular have both generated a great deal of writing over recent years (e.g. Van Dijk Hemmes 1993; Kamionkowski 2003). The sexually explicit, perhaps even pornographic, content has led some critics to consider the book seriously problematic if not downright immoral (cf. Darr 1992; Exum 1995; Moughtin-Mumby 2008).

The place of Ezekiel in modern literature is not insignificant. William Blake's indebtedness to the book was considerable, as is seen in *The Marriage of Heaven and Hell*, where, in one of his "memorable fancies," the prophets Isaiah and Ezekiel dine with the author; Blake also produced illustrations of several scenes from Ezekiel. (On Ezekiel in art more generally, see Beck and Werbeck 1962.) The play *Juno and the Paycock* by the Irish writer Sean O'Casey ends with an anguished plea that Ireland's "hearts o' stone" be replaced with "hearts o' flesh" (cf. Ezek 11:19; 36:26).

Perhaps one of the most bizarre legacies of Ezekiel is found in the legend of the last of the British giants, Gog and Magog, whose statues stand in London's Guildhall; these figures appear to derive their names, by an obscure route, from the Gog of Magog who makes war on the people of Israel in chs. 38–39. The influence of the book remains evident in sayings such as "wheels within wheels" (cf. 1:16) and "like mother, like daughter" (16:44) and in African-American spirituals, such as "Dem Bones" (cf. ch. 37).

Ezekiel has long played an important part in millennial speculation, not surprisingly in view of its historical association with apocalyptic material. Such links were strongly evident in the latter part of the twentieth century (Lieb 1998). As in ancient times so in modern, the opening chapter of Ezekiel has continued to exercise a strangely powerful appeal and influence. Von Däniken's best-selling book *Chariots of the Gods?* (1969) interpreted the passage in terms of extra-terrestrial visitors, and allusions to the same Ezekiel imagery were observed in Steven Spielberg's 1977 film *Close Encounters of the Third Kind.* Ezekiel played a more explicit role in Quentin Tarantino's important film *Pulp Fiction* (1994), of which the oft-repeated refrain is adapted from Ezek 25:17: "I will execute great vengeance on them with wrathful punishments. Then they shall know that I am the LORD, when I lay my vengeance on them." It is sobering to reflect that this proved to be the primary association of the word "Ezekiel" for millions of people around the world at the end of the twentieth century. Though it can hardly be denied that vengeance is a strong feature of the first half of the book, it is sad that brutal vengeance is what the word "Ezekiel" evokes for so many. No one can predict what new associations Ezekiel will gather in this new millennium. One can only hope that they will be truer to the whole of the witness of this great book.

Outline Analysis of Ezekiel

1:1–3:27 *The Prophetic Call of Ezekiel*

1:1–3	Superscription
1:4–28a	The Throne-Chariot Vision
1:28b–3:27	A Series of Commissions

4:1–24:27 *Messages of Judgement upon Judah and Jerusalem*

4:1–5:17	Prophetic Sign-Actions	
6:1–14	Oracle against the Mountains of Israel	
7:1–27	Oracles on the Approaching Judgement	
8:1–11:25	The First Temple Vision	
	8:1–18	Abominations in the Temple
	9:1–11	The Slaying of the Guilty
	10:1–22	The Burning of the Wicked City
	11:1–21	Judgement and Promise
	11:22–25	YHWH leaves his Temple
12:1–20	Prophetic Sign-Actions	
12:21–28	Judgement not Delayed	
13:1–23	Against False Prophets	
14:1–11	Against Idolaters	
14:12–23	Noah, Daniel and Job	
15:1–8	The Allegory of the Vine	
16:1–63	Jerusalem the Unfaithful Wife	
17:1–21	The Allegory of the Two Eagles and the Vine	
17:22–24	The Allegory of the Cedar	
18:1–32	"This proverb shall no more be used by you"	
19:1–9	The Lament of the Lions	
19:10–14	The Lament of the Vine	
20:1–44	"Will you defile yourselves after the manner of your ancestors?"	
21:1–32	The Sword of Judgement	
22:1–31	The Bloody City	
23:1–49	The Two Sisters, Oholah and Oholibah	
24:1–14	The Allegory of the Pot	
24:15–27	Oracle on the Death of Ezekiel's Wife	

25:1–32:32 *Oracles against Foreign Nations*

25:1–17	Oracles against Ammon, Moab, Edom and Philistia
26:1–28:26	Oracles against Tyre
29:1–32:32	Oracles against Egypt

33:1–33 *The Turning-Point*

33:1–20	A Recapitulation of Themes
33:21–22	"The city has fallen"
33:23–29	Judgement on the Non-Exiles
33:30–33	"A prophet has been among them"

34:1–37:28 *Oracles of Blessing upon the Nation*

34:1–31	Bad and Good Shepherds
35:1–36:15	Judgement for Edom; Blessing for Israel
36:16–38	A New Heart and a New Spirit
37:1–14	The Valley of the Dry Bones
37:15–28	Judah and Israel Reunited

38:1–39:29 *Gog, King of Magog*

38:1–9	Invasion by Gog
38:10–23	Plot Doomed to Defeat
39:1–20	Gog's Armies Defeated
39:21–29	Israel Restored to the Land

40:1–48:35 *The Great Temple Vision*

40:1–42:20	A Tour of the Temple	
	40:1–47	The Temple Area, Gates, Outer and Inner Courts
	40:48–41:26	The Temple Itself
	42:1–14	The Priests' Chambers
	42:15–20	The Temple Area as a Whole
43:1–12	The Return of the Glory of YHWH	
43:13–27	The Altar of Burnt Offering	
44:1–31	Temple Ordinances and Priesthood	
45:1–9	The Distribution of Land	
45:10–17	Weights and Measures, and Offerings	
45:18–25	Festival Regulations	
46:1–18	Regulations regarding the Prince	
46:19–24	The Priests' Quarters and the Temple Kitchens	
47:1–12	The River of Life	
47:13–23	Israel's Boundaries and Allotment of Land	
48:1–29	Division of the Land	
48:30–35	The Gates of the City	

Commentary on Ezekiel

CHAPTER 1

The first chapter of Ezekiel—which presents nothing less than a vision of the deity himself—serves as an overture to the entire book. A major feature of the book as a whole is the departure of the glory of YHWH from Jerusalem within chs. 8–11 and its return in ch. 43. But here in the opening vision the deity is already seen in alien Babylonia, the chapter foregrounding his presence with the exiles, even before (in narrative terms) he has left Jerusalem. This is an anticipation of the central theme of the book, as is confirmed when in 43:3 a retrospective reference mentions these passages not in their biblical order but in their logical or temporal order, namely chs. 8–11 before ch. 1: "The vision I saw was like the vision that I had seen when he came to destroy the city, and like the vision that I had seen by the river Chebar." As an overture to the entire book, ch. 1 of Ezekiel may be compared to ch. 1 of Isaiah: themes of the book as a whole are here broached, foregrounded and given priority. The chapter's primacy within the book has been echoed down the centuries by its great importance in reception, within Christianity and even more so within Judaism, where it is the tap root of the Merkabah mystical tradition and also—arguably—of the apocalyptic tradition.

1:1. "In the thirtieth year": the way a book starts is important; if the pattern of Pentateuchal books in the Hebrew Bible were followed, this book might have acquired the title *wayᵉhî bišlōšîm šānâ* ("and it came to pass in the thirtieth year"). In fact, these words constitute a major crux, both in their own terms and in the light of the different time reference that follows in v. 2: the "fifth year of the exile of King Jehoiachin." Some scholars have attempted to ease the problem by textual emendation (Herntrich 1933 and Whitley 1959: "third" year; Bertholet 1936: "thirteenth" year), but there is no manuscript or versional support for such a change. No theory is entirely satisfactory, but there are three plausible contenders: (i) From ancient times some have related the mysterious "thirtieth year" to Josiah's Reform of 621 (giving a date of 593, counting inclusively). This would cohere with v. 2 (so Herrmann 1924), but it is odd that the reform is not mentioned by Ezekiel. (ii) Lindblom (1962) and others (including Origen) proposed a reference to the prophet's personal age. Taylor emphasizes thirty as the age of full initiation to priesthood (cf. Levites at Num 4:3 and 1 Chr 23:3), speaking of Ezekiel's call to prophecy at this age as a kind of compensation for his loss of the active role of priest (Taylor 1969:39). This must be regarded as a real possibility. However, the most natural interpretation is (iii) that the reference is to the thirtieth year of the exile. This theory has the virtue of following the system of dating that characterizes the rest of the book. This date would be later than the other late dates in the book (cf. 40:1: "the twenty-fifth year"; 29:17: "the twenty-seventh year") and would represent the year 568. This thirtieth year of the exile is best understood as the year of the compilation of the book (Howie 1950). Such a view need not rule out further redactional activity on the book during the remainder of the exilic period. Obviously, on this interpretation, the thirtieth year is not the same as the date given in v. 2 (the fifth year) and the attempt to equate the thirtieth and the fifth years must be seen as a gloss aimed at clarifying a confusing opening. The dating formula continues "in the fourth month, on the fifth day of the month." This is typical of the dating schema in this book, which gives year, month and day (see the "Structure" section, above), a system that has also influenced Haggai and Zechariah (Tuell 2000c).

"As I": the autobiographical format of the book is one of its most characteristic features. This was one reason why the book was for a long time, even in the age of modern historical criticism, regarded as a unity containing the authentic words of the prophet himself. But the first person 'I' narrative style of the book can be paralleled in numerous ancient Near Eastern texts that are certainly not autobiographies (e.g. from Mesopotamia, the Epic of Gilgamesh, and, from Egypt, the Story of Sinuhe)—just as we are very familiar with fictional autobiography in the modern novel. "The exiles": Ezekiel's primary audience (see the "Time and Place" section, above). Mein argues that the distinctive situation of the exiles as once-influential elite figures now robbed of autonomy and power is a major determinative factor in the nature of the book (Mein 2001a:257–63). "By the river Chebar": cf. Ps 137:1: "By the rivers of Babylon—there we sat down and there we wept when we remembered Zion." The exiles may have gathered by rivers especially for purposes of ritual cleansing and prayer (cf. Acts 16:13). "The river Chebar" probably refers to a canal, located in the region of Nippur. Absolute identification of the location is neither achievable nor particularly significant; but two things are important. The reference to the river Chebar emphasizes the reality and specificity of the location of Ezekiel's vision (1:1, 3; cf. 3:15) and also serves as a marker for cross-reference throughout the book (3:23; 10:15, 20, 22; 43:3). "The heavens were opened, and I saw visions of God": a remarkably explicit statement! Rowland sees the nature of apocalyptic as characterized by the opened heaven and the visionary experience, and judges this chapter to be crucial in the rise of apocalyptic (Rowland 1982).

1:2. "The fifth year of the exile of King Jehoiachin": this is the date given for Ezekiel's inaugural vision, not to be equated with the date in the previous verse. Jehoiachin was king in Jerusalem for just three months and was exiled at the age of eighteen in 597 (2 Kgs 24:8). We read of his release from prison in the thirty-seventh year of his exile in 2 Kgs 25:27–30. There is no explicit reference to a month here in 1:2, but the text assumes the fourth month of v. 1. According to a lunar calendar, with the year starting in spring (cf. 45:21), the date would be

31st July 593. Several features link 1:1–3; 8:1–3 and 40:1–2, the opening verses of the three great visions of the book. Three key motifs occur together only in these three contexts: the dating formula specific to the day, common in Ezekiel's prophecy; the phrase used for expressing prophetic ecstasy, "the hand of the LORD was on him" (Heb. *wattᵉhî ʿālāyw yad-yhwh*); and reference to *marʾôṯ ʾᵉlōhîm* ("visions of God"). The passages are bound together also by the cross-reference formula of 43:3, alluding to both chs. 8–11 and ch. 1. Parunak, following rabbinic precedent, treated these visionary sections in close relation to each other (cf. Parunak 1980). They function as three great landmarks in the book of Ezekiel.

1:3. "The word of the LORD came to…" and "the hand of the LORD was on him there": these phrases are two recurrent and important formulae for the divine inspiration of the prophet, the latter being especially distinctive of Ezekiel (cf. 3:14, 22; 8:1; 33:22; 37:1; 40:1). We find no reference to "spirit" (*rûaḥ*) until v. 12. "The priest": Ezekiel is explicitly called a priest. This is a determinative feature of Ezekiel and his book, marked by the thought and style of the priestly movement in a way that Jeremiah is not (Jeremiah is linked more indirectly with the priesthood; cf. Jer 1:1: "Jeremiah son of Hilkiah, of the priests who were in Anathoth"). "Ezekiel son of Buzi": we encounter here a rare use of the prophet's personal name (otherwise found only at 24:24). The rarity is for two reasons: first, because of the almost consistent first-person style of the book; and, second, because the prophet is addressed by God not by his personal name but as "Mortal" (*ben-ʾāḏām*, literally "Son of Man"; see on 2:1). Ezekiel is never mentioned elsewhere in the Hebrew Bible (e.g. Kings, Chronicles, Jeremiah; cf. Begg 1986b). A priest of the same name is assigned to David's time in 1 Chr 24:16 (NRSV: "Jehezkel"), and it is possible that this use of the name represents a fictional echo of the sixth-century priestly prophet. The name of the prophet (in Heb. *yᵉḥezqēʾl*) means "God is strong" or "God strengthens." The name is similar in meaning to that of the eighth-century king of Judah Hezekiah (Heb. *ḥizqîâ*, meaning "YHWH is [or makes] strong"). The Hebrew title of the book is simply the name of the prophet, Ezekiel (Heb. *yᵉḥezqēʾl*). The English title is similarly the name of the prophet, in a form derived via Jerome's Vulgate from a latinized form of the LXX Greek. "In the land of the Chaldeans": the territory of the Neo-Babylonians, in the southern part of Mesopotamia (between the two rivers, the Tigris and the Euphrates), corresponding to the southern part of modern Iraq. This is the very area from which Abram was said to derive: "they went out together from Ur of the Chaldeans to go into the land of Canaan" (Gen 11:31). Assuming the typical route around the "fertile crescent" (from Jerusalem up through Syria and then down the river courses into Mesopotamia), this is a long distance from Jerusalem, and such geographical remoteness will have compounded the exiles' sense of dislocation (cf. Ps 137:4: "How could we sing the LORD's song in a foreign land?")

1:4. The opening section of the book complete (1:1–3 serving as a superscription), we move into the account of Ezekiel's throne-chariot vision. In outline, the vision recounts a great cloud with brightness and fire, in the middle of which the prophet glimpses something called in Hebrew *ḥašmal*. Four mysterious living creatures are described, with wheels on the earth beside them. Then over the heads of the creatures a dome is discerned, above that a throne, and seated above the throne "something…like a human form." The ancient versions and modern translations of this chapter tend to domesticate and sanitize what is often difficult and obscure. The obfuscated and contorted language reflects the confusion and distortion that would be expected to accompany any retelling of a dream or vision. There is no good ground for doubting the text's own claim that this is the account of a vision, and while it will of course have been shaped by its cultural context, it is not to be explained away as a stylized and self-conscious piece of writing.

"As I looked, a stormy wind came out of the north": in Ugaritic mythology the god Baal and his consort Anat dwelt on Mount Zaphon, which happened to be in northern Syria. The word *ṣāpôn* became the term for "north" in Hebrew, and some of the mythological associations carried over from the Canaanite context, "the north" sometimes being associated with the transcendent (cf. Ps 48:2 [Heb. v. 3]; cf. Day 2000:107–16). There may be an echo of this at the start of Jeremiah: "Out of the north disaster shall break out on all the inhabitants of the land" (Jer 1:14). In Jeremiah's opening chapter divine judgement is in view; here at the start of Ezekiel we encounter instead the beneficent if awesome presence of God. "A great cloud…and fire flashing forth continually, and in the middle of the fire": the language is reminiscent of the account of the Sinai theophany, for example, in Exod 19:16–19 (cf. 1 Kgs 19:11–12).

"Something like gleaming amber": the word translated as "amber" by the NRSV is Hebrew *ḥašmal*. Its repetition near the end of the vision in v. 27 forms an *inclusio*, underlining its importance, but its meaning is a vexed question. The word is unique to Ezekiel and essentially untranslatable. In stating that the etymology and exact meaning are dubious BDB (365) underplays the difficulty. There are in fact just three occurrences of the word in Ezekiel and none anywhere else. It occurs only once outside this chapter, at 8:2. It is possible that *ḥašmal* is cognate with Akkadian *elmēšu*, a brilliant precious stone. The Greek translates *ḥašmal* by *ēlektron*, and the Latin by *electrum*. Electrum is an alloy of gold and silver, occurring naturally in Turkey and elsewhere, used for some coins in the ancient world and usually (depending on the balance of elements) a good conductor of electricity. The same word (in its Greek and Latin forms) was also used for the substance we call in English, following Arabic, "amber" (the word used to translate *ḥašmal* in English versions of Ezekiel, from AV to NRSV). Amber is a fossil resin, mostly derived from the Baltic coast and used in the manufacture of ornamental objects. It has the power of acquiring an electric charge by friction (in fact it is from the electrostatic properties of amber that the modern English words "electron" and "electricity" derive). These quite separate materials shared a name in Greek and Latin, probably on account of their pale yellow colour. But in truth we do not know what the word *ḥašmal* meant, and nor did the ancients (the Syriac in fact consistently avoids rendering the word). The word *ēlektron* was probably just a guess on the part of the Greek translators, suggested in part by the fact that *nōgah* ("brightness," or "splendour") occurs alongside the word in both vv. 4 and 27, as does *ʿên* ("eye," and thus "gleaming"). The references to *ḥašmal* in vv. 4 and 27 are paralleled by verses referring to various materials. These, like the *ḥašmal* contexts, employ the Hebrew words *kᵉ* ("like") and *ʿên* ("gleaming"). The legs of the living creatures are likened to "bronze" (Heb. *nᵉḥōšet*, v. 7); the wheels are compared to "beryl" (Heb. *taršîš*, v. 16); and the dome to "crystal" (Heb. *qeraḥ*, v. 22). The likening of the throne to "sapphire" (Heb. *ʾeben-sappîr*, v. 26) is similar but lacks the expression *kᵉʿên*, featuring instead *kᵉmarʾê* ("in appearance like"). These formulaic phrases seem to signal major stages within the account, but shed no light on the meaning of the word *ḥašmal*; indeed their form may mimic that of the first *ḥašmal* reference, in v. 4. Since nobody understood this word they took the route of trying to replicate Ezekiel's experience, and such an impetus led on to the Merkabah tradition, within which meditation upon this chapter often led to mystical ecstasy. The word *ḥašmal* had an important place in the tradition, but the opening chapter of Ezekiel was clearly regarded by some as a "dangerous" passage. The Babylonian Talmud (*b. Hag.* 13a), as we have noted, recounts the cautionary tale of a child who was reading the book of Ezekiel at his teacher's house. The child "apprehended what *ḥašmal* was, whereupon a fire went forth from *ḥašmal* and consumed him." One is reminded of Rudolf Otto who in *The Idea of the Holy* wrote of the strange harmony of dread and fascination that characterizes the encounter with the holy (Otto 1923). The imagery is elusive and probably deliberately so, evocative of mystery and the numinous, of excitement and danger. It seems appropriate that Modern Hebrew uses this rare Ezekiel word *ḥašmal* to mean "electricity"!

1:5. "In the middle of it was something like four living creatures": fourfoldness implies completion or fullness (cf. 37:9: "Come from the four winds, O breath"). "Living creatures": *ḥayyâ* means "living thing, beast, animal." Chapter 10 introduces reference to cherubim, with a particular concern to equate them with the figures presented here: "The cherubim rose up. These were the living creatures that I saw by the river Chebar" (10:15; cf. 10:20). Chapter 1 does not feature cherubim (although the Targum introduces them even here, as arguably does Sirach also, in Sir 49:8: "It was Ezekiel who saw the vision of glory, which God showed him above the chariot of the cherubim"). Here it is "living creatures" that we encounter, and the unsystematized nature of this suggests that this is original to the vision. "They were of human form": there is recurrent reference to human form in the chapter. The four living creatures are said to be "of human form" (here in v. 5), and to have "human hands" (1:8; cf. 10:8, 21) and "the face of a human being" (1:10; cf. 10:14; 41:19). True, there are also comparisons to animals: they have wings (1:6), "the soles of their feet were like the sole of a calf's foot" (1:7) and v. 10 refers to a plurality of faces, with "the face of a lion on the right side, the face of an ox on the left side, and the face of an eagle." These animal references are in part merely details of the painting of the picture of the *ḥayyôṯ*, "living creatures," that the prophet has seen in his vision. More significant are the human comparisons, listed above and culminating, as we shall see, when the chapter reaches its crescendo in vv. 26–28.

1:6. "Each had four faces, and each of them had four wings": we have already noted that ch. 10 interprets the living creatures as cherubim, and now the reference to wings echoes Isa 6:2: "Seraphs were in attendance above him; each had six wings: with two they covered their faces, and with two they covered their feet, and with two they flew." One is reminded of other attendants of the deity in the Hebrew Bible, for example, in 1 Kgs 22:19, where "all the host of heaven" stand to the right and to the left of YHWH seated on his throne. These are angels of various kinds. The standard word for angel, *malʾāḵ*, does not appear in this sense in Ezekiel; it originally meant simply "messenger" (as it does in Ezek 23:40), and from there came to be used of a messenger of God, representing an extension of God's personality. As here, there is often some ambiguity between reference to the deity and reference to his attendant representatives (cf. Gen 18; Exod 3:1–6; Judg 6:11–24). Increasingly bold speculation about angels developed, not least in the context of emergent apocalyptic, within which trajectory the present chapter should certainly be placed.

1:7. "They sparkled like burnished bronze": the reference seems to be to the legs as a whole, rather than their parts. "Bronze" (Heb. *nᵉḥōšeṯ*): the element copper, or more likely its common alloy bronze. It is conceivable that there may be an allusion to the word for serpent (*nāḥāš*) or even to the mysterious bronze serpent "Nehushtan" (*nᵉḥuštān*), referred to in 2 Kgs 18:4 (cf. Num 21:6–9). **1:9.** "Their wings touched one another": "one another" is literally "a woman to her sister." Could it be that Ezekiel envisaged the creatures as female? The word *ḥayyâ* ("living thing, beast, animal") is a feminine word, as indeed is the likely immediate referent *kānāp̄* ("wing"). These factors sufficiently explain the feminine forms here without the need for more developed speculation. "Each of them moved straight ahead, without turning as they moved": throughout the passage this emphasis on dramatic and decisive movement is reiterated (cf. vv. 12, 17).

1:10. "As for the appearance of their faces: the four had the face of a human being": human form is reiterated (see on vv. 5, 26), and now with the most personal of features, the face. But there are other faces: "the face of a lion on the right side, the face of an ox on the left side, and the face of an eagle" (cf. 10:14; 41:19). There have been numerous attempts, both traditional and historical-critical, to interpret the significance of each of the faces. Block summarizes well the main biblical associations of each: "the strength and majesty of the lion, the swiftness and mobility of the eagle, the procreative power of the bull, and the wisdom and reason of humankind" (Block 1997:96). **1:11.** "Each creature had two wings, each of which touched the wing of another, while two covered their bodies": again one is reminded of Isa 6 (as also at v. 23). There have been many attempts to describe and even picture these creatures. They are similar to the statues that stood before the holy places and palaces of Mesopotamia, the very context of the exile of Ezekiel and his compatriots. Keel has done much to enrich our understanding, through comparative studies of glyptic or seal art and other ancient Near Eastern depictions (Keel 1977). But the imagery is elusive and probably deliberately so, evocative of mystery and the numinous. We should not squeeze every detail for symbolism, still less for allegory. This is what the visionary Ezekiel saw, or at least his attempt to put it in words. **1:12.** "Wherever the spirit would go, they went, without turning as they went": the first of three "spirit" (*rûaḥ*) references in the chapter (vv. 12, 20, 21). This is an important word in Ezekiel, unlike in Jeremiah (cf. Robson 2006). Not the "stormy wind" (*rûaḥ s^{eʿ}ārâ*) of v. 4, but rather "spirit" in some sense. The reference here could well be to the divine spirit; but see further on vv. 20–21. **1:13.** "In the middle of": NRSV here follows the LXX and the Old Latin; the MT has "And the appearance of" (*ûḏ^{e}mûṯ*). "The fire was bright, and lightning issued from the fire": again reminiscent of the Sinai theophany (cf. v. 4). Note also that the verse features the important word *nōḡah* ("brightness," or "splendour"), as in vv. 4, 27 and 28.

1:15. "I saw a wheel on the earth beside the living creatures": a wheel (*ʾôp̱an*) is symbolic of mobility, the central theme of this chapter, the presence of YHWH in the midst of profane exile. As there are four faces, so there are four wheels, capable of going in any direction (cf. 37:9). The word chariot (*merkāḇâ*) does not occur in this chapter or indeed in the book (as it does in Sir 49:8), but one can certainly understand how that word got attached to this passage in tradition. "One for each of the four of them": so LXX; MT continues "of their faces". **1:16.** "Their appearance was like the gleaming of beryl": recognized for its beauty since prehistoric times, beryl (Heb. *taršîš*) occurs in a range of colours, including green, blue, yellow and red. Another possible translation is "yellow jasper." "Their construction being something like a wheel within a wheel": language is stretched to emphasize the theme of mobility. We are again reminded of the visionary nature of the passage. **1:18.** "The rims of all four were full of eyes all around": the point of the eyes is that YHWH, now universal and omnipresent, is all-seeing. **1:19.** "And when the living creatures rose from the earth, the wheels rose": presumably the reference is to flight by the winged creatures, even though flight is not dramatically described (cf. 10:19, "The cherubim lifted up their wings and rose up from the earth in my sight"). Like the wheels, the wings are a symbol of mobility; perhaps we are to think of flight from Jerusalem (cf. 8:3: "the spirit lifted me up between earth and heaven, and brought me in visions of God to Jerusalem"). **1:20.** "Wherever the spirit would go, they went": this phrase is also found in v. 12, and in both cases the reference could be to the divine spirit. On the other hand, later in this same verse and also in the next it is stated that "the spirit of the living creatures was in the wheels," and it may be that this is the key to the proper understanding of vv. 12 and 20a. However, the sense would amount to much the same, since the creatures are the vehicle of the divine, one might even say an extension of the divine personality. The reference is to the consistency and continuity of the divine purpose. **1:21.** These verses offer classic examples of the repetition and alleged redundancy that mark the book, to be recognized as a feature of the prophet's style (Carley 1975:54; Boadt 1978:489–90). But this and other features of the present chapter may also reflect the visionary situation.

1:22. "Over the heads of the living creatures there was something like a dome": Hebrew *rāqîaʿ* is an expanse or extended surface, hence dome. This is the word used in the priestly creation account of Genesis for the vault of heaven or "firmament," subsequently called "sky" or "the heavens" (Gen 1:6–8). There it separates "the waters that were under the dome from the waters that were above the dome." In the present context also the dome separates that which is below from that which is above, earthly from heavenly. The evocation of this cosmic scale in the smaller context of the present description reminds one of later Jewish notions about the vast body of the deity. "Shining like crystal": Hebrew *qeraḥ* can mean "ice, frost," as well as crystal. BDB (956) has "as if of ice" (cf. *1 Enoch* 14: "And I looked and I saw in it a high throne, and its appearance was like ice and its surrounds like the shining sun and the sound of Cherubim"; Sparks 1984:201–3). Hebrew has the word *nôrāʾ*, "awesome," not present in LXX and omitted by NRSV. **1:24.** "When they moved, I heard the sound of their wings like the sound of mighty waters": the reference to the sound of wings confirms that flight is in view (cf. v. 19). "Mighty waters" presumably refers to the cosmic waters, which fits the reference to a dome and evokes the same primeval creation associations. Towards the end of the book, when the deity returns to the temple, we are again told, "the sound was like the sound of mighty waters" (43:2). "Like the thunder": cf. "fire flashing forth," v. 4. "The Almighty": Hebrew *šadday*; cf. 10:5, which in a similar context features the fuller form *ʾēl-šadday*, "God Almighty." It is noteworthy to have reference to a divine title here, anticipating the direct reference to YHWH in v. 28, though we have already been told overtly in v. 1 that this chapter concerns *marʾôṯ ʾᵉlōhîm*, "visions of God." The title *ʾēl-šadday* is presented in Exod 6:3 as the name of the God of the patriarchs before the revelation of the name YHWH to Moses; but the actual origins of this divine title are obscure (van der Toorn, Becking and van der Horst 1998; Lutsky 1998). "A sound of tumult like the sound of an army": an echo perhaps of another divine title: *yhwh ṣᵉḇāʾôṯ*, "Lord of Hosts." "When they stopped, they let down their wings": repeated in v. 25 (cf. v. 19); further confirmation that the creatures have flown. **1:25.** "And there came a voice from above the dome over their heads": this may be the divine command to halt. This verse anticipates a similar reference in v. 28, which will introduce speech.

1:26. "And above the dome over their heads there was something like a throne": the throne as the seat of the deity features in other classic theophany accounts, notably 1 Kgs 22:19, "I saw the LORD sitting on his throne, with all the host of heaven standing beside him to the right and to the left of him," and Isa 6:1, "I saw the Lord sitting on a throne, high and lofty; and the hem of his robe filled the temple." There are only four references to "throne" (*kissēʾ*) in Ezekiel, but they are found at key locations relating to the presence of the deity: at 10:1, in the context of the departure of YHWH from the temple; at 43:7, where he returns to the sanctuary; and here in 1:26 (twice). This first chapter both anticipates the account of the divine departure from the temple and yet also announces the deity's coming to his people. The throne is linked with the cherubim at 10:1, and more generally in the Hebrew Bible the cherubim are associated with the Ark as the seat of the deity (cf. Exod 37:9; 1 Sam 4:4). But here at the end of the present chapter we are reminded of the non-use of the word "cherubim" in this context. The picture of a throne on wheels expresses a dual affirmation: YHWH reigns and moreover he does so universally, without restriction of mobility. It is telling to contrast with this vision of YHWH's active reign, even in Babylonia, the reference in the same chapter to the passive deportation of King Jehoiachin (Ezek 1:2). One is reminded again of Isa 6, with its contrast between the reported death of the human king Uzziah and the vision of "the King, the LORD of hosts," seated on a throne and reigning in the temple (Isa 6:1, 5). Now YHWH continues to reign in exile, unlike the humiliated Jehoiachin. "In appearance" the throne is like "sapphire" (Heb. *ʾeḇen-sappîr*; cf. 10:1; 28:13). Although English derives the word "sapphire" from Hebrew *sappîr*, it is probable that the sapphire of the Bible was lapis lazuli, which was prized as a gemstone from very early times in the ancient Near East. Deep blue in colour and opaque, it had royal associations, featuring prominently in many of the treasures recovered from pharaonic tombs. As well as in jewellery and ornaments, it is found in architecture, as in the columns of palaces. Exodus 24:10 affords a comparable example of a theophany account featuring reference to this material: "And they saw the God of Israel. Under his feet there was something like a pavement of sapphire stone, like the very heaven for clearness."

"And seated above the likeness of a throne was something that seemed like a human form": a similar figure appears at the start of the temple vision of chs. 8–11 (8:2). I have noted the striking human comparisons made earlier in the present account (see on v. 5), and the anthropomorphic nature of the chapter as a whole is now reinforced as the passage reaches its crescendo. One is reminded of Dan 7:13: "I saw one like a human being coming with the clouds of heaven. And he came to the Ancient One and was presented before him." But whereas the identity of that figure remains obscure and ambiguous, it is made clear in v. 28 of the present chapter that the reference here is to an appearance of YHWH. Ironically, the references to human likeness throughout the chapter seem to anticipate the overt revelation of the divine at the end of the chapter. In the Priestly work humanity is made in the image of God (Gen 1:26–27; 9:6; cf. 5:1–3). Kutsko persuasively argues that, while Ezekiel never directly uses the phrase "image of God" (*ṣelem ʾᵉlōhîm*) to refer to humans, this priestly prophet knows and tacitly exploits in various ways a usage similar to that which we find in

Genesis (Kutsko 2000b). As he struggles to find appropriate language that indicates both human likeness and divine incomparability, Ezekiel here refers to "something that seemed like a human form" (*dᵉmûṯ kᵉmarʾê ʾāḏām*), employing, as he will again in v. 28, the word *dᵉmûṯ* ("likeness"), so closely associated with the language of the "image" of God in Gen 1:26. The anthropomorphism of Ezekiel has often been noted. Mettinger writes that Ezekiel offers a more "humanoid" picture than the Priestly writer (Mettinger 1982:113; cf. Kasher 1998a), while Middlemas explores the tension between Ezekiel's marked anthropomorphism and his role in articulating a thoroughgoing aniconism (Middlemas 2010).

1:27. "Upward from what appeared like the loins": this reference to "loins" (Heb. *moṯnayim*, as at 8:2) is a particularly daring example of anthropomorphic language, since the reference is to the middle of the body. "I saw something like gleaming amber": see on v. 4. The references to *ḥašmal* (NRSV: "amber") there and now here form bookends around this amazing vision account. "I saw something that looked like fire": fire is seen both above and below (cf. on v. 4). Hebrew *nōḡah* ("brightness," or "splendour") appears here, as in v. 4, alongside *ḥašmal*.

1:28. "Like the bow in a cloud on a rainy day": the full spectrum of colour is now added to the rich panoply of the various materials mentioned earlier ("bronze"; "beryl"; "crystal"; "sapphire"), further evidence of the visionary nature of the chapter, as the prophet reaches for language to do justice to his experience. Whether this is an allusion to the priestly tradition of Gen 9:16 ("When the bow is in the clouds, I will see it and remember the everlasting covenant between God and every living creature of all flesh that is on the earth") or just a reference to the natural phenomenon is impossible to say, and of course unnecessary to decide. "Such was the appearance of the splendour all around": again Hebrew *nōḡah* ("brightness," or "splendour") in close proximity to *ḥašmal* (v. 27).

And now we come to the explicit summary point of the chapter: "This was the appearance of the likeness of the glory of the LORD." "Glory" (Heb. *kāḇôḏ*) is a key term linking the accounts of the divine appearance in the book (3:12, 23; 8:4), and serving as a thread uniting the narrative of the departure of the deity from his temple (9:3; 10:4, 18, 19; 11:22, 23) and his eventual return (43:2, 4, 5; 44:4). The motif is shared with the priestly material of the Pentateuch (Lev 9:23; Num 20:6). The basic idea underlying "glory" is one of heaviness, hence here the deity is envisioned as though heavy with honour; but beyond this the "glory" has become a mode of the presence of God, a form of personification if not a hypostasis (cf. Mettinger 1982). The statement is unambiguous in affirming a vision of the deity, as is the retrospective reference of 10:20 ("These were the living creatures that I saw underneath the God of Israel by the river Chebar"). Ezekiel affirmed nothing less than the presence of the God of Israel in alien Babylonia, far from the temple site. This is a bold gambit, and this boldness is reflected in the note of awkwardness that seems to attend the claim. Unambiguous indeed, but note the circumlocution of v. 28: "such was the appearance of the likeness of the glory of the LORD." There are at least three levels of circumlocution here (*at least* three, because it would be a mistake to imagine that the tetragrammaton itself is ever an exhaustive and univocal summation of the deity). We sense the audacity of what is being claimed—we might almost speak of a "blush" as the prophet dares to refer to YHWH himself becoming present to the exiles. There is a dialectic at work here, affirming and yet qualifying, for all God-talk must have its qualifiers. (Compare 11:16, where the boldness of speaking of YHWH as a "sanctuary" [*miqdāš*] to the exiles is qualified by the word *meʿaṭ* ["small"].) We may see this declaration as a daring attempt to deal with exiled Israel's physical, psychological and above all theological dislocation. The sovereign transcendence of the deity is reaffirmed in a radical way (paradoxically through his freedom in establishing new modes of presence). This expedient played its part in enabling exiled Israel to come through its dislocation to eventual restoration to the land, and, perhaps even more importantly, in the longer term it also had a vital role in helping Israel come to terms with an ongoing diaspora situation, as the people of a transcendent and universal God. Ezekiel, in spite of his priestly and Jerusalem-based formation, was able to articulate a theology of divine presence that took account of the exile. The exile and YHWH's departure from Jerusalem was not only punishment for the sins of the nation, but became the occasion for a discovery that YHWH was present to his people even in alien Babylonia.

"When I saw it, I fell on my face": Ezekiel responds in the same way upon being confronted by the divine at 3:23; 43:3 and 44:4 (cf. 9:8; 11:13). "And I heard the voice of someone speaking": cf. v. 25, where no actual speech is reported. Both references are like the *baṯ-qôl*, the divine voice from on high, of later Jewish tradition. This time reported words do follow, with the start of the new chapter.

Ezekiel 3:23 explicitly alludes to the theophany account of ch. 1, in keeping with the fact that chs. 1–3 constitute the first main section of the book. Thereafter the themes are picked up in 8:2 (featuring the only other *ḥašmal* reference) and 8:4, at the beginning of the second of the great vision accounts of the book.

CHAPTER 2

After the dramatic throne-chariot vision of ch. 1, the next two chapters are devoted to a series of commissions of the new prophet. Commentators differ in their divisions between them, but they form a loosely integrated sequence, resting upon the shared foundation of the inaugural vision.

2:1. "He said to me": this refers to "the voice of someone speaking" that was introduced at the end of ch. 1. The scene of that chapter continues and we are to understand this as the divine voice. The first of the commissions is introduced. "O mortal": Hebrew *ben-ʾāḏām*, literally "Son of Man." Ezekiel is so addressed throughout the book. The phrase occurs ninety-three times in Ezekiel, many times more than in the rest of the Hebrew Bible put together (in contrast to the two times the name Ezekiel is used in the book, never in address to the prophet). "Mortal" is always used in address by God or his representative in Ezekiel, and never by any human being. The NRSV avoids the traditional rendering "Son of Man" in the interests of gender-neutral language, but "mortal" is a good translation: in contrast to the awesome grandeur of Ezekiel's holy God, the prophet's finite dependence and insignificance are emphasized. The use of the address is relational: it is important that Ezekiel is not addressed by his personal name, which would place the emphasis on him, but by a title that serves further to present YHWH himself as holy and other, in keeping with the book's radical theocentricity. Daniel 8:17 is similar to Ezekiel's usage and may well be dependent upon it; Gabriel addresses Daniel: "Understand, O mortal (Heb. *ben-ʾāḏām*), that the vision is for the time of the end." The developed use of "Son of Man" language in Enoch is very different, but, given the many other continuities between Ezekiel and the Enochic literature, it is not unlikely that Ezekiel has influenced the development of the title. Later still, the Gospels are heir to a long tradition, combining many facets of "Son of Man" usage. "Stand up on your feet": Ezekiel had fallen on his face before the deity in 1:28.

2:2. "A spirit entered into me and set me on my feet": "spirit" (*rûaḥ*) is not accompanied by the definite article or otherwise qualified (likewise 8:3), but the reference is clearly to animation by the divine (cf. 11:5; 37:1); this is classic inspiration language, more typical of so-called "pre-classical" prophecy (cf. 1 Sam 19:23; 1 Kgs 18:12). **2:3.** "I am sending you to the people of Israel": the exiled community in Babylonia is Ezekiel's primary audience (see the "Time and Place" section, above). He sometimes addresses the exiles as "House of

Israel" (e.g. 18:25). But his address is sometimes broader too, and can include the community back in Jerusalem (cf. 12:1–16). As Childs argued, the specificity of Ezekiel's situation and his audience is occasionally blurred because of his theocentric concentration, in what may be seen as the beginnings of the canonical process toward the final form of Scripture (Childs 1979:361–62). "To a nation": NRSV amends to the singular following the Syriac; the Hebrew plural "to nations" is tolerable in view of the book's oracles against the nations, but if retained would have to be regarded as a parenthesis, since the following words clearly refer to Israel. "Of rebels": rebellion is a recurrent charge in the chapter (cf. on v. 5; also Jer 2:29; 3:13). "They and their ancestors have transgressed against me to this very day": chs. 16, 20 and 23 tell the story of the long history of national sin in detail. The words "they" (that is, the people to whom Ezekiel is now sent) and "to this very day" are important and they are picked up in the following verse with the statement, "The descendants are impudent and stubborn." Chapter 18 is devoted to making it clear that the present generation is punished for its own sins and not for the sins of previous generations. Ezekiel is consistent about this elsewhere too; the past is only ever *illustrative* of the nation's propensity to sin (cf. 16:44; 20:30).

2:4. "Thus says the Lord GOD": frequent use of the double divine name, *ʾᵃḏōnāy yhwh*, characterizes the Hebrew text of Ezekiel. The probability is that the double name usage is original to the MT, and that the single Greek word *kurios* should be seen as the original consistent LXX practice, with a later, albeit uneven, trend in the Greek to assimilate to Hebrew's double usage (see further the "Text and Versions" section, above). The theological impact of the double divine name is to reinforce the sense of YHWH's awesome presence. **2:5.** "Whether they hear or refuse to hear": apparently open to the possibility that they might respond, but a negative expectation is encouraged by the words "they are a rebellious house" (Heb. *bêṯ mᵉrî*). The house of Israel is so described at 2:5–8; 3:9, 26–27; 12:2–3, 9, 25; 17:12; 24:3; 44:6. The designation is found with the phrase "whether they hear or refuse to hear" both here and in v. 7, and with the phrase "let those who will hear, hear; and let those who refuse to hear, refuse" at 3:27; but by 12:2 only the negative aspect remains: "a rebellious house, who have eyes to see but do not see, who have ears to hear but do not hear." "They shall know that there has been a prophet among them": very similar is 33:33, which reads "When this comes—and come it will!—then they shall know that a prophet has been among them." And both echo Ezekiel's characteristic "Recognition Formula" (see the "Theological Themes" section, above; cf. 24:24). **2:6.** "Do not be afraid of them": it is significant that, whereas in the call narratives of Moses and Jeremiah (Exod 4:10; Jer 1:6) diffidence is expressed by the one called, here this theme appears in the form of divine address, typical of the theocentricity of Ezekiel.

2:8. "Do not be rebellious like that rebellious house": the prophet himself is now warned, as also in ch. 3 ("their blood I will require at your hand," 3:18, 20). This introduces a focus on the call of the prophet himself. "Open your mouth and eat what I give you": cf. Ps 81:10 (Heb. v. 11), "I am the LORD your God, who brought you up out of the land of Egypt. Open your mouth wide and I will fill it." Glazov sets Ezekiel's usage in the context of the rich semantic field of language of the opening of the mouth in the ancient Near East (Glazov 2001:232–34). **2:9.** "A hand was stretched out to me": anthropomorphic language, as in ch. 1. **2:10.** The written scroll "had writing on the front and on the back": whether the image is of a scroll that has been used and reused or simply one that has been fully used, the point is clear: there are very many words and so every inch has been covered. "Words of lamentation and mourning and woe" (*qinîm wāheḡeh wāhî*): a fair summary of the message of Ezek 4–24, which contains a sustained and devastating critique of the nation. The fact that the chapter ends here, whereas the episode of the scroll continues through to 3:3, serves to highlight these words of judgement.

Chapter 3

3:1. The episode of the scroll continues. "Eat this scroll, and go, speak to the house of Israel": note the close link between the consumption of the word and the command to go and address the people. **3:3.** "In my mouth it was as sweet as honey": in spite of the contents of the scroll ("lamentation and mourning and woe," 2:10), Ezekiel experiences it as "sweet as honey." This is because it is God's word (cf. Ps 19:10 [Heb. v. 11]; 119:103). The internalization of the word of God is one of many motifs shared by Jeremiah and Ezekiel (Jer 1:9, "Then the LORD put out his hand and touched my mouth; and the LORD said to me, 'Now I have put my words in your mouth'"; Jer 15:16, "Your words were found, and I ate them, and your words became to me a joy and the delight of my heart"). The eating of the scroll indicates that God has supplied Ezekiel with fixed oracles that cannot be changed (cf. Zech 5:1–4). Ezekiel must speak only what YHWH has written. By incorporating God's words into his body, he becomes fully aligned with the divine word of judgement. Instead of speaking his own words or those of the people, he has become completely absorbed by God, speaking the deity's words alone (cf. v. 4). Davis uses "swallowing the scroll" as a metaphor for the shift from orality to textuality in the prophetic tradition, a move that she associates specifically with Ezekiel (Davis 1989a, 1989b). She understands the book of Ezekiel as a literary text first and foremost; while not altogether denying a "live" ministry, her emphasis is strongly on Ezekiel the *writer*. It may be acknowledged that Ezekiel plays a role in the emergence of prophecy as a written medium, but Davis overstates her case (cf. Joyce 1991). Graffy (1984) rightly highlights the importance of the prophet's confrontation with his people and the "disputation speech" as a major vehicle of this.

3:4. "Go to the house of Israel and speak my very words to them": a second commission begins here (cf. 2:1). **3:5.** "You are not sent to a people of obscure speech and difficult language": Ezekiel and his fellow exiles in Babylonia would have been surrounded by the alien languages not only of their captors (cf. Isa 28:9–13), but also of the other national groups of deportees. **3:7.** "The house of Israel will not listen to you, for they are not willing to listen to me": not merely rhetorical hyperbole but the realistic truth; it is too late. **3:8.** "See, I have made your face hard against their faces, and your forehead hard against their foreheads": the name of the prophet, Ezekiel (Heb. *yᵉḥezqēʾl*), means "God is strong" or "God strengthens"; the motif of the hardening of Ezekiel's face and forehead is in keeping with this. **3:9.** "Harder than flint, I have made your forehead": more than a match for the hardness of the people. Verses 8–9 find a parallel in Jer 1:18–19, where YHWH fortifies the prophet against resistance. **3:10.** Verses 10–11 could be seen as a separate commission (because of the formula "He said to me: 'Mortal…'"), but they are better seen as the rounding off of this passage. "All my words that I shall speak to you receive in your heart and hear with your ears": further ways of expressing the internalization of the divine word. **3:11.** "Go to the exiles, to your people": reinforcing the point that Ezekiel's primary audience is his fellow deportees, and also his solidarity with them. "Say to them, 'Thus says the Lord GOD'": an encapsulation of the message Ezekiel is to preach; it is as though no more is needed, as with Ezekiel's most characteristic formula "they shall know that I am the LORD" (cf. v. 27).

3:12. Verses 12–15 provide a narrative interlude, picking up the story from the end of ch. 1, with a return of much of that chapter's imagery. "As the glory of the LORD rose": NRSV here follows the Greek. The Hebrew has a doxology, "blessed be the glory of the LORD." This doxology seems out of place, particularly as the words "from its place" follow, and may well be a case of an early corruption of the original Hebrew, from "in the rising" (*bᵉrûm*) to "blessed" (*bārûḵ*) (Hitzig 1847:24). **3:14.** "I went in bitterness in the heat of my spirit, the hand of the LORD being strong upon me": Ezekiel the prophet is no urbane moralist but rather stands in the long tradition of ancient Near Eastern prophecy, including the so-called pre-classical prophets of earlier Israelite centuries (Lindblom 1962:197). **3:15.** "I came to the exiles at Tel-abib (Heb. *tēl ʾāḇîḇ*)": the name of this Jewish settlement near Nippur derived from Akkadian *til abûbi*, "mound of the flood," but has been hebraized to mean "mound of spring (produce)." The city in modern Israel takes its name from this verse. "Who lived by the river Chebar": NRSV abbreviates the repetitive Hebrew text, on the basis of two Syriac mss. "I sat there among them, stunned": one of the many references that have encouraged speculation about Ezekiel's mental health (e.g. Broome 1946). Carley wisely argued that such oddness on Ezekiel's part should rather be explained by reference to his affinities with so-called pre-classical prophecy (Carley 1975:69–81; cf. Zimmerli 1965), while Smith-Christopher emphasizes not Ezekiel's personal psychology but rather the trauma that affected the exiles as a social group (Smith-Christopher 2002:89).

3:16. "At the end of seven days, the word of the LORD came to me": vv. 16–21 constitute a third commission. **3:17.** "Mortal, I have made you a sentinel (Heb. *ṣōpeh*)": RSV translated "watchman." This is an important motif, found also in 33:1–9 (with the language picked up also in the remainder of ch. 33). Chapter 33 has an important relationship with ch. 3. Although some elements of ch. 3 may have been placed here during the redactional development of the book (so, e.g., Zimmerli 1979a:144), in the final form of the text chs. 3 and 33 form "bookends" around the first "half" of the ministry. Chapter 33 recapitulates various themes before the second "half" of the ministry (and of the book) begins. We should note also a link with ch. 18, with which language and also some ideas about responsibility are shared. The motif of the sentinel provides yet another parallel with Jeremiah (cf. Jer 6:17: "Also I raised up sentinels for you: 'Give heed to the sound of the trumpet!' But they said, 'We will not give heed'"; also Hos 9:8). "For the house of Israel": a strongly corporate perspective, in keeping with the general emphasis of the book. Ezekiel's warnings are for the people as a whole, just as a sentinel serves a community rather than alerting individuals. "Whenever you hear a word from my mouth, you shall give them warning from me": this imperative, laid upon the prophet in the context of his call, is crucial. He is twice warned (vv. 18, 20) that if through his failure to fulfil his task the wicked die, their blood will be required at his hand; in other words, the prophet will bear the responsibility for the death, even though the wicked had deserved to die. This fearsome responsibility laid upon the prophet is a major feature of this unit.

3:18–21. In this sequence there is a disproportionate emphasis on the negative outcome, in other words death, which features in three cases out of four (vv. 18, 19, 20) and, although it is said in v. 21 that if the righteous one stays faithful he will live, we never have the case of the wicked turning and avoiding death. This is arguably implied as an unvoiced possibility in vv. 18–19 and it appears overtly in the other "sentinel" passage at 33:5 (cf. 33:12, 14–16, 19; cf. also 18:21–22, 27–28), but here it never occurs. This omission and the emphasis of the present passage are very significant. The motif of the "sentinel" is not as straightforward as it might seem. Superficially, an open call to repentance appears to be offered. The metaphor seems to be that of the watchman or look-out who calls out (or blows the trumpet), so that the warning can be acted upon, to fight off thieves, wild animals or military attack. However, what is actually said through the sentinel? It is: "You shall surely die" (3:18; cf. 33:8). This is not the call of a sentinel but rather a term from the context of law, indeed it is nothing other than the formal declaration of the sentence of death. Wilson rightly argues that the prophetic task here is not to call the people to repentance, but "to deliver to the accused a legal decision which Yahweh has already given" (Wilson 1972:96). This mixture of metaphors is revealing. In addition to emphasizing the responsibility of the prophet, the purpose of this passage is to reinforce the absolute justice of the current judgement, underlining the culpability of Israel for the now inevitable (indeed already present) disaster. Israel has had every warning and is wholly to blame for the crisis that is even now engulfing her.

3:22. "Then the hand of the LORD was upon me there; and he said to me": a fourth and final commission. "Rise up, go out into the valley": the word used for "valley" (Heb. *biqʿâ*) could also mean "plain." Ezekiel 8:4 refers back to this location and to the vision here reported, and "the valley" is also given as the setting for the vision of the "dry bones" (cf. 37:1–2). It is not clear that anything more specific than the lower Mesopotamian valley is intended in either case.

3:23. "The glory of the LORD stood there, like the glory that I had seen by the river Chebar": the book's cross-references to visionary appearances (8:4; 10:15, 20, 22; 43:3), possibly editorial, help bind it together by highlighting the golden thread of theophany. "And I fell on my face": cf. 1:28; 43:3; 44:4. **3:24.** "The spirit entered into me, and set me on my feet": cf. 2:2. "Go, shut yourself inside your house": the elders sit before Ezekiel in his house at 8:1 (cf. 14:1; 20:1). **3:25.** "Cords shall be placed on you, and you shall be bound with them": Zimmerli suggested that this reference to the binding of Ezekiel may be the basis of the later tradition that Ezekiel experienced opposition in Babylonia, as in the *Lives of the Prophets* (Zimmerli 1979a:158–59; cf. Stone, Wright and Satran 2000:69–94).

3:26–27. "I will make your tongue cling to the roof of your mouth, so that you shall be speechless and unable to reprove them… But when I speak with you, I will open your mouth": the theme of the dumbness of Ezekiel is a perplexing one, since the prophet gives many oracles in the chapters that follow the report that he is to be speechless. His dumbness is said to end when the news reaches him of the fall of the Jerusalem Temple (some seven and a half year later). Ezekiel 24:25–27 says that a refugee will come to report the news of the final collapse, and "on that day your mouth shall be opened to the one who has escaped, and you shall speak and no longer be silent" (24:27), and then in 33:21–22 it is reported that "the hand of the LORD had been upon me the evening before the fugitive came; but he had opened my mouth by the time the fugitive came to me in the morning; so my mouth was opened, and I was no longer unable to speak" (33:22). Some scholars argue that the dumbness began immediately after the prophet's call, but that the loss of speech was either intermittent (Bertholet 1897:22–23) or symbolic (Herrmann 1924:25–27). Many contend that this unit originally belonged later in the book (e.g. Cooke 1936:46–48, 367) and this often goes with the notion that the dumbness was of short duration (Vogt 1970). Some have linked the dumbness with alleged mental illness on the part of the prophet (e.g. Halperin 1993:185–216). But the most satisfactory overall explanation is again that given by Wilson (1972; Glazov [2001:220–74] offers a sophisticated development of Wilson's position). Wilson focused on the key phrase of v. 26, which is translated in the NRSV "you shall be…unable to reprove them," literally, "you will not be to them an *ʾîš môḵîaḥ*." Much turns on the precise meaning of this Hebrew phrase. Wilson shows that when the word *môḵîaḥ* is used in legal contexts it refers primarily to a mediator or an arbitrator, rather than to a reprover or judge (Job 9:33; cf. Gen 31:37). Ezekiel is forbidden to act like a legal mediator for the people; he can no longer intercede with YHWH on behalf of the people to make sure they receive a fair trial, much as Jeremiah too was told not to intercede for the people (e.g. Jer 7:16; 11:14). Ezekiel can deliver the deity's judgements to the people, for when YHWH speaks to the people through the prophet his mouth will be opened (3:27). But communication can now move in only one direction, since the time for a fair trial has passed. This is of a piece with Wilson's insight that the role of the watchman ("sentinel") is to deliver the sentence of the divine judge, and it also explains why when the people approach the prophet to consult YHWH at 14:1–3 and 20:1, they on both occasions receive a rebuff. This situation lasts until the judgement is complete with the fall of the city. After that, YHWH again allows the people to seek him, and he indicates that their requests will be granted (36:37).

"Let those who will hear, hear; and let those who refuse to hear, refuse": as in v. 11 there still appears to be the theoretical possibility of positive response from the people, but the real purpose of this motif is to underline that Israel has had every chance and so is totally deserving of her fate, "for they are a rebellious house."

CHAPTER 4

Ezekiel was perceived by his contemporaries as a "maker of allegories" (21:5 [20:49]) and a "singer of love songs" (33:32). He was, in short, seen as a performer. Prophetic sign-actions play an important role in his ministry. Chapters 4 and 5 report a series of such actions (four in all) describing the coming siege of Jerusalem. The four are distinct and yet interrelated, with some cross-referencing. In the redactional development there may have been some elaboration of the basic accounts, perhaps especially in the provision of explicit interpretation (as with the Gospel accounts of the parables of Jesus). Stacey (1990) emphasized the dramatic dimension of such prophetic sign-actions, Lang (1986) even spoke of Ezekiel as an exponent of "Street Theatre." Friebel (1999) explored Ezekiel's sign-actions as "Rhetorical Nonverbal Communication." They are not, however, to be thought of merely as illustrations or teaching aids. Lindblom rightly emphasized that "such an action served not only to represent and make evident a particular fact, but also to make this fact a reality," and also that "the prophetic actions were akin to the magical actions which are familiar in the more primitive cultures throughout the world" (Lindblom 1962:172). This insight (and, of course, its expression) will be uncongenial to some, but the onus is on any who would deny Lindblom's basic understanding of the prophetic sign-actions. Ezekiel has swallowed the scroll (2:3) and thereby internalized the divine word, which he now embodies and acts out. It would not be accurate to say that he performs the sign-actions because he cannot speak the word of judgement, since, as we have seen, his dumbness amounts to not interceding with God on behalf of the people and does not interrupt his oral pronouncement of the word of judgement. The intention is not to elicit repentance but rather to enact the now irrevocable judgement by visual representation. Ezekiel puts his own shoulder to the wheel of divine indictment, and thereby participates in its coming to pass.

4:1–3. The first sign-action. **4:1.** "Take a brick": a sun-dried brick, common in Babylonia. "On it portray a city, Jerusalem": the book's first reference to Jerusalem, seat of the temple and symbolic representation of the nation. Within this sequence of sign-actions it is also mentioned at 4:7, 16 and 5:5. The once great city (cf. Pss 46; 48) is now humbled, and threatened with worse. **4:2.** "Put siegeworks against it": the famous reliefs depicting the siege of Lachish are a remarkable witness to how the ancient siege of such a city might look (Hall 1928). **4:3.** "Place it as an iron wall between you and the city": the iron plate is an external expression of Ezekiel's personal demonstration. YHWH himself is attacking his own city in a dramatic inversion of Holy War language (cf. Jer 21:5). "Set your face": a common phrase in Ezekiel as an introduction to prophetic denunciation (cf. 4:7; 6:2; 13:17; 14:8; 15:7 [twice]; 20:46 [Heb. 21:2]; 21:2 [Heb. v. 7]; 25:2; 28:21; 29:2; 35:2; 38:2). "A state of siege": Ezekiel had experienced the siege of 597, as the immediate prelude to his deportation; a more dreadful siege is to come. "This is a sign": Hebrew *ʾôṯ*. The only occurrence of the word in chs. 4–5 (cf. 14:8; 20:12, 20). Particularly similar to this verse are 12:6, 11 (where Ezekiel performs a comparable sign-action representing the deportation of those still in Jerusalem) and 24:24, 27 (where Ezekiel's non-mourning of his deceased wife is said to be a "sign" to the people), but these two passages use the Hebrew word *môpēṯ* (also "sign" in these cases in NRSV). "For the house of Israel": a sign for all, not just those in Jerusalem. In Ackroyd's words: "The exiles in Babylonia, who are the prophet's primary audience, are the disobedient to whom it must be said that the judgement upon Jerusalem is the judgement upon themselves" (Ackroyd 1968:109).

4:4–8. A second sign-action. Crucial to interpretation here is the meaning of the phrase *nāśāʾ ʿawōn* (translated in the NRSV as "bear the punishment of"). The phrase can have a range of senses, of which two may be confidently excluded. There is no reasonable way it could have its sense of "forgive" here. Also there is no place here for vicarious or expiatory suffering (contra Brownlee 1986:66), with Ezekiel bearing the nation's punishment in a manner arguably akin to the "servant" material of Isa 40–55. Such notions are excluded by Ezekiel's consistent emphasis on the punishment for sin being borne by the sinner (ch. 18). The Hebrew word *ʿāwōn* can convey both "sin" and "punishment," so the phrase could mean, in one sense or another, "to bear the sin" or "to bear the punishment." The NRSV's translation "punishment," used throughout this section, raises the problematic question of what could be meant by the punishment of Israel for as long as 390 years. (If the northern exile of 721 were the starting point, taking 390 off 721 gives 331 B.C.E., prompting the intriguing if implausible thought of an allusion to the conquests of Alexander as in some sense signalling the end of the punishment of Israel!) The Greek text offers a rationalization, involving changing 390 to 190, a number that accommodates an interpretation of the punishment of the northern kingdom in the period between the Assyrian conquest and Ezekiel's day. But this does nothing to help elucidate the sense of the Hebrew, where the most likely interpretation involves the two senses of the word *ʿāwōn* in turn, sin (v. 4) followed by its punishment (v. 5). Another key issue here involves the meaning of "Israel" in v. 4. The parallel between Israel (vv. 4–5) and Judah (v. 6) might suggest that the reference is to the two kingdoms, northern and southern, a possibility encouraged by the fact that, according to ancient Israelite geographical perceptions, "left" can represent "north" as "right" can represent "south." But wider usage of the word "Israel" in Ezekiel suggests that this is incorrect, for wherever else Israel and Judah are found together in Ezekiel they are used interchangeably (e.g. 8:6, 17) and where the two kingdoms are contrasted a term other than "Israel" is used for the north, as in 23:4, "Samaria," and 37:16, "Joseph/Ephraim." Israel here, then, should be taken to refer to the people of YHWH as a whole (in other words, "Israel" and "Judah" stand in a relationship of synonymous parallelism). As for the notion of days corresponding to years, this is very like Num 14:34, where forty days of sin lead to forty years of punishment.

The meaning of the sign-action seems to be that Ezekiel first in vv. 4–5 dramatically presents the sin of the nation (as he does in verbal terms in chs. 16, 20 and 23) and then in v. 6 acts out its punishment. The number 390 is best understood to refer to the period of national sin from the united monarchy down to Ezekiel's time (not covering, it must be conceded, Israel's sin in Egypt, reported in Ezek 20:8). The number "forty" refers to the current punishment of the nation, that is, the Babylonian exile. We should not be distracted by the thought that the period of punishment seems disproportionately short compared with the long history of sin, but should remember that for Ezekiel the past is only ever *illustrative* of the nation's propensity to sin (cf. 16:44; 20:30). The number "forty" indicates that this section was composed before the end of the exile. If we assume a starting date for the exile of 597 (as with the dating scheme of the book), forty years would take us only to 557 (and dating from the second deportation of 587 would similarly yield a date of 547), well short of the decree of Cyrus that in 539 heralded the end of the exile proper. Forty years is too short a period for the exile, just as Jeremiah's seventy years (Jer 25:11, 12) is too long, the inaccuracy of both signalling that they are original and exilic. Perhaps "forty" simply echoes the forty years in the wilderness (Num 14:33–34) and similarly represents a generation, during which the sinners had time to pass away. **4:7.** "Set your face toward the siege": since the second siege of Jerusalem was some years off (at least according to the literary location of this section), this probably refers to the representation of siege referred to in vv. 1–3, an example of the interrelatedness of the various units of this sequence of sign-actions. "With your arm bared": as in military attack. "You shall prophesy against it": a verbal complement to the sign-action. **4:8.** "I am putting cords on you": the prophet is bound to his task (cf. binding in 3:25). Is it credible that Ezekiel was engaged in this sign-action for well over a year? We should not be sceptical about the prophet actually carrying out long-term sign-actions of this kind. Isaiah is said to have walked naked and barefoot for three years (Isa 20:3); and cross-culturally there are well-documented cases such as that of St Simeon Stylites, a Christian ascetic saint of the fifth century who lived for 37 years on a small platform on top of a pillar in Syria.

4:9–17. A third sign-action, also referring back to the previous one. **4:9.** Ezekiel is commanded to eat a meal of mixed produce, scraped together from meagre resources. **4:10–11.** He is to be permitted limited amounts of food and drink, at specific times only. The instructions to Ezekiel are ironically rather reminiscent of the so-called "Ration Tablets" from contemporary Babylonia, which give an account of the provisions to be permitted to Jehoiachin under detention (cf. *ANET*, 308). **4:12.** "Baking it in their sight": the public and demonstrative nature of the sign-action is made explicit here. "On human dung": ritually unclean (cf. Deut 23:12–14), a matter of particular horror to a priest such as Ezekiel. **4:13.** The sign-action is explained as referring to eating unclean food in exile. Ezekiel is to model the fate of the people, as in another sense he already does as one of the deportees of 597. **4:14.** The priestly prophet protests (cf. 9:8), more it seems for reasons of his own scruples (cf. Lev 17:10–16) than out of concern for others; this does not constitute intercession on behalf of the people. **4:15.** The prophet is granted the concession of using cow dung, actually a common fuel. Compare the amelioration of the extremity of exile by the divine presence as a sanctuary "in some measure" (11:16). **4:16–17.** "I am going to break the staff of bread in Jerusalem": here the reference is to the impending siege. Food and drink were certainly extremely scarce during both Jerusalem sieges of this period (indeed some were to be reduced to cannibalism; cf. 5:10; Jer 19:9; Lam 2:20; 4:10).

Chapter 5

5:1–4. The sequence continues from ch. 4, with a fourth sign-action. **5:1.** "Take a sharp sword": a doubly appropriate image, the sword of judgement (cf. ch. 21), but more immediately to be used as a barber's razor (cf. Isa 7:20). **5:2.** The shorn hair is to be divided in three, for burning, for further cutting, and for scattering to the wind, all images of judgement, probably not to be pressed for more specific meaning. "Inside the city, when the days of the siege are completed": the kind of reference that has prompted questions about the location of the prophet (cf. the "Time and Place" section, above, and also on 2:3. "All around the city": Hebrew has simply "all around it." **5:3.** "Take from these a small number": this could represent some redactional elaboration of the simpler basic image; but Ezekiel does feature recurrent reference to unexpected survivors (see on 6:8). **5:4.** "From these, again, you shall take some": a further selection; but in this context, it seems, survival only for eventual judgement. "From there a fire will come out against all the house of Israel": judgement will engulf the whole nation (cf. 20:45–49 [Heb. 21:1–5]; Isa 6:13; Zech 13:8–9). Later in the chapter, v. 12 appears to give an interpretation of the basic sign-action.

5:5. The rest of the chapter is more oracular in style, rather than presenting further sign-actions. Jerusalem is set "in the centre of (Heb. *b*ᵉ*ṯôḵ*) the nations" (cf. 38:12). This is of a piece with the great dignity accorded to Jerusalem in the Zion Psalms (e.g. Pss 46 and 48) and perhaps reflects also its pre-Israelite reputation. But how are the mighty now fallen (cf. Lam 1:1). The pattern found here, wherein a position of great honour is tragically lost, will be echoed in the pattern of ch. 16, the story of the falling into disgrace of YHWH's bride, Jerusalem. It is a measure of Ezekiel's critique of and his transcending of the Zion tradition that he never once uses the word "Zion" (cf. Renz 1999b). **5:6.** "More wicked than the nations and the countries all around her": the notion that Judah has sinned more than others is found in Ezek 16:47–52; 23:11. **5:7–8.** These verses are typical of Ezekiel in the way they follow a classic pattern of giving a reason for punishment ("because") followed by the announcement of punishment ("therefore"), but they also significantly elaborate the pattern (Hals 1989:31). **5:8.** "Thus says the Lord GOD: 'I, I myself' ": typical of Ezekiel's theocentric presentation (as also vv. 13, 15, 17, "I, the LORD, have spoken"). "In the sight of the nations": an important motif, which Reventlow has wrongly seen as evidence of a marked universalism on Ezekiel's part. The role of the nations in such cases is merely to witness the self-vindication of YHWH (see the

"Theological Themes" section, above). **5:9.** The first occurrence in the book of the word "abomination" (Heb. *tôᶜēḇâ*), a word of central theological importance in Ezekiel (found on thirty-five occasions), an aspect of his indebtedness to deuteronomistic influence. **5:10.** "Parents shall eat their children in your midst, and children shall eat their parents": including as it does the eating of the flesh of parents, this is deliberately shocking, surpassing the horrors of Lev 26:29; Jer 19:9; Lam 2:20; 4:10. This is grim punishment as well as heinous sin (cf. the bizarre motif of the giving of "statutes that were not good" in 20:25–26). "Any of you who survive I will scatter to every wind": cf. v. 2. **5:11.** "As I live, says the Lord GOD": an adaptation of the oath formula. "You have defiled my sanctuary with all your detestable things": this charge will be illustrated vividly in ch. 8. "Abomination" (Heb. *tôᶜēḇâ*), is found especially in the context of anti-idol polemic in the deuteronomistic literature, as it is here. "I will cut you down": Hebrew has the verb *grᶜ*, to "diminish, restrain, withdraw," and no object; here it is best taken in the further sense of "shave" or "shear" (as in Isa 15:2; Jer 48:37), which would pick up the imagery of v. 1. "My eye will not spare, and I will have no pity": this absoluteness of judgement characterizes chs. 4–24. **5:12.** This verse gives an explicit interpretation of v. 2, with which it shares the threefold pattern and relative simplicity (perhaps confirming the suspicion that the original has been elaborated in vv. 3–4); however, it refers to "pestilence" and "famine" rather than to the "fire" of v. 2.

5:13. "My anger shall spend itself, and I will vent my fury": such passionate language used of YHWH's judgement is again characteristic of chs. 4–24. "They shall know that I, the LORD, have spoken in my jealousy": a variation on the "Recognition Formula," found at 6:7 and very many times in Ezekiel (see the "Theological Themes" section, above). **5:14.** "An object of mocking among the nations around you, in the sight of all that pass by": similar language is used in 36:15, 34 (cf. Jer 24:9–10). A key factor in the theology of Ezekiel is YHWH's own desire to avoid being misrepresented by the nations; in 36:20–22 we see the vindication of his name to be the fundamental reason YHWH acts to deliver his people. **5:15.** "You shall be": NRSV follows LXX, Syriac, Vulgate and Targum; Hebrew has "It shall be," and does not require emendation. "A warning and a horror, to the nations around you": against Reventlow, it is not evident that the nations are expected to learn lessons (see the "Theological Themes" section, above). **5:16.** "When I loose against you": Hebrew has "them," rather than "you," but this is clearly intended to refer to Israel. "More and more famine": this grim and very realistic theme is highlighted and escalated, with the reprise, here and in the following verse, of several recurrent motifs of chs. 4–5: "famine"; "break your staff of bread"; "pestilence"; "the sword." **5:17.** The language of this verse is close to the fourfold punishment of 14:21. "They will rob you of your children": a scourge that will be removed only in the context of restoration after the exile (cf. 36:13–14). The devastating announcement of judgement presented in ch. 5 is bleak and overwhelming, but it is vital to see that the prophet is not willing this cataclysm upon his own people. If one may step outside the book's theocentric perspective for a moment and view the prophet's task in human terms, he is offering a theodicy, justifying the ways of YHWH, by providing an interpretation of what is already happening and shedding the light of theological explanation upon the very present horrors of siege and exile.

CHAPTER 6

The entire chapter is devoted to an oracle against the mountains of Israel. The important interrelation between this chapter and chs. 35–36 (where the oracle is reversed in the announcement of blessing upon the mountains) has been helpfully explored by Simian (1974) and Gosse (1989).

6:2. "Set your face": see on 4:3. "Toward the mountains of Israel": Ezekiel prophesies from Babylonian exile. Brownlee (1983) was misguided in claiming that the "set your face" formula meant that the prophet actually travelled to the places that are condemned. **6:3.** "Mountains of Israel, hear": the mountains are personified, in a manner similar to the appeal to inanimate witnesses ("heavens" and "earth") in Isa 1:2. "A sword": a dominant motif in chs. 5 and 21. "I will destroy your high places": the "high place" (Heb. *bāmâ*) was the hill-top shrine of Canaanite religion (cf. Vaughan 1974). The word comes to symbolize syncretism and cultic deviation within the Hebrew Bible, and that is why this oracle is addressed to the mountains of Israel. **6:4.** "Altars" and "incense stands" represent the paraphernalia of syncretistic religion; the deuteronomistic reforms of around 621 had attempted to suppress all local worship of this kind in favour of a Jerusalem-only sacrificial cult (cf. 2 Kgs 22–23). "Idols": Hebrew *gillûlîm*, a favourite word of Ezekiel, occurring thirty-nine times. Literally "dung balls." **6:4–5.** There is irony in the notion that the slain will be thrown down and the corpses of Israel lain down in front of the idols before which they had prostrated themselves. **6:6.** "Your altars will be waste and ruined": NRSV "and ruined" follows Syriac, Vulgate and Targum. Hebrew has *wᵉyeʾšᵉmû*; this would normally mean "and be held guilty," but in the light of Milgrom (1991:339–41) could be translated "and be desecrated," which sense would fit well here. "Your works": this could refer to the sacred pillars or standing stones of Canaanite religion, but is probably intended as an inclusive summary word for cultic paraphernalia as a whole. **6:7.** "Then you shall know that I am the LORD": the first standard occurrence of the "Recognition Formula" (of which a variation has already occurred at 5:13). The formula is found some fifty-four times in Ezekiel in its basic form and over twenty more times with minor variations. It is the most characteristic expression of the radical theocentricity of this prophet and of the tradition that he shaped. (See the "Theological Themes" section, above, and also Joyce 1989:91, where all the uses of the formula are tabulated.) Within this chapter, see also vv. 10, 13, 14.

6:8. "I will spare some. Some of you shall escape…": the recurrent "survivor" motif of Ezekiel typically illustrates the deserved and just nature of the punishment that has taken place (cf. 5:3; 7:16; 12:16; 14:22–23). **6:9.** "Those of you who escape shall remember me among the nations where they are carried captive": not to be understood in the sense of proselytizing the nations but related rather to the motif of self-loathing. "How I was crushed": Hebrew *nišbartî*. NRSV's translation sounds too vulnerable for Ezekiel's God; AV's "because I am broken" is better. "By their wanton heart": "heart" (Heb. *lēḇ*) is an important word in Ezekiel (as also in the deuteronomistic literature), both positively and also—as here—negatively (see on 11:19). "Wanton," used here both of the heart and the eyes, means "like a prostitute," though the key to this metaphorical language is provided in the following phrase, "that turned after their idols." "They will be loathsome in their own sight for the evils that they have committed": the recurrent motif of self-loathing on the part of survivors, whether accidentally spared or the recipients of God's undeserved deliverance, serves to make evident the sinful and undeserving nature of those involved and thereby to vindicate the justice of YHWH's actions. Self-loathing is found also at 20:43 and 36:31. The related motif of shame is found at 16:52, 54, 61, 63; 36:32 (cf. 7:18; 43:10–11; 44:13). **6:10.** "I did not threaten in vain to bring this disaster upon them": evidence of YHWH's effectiveness is to be provided; compare the need to correct the perceptions of the nations in 36:20–22.

6:11. "They shall fall by the sword, by famine, and by pestilence": cf. the tripartite formulations of 5:2, 12. **6:12.** "Any who are left and are spared shall die of famine": a variant of the survivor motif (cf. 5:3–4). **6:13.** "When their slain lie among their idols around their altars, on every high hill, on all the mountain tops, under every green tree, and under every leafy oak, wherever they offered pleasing odour to all their idols": the densest concentration of deuteronomistic language to be found in Ezekiel (see further the "Unity, Authorship and Redaction" section, above). **6:14.** "From the wilderness to Riblah": Hebrew actually has *diḇlâ*, "Diblah," but this is otherwise unattested as a place name, and a scribal error in the writing of the initial letter is easily explained. The "wilderness" is the southern desert of the Negeb, and Riblah is in central Syria. The phrase means "from south to north," with a sense of inclusive completeness, as with certain other formulae: within Ezekiel, 20:49 (Heb. 21:5) and 21:4 (Heb. v. 9) speak of judgement "from south to north." Elsewhere in the Hebrew Bible, cf. Gen 15:18, "from the river of Egypt to the great river, the river Euphrates"; Exod 23:31, "from the desert unto the river"; 1 Kgs 8:65, "from Lebo-hamath to the Wadi of Egypt."

Chapter 7

This chapter has many poetic features, and indeed the NRSV presents most of this chapter as verse. In spite of this, the chapter was not included by Hölscher (1924) in his small core of authentic material from Ezekiel "the Poet." But there is in fact every reason to regard this material as going back to the prophet himself. It addresses his primary theme of judgement upon the nation in the most characteristic of language. Cahinga (2003) declares that in this key chapter are found all the judgements announced both before it and after it within the book.

The text of the chapter is among the most difficult in the book, and it is clear that at points corruption of the original Hebrew has occurred. There are a number of cases where we do not know what the Hebrew means, though it should be stressed that nowhere is the general thrust unclear. The LXX preserves an edition of the chapter that is in a different arrangement and significantly shorter than that reflected in the MT. This is most plausibly explained as due to the interpolation of marginal variants and the accumulation of glosses on the difficult Hebrew text (Cornill 1886; Tov 1986). Some scholars have argued that the LXX's *Vorlage* preserved an earlier edition of the Hebrew, and that some of the differences between MT and LXX can be explained as the result of intentional editorial additions to the ancestor of MT aimed at introducing a specific agent of YHWH's judgement during the Hellenistic era (Lust 1986a; Bogaert 1986).

In its eschatological language the chapter manifests a debt to the eighth-century prophets Amos (5:18–20; 8:2) and Isaiah (2:6–22), and in turn it has influenced later books, including Joel and Daniel. Cahinga (2003) presents an apocalyptic interpretation of the chapter, exemplifying Ezekiel as a pioneer of apocalyptic writing.

7:2. The divine word is directed "to the land of Israel" (cf. also v. 7), but the implications of the judgement are for Ezekiel's primary audience in exile. "An end! The end": Hebrew *qēṣ* (cf. vv. 3, 6). Very similar to Amos 8:2: "The end (Heb. *qēṣ*) has come upon my people Israel." In fact, this language is not common in the Hebrew Bible generally, which makes the place it gains in Daniel the more significant (e.g. 8:17; 12:4). "Has come": the end is indeed already a reality, in that Jerusalem has fallen in 597 and a significant group of the elite has been transported. The "end" also carries the sense of the end of sin, destroyed by God. "The four corners": a way of expressing inclusive completion (cf. 37:9).
7:3–4. These verses (cf. also vv. 8–9) are replete with typical Ezekiel ideas and language: "according to your ways"; "my eye will not spare"; "I will have no

pity"; and, of course, the "Recognition Formula." "I will let loose my anger upon you": cf. Ps 78:49. **7:5.** "Disaster after disaster!": Heb: *rāʿâ ʾaḥaṯ rāʿâ*. This phrase might serve as a summary of chs. 4–24 (cf. v. 26; also 2:10). **7:6.** "The end has come…see, it comes!": NRSV captures well the tension between present and impending judgement.

7:7. "Your doom": the meaning of Hebrew *ṣᵉpîrâ* here and in v. 10 is uncertain; the word is best taken in both verses, contrary to NRSV, as "diadem" or "crown," on the basis of the only other occurrence in the Hebrew Bible, at Isa 28:5: "In that day the LORD of hosts will be a garland of glory (*ʿᵃṭereṯ ṣᵉḇî*), and a diadem of beauty (*ṣᵉpîraṯ tipʾārâ*), to the remnant of his people." And so a royal sense is likely (supported also by use alongside *hammaṭṭeh*, "staff," in v. 10). Here in v. 7 the reference is presumably to a hostile king who "has come," or is about to come, the natural assumption being that he is Babylonian. Lust notes that the LXX has no counterpart to *ṣᵉpîrâ* either here or in v. 10 (Lust 1986a:18; cf. Bogaert 1986). He too interprets as a coming king but he proposes a word-play link with the male goat (*ṣāpîr*) of Dan 8:5, 8 (identified in 8:21 as "the king of Greece"), and goes on to suggest that the Hebrew text has been developed to allude to Alexander the Great. But this is all too speculative, and the more natural assumption is that the reference is to a Babylonian king. "The day is near": cf. 7:10, 12, 19; also 13:5; 21:25 (Heb. v. 30), 29 (Heb. v. 34); 22:4. "The day" (Heb. *hayyôm*) is an important term, both in earlier eschatology and in later proto-apocalyptic material, with Ezekiel an important mediator between the two (cf. Amos 5:18, 20; 8:9–10; Isa 2:11, 12, 17; Joel 1:15; Mal 4:1 [Heb. 3:19]). "Of tumult, not of revelling on the mountains": "tumult" may refer to dramatic invasion, "revelling" could include cult-related activity. This antithesis is similar to the "darkness, not light" of Amos 5:18, 20. **7:8–9.** These verses closely mirror vv. 3–4. This is for rhetorical effect, and is typical of Ezekiel's tendency to repetition. "Then you shall know that it is I the LORD who strikes": an unusual variation on the "Recognition Formula" (cf. Lust 1986a:17).

7:10. "Your doom": The meaning of the Hebrew word *ṣᵉpîrâ* is again uncertain, as in v. 7; "diadem" is the likely sense here in v. 10 too, referring to a royal figure (note the parallel with *hammaṭṭeh*, "staff," here), who has "gone out." The reference is possibly to Davidic monarchy, with a contrast between two royal houses, one arriving (v. 7, Babylonian) and the other departing (v. 10, Judahite). The references to pride, violence, wickedness, abundance and wealth (vv. 10–11) all cohere with the theme of critique of Davidic monarchy, though it must be acknowledged that these lines are fragmented and difficult. **7:11.** "No pre-eminence among them": the meaning of the obscure Hebrew word *nōah*, found only here, is uncertain; the sense "pre-eminence," "distinction," is variously derived from Hebrew root *nwh*, "to beautify, adorn," or from an Arabic root meaning "to be high." Such textual difficulties as these in vv. 10–11 make for ambiguity and multivalency. As Cahinga notes, Ezekiel's vocabulary in this chapter is often "negative, abstract and ambiguous," but this also makes for universal applicability (Cahinga 2003).

7:12. "Let not the buyer rejoice, nor the seller mourn": quite possibly a proverb in origin. The prospect of an end to all activity imposes a critical equality (cf. Isa 24:1–3, and also the implications of the Jubilee in Lev 25). **7:13.** "It shall not be revoked": Dijkstra defends the originality of this phrase (Heb. *lōʾ yāšûḇ*), and elucidates it in the light of legal irrevocability in the context of civil and religious law (Dijkstra 1989). **7:15.** "Sword...pestilence and famine": a return to some recurrent motifs of chs. 5–6. **7:16.** "If any survivors escape...moaning over their iniquity": on Ezekiel's theme of chance survivors, see on 6:8; contrast v. 11 here, "none of them shall remain". The moaning is that of selfish regret, rather than genuine repentance. **7:17.** "All hands shall grow feeble, all knees turn to water": cf. 21:7, "Every heart will melt and all hands will be feeble, every spirit will faint and all knees will turn to water." **7:18.** "Sackcloth...baldness": the standard signs of mourning (cf. Isa 15:2; Jer 16:6).

7:19. "Their silver and gold cannot save them": cf. Zeph 1:18. As in vv. 12–13, eschatological urgency undermines standard assumptions (cf. 14:14, 20, where not even paragons of virtue will be able to save their own children). "Silver" and "gold" here have the double sense of now useless wealth and also ineffectual idols fashioned of these metals. **7:20.** "From their": NRSV follows Syriac and Symmachus; but Hebrew "from his" makes adequate sense if taken to refer to the deity. "Beautiful ornament...abominable images": temple treasures have been used to manufacture idols. **7:21.** "I will hand it over to strangers as booty...they shall profane it": YHWH will allow foreigners to desecrate the temple. **7:22.** "I will avert my face": Hebrew verb *sbb* followed by *pānîm*, to "turn away the face," here has much the same sense as the more common Hebrew Bible phrase that employs the verb *str* with *pānîm*, to "hide the face"; cf. Balentine 1983:16–17. This being so, "from them" would refer to the Judahites, and "they" to the Babylonians. "Profane my treasured place": the word for "treasured" here (Heb. *ṣᵉpûn*, from a root meaning to "hide") could be translated "secret." There may also be an allusion to *ṣāpôn*, "north" (cf. Ps 48:2 [Heb. v. 3], and see on 1:4). The reference is presumably to the city (of Jerusalem), as is suggested by the feminine suffixes that follow. "The violent shall enter it, they shall profane it": cf. Pss 74 and 79, which allude to desecrations of the sanctuary of unknown date. **7:23.** "Make a chain!": Hebrew *rattôq*; a unique occurrence of this word from root *rtq*, to "bind." The obscure reference may be to the chains of deportation. **7:24.** "I will bring the worst of the nations": contrast 5:6, where Judah is more wicked than the nations. This reference to "the worst of the nations," absent from the LXX, is taken by Lust to refer to the Greeks (Lust 1986a:18; cf. on v. 7). But this is again unnecessarily speculative, and the more natural assumption is that the reference is to the Babylonians. "Their holy places shall be profaned": illicit sanctuaries (as in ch. 6), rather than the temple (as in vv. 21–22). **7:25.** "They will seek peace, but there shall be none": cf. Isa 48:22; 57:21. **7:26.** "Disaster comes upon disaster": Hebrew *howâ ʿal-howâ* (cf. v. 5, which however employs different words, Hebrew *rāʿâ ʾaḥaṯ rāʿâ*; also cf. 2:10). Honoured sources of authority will fail: "vision" (Heb. *ḥāzôn*) from the prophet, "instruction" (*tôrâ*) from the priest, and "counsel"

(*ʿēṣâ*) from the elders (cf. the similar threefold expression of traditional authority at Jer 18:18). **7:27.** "The king shall mourn, the prince shall be wrapped in despair": cf. Jer 4:9. "Prince" (*nāśîʾ*) in this context is probably a collective term for the nobility. "The people of the land": cf. on 22:29. "Shall tremble": cf. v. 17. The chapter closes on a summary note employing classic Ezekiel language and ideas: "According to their way I will deal with them; according to their own judgements I will judge them. And they shall know that I am the LORD."

CHAPTER 8

Chapters 8–11 constitute the second of the major vision accounts of the book. We may call this the first temple vision, as distinct from the great temple vision of chs. 40–48. As we have seen, 8:1–3 shares with 1:1–3 and 40:1–2 three key motifs: the dating formula specific to the day; the phrase for expressing prophetic ecstasy, here "the hand of the Lord GOD fell upon me" (Heb. *wattippōl ʿālay yad ʾadōnāy yhwh*); and also reference to "visions of God" (Heb. *marʾōt ʾelōhîm*). These three visionary sections stand in close relation to each other (cf. Parunak 1980).

Chapter 8 recounts the abominations being performed in the temple, to be followed in the subsequent chapters of the visionary account by scenes of judgement and the narrative of the withdrawal of the glory of YHWH. Whereas the Deuteronomistic History portrays Manasseh's reign as one of great sin (2 Kgs 21), it reports his grandson Josiah as reforming the worship of the nation in 621 (2 Kgs 22–23). So, were such offences as are described here in ch. 8 really still going on in the temple in Ezekiel's day? Greenberg argued that, although idolatry continued in the private realm until 587, Ezekiel misrepresents the facts with regard to the official cult, since the prophet's theological position requires him to show that public idolatry persisted down to 587 so that the present generation is punished for its own sins (Greenberg 1970:27–28). Morton Smith (1975) attempted to vindicate the veracity of Ezek 8, finding some corroboration in Jer 44:18, "But from the time we stopped making offerings to the queen of heaven and pouring out libations to her, we have lacked everything and have perished by the sword and by famine." The latter has generally been interpreted (including by Greenberg) to refer to Josiah's reform of 621, but Morton Smith plausibly took it to refer to the suspension of the non-Yahwistic cult during the final stages of the siege of Jerusalem.

8:1. "In the sixth year, in the sixth month, on the fifth day of the month": 17th September 592. "As I sat in my house, with the elders of Judah sitting before me": cf. 14:1; 20:1. **8:2.** "A figure that looked like a human being": the figure is described very much as in the vision of YHWH in 1:26–28. But whereas 1:26 has *ʾādām*, "a human being," the Hebrew of the present verse has *ʾēš*, "fire," a word that in appearance looks very like *ʾîš*, another word meaning "a human being." LXX reads *andros*, "a man," and is followed by NRSV. "Fire" (Heb. *ʾēš*) certainly has an important place in the vision of ch. 1 (cf. vv. 4, 13, 27), but it would be unusual in this precise context (especially since the word is used later in this same verse) and it is more likely that a scribe has introduced the word here to replace the bolder *ʾîš*. "Like gleaming amber": this is the third and last *ḥašmal* reference (cf. 1:4, 27), ushering in the second of the great vision accounts of the book. A marked continuity between ch. 1 and ch. 8 is clearly intended. "Brightness" here is not *nōgah*, which occurs alongside the two *ḥašmal* references in ch. 1, but rather *zōhar* ("shining, brightness"), a word that was to have its own rich place in the history of Jewish mysticism. **8:3.** "It stretched out the form of a hand": a striking anthropomorphism; v. 1 refers explicitly to "the hand of the Lord GOD." "The spirit lifted me up between earth and heaven, and brought me in visions of God to Jerusalem": I have argued that this chapter should not be taken as evidence that Ezekiel exercised a ministry in Jerusalem (see the "Time and Place" section, above). The chapter reflects the local knowledge of Ezekiel, a priest in Jerusalem until 597, and possibly the reports of refugees or visitors to Babylonia, as well as, of course, elements of ideology and polemic.

The chapter recounts four separate cultic offences, using Ezekiel's favoured word "abominations" (Heb. *tôʿēḇôṯ*) repeatedly (vv. 6 [twice], 9, 13, 15, 17). Ackerman (1992:37–99) offers a valuable discussion, as does Mein (2001a:119–35). "To the entrance of the gateway of the inner court that faces north": "inner court" (Heb. *happᵉnîmîṯ*) is not represented in LXX, and is removed by Zimmerli (1979a:217, 237) and Ackerman (1992:39, 53–55), so that the reference is to the gate of the city; this affords a progression within this chapter from outside the city to inside the temple (cf. vv. 7, 14, 16). However, Hebrew *happᵉnîmîṯ*, "inner court," is better retained, with Eichrodt (1970:122) and Greenberg (1983a:168); logical progression is not necessarily to be expected of a visionary sequence and there is appropriateness in the shocking "image of jealousy" being close to the heart of the temple. This image, mentioned here and also in v. 5, is the first of the specific abominations. It is widely taken to refer to a statue of the goddess Asherah (Eichrodt 1970:122–23; Greenberg 1983a:168). Lutzky (1996), favouring the Asherah interpretation, changes the root *qnʾ*, "to be jealous," to *qnh*, "to (pro)create," so that Asherah's statue is given the title "the Creatress." Day persuasively rejects this reading, while judging the Asherah reference itself possible but uncertain (Day 2000:62–63). Odell has offered a fresh alternative to the Asherah interpretation. She proposes a votive statue, finding here a reference to the *mlk* sacrifice and suggesting that the Phoenician practice of dedicating statues of children to the god Eshmoun as a substitute for real children may have been adopted into the worship of YHWH (Odell 2004; 2005:104–108). **8:4.** "The glory of the God of Israel was there, like the vision that I had seen in the valley": a cross-reference back to Ezek 3:23 (cf. 43:3). **8:5.** "Then God said to me": Hebrew has just "he," but it is clear that the deity speaks. "I lifted up my eyes toward the north, and there, north of the altar gate, in the entrance": it is possible that "north" implies an allusion to Canaanite ideas (see on 1:4), but a literal interpretation is more likely. **8:6.** "Do you see what they are doing?": the chapter features a sequence of such questions (cf. vv. 12, 15, 17). "To drive me far from my sanctuary": NRSV in this translation anticipates YHWH's departure (chs. 10–11), but the Qal infinitive more naturally here refers to sinners "going far"; thus Greenberg "removing themselves" (1983a:164, 168–69; cf. 11:15;

44:10). Wong (2001b) takes a similar position, keen to emphasize that YHWH's departure is never described as being forced by the cultic offences that render the sanctuary impure. "You will see still greater abominations": this refrain is repeated through the chapter (cf. vv. 13, 15).

8:7. The second of the abominations concerns a secret room of reliefs. Though the details are difficult to elucidate, the episode clearly depicts idolatry by a representative group of the nation's elite. "There was a hole in the wall": with particular attention to these words, Halperin gives extended attention to this passage in his thoroughgoing psychoanalytical reading of Ezekiel (Halperin 1993:81–117; cf. Joyce 1995b). **8:8.** "I dug through the wall": cf. 12:1–16. **8:10.** "Portrayed on the wall all around": the word represented in NRSV by "portrayed" is Hebrew *mᵉḥuqqeh*, a rare word meaning "carved"; it is found only in 1 Kgs 6:35, apart from here and at 23:14. "Kinds of creeping things and...animals": these words (Heb. *tabnîṯ remeś ûbᵉhēmâ*) are not represented in LXX and could constitute a gloss (cf. Deut 4:17–18); but the reference to animals is probably a correct interpretation of "all the idols of the house of Israel." Ackerman argues that Ezek 8:7–13 reflects the features of a *marzēaḥ* banquet, taking "loathsome" (Heb. *šeqeṣ*) to refer to food (Ackerman 1989); but this is rightly contested by McLaughlin on the grounds that the religious activity here is secretive and also that drinking is not featured (McLaughlin 2001:196–213). **8:11.** "Seventy of the elders of the house of Israel": cf. the seventy leaders in the wilderness (Exod 24:1, 9; Num 11:16, 24–25); this seems to reinforce the sense that the actors in this unit are representative of the Jerusalem leadership. "Jaazaniah son of Shaphan": possibly the son of the secretary at Josiah's court (2 Kgs 22); if so, he has certainly gone astray from his father's ways. **8:12.** "In the dark": the covert nature of this episode is noteworthy in comparison to the other sections of the chapter. Eichrodt saw this as evidence that the particular practice was an Egyptian one, with a political dimension (Eichrodt 1970:124–25). "The LORD does not see us, the LORD has forsaken the land": cf. 9:9; both verses speak as though YHWH has already abandoned Jerusalem, even though in narrative terms this is not accomplished until 11:23. We are reminded of the fact that ch. 1 has anticipated YHWH's movement to be with the exiles. It may seem somewhat strained that the figure of 8:2, already seen in Babylonia, plays a role in bringing Ezekiel back (in vision) to Jerusalem (v. 3), and that we are then told (v. 4) that the glory of the God of Israel is there in Jerusalem, even as reference is made to the vision in the Babylonian "valley" of 3:22–23. However, Ackroyd rightly warned against an over-literal interpretation of the withdrawal of the glory of YHWH from the temple, which would imply an excessively crude notion of physical movement. He preferred to speak of "a denial of that protective presence which maintained the people's life and well-being through the Temple" (Ackroyd 1968:28). The use of quotation, putting words in the mouths of interlocutors and others, often with the use of caricature, is particularly characteristic of Ezekiel (cf. 9:9; 11:15; 12:27; 18:2, 19, 25, 29; 20:32; 33:10, 24; 37:11). (Isa 14:13–14 looks like a precursor, but in fact it may well be post-exilic and indebted to Ezekiel; cf. Kaiser 1974:29–32.)

8:14. The third specific abomination, briefly treated, concerns Tammuz, the only pagan deity explicitly mentioned by Ezekiel. "Women": cf. Jer 7:18; 44:19; and especially Ezek 13:17–23. Feminist-critical discussion, especially of chs. 16 and 23, has made us aware that issues relating to the feminine are particularly problematic in Ezekiel; and so even the presentation of women in a verse like this can no longer be read naïvely. "Were sitting": the traditional pose for mourners; cf. Ezek 26:16; Lam 2:10. "Weeping for Tammuz": Tammuz was the young fertility god of Mesopotamia (Sumerian Dumuzi), taken into the underworld in the summer, when all the vegetation died. His consort Ishtar (Sumerian Inanna) subsequently descended to rescue him, and a sacred marriage was followed by the return of vegetation and fertility. Women had a special role in cultic weeping for Tammuz. However, this traditionally took place in the fourth month of the Babylonian year (i.e. June/July), which derived its name, Tammuz, from the god, rather than in the sixth month mentioned in v. 1. This might dispose one to consider Block's proposal that what is referred to here is not "weeping for Tammuz" but "weeping *the* Tammuz," a special genre of lament, only indirectly related to the Babylonian cult (Block 1997:294–96). This is worth entertaining, though such a theory is not necessitated by the definite article before Tammuz, since we find the article used with other deities (Baal, and—more controversially—Asherah; cf. Day 2000:43). Odell takes up Block's suggestion positively and links it with the idea that the weeping may be connected with royal child sacrifice (Odell 2005:110–12).

8:16. The fourth offence is bowing down to the sun. "At the entrance of the temple of the LORD, between the porch and the altar": this abomination takes place close to the heart of YHWH's sanctuary; cf. Joel 2:17. "Twenty-five men": as in 11:1, but the surprising approximation "about" differs from the precise numbers of 8:11; 11:1. "Their faces toward the east, prostrating themselves to the sun": The worship of the sun was widespread throughout the ancient Near East. Many of the references to this in the Hebrew Bible seem to date from the seventh and sixth centuries, but Day argues that the cult is Canaanite in origin, rather than Mesopotamian (Day 2000:151–54). Taylor contends that YHWH was actually equated with the sun (Taylor 1993), but this is contested by Day, who argues that the sun would have been regarded as part of the host of heaven, subordinate to YHWH (Day 2000:157–61). "Their backs to the temple of the LORD": their rejection of YHWH is perhaps compounded by the insult of exposing their buttocks to him. **8:17.** "Is it not bad enough that the house of Judah commits the abominations done here?": this time we do not have the familiar refrain promising still greater abominations. The sequence is at an end. The question "Must they fill the land with violence and provoke my anger still further?" complements the cultic emphasis of the chapter by adding an ethical dimension, referring to social wrongdoing. "Violence" (Heb. *ḥāmās*) is one of Ezekiel's favoured words in this context (e.g. 7:11, 23; 12:19; 45:9), though less distinctive than his common use of "bloodshed" (Heb. *dāmîm*) (cf. Mein 2001a:94–99). "Putting the branch to their nose": this should not be seen as a fifth specific abomination of the sequence; Zimmerli was right to emphasize that the number four represents completeness (Zimmerli 1979a:252). The "branch" (*z*ᵉ*môrâ*) is widely seen as a phallic symbol (Saggs 1960); and this suggests some kind of obscene gesture. An expression of contempt is implied, referring either to the social wrongdoing of v. 17 or more likely to the offences recounted in the chapter as a whole. **8:18.** "Therefore I will act in wrath; my eye will not spare, nor will I have pity": now familiar threats (cf. 5:11; 7:4), to which is added a new one, "I will not listen to them." It is possible that there is a play here on the name of Jaazaniah (Heb. *ya*ʾᵃ*zanyāhû*, "YHWH hears") in v. 11.

The last verse of ch. 8 sets the scene for the slaughter of ch. 9 and the burning of ch. 10. Zimmerli argued persuasively that this sequence reflects the form of prophetic declarations in the context of Holy War (cf. 1 Kgs 20:13, 28), with ch. 8 corresponding to the "legitimation" and ch. 9 to the "announcement of judgement" (Zimmerli 1982a:107).

CHAPTER 9

9:1. "Then he cried": the deity is the speaker. "Draw near, you executioners of the city": "executioners" (Heb. *p^{e}quddôṯ*) is in this context a better translation than the main alternative, "overseers" (AV: "them that have charge"), as is suggested by the weapon each holds. They may be modelled on various ancient Near Eastern divinities (cf. Bodi 1991:95–110), but here they are unambiguously subordinate agents of the judgement of YHWH; cf. "the destroyer" (Heb. *hammašḥîṯ*) of the Passover tradition (Exod 12:23). **9:2.** "And six men came… among them was a man clothed in linen": the man seems to be additional to the six, rather than one of their number; he and they have quite distinct tasks. The figure introduced here is very different from the divine figure of 8:2 (who is clearly equated with that of 1:26–28); he shares much with the "man…with a linen cord and a measuring reed in his hand," introduced at 40:3. His scribal function may reflect that of Nabu within the Babylonian pantheon. "Linen" is associated elsewhere with priests (e.g. Lev 6:10) and with angels (Dan 10:5). "From the direction of the upper gate, which faces north": the direction of YHWH's theophanic manifestation; cf. on 1:4. "The bronze altar": cf. 1 Kgs 8:64; 2 Kgs 16:14–15; 2 Chr 4:1.

9:3. "Now the glory of the God of Israel had gone up…to the threshold of the house": this picks up the reference to the glory in 8:4. The long withdrawal of the glory from the temple begins here; its further movements within this vision are recorded in 10:3–4, 15, 18–19; 11:22–23. "From the cherub on which it rested": the first occurrence of "cherub" (singular) in Ezekiel; for similar singular references in this context, see 10:4, 7, 9, 14. The remaining three Ezekiel references to "cherub" in the singular are very different: 28:14, 16 (in a mythological context within the Tyre material) and 41:18 (in the context of temple decoration). For the plural usage, see on 10:1. **9:4.** "Put a mark on the foreheads": the Hebrew letter *tāw*, originally written as an "X" or cross; cf. the blood on the lintel and the doorposts in Exod 12. "Those who sigh and groan over all the abominations that are committed in it": a very minimal definition of those who might qualify to be spared, not all except the actively wicked, but only those who positively dissociate themselves from the abominations. **9:5.** "Your eye shall not spare, and you shall show no pity": the executioners are to behave just as YHWH whose bidding they are doing (cf. v. 10). **9:6.** "Old men, young men and young women, little children and women": This list, including, as it does, categories that one might have expected to be exempt, seems to be designed to convey a sense of the inclusive nature of the coming judgement. We may compare similar lists in Ps 148:11–12; Joel 2:28–29 (Heb. 3:1–2); Deut 29:10–11 (Heb. vv. 9–10). Particularly close to the present example are Jer 6:11 and 1 Sam 15:3. "Begin at my sanctuary": the sanctuary is the source and focus of the holiness that is the foundation of YHWH's judgement. This also means that the temple will be defiled with dead bodies (v. 7). "They began with the elders": cf. 8:11, 16. "The house": a reference to the temple. **9:8.** "I fell prostrate on my face": cf. on 1:28. "Ah Lord GOD! will you destroy all who remain of Israel?": cf. 4:14. The prophet's reaction is one of shock rather than protest; this does not constitute intercession on behalf of the people (compare discussion of dumbness motif in 3:26). **9:9.** The answer given by YHWH appears to be in the affirmative: "The guilt of the house of Israel and Judah is exceedingly great." "Bloodshed": Hebrew *dāmîm*; cf. on 8:17. "The LORD has forsaken the land, and the LORD does not see": cf. on 8:12. **9:10.** "As for me, my eye will not spare, nor will I have pity": the theme of neither sparing nor pitying is a recurrent one, found in the verse that precedes this chapter (8:18), in the middle of the chapter (9:5) and here again at the end (9:10).

9:11. "I have done as you commanded me": the fact that one man was to mark individually the foreheads of any righteous led one to expect that they were likely to be few, but now that he has returned, we are not even told whether he in fact found any deserving the mark. Compare the familiar theme of the call narratives: "All the house of Israel are of a hard forehead and of a stubborn heart" (3:7), and also 22:30, "I sought for a man among them who should build up the wall and stand in the breach before me for the land, that I should not destroy it; but I found none." However, it would be a mistake to press for an answer to the question whether the man clothed in linen actually found any who "sighed and groaned" (by asking, for example, where Jeremiah was that day); the instruction to mark any righteous occurs, after all, within an account of a vision. The important point is precisely that we are not told whether any were found; the central concern is not with the possibility of exemption from punishment for any righteous. What we do know is that, now the man clothed in linen has completed his task, all hope of escape for the guilty is past. We heard in v. 5 that the executioners were to pass through the city after him, and we read in vv. 7 and 8 that they were already smiting. In the next chapter, even the man clothed in linen turns destroyer.

The motif of the marking of the foreheads of the righteous has contributed to the popular notion that "individual responsibility" is an important part of the message of Ezekiel. It is important, though, to recognize that it is subordinated to the overall theme of the thorough punishment of the wicked. The exhaustive list of the categories of people who are to be slain (v. 6) confirms the absolute nature of the impending punishment.

The positive role of the marking motif in the chapter may be said to consist in three elements: (i) the instruction to exempt any active righteous makes it clear that the merciless slaughter is in fact a just act of judgement; (ii) the very minimal definition of those who are to receive the sign (not all except the actively wicked, but only those who by "sighing and groaning" positively dissociate themselves from the abominations) emphasizes the thoroughgoing nature of the impending punishment; (iii) the marking of any righteous means that there can now be no hope of escape for the guilty.

While an element of individualism is certainly to be recognized, the motif of the marking of foreheads takes for granted the notion that ideally the righteous should be spared in a general punishment (cf. Gen 6:5–8; 18:25). It is most unlikely that the motif is to be regarded as in any sense an innovation. We also find here material that represents a rather more collective notion of responsibility. The inclusion of little children in the punishment recalls the emphasis on family solidarity and collective retribution that is a feature of many Hebrew Bible narratives (e.g. Josh 7:24–25; Num 16:32). Also to be noted is the collective emphasis of 9:9, referring as it does to the house of Israel and Judah, the land and the city. As Kaufmann wrote of this chapter, "collective and individual retribution are spoken of in the same breath" (Kaufmann 1961:439). If we recall the historical setting of Ezekiel's ministry, namely the subjugation of Judah by Babylonia, such complexities are readily understandable. Though the prophet might well feel some concern for the fate of the righteous in a general punishment, the nature of this great catastrophe was such that, in one way or another, all were inevitably involved.

Chapter 10

Chapters 1 and 10 have much of their imagery in common (cf. Keel 1977); but we shall note a number of particular differences.

10:1. "Above the dome...appeared...a throne": see on 1:26. "Cherubim": the plural (Heb. *kᵉrubîm*) is introduced for the first time in MT here (for singular "cherub," see on 9:3). Verses 15 and 20 are at pains to equate the figures presented here with the "living creatures" of ch. 1 (Heb. *ḥayyôṯ*; see on 1:5). In the present context Ezekiel co-opts a feature of the temple (e.g. 1 Kgs 8:6–7), skilfully exploiting the earlier associations of the "cherubim" with the mobility of the Ark of the Covenant in pre-temple times (cf. 1 Sam 4:4) as he presents his narrative of the movement of the deity to be with his exiled people. The word "cherubim" occurs sixteen times in ch. 10 alone. The one reference in ch. 11 (v. 22) is very similar to those in ch. 10, whereas the other three references are in the different context of temple decoration (41:18, 20, 25). "Throne": Hebrew *kissēʾ*; one of only four references to "throne" in the book, the others being at 1:26 (twice) and 43:7. In other words, it is used at a key point in each of the three major visions in the book. Elsewhere in the Hebrew Bible, YHWH is said to be "enthroned on the cherubim" (Heb. *yōšēḇ hakkᵉrubîm*) (1 Sam 4:4; 2 Sam 6:2) and there are many references to the spread wings of the cherubim overshadowing the "mercy seat" (Heb. *kappōreṯ*) on the top of the Ark (e.g. Exod 25:20).

10:2. "He said": the deity addresses the man clothed in linen. "Wheelwork": Hebrew *galgal*; a different word from that used for wheel (Heb. *ʾôpan*) in ch. 1. Verse 13 is insistent upon equating the two. "Burning coals": Hebrew *gaḥᵃlê-ʾēš*, literally "coals of fire," as in 1:13. "Fire" (Heb. *ʾēš*) has an important place within the theophany of ch. 1 (vv. 4, 13, 27; cf. 8:2) and a quite separate role as a method of judgement in 5:2, 4. Now these two motifs are brought together, with coals from among the cherubim taken out to burn down the city. For judgement by fire, compare the destruction of Sodom and Gomorrah in Gen 19:24–25. **10:3.** "And a cloud filled the inner court": here and in the following verse, the use of the word "cloud" (Heb. *ʿānān*) echoes other narratives of the divine presence (e.g. Num 10:34). **10:4.** "Then the glory of the LORD rose up from the cherub to the threshold of the house": cf. 9:3. "The house was filled with the cloud and the court was full of the brightness of the glory of the LORD": compare, within the priestly culmination of the book of Exodus, Exod 40:34,

"Then the cloud covered the tent of meeting, and the glory of the LORD filled the tabernacle" (cf. Exod 16:10; Num 16:42). "Brightness": Hebrew *nōgah*; an important link with ch. 1, where this word occurs alongside *ḥašmal* (NRSV "amber") in vv. 4 and 27. "The glory of the LORD": Hebrew *kᵉbôd yhwh*; these words echo the crescendo of ch. 1 in v. 28. It is almost as though the divine presence in the temple is manifested for one last time here before the deity abandons his sanctuary. **10:5.** "God Almighty": Hebrew *ʾēl-šadday*: see on 1:24.

10:7. "The man…took it and went out": the destruction by fire begins. **10:12.** "Their entire body, their rims, their spokes, their wings, and the wheels—the wheels of the four of them—were full of eyes all around": an elaboration of the language of 1:18. **10:13.** "As for the wheels, they were called in my hearing 'the wheelwork'": see on v. 2. Halperin, exploring the exegetical character of vv. 9–17, saw the divergences from ch. 1 as reflecting the beginnings of later angelological understanding of the "wheels" (Heb. *ʾôpannîm*) (Halperin 1976). **10:14.** "Each one had four faces": it appears that here each of the cherubim has four of the same face (the form of the face differing from cherub to cherub), whereas in 1:10 each creature has a set of four different faces. Moreover, the face of an "ox" in 1:10 has been replaced by the face of a "cherub." The removal of the ox's face was explained by the rabbis as due to its association with the golden calf incident in Exod 32 (*b. Ḥag.* 13b). Why the face of a cherub has replaced it is unclear. It may be because, the "living creatures" (Heb. *ḥayyôṯ*) of ch. 1 having been replaced by the "cherubim" (Heb. *kᵉrubîm*) in ch. 10, it seemed fitting that the face of a "cherub" should feature. This explanation is favoured by the fact that the cherub's face is listed first here and that "cherub" (alone of the four) is preceded by the definite article (Heb. *hakkᵉrûḇ*).

10:15. "The cherubim rose up. These were the living creatures that I saw by the river Chebar": an explicit cross-reference to ch. 1. **10:19.** "The cherubim lifted up their wings and rose up from the earth": flight appears to be envisaged here, as in v. 16, anticipating perhaps the long journey to Babylonia. One may compare Ps 18:10 (Heb. v. 11) (= 2 Sam 22:11), "He rode on a cherub, and flew; he came swiftly upon the wings of the wind." The context there includes reference to "fire" (Heb. *ʾēš*), "burning coals" (Heb. *gaḥᵃlê-ʾēš*) and "brightness" (*nōgah*), all features of the present passage. "They stopped at the entrance of the east gate of the house of the LORD": this verse, together with v. 18, represents a further stage in the withdrawal of the divine glory. After this reference, that narrative does not feature again until its culmination is reported in 11:22–23. "The east gate": the main processional gate into the temple precinct; also significantly the gate that pointed in the direction of Babylonia.

10:20. "These were the living creatures that I saw underneath the God of Israel by the river Chebar; and I knew that they were cherubim": another explicit cross-reference (cf. v. 15). **10:22.** "They were the same faces whose appearance I had seen by the river Chebar": this is the fourth case of an insistence that ch. 1

and ch. 10 refer to the same phenomena (cf. vv. 13, 15, 20). These may well come from the hand of a harmonizing glossator. In the present case, the claim of consistency with regard to the faces actually contradicts the earlier v. 14. Of course, this was always recognized; and the present affirmation of consistency is a sophisticated one, attesting that in spite of apparent difference the two visions witness to the same divine reality.

CHAPTER 11

11:1–13: This passage in some respects stands awkwardly in its present setting. It is odd to find Ezekiel addressing twenty-five men outside the temple after the references to the six executioners in ch. 9 and to the man clothed in linen scattering burning coals in ch. 10. Also, these verses interrupt the account of the departure of the glory of YHWH (indeed it is noteworthy that we hear nothing of the movement of the glory between 10:19 and 11:22). It is probable that this unit (vv. 1–13) was introduced into its present position some time after the composition of the basic account of the extended vision of chs. 8–11, though a number of possible links with the present context will be noted (see on vv. 3 and 20 below).

11:1. "The east gate of the house of the LORD": Ezekiel is brought to where the cherubim and the glory had moved in 10:19. "Twenty-five men" were there: cf. the seventy elders at 8:11; and "about twenty-five men" at 8:16. Two of them are named as "officials of the people": one is "Jaazaniah son of Azzur" (cf. 8:11, "Jaazaniah son of Shaphan"), the other "Pelatiah son of Benaiah"; they are otherwise unknown. **11:2.** "Men who devise iniquity and who give wicked counsel": elite crimes, in keeping with their being "officials of the people" (Heb. *śārê hāʿām*, "princes of the people"). It is possible that they were involved in plotting an alliance with Egypt, seen as a basis for optimism (cf. Jer 27; 37). **11:3.** "The time is not near to build houses": one expects to find words of complacency here; accordingly, Rashi and Kimḥi understood "not near" to refer to the judgement: "The judgement predicted by the prophets is not near, so let us build houses…" However, it is better is to take the words as in NRSV; the point may be that these leaders have already acquired the property of the exiles, which would cohere with v. 15 (a potential point of contact between vv. 1–13 and vv. 14–21), and so they have no need to build houses. "This city is the pot, and we are the meat": Hebrew just has *hîʾ*, "this" (feminine), here and in vv. 7 and 11, but "city" (appearing at the end of v. 2) is probably intended. The pot (Heb. *sîr*) seems to represent the city walls, within which they imagine themselves secure; cf. the allegory of the "pot" (same Hebrew word) in 24:1–14, where in v. 6 the equation with the city is explicit: "Woe to the bloody city, the pot whose rust is in it…" Graffy finds in this chapter two examples of the "disputation speech," properly limited to cases in which the prophet quotes the people's speech in order to refute them. Of Graffy's sixteen cases, nine are from Ezekiel. In addition to 11:2–12 and 11:14–17, he lists 12:21–25, 26–28; 18:1–20; 20:32–44; 33:10–20, 23–29; 37:11b–13 (Graffy 1984).

11:5. "This is what you think…I know the things that come into your mind": cf. 20:32. **11:6.** "You have killed many in this city": see the reference to violence (*ḥāmās*) in 8:17, and comments there; cf. also ch. 22. "Filled its streets with the slain": a hyperbolic reference, probably including both victims of political murders and those who have died of the indirect effects of bad leadership. This reads oddly coming after the divinely ordained slaying of ch. 9, which may lend weight to the hypothesis that this unit was not originally located here. **11:7.** "The slain whom you have placed within it are the meat": in a development of the metaphor, the prophet suggests that the leaders are cooking their victims. "You shall be taken out of it": the city will not provide them with the security they seek. **11:8.** "I will bring the sword upon you": the "sword" of judgement is an important theme of Ezekiel (cf. chs. 5, 6 and especially 21). **11:10.** "I will judge you at the border of Israel": the reference may be to events at Riblah (at Israel's northern extremity; see on 6:14), as recounted in Jer 52:24–27, in which case this may be a note added after the event. **11:11.** The repetition is typical of Ezekiel and not grounds for trimming the text. **11:12.** A particularly extended example of Ezekiel's "Recognition Formula," in contrast to the basic formula found here in v. 10; cf. on 6:7. "Whose statutes you have not followed, and whose ordinances you have not kept": cf. the reasons for divine judgement given in Isa 42:24. "You have acted according to the ordinances of the nations that are around you": a play on the word "ordinances" (*mišpāṭîm*)—they have become no better than pagans. **11:13.** "While I was prophesying, Pelatiah son of Benaiah died": outside the oracle itself is given a note reporting what happened; this may be another addition (cf. on v. 10). Rationalizing explanations of what might have happened to Pelatiah are of no relevance; within the context of the book of Ezekiel, the awesome and numinous impact of the word of God is all that matters. "I fell down on my face": cf. on 1:28. For further comment on v. 13 see below.

11:14–21. This unit is of particular importance within the theology of Ezekiel and demands especially detailed treatment. It is a positive section standing isolated in the midst of material concerning judgement upon Jerusalem and Judah, one of only four short passages in the first half of the book that contain an element of hope for the future (the others being 16:59–63; 17:22–24 and 20:40–44). In response to the arrogant presumption of the Jerusalem community (v. 15), the prophet declares that the favour of YHWH is to be granted to the exiles. This seems to be a self-contained unit that may not always have occupied its present position at the end of the extended vision account of chs. 8–11. The connection between the address to the leaders of Jerusalem in vv. 1–13 and the oracle of vv. 14–21 appears tenuous. Although the two passages share the theme of the arrogant presumption of the leaders of Jerusalem (and some other possible connections), there are significant differences, chief among which is that 11:1–13 is entirely focused upon Jerusalem and makes no reference to those already in exile. It may well be that the shared theme of the arrogance of the Jerusalem community was one of the factors that prompted the attachment of an originally independent oracle (vv. 14–21) to 11:1–13.

Ezekiel 11:14–21 shares some features with 33:23–29 (which occurs just after the announcement of the fall of the city). Those verses read: "The word of the LORD came to me: 'Mortal, the inhabitants of these waste places in the land of Israel keep saying, "Abraham was only one man, yet he got possession of the land; but we are many; the land is surely given to us to possess"'" (33.23–24). The divine response comes in v. 25: "You eat flesh with the blood, and lift up your eyes to your idols, and shed blood; shall you then possess the land?" On the grounds of similarity to this passage, Eichrodt regarded 11:14–21 as from after 587, as did Brownlee too, interpreting the unit in the light of the reference in Jer 39:10 to Nebuzaradan giving Judahite vineyards and fields to the poor people left in the land after 587 (Eichrodt 1970:143; Brownlee 1986:163). However, Zimmerli and Greenberg rightly saw that the original setting of 11:14–21 was before the fall of Jerusalem in 587 and that 33:23–29 does not provide evidence to the contrary (Zimmerli 1979a:263; Greenberg 1983a:203–4). The case for this conclusion rests on three points. First, whereas 33:24 speaks of "the inhabitants of these waste places in the land of Israel," 11:15 still refers to "the inhabitants of Jerusalem." Second, 11:15 pictures a complacent Jerusalem community: these people imagine that their lot is much better than that of the exiles. This best fits a setting in the period between 597 and 587, when the situation of the two communities could most sharply be contrasted. While 33:23–29 certainly bears witness to the continuing pretensions of the Jerusalem community after 587, the mocking derision of the exiles found in 11:15 has gone. Third, the self-sufficient arrogance on the part of the Jerusalemites in 11:15 has given way to a more dependent appeal to the promises to Abraham in 33:24.

Is it credible that Ezekiel uttered hopeful oracles before the final collapse of Jerusalem in 587, given that they are hardly ever to be found in the first half of Ezekiel, set as it is before the news of the final collapse of Jerusalem? In broad terms it is certainly true that Ezekiel's message before 587 was one of judgement and after 587 one of promise; but the consistency with which the first half of the book is concerned with condemnation and the second with deliverance may owe something to a firm editorial hand during the redactional development of the book. We should resist a dogmatic assumption that the prophet cannot have preached any word of hope before 587 and that any hopeful material found before the fall of Jerusalem must be, as it were, "out of place." It may be conceded that the positive verses at the end of chs. 16, 17 and 20 may well be secondary additions. However, for the reasons outlined above, it seems probable that 11:14–21 presupposes a situation before the fall of Jerusalem in 587. This unit constitutes one case—the only case—where the prophet anticipates the more positive themes of the later part of his ministry. It is important to note that this word of hope for the exiles appears in the context of the condemnation of the Jerusalem community and by way of contrast to their fate, emphasized in v. 21; thus even this unit ends on a note of judgement. Though 11:14–21 may not originally have been in its present position at the end of the extended vision account of chs. 8–11, this self-contained unit presumably found a place in the first half of the book, despite its hopeful content and contrary to the editorial schema, because it was evident that it assumed a situation that obtained only before the final disaster of 587.

The immediate context of 11:14–21 is now provided by Ezekiel's cry in v. 13, "Ah Lord GOD! will you make a full end of the remnant of Israel?" This is to be seen as parallel to the very similar words of 9:8 (as there, the prophet's reaction is one of shock rather than protest; and does not constitute intercession on behalf of the people). In 9:8, in response to the slaughter carried out by the six executioners, the prophet asks: "Ah Lord GOD! will you destroy all who remain of Israel as you pour out your wrath upon Jerusalem?" In response to this question (which, it should be noted, is related specifically to the non-exiles), YHWH gives an answer that appears to be in the affirmative: "The guilt of the house of Israel and Judah is exceedingly great… I will bring down their deeds upon their heads" (9:9–10). In contrast to this, the parallel question in 11:13 becomes the occasion (at least in the present arrangement of the text) for a word of hope, albeit good news for the exiles alone, at the expense of the Jerusalem community. This contrast is stark indeed, and may be compared to the image of the good and the bad figs in Jer 24, representing the exiles and the non-exiles respectively.

11:15. "Your kinsfolk, your own kin, your fellow exiles, the whole house of Israel, all of them": these are the butt of the Jerusalem community's gibe. The context makes it evident that the group in question is constituted by the exiled community. However, the details are more difficult. They are described as "your brothers" (Heb. *ʾaḥêḵā*; NRSV: "your kinsfolk"). The word is repeated for emphasis, as indeed is the word for "all" (Heb. *kullō*) later in this same verse; we should resist the temptation to prune the text to suit our own literary tastes, and rather, in both cases, let the repetition stand. Does this mean "kinsfolk" in the literal sense, that is, family, or in some more general metaphorical sense? The phrase that follows suggests the more literal interpretation, for they are described next in the Hebrew phrase *ʾanšê g*ᵉʾ*ullāṯeḵā*, "the people of your redemption." Some ancient versions (e.g. LXX and Syriac) and some modern translations prefer to read "the people of your exile" here (so NRSV: "your fellow exiles"), assuming the Hebrew *ʾanšê gālûṯeḵā*, but, though difficult, the MT yields tolerable sense (referring to those with whom the prophet shares the reciprocal duty to act as a *gōʾēl*, a redeemer of property) and in fact coheres with the earlier reference to "kinsfolk." The primary reference, then, seems to be to close relatives of Ezekiel in exile, dispossessed of lands by non-exiles back in Judah. The reference is explicitly broadened out beyond the narrow circle of Ezekiel's relatives by the words "and the whole house of Israel" (Heb. *w*ᵉ*ḵol-bêṯ yiśrāʾēl*). It is possible that these words constitute an explanatory gloss, but even if this is so, they simply spell out the fact that Ezekiel's relatives here symbolize the dispossessed exiles as a whole. It is noteworthy that "Israel" is used here to mean the exiled community in contrast to those in Jerusalem: it is the exiles who now constitute the Israel of God and of the future.

'They have gone far from the LORD; to us this land is given for a possession": the words of the gibe uttered by the inhabitants of Jerusalem (cf. 8:6). The MT has *raḥ^{a}qû*, imperative ("Get you far [from the LORD]"). This is best amended to the perfect indicative, *rāḥ^{a}qû* ("They have gone far [from the LORD]"). This is more appropriate, since the reference is to the deportees of 597, who are clearly already in exile. The point is not just that they have gone far geographically; the Jerusalemites' taunt assumes that YHWH is localized and that physical removal necessarily means alienation from his presence. Such assumptions were deeply rooted (compare the words attributed to David in 1 Sam 26:19, and to Naaman in 2 Kgs 5:17). The attitude of the Jerusalem community is, in a sense, very understandable: the temple (still standing until 587) was the particular token of YHWH's favour and presence. The words "They have gone far" here in v. 15 parallel the Hiphil perfect of the same root, found in v. 16, *hirḥaqtîm*, "I removed them," referring to YHWH's deportation of the exiles of 597. This reveals a further nuance, highlighting the deserved nature of the exiles' fate. Balentine likens this to the *lex talionis*, and translates; "Because they have gone far from me, therefore I have removed them far from me" (Balentine 1983:156–57). Read more politically, 11:14–21 constitutes a revealing encapsulation of the two Judahite communities' rival claims.

11:16. The response features three verbs of which the subject is YHWH. As we have seen, the first, *hirḥaqtîm*, takes up the word of the taunt and assumes divine responsibility for the deportation of 597: "I removed them." The next serves much the same function: *h^{a}pîṣôṯîm*, "I scattered them." The third and last is *wā$^{\supset e}$hî*, "yet I have been (or become)." The first two verbs are preceded by *kî*, which seems here to have some such sense as "though" or "whereas." Whichever precise English word one chooses here, it is clear that these first two verbs anticipate what we might describe loosely as an apodosis, introduced by a further verb which will be the real point of the sequence. The difficulty is in knowing whether this is provided by the verb "to be" in v. 16, or whether we must wait for the references to the physical restoration of the exiles that follow in v. 17, as Davidson, Lofthouse and Greenberg contend. They take the verb "to be" as directly parallel with the two preceding verbs, in spite of the absence of a third *kî*. Davidson pressed this line of interpretation furthest, arguing that until restoration from exile comes the taunt of the Jerusalemites is accurate: the exiles are indeed all but cut off from YHWH's presence (Davidson 1892:74; Lofthouse n.d.:115; Greenberg 1983a:186, 204). However, in view of the absence of a third *kî*, it is preferable to take *wā$^{\supset e}$hî* as providing the genuine culmination of the sequence of verbs found in v. 16, with the *wā* taken as a disjunctive, "yet" (as NRSV). This places positive weight on the enigmatic motif of YHWH as "a sanctuary…for a little while" (NRSV; Heb. *miqdāš m$^{e c}$aṭ*) to the exiles, and is to be preferred to a reading that reduces this clause to merely a negative preamble to the future blessing described in v. 17.

Hebrew *miqdāš* means "sanctuary" and would normally suggest the Jerusalem temple, as the place of encounter with YHWH. The concept of holiness and in particular the root *qdš* are of special importance in Ezekiel's theology. We find frequent mention of YHWH's "holy name" (e.g. 20:39: "But my holy name you shall no more profane") and recurrent reference to YHWH acting to vindicate his holiness (e.g. 36:23: "when through you I display my holiness before their eyes"). Holiness is associated in an especially intimate way with the person of YHWH, and this is important in understanding 11:16. Some material from elsewhere in the Hebrew Bible may shed further light on this. Twice in the Holiness Code we find a particularly striking phrase. In Lev 19:30 and 26:2, together with the command to "keep my sabbaths," there appears the injunction to "reverence my sanctuary." This phrase uses the Hebrew verb *yrʾ*, "to fear," a word more normally used with reference to YHWH himself (e.g. Deut 25:18). It may be that this phrase provides a parallel to the motif of YHWH himself becoming a "sanctuary" in Ezek 11:16. It is also germane to recall the motif of the tabernacle in the wilderness (e.g. Exod 26); given that it probably owes much to the hands of priests in the exilic age, attempting to come to terms with the loss of the Jerusalem temple, there may here be a significant parallel with Ezekiel's *miqdāš mᵉʿaṭ*. A further text to note is Isa 8:13–14: "But the LORD of Hosts, him you shall regard as holy; let him be your fear and let him be your dread. He will become a sanctuary…"

The use in Ezek 11:16 of the verb "to be" (*hyh*) followed by the repeated use of *lᵉ* ("to," "for") is reminiscent of the so-called covenant formula, widely attested in Priestly and other literature: literally, "I will be to you for a God and you shall be to me for a people" (e.g. Lev 26:12). The covenant formula occurs in the present context at v. 20, as the apparent culmination of this oracle of blessing upon the exiles: "Then they shall be my people, and I will be their God." Zimmerli believed this verse to express the full articulation of God's blessing upon Israel, of which the reference in v. 16 is only a partial, though real, foretaste. On this basis, he postulated a hypothetical priestly variant of the covenant formula: "I will be to them a sanctuary" (Zimmerli 1979a:262).

The word *mᵉʿaṭ* could refer to time ("a sanctuary…for a little while," as NRSV), or to degree ("a sanctuary in small measure" or "to some extent"). The latter is to be favoured, for two reasons. First, as I have argued, v. 16 should be read as complete in itself, rather than simply as a prelude to v. 17. The case for a "time" interpretation would be stronger if v. 16 were subordinate, leading up to the promise of physical restoration in v. 17. Second, usage elsewhere would certainly permit a "degree" sense here (note especially 2 Kgs 10:18; Zech 1:15; cf. Exod 23:30; Deut 7:22; 2 Chr 12:7). We should then translate: "Yet I have become to them a sanctuary (albeit in small measure)" (see further Joyce 1996). This is a positive, if qualified, statement of divine blessing in exile. In what did this consist? The Targum, somewhat anachronistically, interprets Ezek 11:16 as referring specifically to the establishment of synagogues (Sperber 1962:283). Lofthouse stresses the observance of sabbaths and circumcision (Lofthouse n.d.:115). Allen emphasizes the possibility of prayer to YHWH in exile, comparing

Jer 29:12–14 and Dan 6:10 (Allen 1994:164). Another possibility is that the very presence of Ezekiel witnessed to the fact that YHWH maintained a relationship with those whom he had smitten (cf. 33:33). But there is another important clue to the fullness of what is meant by YHWH becoming a "sanctuary" to the exiles, and this is provided by the throne-chariot vision of ch. 1. Ezekiel established through that vision a vital surrogate for the Jerusalem temple. The word *meᶜaṭ* in 11:16 witnesses to much the same sense of the audacity of what is being claimed as does the elaborate circumlocution of 1:28. As in ch. 1 so here, the sovereign transcendence of the deity is reaffirmed in a radical way, paradoxically through his freedom in establishing new modes of presence, impervious to the machinations of the world's empires. The framing of 11:14–21 between stages of the withdrawal of the glory of YHWH from Jerusalem (in 10:19 the glory is at the east gate of the temple; in 11:22–23 it leaves the city altogether) is especially important here and may be seen as the main reason for its present location as a unit.

11:17. "I will give you the land of Israel": material restoration, emphasized by the scholars noted earlier (Davidson 1892:74; Lofthouse n.d.:115; Greenberg 1983a:186, 204). The shift to second person address could indicate a gloss, but this is not a necessary assumption. **11:18.** The returnees will remove from the land all those things that had led to the judgement, expressed in Ezekiel's characteristic words: all its "detestable things" (Heb. *šiqqûṣîm*) and "abominations" (Heb. *tôᶜēḇôṯ*). **11:19.** The prophet now gives voice to a remarkable divine promise: "I will give them one heart, and put a new spirit within them; I will remove the heart of stone from their flesh and give them a heart of flesh." To be compared closely with this are the similar words of 36:26–27a: "A new heart I will give you, and a new spirit I will put within you; and I will remove from your body the heart of stone and give you a heart of flesh. I will put my spirit within you." The key distinctive features of the promise here in ch. 11 are three. First, it is addressed to "them," whereas 36:26–27 is addressed to "you" (plural). Second, 11:19 refers to "one" heart, in contrast to the "new" heart of 36:26 (see below, on text). And third, 36:27a continues "I will put my spirit within you," words not paralleled in the present context. With these two texts must be compared 18:31: "Get yourselves a new heart and a new spirit!" Like 36:26–27, these words are addressed to "you" (plural) and also refer to a "new" heart as in 36:26, but they differ from both ch. 11 and ch. 36 in being couched as a challenge rather than as a promise.

So important are the words "heart" and "spirit" that a brief survey of their usage is necessary here. This will serve more generally for illuminating their function in Ezekiel, but is particularly relevant to the present passage and the ones in chs. 18 and 36. The Hebrew word for "heart" occurs in two forms, *lēḇ* and the less common longer form *lēḇāḇ*. The great majority of "heart" references in the Hebrew Bible are in relation to human beings, and indeed Wolff described this as "the most important word in the vocabulary of Old Testament anthropology" (Wolff 1974:40). The word is employed in a wide range of senses. It is used of the physical organ that beats in the breast (as in Jer 4:19). The image of the replacement of the "heart of stone" with a "heart of flesh" in Ezek 11:19 (and 36:26) reflects this physical sense, albeit metaphorically. The word is also used, as in the common use of "heart" in English, of the emotions (e.g. 1 Sam 2:1; Isa 40:2; Ezek 36:5). Commoner than either the "physical" or the "emotional" sense is the use of *lēḇ* to mean the rational faculty (e.g. Exod 36:1; 1 Kgs 4:29 [Heb. 5:9]; Ezek 38:10). Of particular relevance to the present context, however, is the use of the word as a designation of the locus of the moral will (e.g. 1 Sam 24:5 [Heb. v. 6]). This "moral" sense is particularly predominant in Ezekiel: the heart of Israel is said to be "wanton" (6:9) and to go after idols in the wilderness (20:16). At the beginning of his ministry, Ezekiel is warned that the people of Israel are, in Hebrew, *ḥizqê-lēḇ* (2:4) and *qᵉšê-lēḇ* (3:7), both phrases meaning "stubborn hearted." It is this unresponsive and insensitive "heart of stone" that is now to be replaced (11:19; cf. 36:26). There is a further nuance of the word *lēḇ* to note. It is used at times to mean reality as distinct from outward appearance, as in Ezek 33:31: "With their lips they show much love, but their heart is set on their gain" (cf. 1 Sam 16:7; Joel 2:13). It is a serious matter, then, when Israel takes her idols right into her heart (Ezek 14:3); and, conversely, to replace the heart is to effect as profound a change as is possible. In 11:19 (and also 18:31 and 36:26), then, two important senses of *lēḇ* converge, the heart as the locus of the moral will and as the symbol of inner reality as distinct from mere outward appearance.

The noun *rûaḥ* ("spirit") is used in the Hebrew Bible frequently of God as well as of humanity; for this reason, Lys spoke of it as a "theo-anthropological" term (Lys 1962:336). This word too is used in a wide range of senses (Robson 2006). It often refers to the wind, particularly as a mighty force at YHWH's disposal (Ezek 13:11, 13; 37:9). In a closely related sense, the word is used of the God-given breath of life: in 37:9, 10, "the breath" (*hārûaḥ*) is summoned to vivify the dry bones. It is also used in a more general sense of the dynamic power of YHWH, inspiring judges, kings and prophets (Judg 3:10; 1 Sam 16:13; Num 24:2). This sense is particularly common in Ezekiel, as in 11:5: "Then the Spirit of the LORD fell upon me." It is *rûaḥ* (generally without the article) that enters into Ezekiel and makes him stand (2:2; 3:24), snatches him up and transports him (3:12, 14; 8:3; 11:1, 24; 43:5). Some relatively late Hebrew Bible passages look forward to an eschatological outpouring of the *rûaḥ* of YHWH (e.g. Joel 2:28 [Heb. 3:1]; cf. Isa 61:1). Ezekiel's usage in 36:27, "I will put my spirit within you," and also 37:14, "I will put my spirit within you, and you shall live" (cf. 39:29), anticipates that development. The word is used of the human spirit too: as the medium both of understanding (as in Ezek 11:5: "I know the things that come into your *rûaḥ* [NRSV: mind]") and of feeling (e.g. Ezek 3:14: "I went in bitterness in the heat of my spirit"). However, most relevant of the various human senses is that which refers to the moral will, both in a positive and in a negative sense. Thus the *rûaḥ* can be "steadfast" and "willing" (Ps 51:10, 12 [Heb. vv. 12, 14]) or it can be "a spirit of harlotry" (Hos 5:4). It is in the light of such expressions that we are to understand the "new spirit" (*rûah ḥᵃḏāšâ*) here in 11:19 (and also 18:31 and 36:26), to refer to the renewal of "the moral will." There is clearly some convergence between this use of *rûaḥ* of the will and what I described as the "moral" sense of the word *lēḇ*.

The promise of 11:19 should not be understood in an individualistic way, for three reasons. First, 11:15 defines the exiles, the recipients of the promise, in the very corporate phrase "the whole house of Israel, all of them." Second, it is important that "heart" and "spirit" (and indeed "flesh") are terms used of aspects of the human person; thus the replacement of the "heart" and the giving of a "new spirit" are indeed strongly "corporate" images. Third, the covenant formula that follows, "they shall be my people, and I will be their God" (11:20; cf. 36:28), underlines the essentially collective nature of the promise.

"I will give them one heart": a few Hebrew manuscripts, Syriac and Targum have "a new heart," probably through assimilation to 18:31 and 36:26. LXX has *heteran* (cf. 1 Sam 10:9, "another heart," Heb. *lēḇ ʾaḥēr*). But "one heart" should be retained (cf. Jer 32:39, "I will give them one heart and one way," Heb. *lēḇ ʾeḥāḏ wᵉḏereḵ ʾeḥāḏ*). What might it mean? One possibility is that the phrase reflects the hopes for the reunification of the people that are found in 37:15–28. If this were so, it might further reinforce the collective emphasis of the passage. A more likely interpretation, however, is suggested by the words of Ps 12:2 (Heb. v. 3): "they speak with a double heart" (Heb. *bᵉlēḇ wālēḇ*)." YHWH will grant an "undivided heart," reliable rather than duplicitous, so as to enable a response that is "wholehearted."

11:20. "So that they may follow my statutes and keep my ordinances and obey them": confirmation that the gift of v. 19 amounts to a renewed capacity to respond to YHWH in obedience. The echoing of v. 12 here constitutes another possible connection between vv. 1–13 and vv. 14–21. The relationship between v. 12 and v. 20 could be seen as analogous to that between Deut 6:4–5 and Deut 30:6, where too first challenge and subsequently divine gift are expressed in consistent language. "They shall be my people, and I will be their God": the "covenant formula" (cf. Rendtorff 1998:35–37). **11:21.** "But as for those whose heart goes after their detestable things and their abominations": this NRSV translation is a good attempt to make sense of the difficult Hebrew *wᵉʾel-lēḇ šiqqûṣêhem wᵉṯôʿᵃḇôṯêhem libbām hōlēḵ* ("And to the heart of their detestable things and their abominations their heart goes"). "I will bring their deeds upon their own heads": the verse should be taken as rounding off the condemnation of the Jerusalem community, rather than as implying any segregation among the restored exiles.

11:22. After a long interlude (from 10:19) we hear again of the movement of the glory. **11:23.** "The glory of the LORD…stopped on the mountain east of the city": the Mount of Olives. And so YHWH has abandoned his sanctuary and will not return until we read in 43:2: "And there, the glory of the God of Israel was coming from the east." Bodi has helpfully highlighted the importance of the Akkadian *Poem of Erra* for the motif of the absence of the deity (Bodi

1991:183–218). More generally, there has been much valuable discussion of the absence and presence of God in Ezekiel (e.g. Block 2000b; Kutsko 2000a; Tuell 2000a). In narrative terms, the divine glory now departs to Babylonia, where it will be experienced by the exiles as a "sanctuary (albeit in small measure)" (v. 16). This is in no way to deny the ongoing presence of the deity in his heaven; indeed it is that very transcendence that undergirds his freedom to manifest himself where he wills. **11:24.** "The spirit lifted me up and brought me in a vision by the spirit of God into Chaldea, to the exiles": the prophet's journey of 8:3 is reversed. **11:25.** "And I told the exiles all the things that the LORD had shown me": the *inclusio* is complete, as Ezekiel reports his vision to the "elders of Judah" sitting before him (cf. 8:1).

CHAPTER 12

This chapter presents two further prophetic sign-actions (vv. 1–16, 17–20); cf. chs. 4–5, and discussion there. There is the possibility here, as there, of some redactional elaboration, perhaps especially in the provision of explicit interpretation (e.g. vv. 10–14). Many now-familiar features occur in this and successive chapters; they will not always be highlighted or cross-referenced.

12:1–16: Ezekiel enacts the coming exile of the prince and those in Jerusalem. Ezekiel is told what to do in vv. 3–6, and in v. 7 reports that he has done as commanded. **12:3.** "An exile's baggage": cf. Jer 10:17–18. "Perhaps they will understand": v. 9 reveals that they do not. **12:6.** "Cover your face, so that you may not see the land": see on v. 12. "I have made you a sign": Hebrew *môp̱ēṯ*, here and in v. 11 (cf. 24:24, 27). It means much the same as Hebrew *ʾôṯ*, "sign" (cf. 4:3; 14:8; 20:12, 20). **12:8.** "In the morning": note the "day," "evening," "dark," "morning" sequence in vv. 7–8; escalating crisis is followed by calm explanation. **12:10.** Failure to understand (v. 9) is met with interpretation (cf. 17:12). "Prince": Hebrew *nāśîʾ*; the reference is to Zedekiah, placed on the throne by the Babylonians after the 597 humiliation of Judah; the word *nāśîʾ* is used here with the intention of disparaging his status, emphasizing his role as mere vassal (Joyce 1998:323–24, 331). Ezekiel models the prince in particular, as well as more generally the non-exiled community. "In Jerusalem": this sign-action might be thought to make more sense if performed in Jerusalem; note also "in their sight" in vv. 3–6 (cf. the "Time and Place" section, above), but this chapter does not demand a Jerusalem setting for any part of Ezekiel's ministry: "Ezekiel speaks in exile about the fate of those who remain in Jerusalem, who are threatened by the divine judgement which the exiles, whose hope depends on the continued existence of Jerusalem, refuse to see" (Zimmerli 1979a:269). **12:11.** "I am a sign for you": cf. v. 6; a sign for all Israel, whether already exiled or not. **12:12.** "In the dark": possibly an allusion to Zedekiah's flight by night, just as the phrase "yet he shall not see it" in v. 13 may refer to the putting out of his eyes (cf. 2 Kgs 25:4, 7; Jer 39:4, 7; 52:7, 11). This passage seems to have been revised to align it with the details of Zedekiah's fate in 587. "He": so LXX and Syriac; Hebrew has "they." "He shall cover his face, so that he may not see the land with his eyes": picking up the words of v. 6, this enigmatic statement could refer to an expression of shame or grief, an attempt at disguise, or perhaps an allusion to Zedekiah's blinding. Block, with reference to Jer 22:10–12, finds here a symbol of the permanent separation from the land that was beginning

(Block 1997:375–76). **12:13.** "I will spread my net over him and he shall be caught in my snare; and I will bring him to Babylon": a remarkable reference to YHWH himself taking directly the role of transporting power. For the reference to the "net" (Heb. *rešeṯ*), cf. 17:20; 19:8. **12:14.** "I will scatter to every wind… unsheathe the sword behind them": cf. 5:2, 10, 12. **12:16.** "But I will let a few of them escape": the recurrent motif of survivors, cf. on 6:8. It is important that the nations should not misunderstand YHWH's action (cf. 36:20). "Sword, famine, pestilence": cf. 5:12, 17; 6:11–12; 7:15.

12:17–20. A second sign-action, enacting the people's terror at the approaching invasion. **12:18.** "Eat your bread with quaking, and drink your water with trembling and with fearfulness": cf. 4:16–17. **12:19.** "The people of the land": Hebrew *ʿam hāʾāreṣ*; see on 22:29. Here the usage seems ironic, for it is employed with reference to Ezekiel's immediate audience, the exiles, who are by definition a people without a land (Block 1997:382).

12:21–25. In response to popular scepticism, these verses emphasize that YHWH's word will soon be fulfilled. **12:22.** "What is this proverb…?": an example of Ezekiel's characteristic technique of citing a proverb (*māšāl*), followed by a statement rejecting the validity of the proverb (cf. 18:2–3). "The days are prolonged, and every vision comes to nothing": cf. Jer 5:13; 17:15. **12:23.** "The days are near, and the fulfilment of every vision": a direct contradiction of the proverb; cf. vv. 27–28. **12:24.** "False vision": Hebrew *ḥ*ᵃ*zôn šāw*ᵉʾ; "flattering divination": Hebrew *miqsam ḥālāq*; cf. ch. 13 for similar subject matter and language. For eschatological hope of an end to false prophecy, cf. Zech 13:2–6. **12:25.** "I the LORD will speak the word that I speak…": the message of the section is reinforced through the technique known as *idem per idem*, whereby a verbal root (here Heb. *dbr*, "to speak") is repeated in both principal and subordinate clauses, connected with a relative (Ogden 1992:112).

12:26–28 recapitulates vv. 21–25. **12:27.** "The vision that he sees is for many years ahead…": another saying placed in the mouth of the people, not this time explicitly described as a "proverb" (cf. Isa 22:13). The earliest LXX text, P. 967, lacks 12:26–28, and it is possible that these verses result from elaboration of the earliest Hebrew text (cf. Filson 1943; Lust 1986a:15; see the "Text and Versions" section, above).

CHAPTER 13

The chapter divides into two parts, vv. 1–16 "against the prophets of Israel" and vv. 17–23 "against the daughters of your people, who prophesy." There are close parallels with the general issue of so-called false prophecy in Jeremiah and more especially with Jer 23. This was a controversy characteristic of the age (cf. Deut 13; 18). More generally, the issue raises profound questions about the discernment of truth in the absence of objective or agreed criteria (cf. Carroll 1979, 1981; Moberly 2006).

13:1–16. 13:2. "Prophesy against the prophets": a deliberately paradoxical expression, both here and in v. 17. Ezekiel contrasts the prophets' "own imagination" (Heb. *lēḇ*, "heart"; cf. on 11:19)—or, in v. 3, "their own spirit" (*rûaḥ*, "spirit"; cf. on 11:19)—with divine inspiration. **13:3.** They are "senseless" (*nāḇāl*, "foolish"), for they "have seen nothing" (cf. v. 6). **13:5.** "They have not gone up into the breaches…": note the close parallel with 22:30. "A wall": Hebrew *gāḏēr*; the word used for "repair" here is the cognate verb *gdr*. A city wall is intended (cf. Mic 7:11), even though Ezekiel does not use the normal word (Heb. *ḥômâ*). "Stand in battle on the day of the LORD": cf. on 7:7. **13:6.** This and the following verses (vv. 6–9; cf. v. 23) speak of "false prophecy" using recurrent verbal roots (notably *ḥzh* and *qsm* of prophecy, in the broadest sense; *šwʾ* and *kzb* of falsehood), for example, here "falsehood" (Heb. *šāwᵉʾ*) and "lying divination" (Heb. *qesem kāzāḇ*). For divination, see also 12:24 and especially 21:21, 23 (Heb. vv. 26, 28). The prophets are indeed "senseless" (v. 3) to "wait for the fulfilment of their word" (cf. the criterion of truth in Deut 18:21–22), since "the LORD has not sent them" and (v. 7) "did not speak"; cf. Jer 23:21. **13:7.** They have seen a "false vision" (Heb. *maḥᵃzê-šāwᵉʾ*), uttered a "lying divination" (Heb. *miqsam kāzāḇ*), and (v. 8) "envisioned lies" (Heb. *ḥᵃzîṯem kāzāḇ*). **13:8.** "I am against you, says the Lord GOD": cf. the declaration against the shepherds in 34:10. **13:9.** Those who see "false visions" (Heb. *ḥōzîm šāwᵉʾ*) and utter "lying divinations" (*qōsᵉmîm kāzāḇ*) shall not be enrolled in "the register of the house of Israel." Davies (1994) presents much comparative evidence for census-taking in the ancient Near East (cf. Ezra 2:62; Neh 7:64; see also Exod 32:32–33; Dan 12:1). "Nor shall they enter the land of Israel": suggests a Babylonian location, as one would expect; cf. 20:38. **13:10.** "Misled my people": cf. Jer 23:13b. "Saying, 'Peace,' when there is no peace": also v. 16; cf. Jer 6:14; 8:11.

"When the people build a wall": Hebrew *ḥayiṣ* is used here alone in the Hebrew Bible, whereas the common Hebrew word *qîr* is used for "wall" in the following verses. The wall of a residential building is probably the primary image, but it serves as a metaphor for the state of the nation and also evokes the wall of Jerusalem (cf. v. 5). "These prophets": Hebrew has simply "they"; this ambiguity persists to v. 16, and that verse could well be an interpretative gloss (so Zimmerli 1979a:290). "Whitewash": Hebrew *tāp̱ēl.* The word is found in two contexts in Ezekiel, here at 13:10–15 and at 22:28. NRSV takes it to refer to smearing "whitewash" on a wall, its translation influenced perhaps by the Gospel motif of the "whitewashed tomb" (Matt 23:27), but it is better translated as "plaster" (Davies 1994). The prophets' reassuring oracles improve appearances but only superficially and temporarily. Propp has argued that Ezekiel uses the word in the sense of "vanity" or "folly" (Propp 1990; cf. Theodotion). **13:11.** "It shall fall": cf. Isa 30:13. "Rain": Hebrew has "rain and you." "Hailstones": cf. 38:22; Josh 10:11. **13:12.** "Whitewash": a different Hebrew noun is used in this verse: *ṭîaḥ*; the cognate verb *ṭwḥ*, to "smear," is used throughout this passage (and also in 22:28). **13:14.** "When it falls, you shall perish within it": this might be taken to imply a Jerusalem setting. Davies suggests that whereas vv. 2–9 are directed against prophets in the exile, vv. 10–16 are against prophets still in Jerusalem (Davies 1994). But this should not be pressed, as lack of clarity in such matters is typical of Ezekiel (see on 2:3).

13:17–23. An oracle against "the daughters of your people, who prophesy." **13:17.** "Set your face": see on 4:3. "Their own imagination": cf. v. 2. Zimmerli contends that the absence here of the term "prophetess" (Heb. *n*^{e}*ḇîʾâ*; Exod 15:20; Judg 4:4; 2 Kgs 22:14; Isa 8:3; Neh 6:14; 2 Chr 34:22) indicates their unofficial status (Zimmerli 1979a:296). But it should not be assumed that the practices referred to here were outside the range of Yahwism, which was no doubt a good deal broader than the received Hebrew Bible would suggest. On the feminine in Ezekiel, see on 8:14 (cf. Bowen 1999). **13:18.** In contrast to vv. 1–16, these people seem to be involved with individuals rather than with the nation or community as a whole. They sew "bands" (Heb. *k*^{e}*sāṯôṯ*) on all wrists, and make "veils" (Heb. *mispāḥôṯ*), but these will be torn off (vv. 20–21). The details of the practices referred to here remain obscure (cf. Isa 8:19–20). Herrmann persuasively related Hebrew *k*^{e}*sāṯôṯ* and *mispāḥôṯ*, which occur only in this passage, to the Akkadian verbs *kasû* and *sapāḫu*, which mean respectively "to bind" and "to loose," in the magical sense (Herrmann 1924:81, 86; cf. Davies 1994). This fits in well with the concerns of this passage with the preservation and destruction of life. **13:19.** "You have profaned me": Hebrew verb *ḥll*; a characteristic Ezekiel theme. "For handfuls of barley and for pieces of bread": a disparaging reference to payment. "Putting to death persons who should not die and keeping alive persons who should not live": usurping the role of YHWH. **13:20.** YHWH's judgement is announced; cf. v. 8. "I am against your bands with which you hunt lives": so LXX and Syriac; Hebrew has "lives for birds," thus referring to "birds" (Heb. *pōr^{e}ḥôṯ*) here as well as at the end of the verse; Korpel (1996) compares evidence for avian spirits at Ugarit.

Verses 22–23 are an elaboration of vv. 17–21, also picking up the language of vv. 1–16. **13:22.** "You have disheartened the righteous… encouraged the wicked": these words (and also v. 19) echo the terminology of chs. 3, 18 and 33. They do the opposite of YHWH's will (cf. Jer 23:22). It is possible that the reference here is to the formal subverting of justice. "Falsely" is an adverbial use of Hebrew noun *šeqer*, "lie," "falsehood." This is the single use in Ezekiel of a word that is used 37 times in Jeremiah, often in the context of "false prophecy" (as also 1 Kgs 22:22–23). **13:23.** This final verse recalls the language of vv. 6–9, with variations on the same verbal roots. "I will save my people from your hand": cf. vv. 20–21; and also 34:22, 27.

CHAPTER 14

This chapter falls into two parts, vv. 1–11 and vv. 12–23. Although both sections reflect the influence of the priestly case law format and also manifest a strong emphasis on Israel's responsibility for her fate, there is otherwise little continuity in content.

14:1–11. Elders come to Ezekiel to "consult" YHWH (that is, they seek a favourable oracle from the prophet). **14:1.** This opening verse shares much with 8:1 and 20:1 (though surprisingly, unlike these verses, has no date). These affinities prompted Nay to a thorough investigation of 14:1–11 in the light of chs. 8–11 and ch. 20 (Nay 1999). **14:3.** YHWH declares the elders' approach presumptuous and unacceptable (cf. 20:3, 31). The inevitability of the disaster is highlighted by this refusal of YHWH to be consulted by the elders. This is thoroughly consistent with the command that Ezekiel should not be a mediator (see on 3:26, the "dumbness" motif). "These men have taken their idols into their hearts": cf. 11:21. Mein takes this verse as a classic example of what he calls the "domestication of ethics" within the exile, whereby the moral horizons of elite Judahites formerly responsible for foreign policy and the national cult are reduced to smaller-scale and yet still serious matters (Mein 2001a:177–215). On "idols" (Heb. *gillûlîm*), see on 6:4. **14:4.** "Any of those of the house of Israel who…": the statement of how YHWH deals with idolatry is couched in terms of a discussion of a particular legal case (as also v. 7). In an important study of these verses, Zimmerli showed that this language is indebted to that of priestly law; cf. Lev 17:8 (Zimmerli 1954b). "I the LORD will answer those who come with the multitude of their idols": this will not be the kind of consultation they sought. **14:5.** "That I may take hold of": Hebrew *tpś*, "seize": implies an aggressive act of claiming; BDB has "terrorize" (BDB, 1074). "The hearts": cf. on 11:19. "The house of Israel, all of whom are estranged from me": the estrangement is total and national.

14:6. "Repent and turn away": a rare reference to repentance in Ezekiel; cf. 18:30–31. This comes as a surprise after vv. 3–5, which seem to anticipate a declaration of absolute judgement, and indeed after the preceding chapters with their strong emphasis on imminent cataclysm. Fohrer (1951) proposed to remove v. 6 (together with vv. 3b and 7) as a gloss, but there is no good ground for this. How is the call to be explained? The repentance motif serves two functions: in the first instance it is a rhetorical device, underling Israel's responsibility for the inevitable disaster. Israel's condemnation is fully deserved—repentance now will not avert the collapse of Jerusalem, but the reference to repentance serves as a reminder of why the end has come. The repentance theme is not simply, however, a device to highlight responsibility. Its second function is to testify to an earnest desire on the part of the holy and just God for the obedience of his people. The call to repentance here offers just a hint of the possibility of a new future. Yet no new beginning can be envisaged until after the judgement is complete—and then it will depend not upon Israel's own response but upon the obedience that YHWH himself will grant as a gift (cf. 11:19; 36:26–27). Meanwhile, the exiles are called to right behaviour, within their now constrained circumstance as exiles, even though such obedience will neither avert disaster nor hasten restoration (see further the "Theological Themes" section, above). **14:7.** "The aliens who reside in Israel": Hebrew *gēr*, "alien"; cf. 22:7, 29; 47:22–23. High expectations were placed on proselytes; but in the present exilic context, this reference reads oddly and the phrase may have been carried over from the adapted priestly legislation (cf. Lev 17:8; so Greenberg 1983a:249). The repetitive nature of much of this verse is not ground for deletion, but further evidence of Ezekiel's style. **14:8.** "I will set my face against them": cf. on 4:3. "I will make them a sign": Hebrew *ʾôṯ*; again, see on 4:3. "A byword": Hebrew *māšāl*. "Cut them off from the midst of my people": another priestly phrase; cf. Lev 17:10. These words (and the similar ones in the next verse) imply not that the legal death penalty is to be imposed by human agency, but rather that the guilty party will suffer a direct blow from YHWH himself (Zimmerli 1979a:303–5).

14:9. "If a prophet is deceived and speaks a word…": again the hypothetical style is adapted from priestly case law; the reference appears to be general but is actually focused on Ezekiel; cf. again the "dumbness" motif of 3:26. "I, the LORD, have deceived that prophet": of a piece with Ezekiel's theocentric emphasis; cf. 20:25–26. **14:10.** The phrase "they shall bear their punishment" (Heb. *nāśᵉʾû ʿᵃwōnām*) seems to be another reference to YHWH himself dealing a punitive blow against the offender, rather than the juridical death penalty (Zimmerli 1979a:303–5). In such a case, the role of the community is to exclude the doomed sinner from the circle of fellowship; in this respect, these phrases are related to the practice of excommunication. "The punishment of the inquirer and the punishment of the prophet shall be the same": cf. the penalty for failure as a "sentinel" (3:18, 20; 33:6, 8).

To what extent is it the responsibility of the individual that is envisaged in 11:1–11? Individualistic elements certainly feature, but on closer inspection we find the passage to be overwhelmingly collective. There is reference to the "house of Israel" throughout and also to "my people" (vv. 8–9). Moreover, I have noted that the priestly formulae used here seem related to the practice of excommunication. A paradoxical feature of such language is that it involves a strong sense both of individual responsibility and also of the importance of the community: the guilty individual is singled out for punishment, but for the very purpose of the ultimate preservation of the community. Furthermore, the passage may be even less individualistic than this suggests. We read in 14:5 that the house of Israel are "all" estranged from YHWH through their idols. This is difficult to relate to the notion of the exclusion of individual idolaters from the community, and would seem to imply that the whole house of Israel, as a collective group, is judged wicked and deserving of punishment. How are we to explain this? Crucial here is Zimmerli's insight that Ezekiel reapplies language that originally dealt with individual legal cases to collective groups and above all to the nation of Israel: "The divine saying does not restrict itself with this threat of judgement to individual men, but shows immediately the deeper truth that this holy wrath has in mind 'Israel' when speaking about the individual sinner" (Zimmerli 1979a:307). If this is correct, it is nothing less than the "cutting off" of the nation as a whole that is envisaged.

14:11. "So that the house of Israel may no longer go astray from me": YHWH cannot, it seems, allow the "cutting off" of Israel to be the last word. "They shall be my people, and I will be their God": the "covenant formula"; cf. on 11:20. While this verse could be seen as a more optimistic addition, it is better understood as illustrating the tensions within Ezekiel's perception of the divine purposes.

14:12–23. Like vv. 1–11, this section adapts the priestly case law format. These verses at first appear to lay down a general principle according to which YHWH deals with any land that sins against him. **14:13.** "When a land sins against me…": there follows reference to four forms of punishment, the first being "famine" (cf. 5:12, 16–17; 6:11–12; 7:15; 12:16; 36:29–30). "Human beings and animals": cf. v. 17, 19, 21; a colloquial phrase conveying inclusion (cf. RSV's "man and beast"). Ezekiel employs a range of such phrases (e.g. 21:4 [Heb. v. 9]; 22:5). **14:14:** In each of the four cases, it is said that even if figures of exemplary righteousness were present (cf. Jer 15:1), they would save only their own lives (vv. 14, 16, 18, 20). Three paragons of virtue are named (explicit only in the first and last cases, vv. 14, 20): Noah, Daniel and Job (cf. Spiegel 1945; Noth 1951). It is interesting to note that all three are in some sense international figures; this coheres with the general case law format. "Noah": the righteous hero of the Genesis Flood story; there Noah's close family are spared (Gen 6:18; 7:1, 7), even though it seems to be Noah alone who had found favour with God (Gen 6:8, 9; 7:1). Noah lives before the call of Israel through Abram (Gen 12:1–3) and so is non-Israelite; also there are affinities with several ancient Near Eastern traditional figures, including the Babylonian Atraḫasis and Utnapishtim (cf. Wahl 1992). "Daniel": Block favours the hero of the biblical book of Daniel, who is presented as among the sixth-century Judahite exiles in Babylonia (Block 1997:449). But this would be more likely (assuming a historical basis for the narratives of Dan 1–6) if Daniel came third in the list, and a more ancient figure is more probable (cf. Day 1980). Daniel features as a paragon of wisdom in Ezek 28:3, in an oracle against the king of Tyre. The spelling of the name there, as in the present chapter, lacks the middle letter *yôḏ* (unlike the fuller spelling found in the book of Daniel). This might suggest the legendary king Danʾel (*dnil*), as found in the tale of Aqhat from the Ras Shamra tablets from twelfth-century B.C.E. Ugarit (which would fit the Tyre context especially well). A figure of the same name is listed as the grandfather of Methuselah in *Jub*. 4:20. "Job": the righteous hero of the biblical book of Job is said to be of the land of Uz (Job 1:1), probably Edom and so non-Israelite (cf. Goshen-Gottstein 1972). Sirach 49:9 can be construed to say that Ezekiel mentioned Job, which would presumably be an allusion to the present chapter.

14:15. The second form of punishment is "wild animals," or "evil beasts" (Heb. *ḥayyâ rāʿâ*; cf. 5:17; 33:27; 34:25). **14:16.** Verses 16, 18 and 20 elaborate upon v. 14 to say that the paragons would not deliver sons and daughters. Though the Hebrew does not employ possessives here, it is likely that this means "their own sons and daughters." These, being among the closest relatives, represent those one would think most likely to be spared, if any one at all were to be spared with the righteous. This is very similar to 9:6, where even "little children" who do not bear the mark on the forehead are to be slain. "As I live, says the Lord GOD": an intensifying oath, which accompanies the three references to offspring not being spared; cf. vv. 18, 20. **14:17.** The third form of punishment is the "sword," a very common motif in Ezekiel (especially in chs. 5; 6; 21; 32; 33). **14:19.** The fourth and final form of punishment is "pestilence": cf. 5:12, 17; 6:11–12; 7:15; 12:16; 33:27. **14:21.** The general principle is now related specifically to the fate of Jerusalem in particular. "How much more": Hebrew *ʾap̱ kî-*; cf. 15:5, where it means "how much less." "My four deadly acts of judgement": repeats the four of vv. 13–19, but the order is modified; the "sword" is here brought to the head of the list for rhetorical effect, the others maintaining their sequence. This reflects the great frequency of the word "sword" in the book as a whole (cf. on v. 17), and also perhaps the fact that it is the mode of punishment most evocative of Babylonian conquest.

Ezekiel 14:12–21 has often been understood to be strongly individualistic (e.g. Stalker 1968:34; Taylor 1969:45), but this is a misreading. The basic idea that the righteous should be spared in a general punishment seems to be taken for granted here, as in Ezek 9, rather than advanced as a new principle. It is conceivable that vv. 13–14 are intended actually to assert (rather than to assume) that Noah, Daniel and Job would save at least themselves, since the Hebrew word *l*e*ḇaddām* ("alone," "only"), which is found in vv. 16 and 18, is not found in v. 14 (in spite of the NRSV supplying "only"); moreover, there is in v. 14 no reference to the fact that the three righteous ones would save neither sons nor daughters, as is stated in vv. 16, 18 and 20. Thus the purpose of vv. 13–14 could possibly be to establish the basic principle that at least the righteous would be spared, before the subsequent verses make the point that they would deliver no one else. However, it is more probable that the four cases (vv. 13–14, 15–16, 17–18 and 19–20) are intended to be parallel with each other, and that, as in the other three cases, vv. 13–14 should be understood to mean that the three hypothetical righteous ones would save "but their own lives." This seems the more likely since v. 20 (which, like v. 14, lacks the word *l*e*ḇaddām*, "alone," "only") undoubtedly has this sense, as is shown by the reference to neither son nor daughter being spared. It seems to be assumed, then, that Noah, Daniel and Job would deliver their own lives by their righteousness if they were present.

The passage asserts that this old principle of individual responsibility is to be operated with unprecedented rigour, but it is essential to ask why this is so. What is the basic purpose of this passage? Whereas many Hebrew Bible narratives (e.g. Noah and the Flood; Abraham pleading for Sodom and Gomorrah; the Passover story) have the sparing of the righteous as a primary focus, the basic concern of Ezek 14:12–21 is significantly different. The prophet anticipates an imminent judgement that will "cut off man and beast" (RSV; 14:13, 17, 19, 21). His purpose is to stress the thoroughness of judgement; there will certainly be no place for what Daube called "Communal Merit" (Daube 1947:157–58), not even on the basis of family solidarity.

It is important to recognize that we are dealing here with rhetoric. Ezekiel does not envisage segregation between paragons of virtue and their unrighteous offspring actually taking place; rather, the motif is a forceful way of saying to the wicked that justice will be thorough and absolute. The priestly case law format in which Ezek 14:12–21 is presented must not be allowed to obscure this fact. It might at first sight seem that the rigour of YHWH's application of the principle of individual responsibility when punishing lands is presented as a general rule, which is only related specifically to Jerusalem at v. 21, but the theoretical appearance of Ezek 14:12–20 is to be attributed to Ezekiel's adaptation of the case law format. The purpose of Ezekiel here is an *ad hoc* one; he addresses a specific and desperate situation. This is an example of prophetic hyperbole: the sins of Israel are so great (the situation is even worse, it is implied, than at the time of the Flood) that an overwhelming punishment is now imminent, so thorough that the most righteous people who can be imagined would not be able to deliver even their closest relatives.

14:22. "Yet": Hebrew *wᵉhinnê*. A surprise; literally "Yet behold…" "Survivors": Hebrew *pᵉlēṭâ*, "escape, remnant." The recurrent motif of remnant; cf. on 6:8. "Sons and daughters who will be brought out": the passive wording of the NRSV follows the MT's Hophal participle *hammûṣāʾîm* and implies that the only survivors are children. However, while children are admittedly not normally to be spared (9:6; 14:16, 18, 20), in the present context adult survivors would better vindicate the justice of YHWH's action and so RSV's "to lead out sons and daughters," based on a revocalizing of the Hebrew word as an active form (cf. LXX), is more likely. This would suggest that the chance survivors are adults, who bring children out with them. "When you see their ways and their deeds, you will be consoled": Hebrew verb *nḥm*, here and in v. 23. Davis helpfully proposes "you will change your mind" (Davis 1999:234–5). "For the evil that I have brought upon Jerusalem": the point is one of theodicy; YHWH is justified in executing this terrible judgement. **14:23.** "You shall know…": this sentence is an adaptation of the "Recognition Formula."

At first sight, these last verses of the chapter seem to conflict with what has gone before, for they contain two surprises. First, they refer to the survival of an undeserving remnant; and, second, these survivors lead out sons and daughters. This has led some to regard vv. 22–23 as a secondary addition (e.g. Wevers 1969:114). However, these verses not only have an integral place but actually clarify the meaning of the passage. The "survivors" of vv. 22–23 are not in the same category as the three hypothetical righteous of vv. 14–20, but are chance left-overs (cf. Amos 3:12; Isa 17:6), whose appearance does not, strictly speaking, contradict what has been asserted in vv. 12–21. The "sons and daughters" also survive by chance rather than family solidarity (if sons and daughters cannot share in the benefits of their parents' righteousness at 14:16, 18 and 20, they will not profit from their parents' sheer luck here in vv. 22–23). But even if these verses are not actually incompatible with what has gone before, what is their purpose? Three observations can be made. First, the survival of a few sinners will provide evidence of the justice of the general punishment. This both underlines the responsibility of Israel for her fate and vindicates YHWH's name and actions. Second, vv. 22–23 confirm our insight that Ezekiel is not promulgating a general theory of responsibility but rather addressing the concrete realities of his own day. (If vv. 12–21 really were intended to advance a definitive doctrine, the place of vv. 22–23 would be difficult to explain, as they would then indeed appear to undermine the purpose of the preceding verses.) Third, vv. 22–23 take it for granted that any survivors will be undeserving ones (in other words, that there will be no Noahs, Daniels or Jobs), another indication that 14:12–21 is to be understood as an example of hyperbole rather than as an anticipation of actual segregation. It is clear that Ezekiel regards his people as sinful virtually "to a person" (cf. 3:7; 9:8–9; 22:30) and anticipates an imminent punishment that will be well-nigh total.

Chapter 15

This chapter does not use a word to characterize its genre, but we may speak of it as an allegory. Ezekiel is indeed a "maker of allegories," Hebrew *m^{e}maššēl m^{e}šālîm* (20:49 [Heb. 21:5], employing there the word *māšāl*, often translated "proverb"). Allegories of various kinds characterize many of the chapters between this point and ch. 23, with others to follow later in the book. Ezekiel's allegories often subvert familiar positive images (e.g. a bride turns whore in ch. 16; a noble merchant ship becomes a wreck in ch. 27). The vine is often a positive image in the Hebrew Bible (e.g. Judg 9:13), but here its wood is presented as a thing of no purpose. Simian-Yofre (1986) provides a focused study of this shortest chapter of the book. It is possible that vv. 2–5, which have poetic features including some parallelism, may originate in a wisdom poem (cf. Isa 28:23–29).

15:2. "How?": in the sense of "in what way, if any?" A series of rhetorical questions is posed, each expecting the answer "none" or "no" (cf. Amos 3:3–8). "Among the trees of the forest": the wild vine may be in view; cf. Jer 2:21. **15:4.** "It is put in the fire for fuel…": a use of sorts, but it does not burn well. **15:5.** "How much less": Hebrew *ʾap̱ kî-*; see on 14:21. It is less than useless after its poor service as fuel. **15:6.** "Therefore": the judgement is presented in more prosaic form. As the worthless wood is given for fuel, so YHWH will give up the inhabitants of Jerusalem. The nation is often likened to a vine or vineyard (e.g. Isa 5:1–7; Hos 10:1; Ps 80:8–13). Fire now becomes a means of judgement (cf. 5:2, 4; 10:6–7). A significant parallel is found in 19:10–14, where a vine, representing Judah, is consumed by fire. **15:7.** "Set my face": see on 4:3. "Although they escape": as many had survived the events of 597 and others would escape even the judgement of 587. "The fire shall still consume them": cf. 5:3–4; Isa 6:13. "You shall know that I am the LORD, when…": a development of the "Recognition Formula." **15:8.** "I will make the land desolate, because they have acted faithlessly": a pithy summary of exilic judgement theology; cf. Isa 42:24.

CHAPTER 16

The shortest chapter is followed by the longest. This is one of three great narrative surveys of the history of the nation in Ezekiel, the others being chs. 20 and 23. Like ch. 23, this chapter is presented through female personification. Models are found in both Hosea (e.g. 2:2–13 [Heb. vv. 4–15]) and Jeremiah (e.g. 3:6–14). Moughtin-Mumby (2008) presents an incisive review of sexual and marital metaphors in the Prophets.

16:2. "Make known to Jerusalem her abominations": Jerusalem represents the nation as a whole. Personification of Jerusalem as a woman is facilitated by the feminine gender of the Hebrew word for "city," *ʿîr*. Galambush (1992) presents a focused study of Jerusalem as YHWH's wife in Ezekiel. The narrative tells of a baby girl, found and adopted by YHWH, who marries her and makes her his queen, only to see her degenerate into prostitution. Dreadful punishment follows. For Ezekiel, the past is only ever *illustrative* of the nation's propensity to sin (cf. 18:2–4; 20:30). The point of this long portrayal of national apostasy becomes clear in v. 44: "Like mother, like daughter." **16:3.** "The land of the Canaanites": Jerusalem and her people were a bad lot from the start (cf. 20:8; Israel sinned even in Egypt). Although Jerusalem was indeed a Canaanite (specifically Jebusite) city by origin, the intention here is to insult. Moreover, in so far as the city represents the nation, this ignores the Patriarchal tradition of origins, though this is clearly known (cf. 33:24). This is a bold handling of tradition, comparable with Amos 9:7. Incidentally, one is reminded also of modern historical theories about the emergence of Israel from Canaan (Mendenhall 1962; Gottwald 1979). The "Amorites" and the "Hittites" are both listed among the inhabitants of the land of Canaan (e.g. Josh 3:10). The word Amorite is sometimes used as a synonym for Canaanite (cf. Deut 1:20) and is also used by historians to refer to Semitic movements into the fertile crescent in the second millennium B.C.E. There is no consensus as to how the Hittites in Canaan (cf. Gen 25:9; 2 Sam 11:3) were related to the Indo-European people of this name based in central Anatolia (now in modern Turkey). The tradition of Jerusalem being taken over from the Jebusites by David is recorded in 2 Sam 5:6–10. **16:4.** "Your navel cord was not cut": in a range of respects the baby is neglected, but this could also symbolize the fact that the link with the pagan past was not severed. This verse witnesses to ancient practices and expectations with regard to childcare. **16:5.** "No eye pitied you, to do any of these things for you out of compassion for you": by contrast YHWH's action was compassionate (v. 6), though that is not characteristic of Ezekiel, where divine non-pitying is a recurrent theme (e.g. 7:4–9). "You were thrown out in the open field": the exposure of babies was commonplace in the ancient world. **16:6.** "As you lay in your blood, I said to you, 'Live!'": Hebrew gives these words twice (*wāʾōmar lāḵ bᵉḏāmayiḵ ḥᵃyî*); this is a case of accidental dittography. Malul helpfully discusses legal metaphors in vv. 1–7 in the light of the adoption of foundlings elsewhere in the Bible and in Mesopotamian documents (Malul 1990). **16:7.** "And grow up": so LXX and Syriac. The Hebrew *rᵉḇāḇâ nᵉṯattîḵ* means "I made you a myriad (that is, ten thousand)," in other words "I caused you to flourish"; this does not require emendation. "Full womanhood": the Hebrew *ᶜᵃḏî ᶜᵃḏāyîm* means literally "ornament of ornaments." Greenberg takes this phrase to refer specifically to the secondary sexual features, the breasts and the pubic hair (Greenberg 1983a:276). "Yet you were naked and bare": the explicit sexual language of this chapter proved controversial in some rabbinic quarters; Rabbi Eliezer is reported as saying that the chapter is not to be used as a reading (*m. Meg.* 4:10). The same and related features have been subjected to modern feminist criticism, which has highlighted a discourse of gratuitous titillation (e.g. v. 7), humiliation (e.g. v. 37) and abusive violence (e.g. v. 40), with the female figure presented as a possessed object (v. 8) dominated by her own insatiable sexual appetite (e.g. v. 28) (cf. Darr 1992; Carroll 1995, 1996; Exum 1995, 1996; L. Day 2000, P. L. Day 2000a, 2000b). **16:8.** "You were at the age for love": puberty; the emphasis here is more on sex than affection (Shields 1998a; 2001b). "I spread the edge of my cloak over you": Kruger (1984) explores the meaning of the symbolic gesture here and in Ruth 3:9, not merely an act of charity but a declaration of a new relationship. "Entered into a covenant": a double sense, referring both to marriage and to a theological covenant (Heb. *bᵉrîṯ*). **16:10.** "Embroidered cloth…": we have moved beyond commonplace care to special clothing. "Sandals": a reference to footwear is often found here because the only other case of the verb *nᶜl* (2 Chr 28:15) refers to the provision of sandals. "Fine leather": Hebrew *tāḥaš* is used otherwise only of the cover of the tabernacle (e.g. Num 4:6); its meaning is far from certain. Dalley (2000) relates Hebrew *tāḥaš* to Mesopotamian evidence of beading, suggesting the translation "decked you in beaded work." **16:12.** "A beautiful crown": the foundling girl has become a queen, the consort of YHWH, as is made explicit in the next verse. **16:14.** "Your fame": Hebrew *šēm*, "name." Perhaps the age of Solomon is in view here (cf. 1 Kgs 10:1). "Because of my splendour that I had bestowed": a double emphasis on the derived nature of her beauty.

16:15. "But": here the key changes from major to minor. "You trusted in your beauty": as though it derived from herself, rather than being a result of relationship with YHWH; cf. self-reliance as a sin elsewhere in Hebrew Bible (e.g. Isa 5:11–12). "Played the whore": a double sense, with sexual promiscuity a metaphor for cultic syncretism and more general apostasy. "Lavished your whorings on any passer-by": indiscriminately taking the initiative (cf. Hos 4:13–14). **16:16.** "You took some of your garments": these were God-given, and so special

(vv. 10–13; cf. Amos 2:8). "Made for yourself colourful shrines": as in the "high places" (Heb. *bāmôṯ*; cf. on 6:3). **16:17.** "My gold and my silver that I had given you": again explicit reminders of her indebtedness. "Male images": phallic symbols (cf. Isa 57:8). **16:18.** "My oil and my incense": that which is properly designated for the worship of YHWH. **16:20.** The degeneration now escalates rapidly, to include child sacrifice; cf. on 20:25–26. "Your sons and your daughters whom you had borne to me": picking up the earlier sexual and marriage images. **16:22.** "You did not remember": "remembering" is an important motif, in a variety of ways, in this chapter; cf. vv. 43, 60–61, 63. "The days of your youth": cf. vv. 6–7; a time of vulnerable dependence on YHWH, rather than a time of pristine virtue. **16:24.** "You built yourself a platform and made yourself a lofty place": cf. Prov 9:13–18; there may also be an allusion to the "high places" (Heb. *bāmôṯ*); cf. on 6:3. **16:26.** "You played the whore with the Egyptians": a specific allusion to political alliances; cf. on 8:12.

16:27. "Therefore I stretched out my hand against you": a new phase, with the first reference to punishment. "The daughters of the Philistines": the neighbouring, non-Semitic arch-enemies of Israel; presented as female here to underline Jerusalem's humiliation, they are also rivals for the attentions of her lovers. "Who were ashamed of your lewd behaviour": so wicked was Jerusalem; cf. v. 48. **16:28.** "The Assyrians": the two great Mesopotamian powers are now mentioned in turn, in order of their historical dominance and with elements of parallelism in their presentation. **16:29.** "Chaldea": Babylonia. "The land of merchants": cf. 17:4. **16:30.** How sick is your heart": cf. on 11:19. "Brazen": Hebrew *šalleṭeṯ*. In the Elephantine Papyri a cognate word is used of a woman authorized to dispose of property (Greenfield 1982). **16:31.** "Your platform…your lofty place": cf. vv. 24–25. "You were not like a whore, because you scorned payment": deemed even worse than regular prostitution (cf. Hos 8:9). This puzzled LXX, which rendered as "gathering" payment. "Scorned": Hebrew *qls*. Piel is found here alone in the Hebrew Bible; this enabled identification of the Qumran fragment of Ezek 16 known as 3QEzek (3Q1) (Lust 1986c:90). **16:32.** "Adulterous wife": the emphasis has moved from prostitution, to reinforce from a different perspective the rhetorical appeal to male readers.

16:35. "Therefore, O whore, hear the word of the LORD": judgement is announced again; cf. v. 27. **16:36.** "Because your lust was poured out": this may be an allusion to female ejaculation. Here and elsewhere in this chapter the NRSV translation euphemistically masks the most graphic of sexual language. Kamionkowski (2001a, 2003) explores the way this chapter works with themes of gender reversal in an age when humiliated Judahite manhood had been emasculated, both metaphorically and in some cases physically. "Your nakedness uncovered": what was once pathetic (v. 7), is now culpable. "Because of the blood of your children that you gave to them": cf. vv. 20–21. **16:37.** "Therefore": resumptive (cf. v. 35), after repeated reference to the grounds for punishment. "I will uncover your nakedness": humiliating punishment, recompensing her self-exposure (cf. v. 36); here, as in v. 39, poetic justice (cf. Barton 1979). **16:39.** "They shall strip you of your clothes": the stripping motif is combined now with deprivation of finery. **16:40.** "They shall stone you": cf. Deut 22:21, 24. "Cut you to pieces with their swords": increasingly violent retribution. **16:41.** "Execute judgements on you in the sight of many women": as a discouragement to others, no doubt. Here (as perhaps already in v. 38) we may see the metaphorical language beginning to break down, so that actual women are in view rather than Jerusalem under the guise of a woman (cf. 23:48). **16:42.** "I will be calm, and will be angry no longer": are fury, jealousy and anger truly spent, or is this just a prelude to a fresh onslaught? Analogies can be drawn with the ugly dynamics of domestic violence (cf. Weems 1995).

16:44. "See, everyone who uses proverbs will use this proverb about you, 'Like mother, like daughter'": characteristic of Ezekiel's use of proverbs, real or invented, but atypical in that this time the proverb is affirmed rather than rejected. It is for the sins of the present generation that Jerusalem is condemned (cf. on v. 2). Here we turn away from history to the present. **16:45.** "You are the daughter of your mother": a very different mother from the Sarah of Isa 51:2. "Loathed…her children": cf. vv. 20–21. "And you are the sister of your sisters": the first reference to sisters, a theme to be developed in the following verses. "Your mother was a Hittite and your father an Amorite": cf. v. 3. The order is reversed here, to emphasize the mother. **16:46.** "Your elder sister is Samaria": Hebrew *šōmᵉrôn*; the city came to represent the northern kingdom. In 23:4 Oholah represents Samaria, there too styled as the elder sister. This may be because the northern kingdom fell first, but "elder" reads oddly since Judah in fact predated the separate northern kingdom. Block eases this by translating "bigger" (Block 1997:507). "Your younger sister…is Sodom": Sodom is hardly parallel to Judah and Samaria; perhaps the point is further to degrade Judah by presenting Sodom as her sister and peer. The introduction of sisters begins to render the theme of the chapter diffuse, but this is not sufficient ground for attributing this motif to secondary elaboration. **16:47.** "You were more corrupt than they in all your ways": cf. 5:6; 23:11; Jer 3:11. **16:48.** "Sodom and her daughters have not done as you": this is saying something, for the people of Sodom were notoriously "wicked, great sinners against the LORD" (Gen 13:13); cf. v. 27, where even the Philistines are "ashamed of your lewd behaviour". **16:49.** It is noteworthy that the sin of Sodom is not defined overtly in relation to sexual immorality. The charges are broadly based: "pride, excess of food, and prosperous ease," "not aiding the poor and needy," and (v. 50) being "haughty" and doing "abominable things." Even this last word (Heb. *tôᶜēḇâ*) may not have sexual practices in particular in view, since it is a very common and inclusive term in Ezekiel. **16:50.** "Therefore I removed them when I saw it": cf. Gen 18–19. **16:51.** "Samaria has not committed half your sins": a polemical barb for the Judahites, given the long-standing rivalry between the two Hebrew kingdoms. **16:52.** "You have brought about for your sisters a more favourable judgement": in relative terms; the purpose is to emphasize the sin of Judah. "So be ashamed":

the motif of shame is found both here and in vv. 54, 61, 63 (cf. 7:18; 36:32; 43:10–11; 44:13). (On the theme of shame in Ezekiel, see Lapsley 2000a:130–56; 2000b; Stiebert 2000, 2002a:129–62; Smith-Christopher 2002:105–23.)

16:53. "I will restore…the fortunes of Sodom and…Samaria": a remarkable development, out of the hyperbolic emphasis on the greater sins of Judah. "I will restore your own fortunes along with theirs": this is still more surprising, especially as it undercuts the rhetorical contrast between Judah and her sisters, which is how we reached this point. For this reason, there is a real question as to whether this section (vv. 53–58) is secondary. **16:54.** "In order that you may bear your disgrace and be ashamed of all that you have done": cf. v. 52; a familiar Ezekiel theme, which looks more original. It should be noted that the shame motif does not only occur in contexts of chance survival, but is found for example in 36:32, at the end of a classic restoration passage. On balance, the grounds for deeming vv. 53–58 secondary fall short of convincing, especially since it concludes on a very judgemental note (vv. 56–58). **16:55.** "Sodom… Samaria, and you…shall return to your former state": meaning the same as the "restored fortunes" of v. 53 (cf. Jer 12:14–17). **16:57.** "A mockery": Hebrew *ḥerpâ*, here "object of reproach." "The daughters of Aram": Hebrew *ʾᵃrām*, "Aram, Syria"; another reading is "Edom" (Heb. *ʾᵉḏōm*), which fits better; cf. 25:12–14; 35:1–36:7. The Edomites occupied Judahite territory after 587 B.C.E. (cf. Lam 4:21–22); this could be a pointer to revision of this verse in the light of later events. "The daughters of the Philistines": cf. v. 27. "Who despise you": Hebrew *šwṭ*, "to despise," a forceful word, found only in Ezekiel (28:24, 26; cf. 25:6, 15; 36:5).

16:59–63. In the case of this last section of the chapter the balance of probability tips with regard to secondary provenance. In literary terms, the original theme has now become diffuse, and this is compounded by the fact that these verses (unlike vv. 53–58) present a positive hope not found elsewhere in authentic Ezekiel material before the fall of Jerusalem (see on 11:14–21 for the single exception). **16:59.** "You who have despised the oath": Hebrew *ʾālâ*, "oath"; this word is usually found in covenant contexts, of the calling down of curses upon oneself, if (as Jerusalem has) one fails to keep the covenant conditions (cf. Deut 29:12, 14, 21 [Heb. vv. 11, 13, 20]; Neh 10:29 [Heb. v. 30]). "Breaking the covenant": the reference to "covenant" (Heb. *bᵉrîṯ*) is made explicit (cf. v. 8). **16:60.** "The days of your youth": cf. vv. 22, 43. "An everlasting covenant": Hebrew *bᵉrîṯ ʿôlām*; cf. 37:26. Renaud (1986) compares this section with the "new covenant" of Jer 31:31–34. **16:61.** "You will remember your ways": a play on the start of v. 60; also see on v. 22. "Be ashamed": a familiar theme (cf. on v. 52). Odell (1992) explores the inversion of shame and forgiveness in vv. 59–63. "When I": so Syriac; Hebrew has "you." "Take your sisters…and give them to you as daughters": to be subordinate to Jerusalem. "Not on account of my covenant with you": meaning "though not because you deserve it." Hebrew lacks "my" before "covenant." **16:62.** "You shall know that I am the LORD": if

vv. 59–63 are indeed secondary, this use of the "Recognition Formula" provides a good example of the way that even redactional material in Ezekiel tends to manifest features of the characteristic style of the prophet. **16:63.** "Never open your mouth again": the Hebrew phrase *piṯḥôn peh* occurs twice in Ezekiel, at 16:63 and at 29:21. Kennedy argues that it constitutes a technical term, the equivalent of the Akkadian *pit pi*, used of the dedication of sacred images for liturgical use, after which the image becomes the source of oracles. In 16:63 the allusion seems to be to the final failure of idolatry (Kennedy 1991; cf. Glazov 2001:351, 380–81). "When I forgive": Hebrew verb *kpr*, "cover, make atonement for"; otherwise found in Ezekiel only in chs. 40–48, of ritual atonement: 43:20, 26; 45:15, 17, 20. The Hebrew verb *slḥ*, "forgive," never occurs in Ezekiel.

CHAPTER 17

Although Garscha attributes only about thirty verses of the entire book to Ezekiel himself, nine of these are in ch. 17, namely vv. 2–10 (Garscha 1974). Moreover, Pohlmann, who also assigns much to redactors, places this chapter among the oldest texts in Ezekiel (Pohlmann 1989; 1992:174–85, 196–204).

17:2. "Propound a riddle (Heb. *ḥîḏâ*), and speak an allegory (Heb. *māšāl*)": Simian-Yofre explores these key words and relates them to the way this passage functions both as an enigma and as a parable (Simian-Yofre 1984). **17:3.** "A great eagle": Nebuchadrezzar of Babylon. "Came to the Lebanon": because that is where cedars are famously to be found; also the normal route from Babylonia to Jerusalem would pass the Lebanon. "He took the top of the cedar…": the Davidic dynasty (cf. Jer 22:5–6). "Its topmost shoot": Jehoiachin, deposed and exiled in 597. **17:4.** "He carried it to a land of trade…a city of merchants": Babylonia, like Phoenicia, was renowned for commerce; cf. 16:29. **17:5.** "He took a seed from the land": Zedekiah, son of Josiah, put in place as king of Judah after Jehoiachin's removal. "Placed it in fertile soil…by abundant waters": a favourable situation; matters should have progressed well. "A plant": Hebrew *qāḥ*; found only here in the Hebrew Bible, and unrepresented in LXX and the Syriac, the meaning of this word is uncertain. It could just be a copied fragment of the initial word of the verse (so Zimmerli 1979a:354–55), but Greenberg persuasively relates it to Akkadian *qū*, "plant" (Greenberg 1983a:310). **17:6.** "Became a vine": often an image for the nation; cf. on 15:6. Here Zedekiah in particular is in view. "Its branches turned toward him": to begin with, Zedekiah is loyal to his Babylonian suzerain. **17:7.** "Another great eagle": the Pharaoh of Egypt, probably Psammetichus II (594–588 B.C.E.), who fomented resistance to Babylonia among the minor western states, rather than his successor Hophra (588–569) (cf. Greenberg 1957). "This vine stretched out its roots toward him": Zedekiah turns his attentions to Egypt and the possibilities of alliance; cf. 16:26. **17:8.** "It was transplanted to good soil by abundant waters": the verb translated "transplanted" by NRSV (Heb. *štl*) does not require the sense "transplant" (contra BDB, 1060). The reference is back to the original planting by the first eagle and does not imply a second planting. **17:9.** "Will it prosper?": this is the key question of the time; what will come of Zedekiah's political flirtation with Egypt? "Will he not pull up its roots?": Nebuchadrezzar will indeed act to punish this disloyalty. "Cause…to rot": NRSV follows LXX; the Hebrew *qss* is found only here in the Hebrew Bible, and its precise meaning (some aspect of the destruction of the fruit) is unclear. "No strong arm or mighty army will be needed to pull it from its roots": the rhetorical point is to emphasize the shallowness of the roots. Nebuchadrezzar did in fact apply considerable military force and the siege of Jerusalem lasted over a year and a half (cf. Jer 52:4–12). **17:10.** "When the east wind strikes it": Nebuchadrezzar. He is portrayed as a great eagle in v. 3 and as an east wind here in v. 10; Wevers concluded unnecessarily that the latter must be an accretion (Wevers 1969:34).

17:11–21. These verses provide an interpretation, possibly redactional or at least subsequent to the original allegory. **17:12.** "Do you not know what these things mean?": cf. 12:9. "Took its king and its officials…to Babylon": the deportation of 597 (cf. 2 Kgs 24:14–16). Ezekiel, it seems, was taken then too. **17:13.** "He took one of the royal offspring": Zedekiah was in fact uncle to the deposed Jehoiachin (2 Kgs 24:17). "Made a covenant with him": the Hebrew word *bᵉrîṯ* ("covenant") could mean a treaty, in fact many scholars have seen biblical covenant language as based on treaty forms, whether Hittite, Assyrian or other (cf. Mendenhall 1973; McCarthy 1973; on covenant in Ezekiel, see Begg 1986a). "Putting him under oath": on Mesopotamian vassal oaths, see Tsevat 1959. **17:15.** "He rebelled against him by sending ambassadors to Egypt": cf. on 8:12; 16:26. "That they might give him horses and a large army": cf. Deut 17:16; Isa 31:1–3. "Will he succeed?… Can he break the covenant and yet escape?": Lang provides a close study of this chapter and material in chs. 12, 19 and 21, in an attempt to expound the politics of Ezekiel, the central position of which is to oppose moves to rebel against Babylon during the reign of Zedekiah (Lang 1981a). **17:16.** He shall die "in the place where the king resides who made him king": this is, Babylon. The Babylonian suzerain had created the vassal king; YHWH had not installed Zedekiah, elsewhere always called merely *nāśîʾ*, "prince"; cf. Hos 8:4. **17:17.** "Pharaoh…will not help him": uncharacteristically, Greenberg deletes "Pharaoh," taking this verse instead as a reference to Nebuchadrezzar taking Jerusalem with relative ease ("with no great force…will he deal with him"; cf. v. 9) (Greenberg 1957:308–9; 1983a:315). But "Pharaoh" is better retained, with Block (1997:545). Pharaoh Hophra (588–569 B.C.E.) offered belated help shortly after his accession (Jer 37:5). This reference may reflect revision of the oracle after this event, but there is no need to deny this to Ezekiel. **17:18.** "He despised the oath and broke the covenant…he gave his hand": Jeremiah too disapproves of Zedekiah's disloyalty to his treaty with Nebuchadrezzar; cf. Jer 27:6. **17:19.** "My oath that he despised, and my covenant that he broke": Greenberg takes this as a reference to YHWH's covenant with Israel and none other (as in 16:59); Zedekiah has gone against YHWH's will, for Babylonia is YHWH's chosen instrument to punish his people (Greenberg 1983a:321–32). But most (e.g. Tsevat 1959) have seen Zedekiah's reneging on his treaty with Nebuchadrezzar as here equated with breaking YHWH's covenant, on the understanding that Zedekiah swore his oath as a vassal in the name of his own God (cf. 2 Chr 36:13, though that text is probably dependent on Ezekiel). **17:20.** "I will spread my net…my snare": cf. 12:13; 19:8. "I will bring him to Babylon": Zedekiah was in fact judged at Riblah before being taken to Babylon (cf. 2 Kgs 25:6–7). "The treason he has committed against me": cf. v. 19.

17:21. "The pick": NRSV, like some of the versions, seems to reflect Hebrew *miḇḥārāyw*, "his choice, picked" (cf. 23:7; Dan 11:15). But MT has Kethiḇ *miḇrāḥô*, "his fugitive"; Qere *miḇrāḥāyw*, "his fugitives"; the latter makes tolerable sense and should be followed. "Fall by the sword…scattered to every wind": cf. 5:2, 12; 12:14.

17:22–24. The allegory of the cedar. These verses pick up the language of the allegory of the two eagles and the vine found in vv. 2–10 (cf. Foster 1958). They constitute one of only four sections of hope within chs. 4–24 (the others being 11:14–21; 16:59–63; 20:40–44). For this reason and also because of their developed messianic interest they may be secondary, though see Levenson (1976:79–80) and Greenberg (1983b) for arguments in favour of Ezekiel's authorship. **17:22.** "I myself": YHWH is the subject. "A sprig from the lofty top of a cedar": cf. vv. 3–4, which referred to Jehoiachin. This section is like an early midrash on those verses, picking up and reworking some of the vocabulary, for example, Hebrew *ṣammereṯ*, "top," Hebrew root *ynq*, of various "twigs," and Hebrew verb *qṭp*, "to break off." "A tender one from the topmost of its young twigs": specially selected, like a quintessence. "A high and lofty mountain": Zion, though Ezekiel never uses that word (cf. Mic 4:1–4; Isa 2:2–4). As in 40:2, there are also resonances here of the cosmic mountain of ancient Near Eastern mythology (Clifford 1972). **17:23.** "The mountain height of Israel": more explicit, but not to be deleted as an explanatory gloss. "Bear fruit, and become a noble cedar": cf. v. 8. For similar imagery, compare the allegory of the cedar in Ezek 31:1–9. **17:24.** "All the trees of the field shall know that I am the LORD": striking anthropomorphism (cf. Isa 55:12); this is the most unusual development of the "Recognition Formula," perhaps further evidence that this section is secondary. "I bring low the high tree, I make high the low tree": cf. 1 Sam 2:7; Isa 2:12–13. "I the LORD have spoken; I will accomplish it": cf. Isa 55:10–11.

Although more explicitly royal language is lacking, a picture of great blessing is here painted, through the picking up and inversion of the language of an oracle of judgement upon the royal house of Judah. It is not inappropriate therefore to describe this as a messianic oracle. For messianic material using "branch" language (similar in concept though not in vocabulary); cf. Jer 23:5–6; 33:15 (Heb. *ṣemaḥ*, "branch"); Zech 3:8 (Heb. *ṣemaḥ*); Isa 11:1 (Heb. *ḥōṭer*, "shoot"; *nēṣer*, "branch"). Levenson shows that an analogy appears to be drawn in 17:22–24. As in vv. 3–4, the eagle (representing Nebuchadrezzar) had taken a sprig (representing the house of David), so now in v. 22 YHWH himself takes a sprig, which becomes a great tree. YHWH is now to the "messiah" as Nebuchadrezzar had been to the Davidic house. "What YHWH does when he raises up the messiah is what a great emperor does when he places a vassal on the throne of a hostile state—he establishes his own sovereignty by restricting the options of the head of state" (Levenson 1976:80). As the Judahite kings had only stayed in place by the sufferance of their suzerains, so the "messiah" will reign only in so far as his rule remains subject to the stated will of YHWH.

CHAPTER 18

The prophet here addresses an audience that is blaming the sins of previous generations for the disaster of exile. He rejects a current proverb and with it his audience's denial of responsibility for their fate (vv. 1–4). To illustrate his case, he draws an analogy with three generations within a family, showing that each generation is judged independently. In this way Ezekiel emphasizes the responsibility of the present generation of Israel for what is happening to them (vv. 5–20). The final section of the chapter explores the theme of repentance; the prophet argues (again by analogy to particular cases) that God always wants his people to repent (vv. 21–32).

This chapter has widely been interpreted as an argument for "individual responsibility" (e.g. Eichrodt 1970:231–49; Brownlee 1986:50, 284, 292). The phrase "individual responsibility" will be used here to mean the moral independence of contemporary individuals; in other words, the notion that particular men and women are judged in isolation from their contemporaries. It is by no means clear that Ezek 18 asserts "individual responsibility" in this sense. Far from constituting an argument for "individual responsibility," the purpose of the chapter is to demonstrate the collective responsibility of the contemporary house of Israel for the national disaster of defeat and deportation.

In order to understand this chapter aright, it is necessary to grasp some key points about its use of language. It is marked by the frequent use of phrases drawn from a priestly legal background, of three main kinds:

(i) *The Test-Case Format*: Ezekiel's response to the proverb is developed through the presentation of test-cases in the style of priestly case law (cf. Lev 20:9, 15), each case illustrating a particular hypothetical situation (e.g. vv. 5, 10, 14, 21, 24, 26, 27).

(ii) *The Statement of Judgement*: In its fullest form this consists of a verdict on behaviour in a particular case followed by a declaration of sentence. Favourable decisions are declared in vv. 9, 17, 19, 21, 22, 27 and 28. Conversely, unfavourable judgements appear in vv. 13, 18, 24 and 26. The latter seem to be an adaptation of the pronouncement of the death sentence in the priestly legal context (e.g. Lev 20:9, 15), but the precise origins of the positive declarations of ch. 18 cannot be demonstrated with certainty. They could represent an adaptation of the priestly statement of acquittal; but while related language is found (cf. Lev 13:17; 18:5), precise parallels to Ezekiel's phrases are not evident. And so both von Rad and Zimmerli argued for an alternative priestly legal background, in the liturgy of entrance at the gates of the Jerusalem temple (cf. Pss 15:1–2; 24:3–4; 118:19–20; cf. Ezek 44:5).

(iii) *Lists of Sins and Virtues*: Within vv. 5–18, the content of righteousness and wickedness is illustrated by the inclusion of a list of sins and virtues. Similar material is to be found elsewhere in Ezekiel, notably at 22:6–12, 25–29 and 33:15. It is likely that such lists are an adaptation of priestly style (cf. Lev 19) and concerns (cf. Gen 9:6; Lev 15:24). Compare also the lists found in liturgies of entrance to the temple, such as Pss 15:2–5; 24:4.

Ezekiel 18 seems indebted, then, to these three features of legal language. this is the language of criminal law; and yet here it is not used in its normal context but adapted to a rather different purpose. It is essential to draw a proper distinction between language about criminal law and that relating to divine retribution, as was shown by Lindars (1965). In criminal law, when a crime has been committed the culprit is sought and, eventually, punishment is imposed (e.g. Exod 21:14; Num 15:32–36). But the discourse of divine retribution starts from the recognition of a particular state of affairs, prosperity or adversity, and then proceeds to attribute this to divine favour or displeasure (cf. Ps 37:25; Job 4:8–9). Ezekiel 18 is clearly concerned with questions about YHWH's punishment of human sin, that is, with divine retribution. Whereas in criminal law evidence can demonstrate that a particular individual is responsible for a crime, it is impossible to demonstrate a direct causal relationship between human sin and divine punishment—hence the considerable scope for those wishing to "pass the buck." So it is that Ezekiel's audience can choose to trace the cause of their sufferings not to their own sins but to those of others.

Ezekiel is engaged not in abstract theological discussion, but in addressing a specific situation of crisis. He advances his argument by drawing upon analogies from the realm of criminal law as applied to particular cases but his purpose in this is to convey the true meaning of great historical events, which inevitably affected the nation as a whole. Recognition of this reapplication of language is the key to the understanding of the chapter.

18:1–20. The moral independence of generations. **18:2.** "What do you mean by repeating this proverb…?": the "sour grapes" saying is described as a *māšāl* ("proverb") here and in v. 3 and is in the form of a poetic couplet (cf. Darr 2004). It appears also at Jer 31:29 and it is probable that it is a current proverb (cf. 12:22; 16:44), which may owe something to the Decalogue (Exod 20:5; Deut 5:9). The Hebrew word *ʿal* in v. 2 should be understood (with the NRSV) to mean "concerning" rather than "on" or "in." The proverb is used by the exiles "concerning" the fate of "the land of Israel" (i.e. defeat at the hands of the Babylonians) rather than being used by people in the homeland itself. As for the chronological setting of this exchange, Zimmerli argued for the situation immediately after 587 (Zimmerli 1979a:377–78), but there are no convincing grounds for abandoning the setting before the fall of the city that the book gives it. "The parents": Eichrodt suggested that the "parents" of the proverb are the non-exiles who are being blamed by the Judahite community in Babylonia (Eichrodt 1970:236–37). It is much more likely that the "parents" are the ancestors of those who are now suffering. Such views were being expressed in

Ezekiel's time (e.g. 2 Kgs 22:13; 24:3; Jer 15:4; Lam 5:7). The "sour grapes" proverb is more than simply an expression of despair; it is also a complaint that YHWH's system of justice is unfair. And implicit in this is a plea of innocence, a denial of responsibility on the part of those who are suffering. Ezekiel's audience revel in the fact that the proverb relieves them of responsibility.

18:3. "This proverb shall no more be used": similar to 12:21–25. Note that at Jer 31:29–30 the "sour grapes" proverb is rejected, but only prospectively as a matter of eschatological hope. This implies that the proverb does apply to Jeremiah's own day, and so the meaning is quite contrary to Ezekiel's. "By you in Israel": the Hebrew words *lāḵem bᵉyiśrāʾēl* should be understood to refer to the exiles in Babylonia citing the proverb, rather than to the current inhabitants of Judah. **18:4.** "Know that all lives are mine; the life of the parent as well as the life of the child is mine": four times this verse uses the Hebrew word *nep̄eš* ("life," "soul," "person"). This statement that all lives belong to YHWH is typical of the radical theocentricity of the book of Ezekiel, in which all things depend on the will of YHWH. "It is only the person who sins that shall die": this apparently austere statement is in fact the beginning of Ezekiel's demonstration that the disaster of exile is not meaningless chaos. It enunciates the legal principle that it is the person who is guilty, and not another, who should be punished, the working basis of criminal law in Israel from the earliest times. However, it is important to remember that in what follows this generally accepted legal principle (which may properly be described as that of "individual responsibility") is reapplied to a realm of discourse very different from that of criminal law, namely discussion of the national crisis of exile.

18:5–18. Three cases are presented, those of a righteous man, his wicked son and his righteous grandson. Behaviour is defined through a combination of positive and negative statements, covering both cultic and ethical conduct (for further discussion, see Matties 1990; Kaminsky 1995:139–78). Each test-case concludes with a verdict, reached on the basis of the principle enunciated in v. 4. Thus it is said that the righteous man shall live: "Such a one is righteous; he shall surely live"; Hebrew *ṣaddîq hûʾ ḥāyō yiḥyeh* (v. 9). His wicked son shall die, despite his parent's righteousness: "He shall surely die"; Hebrew *môṯ yûmāṯ* (v. 13). These first two cases establish a precedent for the third case, that of the righteous son of a wicked man in vv. 14–17, which is crucial because Ezekiel's audience imagine themselves to be the righteous descendents of wicked ancestors. Although a single person is considered in each of the three test-cases, it is the cause of the nation's predicament that is being explored; the proverb blames the sins of previous generations for the sufferings of the present, and accordingly the individuals of the test-cases each represent a generation.

When the legal principle of v. 4 is applied to the case of the righteous son of a wicked man, it is clear what the verdict must be: "He shall surely live"; Hebrew *ḥāyō yiḥyeh* (v. 17). Ezekiel is asserting that if the present generation were righteous they would not be suffering; since they are suffering, this must be because of their own sins. Thus Ezekiel's hearers cannot be the righteous sons of wicked men that they suppose themselves to be. Ezekiel takes for granted the general principle of "individual responsibility" in the realm of legal practice (and employs it in considering his three hypothetical cases), but the possibility of YHWH judging individuals in isolation from their contemporaries is not considered.

18:19. "Why should not the son suffer for the iniquity of the father?": the present verse is the most sophisticated case of Ezekiel's technique of putting words in the mouths of his interlocutors. Ezekiel's audience is pictured as demanding that "the son" should suffer for the iniquity of "the father." These words clearly refer back to the last of the three test-cases, found in vv. 14–17, in which it is said that the righteous son of the wicked man shall live. Ezekiel's audience object: they are righteous and yet suffering, so Ezekiel must be mistaken. The "sour grapes" proverb expresses the complaint that they are suffering for the sins of their ancestors, and yet here in v. 19 the same people are pictured as demanding that "the son" (with whom they identify themselves) *should* suffer for the iniquity of "the father." This is indeed paradoxical and can only be explained on the hypothesis that Ezekiel is suggesting that such a demand is implied by his audience's position. They have a vested interest in the "sour grapes" proverb; unless it can be established that one generation suffers for the sins of previous generations, they will have to admit that they are to blame for the current situation. They complain about the injustice of events, but would prefer to go on believing in their own explanation for the disaster rather than admit responsibility. Hence the paradoxical plea of v. 19, in which Ezekiel's hearers are represented as in effect pleading that they be punished—a *reductio ad absurdum* of their whole position. They would, it seems, prefer YHWH be unjust than admit themselves unjust, a theme that will be taken up in v. 25.

18:20. This verse affirms the basic legal principle of "individual responsibility" upon which verdicts were reached in the three test-cases. It begins with the words with which v. 4 ended, "The person who sins shall die." This is then spelled out in a way that relates it more specifically to the concerns of the chapter. That v. 20 is a statement of legal principle is the more likely in view of its close similarities to Deut 24:16, which reads, "Parents shall not be put to death for their children, nor shall children be put to death for their parents; only for their own crimes may persons be put to death." Ezekiel 18:20 places the statement that "a child shall not suffer for the iniquity of the parent" before the converse statement (in contrast to the order of Deut 24:16). This is appropriate, since it is the question of whether the innocent son suffers for the sins of the father that really concerns Ezekiel (vv. 14–17).

It is important to be clear about the difference between vv. 2 and 20 with regard to the use of the words "parent" and "child." In v. 2, the proverb speaks of YHWH's punishment of sin through his activity in history: the "parents" are the previous generations who are being blamed for the sufferings of the "children," who are the present generation. Verse 20, on the other hand, is (like v. 4) a statement of legal principle: "the parent" and "the child" of the wicked are cited here as examples of closely related contemporaries who might suffer for the iniquity of the wicked; the legal principle of "individual responsibility" states that even these are not to be punished. This principle was intended to prevent any undeserved suffering of the innocent that might happen in the future; Ezekiel's purpose in ch. 18 is to explain the deserved suffering of the wicked that is already happening. By rejecting the notion that the disaster is a punishment for the sins of previous generations, Ezekiel seeks to demonstrate that YHWH's activity in history is every bit as just as the demands of legal practice: the present generation suffers for its own sins.

18:21–32. Ezekiel turns to consider a different but closely related question, namely that of repentance. **18:21–28.** He argues (again by analogy to particular cases couched in the test-case format) that repentance is always possible and that YHWH always wants his people to repent. In v. 21 it is said that if the wicked repent, "they shall surely live; they shall not die." Verse 22 underlines the fact that none of the penitent's past transgressions will be remembered. The opposite case is described in v. 24: if the righteous turn to sin, "they shall die"; previous righteous deeds will not be remembered. In vv. 26–28 both cases are reiterated; v. 26 deals with the apostasy of the righteous and vv. 27–28 with the repentance of the wicked. The consistent message in this section is that what matters is present orientation; the past is forgotten. Righteous and wicked are judged as they are now: there is no "treasury of merit," as Sakenfeld (1978:297) puts it, but conversely none of the sins of the past will be remembered against the penitent. Though this section deals with the dual themes of repentance and apostasy, it is clearly the possibility and value of repentance that dominate. Not only is this theme handled at greater length, but the section is arranged in a chiastic fashion, so as to give prominence to the positive theme. The section opens (vv. 21–22) and closes (vv. 27–28) with the case of turning from evil, rather than with its negative counterpart, which is dealt with in vv. 24 and 26. This positive emphasis is further highlighted in v. 23 (the words of which are echoed also in the final verse of the chapter): "'Have I any pleasure in the death of the wicked,' says the Lord GOD, 'and not rather that they should turn from their ways and live?'"

18:25, 29, 30a. In spite of the dramatic shift to the issue of repentance at v. 21, we apparently return to the issue of responsibility in vv. 25, 29 and 30a. It seems strange, at first sight, to find repentance discussed before Ezekiel has completed the argument for his interpretation of the disaster. However, this is yet another example of the sophisticated way in which he advances his case, introducing the theme of repentance before he has said his last word on the question of whose sins are being punished. The subtlety of the chapter is seen in the way that at v. 21, before he has finished persuading his hearers of their blame, Ezekiel boldly anticipates their acceptance of responsibility and tells of the attractive possibility of a fresh start. In this way he not only broaches the theme of repentance, but also hopes to move his audience a little closer to admitting their responsibility.

Verse 25 reads: "Yet you say, 'The way of the Lord is unfair.' Hear now, O house of Israel: Is my way unfair? Is it not your ways that are unfair?" Verse 29 is virtually identical. They concern the same question as that addressed in vv. 1–20, namely whether Ezekiel's hearers are in fact, as they claim, suffering for the sins of their ancestors. The words "Is it not your ways that are unfair?" clearly indicate that Ezekiel's audience has not yet acknowledged responsibility for the present events. Accordingly, it seems that their words, "The way of the Lord is unfair" express precisely the same complaint as is articulated in the proverb of v. 2, namely that YHWH is punishing the present generation unjustly. By such an interweaving of the themes of responsibility and repentance, Ezekiel attempts to manoeuvre his audience into the position YHWH demands of them. Verses 25 and 29 provide further examples of the technique of placing words in the mouth of the audience, so as to show them the implications of what they are saying. The very words "The way of the Lord is unfair" have a shocking presumption about them, and even by summarizing his audience's position in this way the prophet has dealt a blow against it. In response Ezekiel asks, in the name of YHWH, "Is my way unfair?" and then he puts directly the question that was posed indirectly by the whole of the first section (vv. 1–20): "Is it not your ways that are unfair?" This explicit challenge represents the culmination of that elaborate argument based on the adaptation of case law. Ezekiel here contends that they would rather YHWH be unjust than admit themselves unjust. Either it is the house of Israel that is unjust, or YHWH himself. Which is the more reasonable assumption? Ezekiel demands of his audience a complete *volte-face*; what they need to question is not YHWH's justice, but the basic premise of their whole position, namely the arrogant assumption of their own innocence. Once this premise falls, Ezekiel's own line of argument follows.

Verse 30a, introduced by the Hebrew word *lāḵēn* ("Therefore"), represent a final summary of Ezekiel's response to the "sour grapes" proverb. The Hebrew words *ʾîš kiḏrāḵāyw* (NRSV: "all of you according to your ways") are not to be understood to imply that YHWH will punish individuals in isolation from their contemporaries. Rather, they constitute a third and final reference to the legal principle (enunciated in vv. 4 and 20) whereby in law it is the guilty party who is to be punished. We might paraphrase thus: "Therefore I will judge you, O house of Israel, by analogy to the legal principle whereby each individual is punished for his own crime." Applied to the question at issue, this means that the present generation is being punished for its own sins alone.

18:30b–32. The final words of the chapter focus on the call to repentance, making explicit the challenge that is clearly implied in vv. 21–24 and 26–28. This is one of only two places in the book where the call to repentance is explicit, the other being 14:6. "Get yourselves a new heart and a new spirit!" (cf. 11:19; 36:26–27). See on 11:19, for the key terms "heart" (Heb. *lēḇ*) and "spirit"

(Heb. *rûaḥ*). Two important senses of *lēḇ* converge here: the heart as the locus of the moral will and as the symbol of inner reality as distinct from mere outward appearance. A "new spirit" (*rûah ḥᵃḏāšâ*) refers to the renewal of "the moral will." Gosse (2004a) argues that this verse influenced the conception of the "new covenant" in Jer 31:31–34. The chapter ends on a rhetorical note: "Why will you die?… I have no pleasure in the death of anyone" (vv. 31–32), picking up the language of v. 23. "Turn, then, and live": cf. Deut 30:15–20.

How are we to understand the call to repentance in ch. 18? Exile has already claimed Ezekiel and his immediate audience, and the final judgement upon Jerusalem itself is imminent. Chapter 18 operates on the assumption that the crisis is already being suffered—the children's teeth are already set on edge. The "life" to which the chapter calls the house of Israel (v. 32) clearly cannot mean exemption from the disaster. The motif of the call to repentance serves two functions. The first is to emphasize Israel's responsibility for the inevitable punishment. By emphasizing the demand of YHWH, the call to repentance underlines the fact that Israel has had every warning and is wholly to blame for the crisis that is even now engulfing the nation. The words "Why will you die, O house of Israel?" (18:31) are words of deep pathos: Israel is dying as the prophet speaks—and his purpose is to show that this is the just act of YHWH.

But the repentance motif is by no means only a rhetorical device to emphasize responsibility; it has a second function too. We read in v. 23, "Have I any pleasure in the death of the wicked…and not rather that they should turn from their ways and live?" The disaster may not now be avoidable, but (though he has certainly ordained it) this is not what YHWH would wish for Israel. The call to repentance reveals also the yearning of YHWH for the obedience of his people. Ezekiel's God will not in the end allow the sin of Israel to be the last word. Beyond the disaster—and not before—the prophet looks to a new beginning for his people, in which "life" will consist in the fullness of relationship with God, in contrast to the "death" of estrangement from him. But this new beginning is as yet barely hinted at in the call to the dying Israel to "turn and live." When the new day actually dawns, it will in no way depend upon Israel's own repentance, indeed it will appear in spite of the behaviour of the nation. The challenge to get "a new heart and a new spirit" in 18:31 is followed by the free gift of 36:26–27, "A new heart I will give you, and a new spirit I will put within you." More immediately, the call to repentance represents a concern that even in exile the Judahites should conduct their lives in accordance with God's will. This is well expressed by Wilson, who writes that "even Ezekiel, who proclaimed that Jerusalem's future doom could not be avoided under any conditions, urged the Israelites already suffering the judgement of exile to keep themselves righteous (Ezekiel 18)" (Wilson 1998:216). Mein too reflects on what a realistic call to repentance in the exilic context might mean, arguing that ch. 18 "in the specific examples used…reflects the new lifestyles of the exiles, and the possibilities open to them… [I]t may be that the call to repentance in Ezekiel itself forms part of the evidence for the more limited, domestic scope of the exiles' moral world" (Mein 2001a:212–13).

When considering the earlier section of the chapter (vv. 1–20) it was possible to show that the nation as a collective unit was the subject of discussion; with vv. 21–32, however, it is more difficult to decide, for a number of reasons. First, whereas the consideration of responsibility in vv. 1–20 pertains to a given historical situation which was inevitably corporate, the issue of repentance addressed in vv. 21–32 concerns an open opportunity that could, theoretically, be either a collective or an individual experience. Second, although in vv. 21–32, as in vv. 1–20, we find the use of the test-case format and of legal declarations, an important difference is to be observed. Whereas in vv. 1–20 the three test-cases were discussed as though actual legal cases, from which a theological analogy was then drawn, in the present section the distinction between legal and theological discourse seems to be less rigorously maintained. Thus, while it would seem to be universally true of legal practice that a man who commits a crime is held responsible, regardless of his former righteousness (cf. vv. 24, 26), the statement that when a wicked man repents his past transgressions will not be held against him (vv. 21–22, 27–28) is more surprising. Despite the use of legal terminology, it is clear that here we are already dealing with a statement about how YHWH himself acts. (This is also suggested by the inclusion in the midst of this section of the words, "'Have I any pleasure in the death of the wicked,' says the Lord GOD, 'and not rather that they should turn from their ways and live?'" [v. 23].) So, when in these verses reference is made to an individual penitent, it is not clear whether this is simply because the test-case format characteristically operates in terms of particular cases, or because Ezekiel is indeed concerned with the repentance of independent individuals. It is conceivable, then, that the two halves of the chapter differ significantly in this regard; indeed, Greenberg asserts that at v. 21 the focus shifts "from intergenerational moral autonomy to the liberation of the individual from the burden of his own past" (Greenberg 1983a:340; cf. 334).

There are, however, good reasons for believing that in vv. 21–32 Ezekiel is in fact calling upon the community as a whole. First, Ezekiel's argument to persuade his hearers of their responsibility is not complete at v. 20; he returns to it in vv. 25, 29 and 30a. The references to repentance in vv. 21–24 and 26–28 are thus sandwiched between material that attempts to persuade the present generation of its responsibility for the inevitably communal disaster. Thus it seems likely that in these verses Ezekiel is concerned for the repentance of that same generation as a collective unit. Second, the address to the house of Israel in v. 31 ("Why will you die, O house of Israel?") confirms that it is the community as a whole that is being challenged to repent. And third, the same verse calls upon Israel to get "a new heart and a new spirit"—a corporate image indeed. We conclude, then, that, although the distinction between legal and theological discourse is less rigorously maintained in vv. 21–32 than in the first part of the chapter, it is again the case that the citing of individuals is due to the legal convention of dealing with particular cases. While it is, of course, true that communal repentance would necessarily involve change within particular individuals, it is no part of the purpose of Ezekiel here to argue for the repentance of individuals in isolation from the collective people of God.

Chapter 19

This chapter shares much in style and theme with ch. 17, and like that chapter finds a place among Pohlmann's oldest texts in Ezekiel (Pohlmann 1989; 1992:139–59, 190–97). The chapter falls into two parts, vv. 1–9, the lament of the lions, and vv. 10–14, the lament of the vine.

19:1–9. For focused studies of these verses, see Kottsieper 1993; Beentjes 1996. **19:1.** "Raise up a lamentation": Hebrew *qînâ*, "lamentation." Cf. the coda to the chapter in v. 14: "This is a lamentation, and it is used as a lamentation." The chapter (especially vv. 2–8) well exemplifies the characteristic 3:2 *qînâ* metre. "For the princes of Israel": the Hebrew word for "prince" is *nāśîʾ*; Ezekiel uses this term to disparage the authority of the now disgraced royal family (cf. Joyce 1998). **19:2**. "What a lioness was your mother among lions!": the lion has long been an important symbol of Judah; e.g. Gen 49:9 (Gen 49:8–12 has several features in common with this chapter). **19:3.** "She raised up one of her cubs": Jehoahaz, son and successor of Josiah (2 Kgs 23:30–34). It is said that the cub devoured humans (cf. also v. 6); this may be an allusion to the unjust rule of the Judahite monarchs. **19:4.** "The nations sounded an alarm against him": mention of "the nations" illustrates that allegory and interpretation are rather intertwined here. This chapter does not have a separate interpretation section, like 17:11–21. "Pit…hooks": cf. 12:13; 17:20. "They brought him to the land of Egypt": cf. 2 Kgs 23:34; Jer 22:10–12. **19:5.** "Another of her cubs": there is disagreement about the identity of the second cub (cf. Begg 1989). Block proposes Jehoahaz's successor Jehoiakim (cf. 2 Kgs 23:34–24:6; Block 1997:604–7), whereas Zimmerli favours Jehoiachin (cf. 2 Kgs 24:8–16; Jer 22:24–30; Zimmerli 1979a:395). Eichrodt argues for Zedekiah (cf. 2 Kgs 24:17–25:7; Jer 39:7), who in reality had the same mother, Hamutal, as Jehoahaz (cf. 2 Kgs 23:31; 24:18); on this theory Hamutal can be seen as the "lioness" (Eichrodt 1970:253–55). Greenberg points in the direction of the best approach, critical of any view that "needlessly commits one to a specificity in interpretation of the second cub-king…beyond that which the data allow, thus shifting attention from their typical features to historical details that the allegory is not meant to illumine" (Greenberg 1983a:357). **19:7.** "Ravaged their strongholds": Hebrew has *wayyēḏaʿ ʾalmᵉnôṯāyw*, "he knew his widows," which should be retained, referring to the sexual claiming of the widows of dead victims. "The land was appalled…": this is a much more polemical critique than v. 3; but this is to be explained as the result of escalation of the passage's rhetoric rather than of the greater vices of the supposed royal referent. **19:9.** "Brought him to the king of Babylon": in keeping with the open reading commended by Greenberg, this may be taken as speaking of the fate of the nation as a whole, misled by their leaders.

19:10–14. Now a dramatic change of image, though still focused on "your mother." A second lament tells of a vine, again representing Judah; cf. 15:6; 17:6. **19:10.** "In a vineyard": Hebrew has *b^{e}ḏām^{e}ḵā*, "in your blood," probably a corruption of *karm^{e}ḵā*, "your vineyard." "Fruitful and full of branches": prospects for the vine are good. **19:11.** "Its strongest stem became a ruler's sceptre": the Hebrew *šēḇeṭ*, "sceptre," is often used of royal authority (cf. Gen 49:10); here this is made explicit. The Hebrew has plural forms: "Its strongest stems became rulers' sceptres." The LXX has singular forms, and is followed by NRSV. A plural reference might cohere with the two cubs (vv. 3, 5). But singular subjects predominate in the Hebrew of vv. 11–13, and this (together with the fact that the Heb. of v. 14 features the singular in a phrase very similar to that of v. 11) justifies taking v. 11 as singular. If singular, it could be a reference to Zedekiah (since the following verses employ some of the language used in ch. 17 of the fate of the vine, representing Zedekiah, for example, the "east wind" of 17:10; 19:12). But it is better, with Greenberg, to regard the reference here too as unspecific (cf. on v. 5), beyond this being an oracle on the Davidic house (Greenberg 1983a:356–59). "It towered aloft…": an image not so much of thriving as of hubris, as a prelude to the judgement that is to follow; cf. Isa 2:12–13. **19:12.** "Its strong stem was withered": cf. on v. 11; Heb has the noun in the singular here, in spite of a plural verbal form. **19:13.** "Transplanted into the wilderness": an inversion of v. 10. "A dry and thirsty land": Babylonia, albeit under the guise of a stylized land of exile. **19:14.** "Fire has gone out from its stem": cf. 5:4, "A fire will come out against all the house of Israel"; also 20:45–49 (Heb. 21:1–5); Isa 6:13. "There remains in it no strong stem, no sceptre for ruling": cf. on v. 11; Heb has singular here. Davidic monarchy is finished, a lamentable outcome indeed. "This is a lamentation, and it is used as a lamentation": these words provide an *inclusio* to v. 1.

CHAPTER 20

This chapter shares with chs. 16 and 23 the fact that it is a history of the nation, but it lacks the personification motif of those two reviews. Comparison with the historical survey of Ps 106 is also instructive. In addition to those mentioned below, the following important studies of ch. 20 should be noted: Lust 1967, 1969; Sedlmeier 1990; Allen 1992; Eslinger 1998.

20:1. "In the seventh year, in the fifth month, on the tenth day of the month": 14th August 591. "Certain elders of Israel came to consult the LORD": close to 14:1–3; cf. also 8:1. **20:3.** "I will not be consulted by you": Hebrew *drš*, "seek, consult"; cf. v. 31; also cf. 14:3. **20:4.** "Let them know the abominations of their ancestors": the sins of the forefathers are illustrative of the tendencies of the nation today; it is not suggested that the present generation suffers because of this long history of sin; see below on v. 30.

20:5. "On the day when I chose Israel": Hebrew verb *bḥr*, "to choose," conveys election, as often in Deuteronomy (e.g. Deut 7:7). This happens in this context in Egypt, but the reference to the house of Jacob shows an awareness of the patriarchal tradition as a prelude (cf. Deut 26:5). **20:7.** "Cast away the detestable things": Israel is already sinning in Egypt (cf. 23:3), unlike in the Exodus account and in contrast to those biblical traditions that seem to envisage an early "honeymoon" period in the story of the nation (e.g. Hos 11:1; Jer 2:2). **20:8.** "They rebelled against me": sin is now compounded by active rejection of the divine call. "Then I thought": Hebrew *wāʾōmar*, "I said," in the sense of internal reflection or consideration. "I would pour out my wrath upon them...in the midst of the land of Egypt": again, not a feature of the Pentateuchal accounts before the Exodus from Egypt. **20:9.** "But I acted for the sake of my name": a recurrent refrain in this section (cf. vv. 14, 22). In this chapter it refers to YHWH's gracious forbearance in the past, repeatedly sparing Israel when punishment was fully deserved. Chapters 4–24 in their message of judgement upon contemporary Judah and Jerusalem are characterized by the opposite, an absolute insistence on the exclusion of mercy and pity (e.g. 9:10). Conversely, when after the fall of Jerusalem Ezekiel begins to articulate a positive message, it is couched in terms similar to this recurrent refrain of vv. 9, 14, 22. For example, 36:22: "It is not for your sake, O house of Israel, that I am about to act, but for the sake of my holy name." These verses also share the motif that grounds YHWH's action in the wish to avoid the profanation of his name in the sight of the nations. So the present passage in an indirect way anticipates how YHWH will deal with his restored people (cf. Rendtorff 1986). The cyclical pattern of divine favour, sin, divine consideration of punishment, followed by sparing for the sake of the divine name will be repeated (with variations) several times through the first half of the chapter (vv. 5–22).

20:10. "I led them out of the land of Egypt": a second cycle begins. **20:11.** "I gave them my statutes...": an allusion to the lawgiving at the holy mountain. "By whose observance everyone shall live": as in Lev 18:5, "You shall keep my statutes and my ordinances; by doing so one shall live" (cf. vv. 21, 25). **20:12.** "I gave them my sabbaths": cf. v. 20. Though the predominance of sabbath in this chapter is surprising, there is no good ground for regarding this theme as a secondary addition (contra Cooke 1936:217). Mein argues that whereas the sabbath references in 22:8, 26 and 23:38 are part of the prophet's condemnation of Jerusalem and the abuses of the pre-exilic cult, those in ch. 20 reflect the emerging emphasis on sabbath as a covenantal sign and represent an important step towards its use as a distinctive marker of Jewish identity within a situation of diaspora (Mein 2001a:158). "A sign": Hebrew *ʾôṯ*; cf. on 4:3. **20:13.** "My sabbaths they greatly profaned": Hebrew verb *ḥll* (cf. vv. 16, 21, 24). **20:14.** "I acted for the sake of my name": the second round of the pattern reaches completion.

20:15. "I swore to them in the wilderness that I would not bring them into the land": this third cycle differs in several respects. It begins here not with blessing (as in vv. 5–6 and vv. 10–12) but with threat. This is commensurate with the development of the people's sin. **20:17.** "Nevertheless my eye spared them, and I did not destroy them": again the pattern is varied: instead of YHWH considering punishment before reference to his relenting for the sake of his "name," the sequence is reversed with different formulae used.

20:18. "I said to their children...": a fourth cycle begins with reference to a second wilderness generation. Though the parents have apparently been spared (v. 17), their children are called upon to turn to virtue (cf. 18:14; see Phillips 1982, for a possible analogy with Isa 40:2). "Do not follow the statutes of your parents...": this anticipates the call to Ezekiel's generation not to defile themselves after the manner of their ancestors" (v. 30). In contrast to vv. 15–16, the tone is hortatory rather than threatening. **20:19.** "I the LORD am your God": cf. vv. 5, 7. "Follow my statutes...my ordinances": rather than those of the parents (cf. v. 18). **20:20.** "Hallow my sabbaths": cf. v. 20. Outside chs. 40–48, this is the only case in Ezekiel where the verb *qdš* has a subject other than YHWH (Wong 2003:226). **20:21.** "But the children rebelled against me": now even the second generation turns, in spite of the special appeal (this does not bode well for the responsiveness of Ezekiel's generation). "My ordinances, by whose observance everyone shall live": cf. v. 11. **20:22.** "But I withheld my hand...": the established formulae of vv. 9 and 14 are used for the last time. The cyclical section of vv. 5–22 at an end, the story of the nation will now descend to its nadir.

20:23. "I would scatter them among the nations and disperse them through the countries": an anticipation of the exile, in the manner of Lev 26:32–39 and Deut 4:25–28; 28:36–68. **20:24.** "Their ancestors' idols": again the analogy to the appeal to Ezekiel's audience (v. 30) is to be noted. **20:25.** "Moreover I gave them statutes that were not good and ordinances by which they could not live": a shocking paradox. The chapter has featured recurrent reference to the divine statutes and ordinances, "by whose observance everyone shall live" (vv. 11, 21). Now YHWH compounds the nation's situation by giving laws that cannot give life. One is reminded of the hardening of Pharaoh's heart in Exodus (e.g. Exod 4:21) and of the making dull of the mind of the people in Isa 6:10. **20:26.** "I defiled them through their very gifts, in their offering up all their firstborn": while v. 25 could be self-contained, it is likely that v. 26 is intended to elucidate it (though note that v. 25 uses the plural of "statutes" and "ordinances," so the reader of v. 26 is left with a disturbing sense of uncertainty about which other specific commandments might be "not good").

Child sacrifice appears to be referred to in Ezekiel at 16:20–21; 20:26, 31; and 23:37 (Odell finds allusions also in 8:3, 5; 43:7–9). A word of general background is called for. Biblical law included the categorical statement that all firstborn, whether human or animal, belonged to YHWH: "Consecrate to me all the firstborn; whatever is the first to open the womb among the Israelites, of human beings and animals, is mine" (Exod 13:2). Some Pentateuchal laws allowed for the redemption of human offspring (e.g. Exod 13:13), while others apparently did not (Exod 22:29 [Heb. v. 28]). A related issue in the Hebrew Bible involves various occasions where offerings are made that are defined by the Hebrew letters *lmlk* (e.g. Lev 18:21). While many have understood these to be offerings to a god Molech (e.g. Day 1989; 2000:209–16), others have interpreted them as *mlk*-offerings, child sacrifices similar to those practised in Carthage (Eissfeldt 1935). Stavrakopoulou (2004) has recently argued that the latter were commonplace within mainstream Yahwist circles in Judah.

Whereas in Ezek 16:20–21; 20:31 and 23:37, Ezekiel seems to connect Israelite observance of child sacrifice with the worship of alien gods and idols (though in none of these contexts does the Heb. form *lmlk* occur), in the present verse (v. 26) it appears that the people had correctly understood the law of the firstborn as something prescribed by YHWH. However, that law was evil, given by YHWH to punish his people and guarantee their ultimate destruction (cf. Patton 1996:78–79). Heider notes that the result of Israel's refusal to obey YHWH is as it was for Pharaoh—the death of the firstborn, only this time at the willing hands of the rebels themselves (Heider 1988; cf. Heider 1985:369–75). "That they might know that I am the LORD": the "Recognition Formula" can be used even here, indeed it is integral to this difficult text, for this is the darkest manifestation of Ezekiel's radically theocentric perspective. (For other important contributions on this notorious crux, see Gese 1977 and Hahn and Bergsma 2004.)

20:27. "Therefore": Hebrew *lāḵēn*. This word signals that the passage is coming to its point (the direct challenge of v. 30, where the word is repeated). "Speak to the house of Israel": the contemporaries of Ezekiel. **20:28.** "For when I had brought them into the land": the last episode of the historical review brings the story into Canaan (cf. v. 6). "That I swore to give them": YHWH was true to this oath, in spite of his threats to the contrary (vv. 15, 23). "Wherever they saw any high hill or any leafy tree…": cf. on 6:13. **20:29.** "What is the high place to which you go? So it is called Bamah to this day": the "high place" (Heb. *bāmâ*) was the hill-top shrine of Canaanite religion (cf. on 6:3). Ezekiel is punning on the Hebrew verb *bwʾ*, to "go, come". **20:30.** "Say to the house of Israel": the contemporaries of Ezekiel. "Will you defile yourselves after the manner of your ancestors and go astray after their detestable things?": cf. v. 24. They are being held responsible as a generation, for their own sins that followed the pattern of their ancestors; we see that this chapter does not contradict the message of ch. 18 (cf. 16:44). This is reinforced by the words "to this day" in the following verse. **20:31.** "When you offer your gifts and make your children pass through the fire, you defile yourselves with all your idols": see on v. 26. "Shall I be consulted by you?… I will not": cf. v. 3; this confirms that we have come full circle. This rebuff coheres with the dumbness motif, properly understood (see on 3:26–27).

20:32. "What is in your mind shall never happen": another example of Ezekiel's practice of attributing statements to his interlocutors. "Let us be like the nations…and worship wood and stone": cf. Deut 4:28; 28:36, 64. On vv. 32–44 and their intertextual relationship with Isaiah, see Lust 1997a. Some, including Zimmerli (1979a:414), have argued that in v. 32 the position of the people is one of despair ("We are like the nations"). This amounts to a softening of their position, and the divine reaction is then interpreted in part at least in terms of encouragement. However, it is more likely that the people's position is presented as one of defiance ("We *will* be like the nations"; cf. 1 Sam 8:19–20). This fits naturally within the overall theology of Ezekiel, wherein no move towards repentance plays any part in the process towards the new future that God will eventually grant the people.

20:33. "As I live, says the Lord GOD, surely…": the form of vv. 32–38 is that of the disputation oracle, a form characteristic of Ezekiel (cf. Graffy 1984). Verses 33–38 give the divine rejoinder to the people's thought, beginning with an oath. "With a mighty hand and an outstretched arm, and with wrath poured out, I will be king over you": the familiar language of YHWH's mighty acts (cf. Deut 4:34; 5:15). The language of Holy War is now turned against Israel (cf. Jer 21:5). On vv. 33–34, see Kreuzer 1997. This verse employs royal language of YHWH for the only explicit time in Ezekiel, using the verb *mlk*, "to reign" or "to be king" (cf. Joyce 1998). For Ezekiel in exile, again in a "wilderness" situation (cf. 19:13), with no legitimate human king, it is YHWH who reigns as divine king and who judges his people. That "king" as harsh ruler or judge is here intended is especially clear from the phrase "with wrath poured out" and this confirms the interpretation that v. 32 is to be understood as defiance.

20:34. "I will bring you out from the peoples and gather you out of the countries where you are scattered": the vocabulary of v. 33 ("with a mighty hand and an outstretched arm") already hinted at the "second Exodus" language that shapes our passage, and now in v. 34 this becomes more explicit. Ezekiel shares this reuse of Exodus language with Jeremiah (e.g. Jer 23:7–8) and the so-called Second Isaiah (e.g. Isa 51:10–11; cf. Zimmerli 1960). But Ezekiel's use of it here transforms the model from one of salvation to one of judgement, or at least one that is about judgement before it is about salvation. It is important to recognize that, as with the original Exodus, so now it is the whole generation of Israel that is brought out. This understanding coheres with the collective nature of Ezekiel's presentation of God's dealings with his people.

20:35. "The wilderness of the peoples": this seems to refer to the open desert, the territory of no particular people. Here YHWH will enter into judgement with his own people. "Face to face": Hebrew *pānîm ʾel-pānîm*; intensely, but not necessarily implying any individualistic focus. **20:36.** "As I entered into judgement with your ancestors…so I will enter into judgement with you": as the judgement in the wilderness was generational, so now YHWH judges the present generation, in keeping with Ezekiel's consistent theme (v. 30; cf. 16:44; 18:2–4). "In the wilderness of the land of Egypt": cf. vv. 13, 15–16. **20:37.** "I will make you pass under the staff": the word for "staff" (Heb. *šēḇeṭ*) both picks up the royal language of v. 33 and also evokes the image of a shepherd counting in sheep (cf. Lev 27:32). "I will bring you within the bond of the covenant": Hebrew *wᵉhēḇēʾṯî ʾeṯkem bᵉmāsōreṯ habbᵉrîṯ*. On the basis of the LXX some emend *bᵉmāsōreṯ* to *bᵉmispār*, "by number" (appealing also to 1 Chr 9:28). This position then normally regards *habbᵉrîṯ* as an error, possibly through dittography of the first word of the following verse. Such a view was favoured by Zimmerli (1979a:403), and also the RSV ("I will let you go in by number"). This reading arguably shares echoes of shepherding language with the first phrase of the verse ("I will make you pass under the staff") and might seem to imply individual judgement. However, there is no need to depart from the MT here. It is not at all clear that LXX read *bᵉmispār*—MT's *hapax legomenon māsōreṯ* is not likely to have arisen from the common word *mispār*. NRSV rightly opts (against RSV) for "I will bring you within the bond of the covenant." Covenant language has its place in Ezekiel; it is one of the ways in which God's promise for the future of the nation as a whole is expressed (e.g. 37:26), and the covenant reference here in v. 37 is compatible with others in Ezekiel, albeit more rigorous in tone. The preceding phrase, "I will make you pass under the staff," can be understood as of a shepherd counting in *all* of the sheep, making sure none are left out. Such a reading would cohere with Ezekiel's theology as operating in collective terms and with the future not depending on repentance.

20:38. "I will purge out the rebels among you, and those who transgress against me; I will bring them out of the land where they reside as aliens, but they shall not enter the land of Israel": this verse appears to envisage a segregation between righteous and wicked individuals, and also to posit a conditional element to restoration. If so, then in both respects it runs counter to the overall interpretation of Ezekiel's theology presented in this commentary. Though it does not include a call to repentance, it is clear that the rebels are judged for their wickedness and on that basis separated from the body of Israel and excluded from entry into the land. Mein notes that this is uncharacteristic of Ezekiel, who otherwise consistently presents Israel's future as YHWH's unconditional gift to an undeserving people (Mein 2001a:209). There are no grounds for regarding vv. 32–38 or indeed this verse alone as secondary (theological arguments for theories of secondary elaboration are generally the weakest of all). This verse is unique in the book (the rhetoric of 13:9 does not provide a substantial parallel) and can only be explained as an anomalous case. Within the "second Exodus" context of our passage, a number of Pentateuchal themes are under the surface of the text; in particular, the reference to rebels who are to be purged puts one in mind of the rebellion of Dathan and Abiram. It is possible that the purging motif of v. 38 should be explained entirely in literary terms as an allusion to Num 16, in this way filling out the Exodus imagery. Beyond this, there may be an actual historical referent in the Babylonian exile, but one can only speculate as to what that might be. Ezekiel possibly has in view a dissident group who had turned away completely from Yahwism, presumably in favour of Babylonian deities (cf. v. 32, with its emphasis on idolatry). Such a group would effectively have excluded themselves from the covenant community and from the prospect of a new beginning graciously granted by the God of Israel. The late work *The Lives of the Prophets* (see the "After Ezekiel" section, above) suggests that Ezekiel encountered intractable opposition among the Babylonian exiles, but whether the present verse should be explained in such a way lies beyond our evidence (see further Joyce 2006).

20:39. "Go serve your idols": renewing the emphasis on idols that has characterized the chapter. The verse, which seems to stand alone, is couched in terms of an ironic command to sin (cf. v. 25). "But my holy name you shall no more profane": cf. 36:20–22; 39:7, 25.

20:40–44. A passage of positive hope for the future, the last of only four such passages in chs. 4–24, the others being 11:14–21; 16:59–63 and 17:22–24. Given the disjunction from what precedes it, this passage is possibly secondary, in spite of the presence of the self-loathing motif in v. 43. **20:40.** "On my holy mountain, the mountain height of Israel": cf. 17:22–24. Zion is the setting, though Ezekiel never uses that word (cf. Mic 4:1–4; Isa 2:2–4). As in 40:2, there are perhaps also resonances here of the cosmic mountain of ancient Near Eastern mythology. "All the house of Israel, all of them": the emphasis is collective and inclusive. "Shall serve me...with all your sacred things": an eschatological image of the gathered cultic community; cf. 37:27–28 and chs. 40–48. **20:41.** "As a pleasing odour I will accept you": a spiritualization of cultic language. "I will manifest my holiness among you": this and various features of the following verses, such as the "Recognition Formula," the self-loathing motif and the formula "for my name's sake" are all characteristic of Ezekiel's thought and style, but this observation is not incompatible with the possibility that vv. 40–44 are secondary. They may well provide good examples of the homogeneity of the Ezekiel tradition, primary and secondary (see the "Unity, Authorship and Redaction" section, above).

20:45–49. These verses are vv. 1–5 of ch. 21 in Hebrew. **20:46.** "Set your face": cf. on 4:3. "Preach against the south...": the verse uses three different Hebrew words for "south": *têmān*; *dārôm*; *negeḇ*. The reference is not to Judah, but rather to the territories further south as a symbolic way of emphasizing the dramatic and all-encompassing nature of the judgement (cf. "from south to north" in v. 47). **20:47.** "I will kindle a fire in you": "fire" (Heb. *ʾēš*) has a significant place in Ezekiel as a mode of judgement; cf. 5:2, 4; 10:2. "Every green tree in you and every dry tree": one of several expressions in this passage conveying the inclusivity of the judgement. Allen (1989) regards the mysterious words of 21:10b (Heb. v. 15b) as a misplaced gloss on this verse; he considers the possibility that the "green tree" may represent Jehoiachin and the "dry tree" Zedekiah. **20:49.** "They are saying of me, 'Is he not a maker of allegories?'": a vignette of the popular reaction to Ezekiel (cf. 33:32, "a singer of love songs"). "A maker of allegories" (Heb. *mᵉmaššēl mᵉšālîm*) rings very true as a description of Ezekiel. The phrase employs the noun *māšāl*, often translated "proverb," and its cognate verb. The word *māšāl* is indeed a favourite of Ezekiel (cf. 12:22–23; 14:8; 16:44; 17:2; 18:2–3; 24:3). We have also noted that a range of what might be described as allegorical presentations characterize the book, especially between chs. 15 and 23.

CHAPTER 21

This chapter contains a series of oracles united (with one exception) by the theme of the sword (Heb. *ḥereḇ*). The sword of judgement is a common motif in Ezekiel, especially in chs. 5, 6, 30, 32 and the present chapter. Throughout ch. 21 the English verse numbers are 5 lower than the Hebrew.

21:1–7 (Heb. vv. 6–12). YHWH draws his sword. **21:2**. "Set your face": see on 4:3. "Preach against the sanctuaries…prophesy against the land of Israel": this passage shares with ch. 6 not only the sword motif, but also the object of judgement, the homeland and its syncretistic hill-top shrines. **21:3.** "I am coming against you": Holy War language is turned against YHWH's own people. "I will cut off from you both righteous and wicked": the exilic crisis is a given, affecting the nation as a whole. These words pose a problem for any scholar wishing to present Ezekiel as an exponent of "individual responsibility"; Irwin claimed that the verses must come from early in the prophet's ministry, before he had reached the full maturity of his individualistic view (Irwin 1943:331–32). Such concerns go back even to ancient times; LXX reads *adikon kai anomon*, "both unrighteous and wicked," which Zimmerli describes as a "classical example of a correction for dogmatic reasons" (Zimmerli 1979a:421). Such special pleading (whether in LXX or in Irwin) is unnecessary, for Ezekiel's concerns are in no way systematic. **21:4.** "Against all flesh from south to north": another expression of inclusivity. **21:5.** "All flesh shall know…": cf. 20:48 (Heb. 21:4). "That I the LORD have drawn my sword": another variation on the "Recognition Formula." **21:6.** "Moan with breaking heart and bitter grief before their eyes": we rarely see Ezekiel expressing emotion; contrast 24:15–27, where he is commanded not to mourn. **21:7.** "Because of the news that has come": the announcement of judgement. "Every heart will melt and all hands will be feeble, every spirit will faint and all knees will turn to water": cf. 7:17.

21:8–17 (Heb. vv. 13–22). "The Song of the Sword." Maarsingh (1986) compares this poetic section with motifs in the Neo-Babylonian *Poem of Erra*, as does Bodi (1991:231–57); cf. Jer 50:35–37. **21:10.** "You have despised the rod, and all discipline": the "despised rod" here and in v. 13 (Heb. v. 18) could simply refer to failure to respect chastisement, as in the NRSV. On the other hand, Allen (1989) finds in both verses reference to the doomed Davidic monarchy, described as the "despised rod" or, as he prefers, the "rejected sceptre." **21:12.** "Strike the thigh!": a sign of mourning; cf. Jer 31:19. **21:13.** "If you despise the rod, will it not happen?": see on v. 10. **21:15.** "I have set the point of the sword": NRSV "point" is a plausible guess for the obscure Hebrew *hapax legomenon ʾibḥâ*. "It is polished": MT features here another *hapax legomenon*, *mᵉʿuṭṭâ*; the most likely meaning of this is "wrapped up," which makes poor sense. *BHS* proposes *mᵉruṭṭâ*, "polished" (cf. vv. 9, 11, 28 [Heb. vv. 14, 16, 33]). NRSV follows this, citing the support of the Targum.

21:18–24 (Heb. vv. 23–29). Lang includes the evidence of 21:18–32 (Heb. vv. 23–37) in his study of the politics of Ezekiel (Lang 1981a). **21:19.** "Mark out two roads for the sword of the king of Babylon": Nebuchadrezzar is coming to deal with his rebellious vassal states. What Ezekiel is commanded to do shares some features with the prophetic sign-actions of chs. 4, 5 and 12. **21:20.** "To Rabbah of the Ammonites": Ammon was a minor kingdom to the east of the Jordan; Rabbah its capital was on the site of modern "Amman," whose name is cognate with "Ammon." "Or to Judah and to Jerusalem": so LXX and Syriac; Hebrew has "Judah in Jerusalem." Both Ammon and Judah are on the list for punishment (cf. v. 28); the question is "which first?" **21:21.** "He shakes the arrows, he consults the teraphim, he inspects the liver": three forms of divination; cf. Greenberg 1991. **21:22.** "Into his right hand": the hand that matters. "Comes the lot for Jerusalem": her turn will be first. "Battering rams…siege towers": cf. on 4:2. **21:23.** "To them it will seem like a false divination": cf. 12:21–28. "They have sworn solemn oaths": cf. 17:16, 19.

21:25–27 (Heb. vv. 30–32). An oracle against Zedekiah. This short section is the one unit of this chapter not to feature the word "sword" (Heb. *ḥereḇ*). **21:25.** "Vile, wicked prince of Israel": the disparaging title "prince" (Heb. *nāśîʾ*) is further qualified by two strongly negative adjectives (cf. Joyce 1998). **21:26.** "Remove the turban, take off the crown": the paraphernalia of monarchy are to be stripped away. "Exalt that which is low, abase that which is high": cf. 17:24. **21:27.** "A ruin, a ruin, a ruin": this echoes the language of ch. 7 (cf. 7:2, 5, 26). "Such has never occurred": these words seem to mark the culmination of the judgement. The next words appear more positive, but they are cryptic: "Until he comes whose right it is; to him I will give it." There is no overtly royal or "messianic" language here, but in the context of judgement on the "prince," these words could imply a future, worthy royal recipient of divine favour and blessing (cf. Joyce 1998). Such an interpretation is the more likely in view of a possible allusion here to Gen 49:10b: "Until tribute comes to him; and the obedience of the peoples is his." (I noted the significant influence of Gen 49:8–12 within Ezek 19; see on 19:2.) It is interesting to observe a particular similarity to the Syriac of Gen 49:10, and also to note that in this context the Targum speaks of Gedaliah inheriting Zedekiah's crown, albeit only temporarily. Allen (1989) takes v. 13 (Heb. v. 18), interpreted as a reference to the doomed Davidic monarchy, as a transposed marginal gloss on this verse.

21:28–29 (Heb. vv. 33–34). An oracle against Ammon. "Thus says the Lord GOD concerning the Ammonites": cf. v. 20. This anticipates the oracles against the nations section (chs. 25–32), and specifically 25:1–7. "Concerning their reproach": this could be a euphemistic reference to the Ammonites' god Milkom, but it is more likely an allusion to the post-587 "taunt" referred to in 25:3, 6. "A sword! Drawn for slaughter": the language is close to vv. 9–10. "To consume": the Hebrew has Hiphil of *kwl*, to "contain," which makes poor sense. Block persuasively interprets as a by-form of *kālâ*, "to end" (Block 1997:693). **21:29.** "The vile, wicked ones…whose day has come, the time of final punishment": the language is close to that used of the prince of Israel in v. 25.

21:30–32 (Heb. vv. 35–37). Judgement upon Nebuchadrezzar. **21:30.** "Return it to its sheath!": contrast v. 5. This is a cue that the tables are to be turned on the king of Babylon here at the end of the chapter. "The place where you were created, in the land of your origin": the reference is to the return of Nebuchadrezzar to his homeland for judgement and punishment by YHWH. **21:32.** "You shall be remembered no more": the worst fate that could befall an emperor.

CHAPTER 22

22:2. "Will you judge, will you judge?": cf. 20:4. "The bloody city": Hebrew *ʿîr haddāmîm*; cf. 24:6, 9; used of Nineveh in Nah 3:1. The reference here is, of course, to Jerusalem. "Declare to it all its abominable deeds": cf. 16:2; 20:4. This chapter shares some features with chs. 16 and 20, but it is entirely a contemporary rebuke, without historical survey. **22:3.** "A city! Shedding blood within itself": a "bloody city" indeed. **22:4.** "You have become guilty by the blood that you have shed, and defiled by the idols that you have made": the nature of the "defiling" of v. 3 is here spelled out. "You have brought your day near, the appointed time of your years has come": this verse develops the eschatological theme of v. 3, "its time has come" (cf. 7:7, 10, 12). The chapter is marked by great intensity of expectation of the culmination of the judgement.

22:6. "The princes of Israel": the first of many categories of the nation's leaders who are condemned in this chapter (see vv. 25–29). Compare the critique of the "shepherds" in ch. 34. While princes (Heb. *nᵉśîʾîm*) could here refer to the nobility (cf. 7:27), it is more likely that the reference is specifically to the royal house (Duguid 1994:38–39; Mein 2001a:95). A list of sins is presented in vv. 6–12 (cf. vv. 25–29), with affinities to both the Decalogue and the Holiness Code. Similar material is to be found elsewhere in Ezekiel, notably at 18:5–18 and 33:15. The list features both cultic and ethical transgressions. **22:9.** "Slander to shed blood": the motif of "shedding blood" is recurrent in this chapter (cf. v. 12, "Take bribes to shed blood"; also vv. 3, 4, 6, 13, 27). **22:12.** "Make gain": Hebrew *tᵉḇaṣṣᵉʿî*; see Harland 2000 on the semantic range of the root *bṣʿ* (cf. also v. 27). **22:13.** "I strike my hands together": cf. 6:11; 21:14, 17. **22:15.** "I will scatter you among the nations and disperse you through the countries": explicit reference to exile as punishment; cf. 20:23. "I will purge your filthiness out of you": cf. vv. 17–22. **22:16.** "And I": so LXX, Syriac, Vulgate; MT implausibly has "you." "Shall be profaned through you in the sight of the nations": cf. 20:9, 14, 22; 36:20–22.

22:18. "The house of Israel has become dross to me": so wicked is the nation that it must be purged as in the smelting of metal; cf. Isa 1:22–25; Jer 6:27–30. This is one of a number of places where Ezekiel reveals technical knowledge, another good example being the detailed awareness both of shipcraft and of Tyrian trade exhibited in ch. 27. On metals and their symbolism in the Hebrew Bible, see

Singer 1980. "Silver" appears at the end of the verse in Hebrew; cf. v. 20. **22:19.** "I will gather you into the midst of Jerusalem...as one gathers...into a smelter": cf. the allegorical uses of "pot" language in 11:1–13 and 24:1–14. **22:20.** "In my anger and in my wrath": the divine wrath (here and v. 22, Heb. *ḥēmâ*) is a prominent theme. On 22:20, see further Allen 1986. **22:21.** "The fire of my wrath": this phrase fits the smelting image particularly well. The Hebrew word used for "wrath" here and in v. 31 is a different one (*ʿeb̲râ*). **22:22.** "As silver is melted in a smelter, so you shall be melted in it": characteristic repetition.

22:23–31. In this section, various categories of leader are condemned, in the manner of the reference to "princes" in v. 6. **22:24.** "You are a land that is not cleansed": the image has changed from the "city." "In the day of indignation": see on 7:7. **22:25.** "Its princes": so LXX; Hebrew has "A conspiracy of its prophets." Prophets are dealt with later in this particular passage (v. 28) and, on the whole, the behaviour condemned here seems to cohere better with a reference to "princes." Verses 25–29 list a sequence of sins (see on vv. 6–12); these verses share much with Zeph 3:3–4. **22:26.** "Its priests": Duguid argues that among the leaders of Israel the priests are criticized relatively leniently in Ezekiel (Duguid 1994:72–75). "Have done violence to my teaching": Harland (1997) explores the nature of the violence referred to in this chapter. "Profaned my holy things...no distinction between the holy and the common...the unclean and the clean": precisely the matters priests should have attended to. **22:27.** "Its officials": Hebrew *śārîm*; a reference to the lay leadership, neither royal nor priestly (cf. Duguid 1994:118–19). "Get dishonest gain": Hebrew *bᵉṣōaʿ bāṣaʿ*; see Harland 2000 on *bṣʿ* (cf. also v. 12). **22:28.** "Its prophets": see on v. 25. This reference seems dependent on 13:1–16. "Whitewash": Hebrew *tāp̄ēl*. See on 13:10. "Seeing false visions and divining lies": cf. 13:6–9; 21:29 (Heb. v. 34). "When the LORD has not spoken": cf. 13:6–7; Jer 23:21. **22:29.** "The people of the land": Hebrew *ʿam hāʾāreṣ*. A much-debated phrase that has a range of senses in Hebrew literature. Here, as most commonly in Ezekiel (e.g. 7:27), it seems to refer to a group of powerful figures in Jerusalem, with close ties to the Davidic house (Duguid 1994:119–21); this would cohere with the fact that the objects of their actions here include the "poor and needy" and the "alien." **22:30.** "I sought for anyone among them who would repair the wall and stand in the breach before me on behalf of the land, so that I would not destroy it": cf. 13:5; Jer 5:1. "But I found no one": this is very telling, so close to the culmination of the judgement. At 9:11 the reader was left to wonder whether the man clothed in linen had found any who sighed and groaned over all the abominations committed in Jerusalem. Here all doubt is removed. **22:31.** "Therefore I have poured out my indignation": cf. v. 24. "I have returned their conduct upon their heads": the familiar "just deserts" theme. Verse 31 appears to describe the judgement as accomplished, as though viewed from a post-587 perspective. If so, this is best understood as a proleptic anticipation of the end, in keeping with the eschatological tone of parts of the chapter (especially vv. 3–4).

CHAPTER 23

The third and last of the extended historical surveys of the book is found here, the others being found in chs. 16 and 20. Like ch. 16, it is presented through female personification. (On sexual and marital metaphors in the Prophets, see Moughtin-Mumby 2008). This chapter seems to lack a clear-cut signal (in the manner of 16:44 and 20:30) that it coheres with ch. 18 in judging the present generation for its own sins alone (albeit following the pattern established by the ancestors). Nonetheless, given the cumulative evidence for such an understanding of Ezekiel, there is no cause to question that this chapter too proceeds on that basis. There can also be no reasonable doubt that this chapter goes back to Ezekiel himself. (Well over half of the primary verses acknowledged by Garscha [1974] are found here, in vv. 2–25.)

Like ch. 16, this chapter features very explicit sexual language, which proved controversial in some rabbinic quarters. The same and related features have been subjected to modern feminist criticism, which has highlighted a discourse of gratuitous titillation (e.g. vv. 3, 20), humiliation and abusive violence (e.g. vv. 10, 25), with the female figures presented as possessed objects (e.g. vv. 4, 5) dominated by their own insatiable sexual appetites (e.g. vv. 7, 11). Van Dijk-Hemmes (1993:169) referred to the "androcentric-pornographic character of this metaphorical language." (See also Exum 1995, 1996; Brenner 1996; Shields 1998b, 2001a.) In a sympathetic response to feminist critiques of this chapter, Patton argues that the male audience, having been subjected to the emasculating experience of defeat and exile, is called upon to identify with Oholah and Oholibah (Patton 2000a:237–38). For a more conservative reaction, see Greenberg 1997:493–94.

23:2. "There were two women, the daughters of one mother": cf. 16:3, 44. **23:3.** "They played the whore in Egypt": as in 20:7–8, where (unlike in the Pentateuchal narratives) Israel sins even in Egypt. Egypt is a recurrent theme in this chapter: cf. vv. 8, 19, 21, 27. **23:4.** "Oholah" (Heb. *ʾohºlâ*, "her [own] tent") was the name of the elder (or bigger) sister, representing Samaria, and "Oholibah" (Heb. *ʾohºlîḇâ*, "my tent [is] in her") the name of the younger (or smaller), standing for Jerusalem (Galambush 1992:63–64, 72–78, 109–24). The names probably allude to the illegitimate and legitimate sanctuaries of the north and south respectively. On the surprising designation of Samaria as the elder sister, see on 16:46. "They became mine": YHWH marries the two. Jacob married two sisters (Gen 29), whereas Lev 18:18 forbids this. The development of Ezekiel's allegory seems to override priestly scruple here.

23:5. "Oholah played the whore while she was mine": as well as previously, it seems (cf. v. 3; contrast ch. 16, where there is an initial period before the foundling Jerusalem goes astray). **23:7.** "She bestowed her favours…she defiled herself": she takes the initiative; cf. 16:15. **23:9.** "Therefore": introducing the judgement upon Oholah. "I delivered her into the hands of her lovers": poetic justice (cf. Barton 1979); Samaria fell to the Assyrians in 721 B.C.E. (2 Kgs 17). **23:10.** "These uncovered her nakedness": as in ch. 16, nakedness features in this chapter both as culpable behaviour (v. 18; cf. 16:36) and, as here, as fitting punishment (cf. 16:37). "A byword": Hebrew *šēm*, "a name."

23:11. "Her sister Oholibah saw this": Jerusalem copied Samaria's behaviour, rather than learning from her fate. "She was more corrupt": as in the comparison motif of 16:47; cf. also 5:6; Jer 3:11. **23:12.** "She lusted after the Assyrians": a sequence of Judahite kings paid tribute to Assyria, including Ahaz, who is presented as adopting Assyrian cult practices (2 Kgs 16). **23:14.** "The Chaldeans": the imperial power that would usurp Assyria's dominant position. **23:15**. "A picture of Babylonians whose native land was Chaldea": this may be an explanatory gloss. **23:16.** "Sent messengers to them": cf. v. 40; like her sister, she takes the initiative. It is interesting to contrast with this condemnation of dealings with the Babylonians the critique of Zedekiah's disloyalty to the Babylonian king in 17:16–19. **23:17.** "They defiled her…she defiled herself": through wordplay on the Hebrew root *ṭmʾ*, "defile," Oholibah is portrayed as both victim and culprit. "She turned from them in disgust": the motif is found also in vv. 22, 28; and strikingly in v. 18, where it is YHWH himself who turns in disgust. **23:20.** "Whose members were like those of donkeys, and whose emission was like that of stallions": a dramatic symbolization of the Egyptians' reputation for lewdness (cf. 16:26). Egypt was also noted for its horses (cf. Deut 17:16; 1 Kgs 10:28), and equines were thought of as lascivious (cf. Jer 5:8); so we have here a cluster of interrelated ideas.

23:22. "Therefore, O Oholibah": addressed for the first time. The focus of the judgement is naturally on Jerusalem, the passage relating to Samaria having served as background to this (though note the reappearance of Oholah by name in v. 36). "I will rouse against you your lovers": again, poetic justice. **23:23.** "Pekod and Shoa and Koa": Aramaean mercenaries. "And all the Assyrians": either another reference to mercenaries working for the Babylonians or to be explained as stylized rhetoric. **23:24.** "The north": so LXX; this would make sense as the direction of an invasion and also possibly in terms of its mythological associations (cf. on 1:4). However, the MT reads *hōṣen*, an obscure *hapax legomenon*. Following the Targum, it is best taken as a heading, "weapons" or "arms," for the list that follows (so Block 1997:750–51; Greenberg 1997:481). Several features of the language and imagery of vv. 22–24 remind one of the Gog of Magog material in chs. 38–39. "They shall judge you according to their ordinances": Jerusalem will be treated according to the standards of the nations, a frightening prospect, as is confirmed by the details that follow in vv. 25–26.

23:25. "Indignation": Hebrew *qinʾâ*, "jealousy," different from the word (Heb. *zaʿam*) translated "indignation" at 22:24, 31. "In order that they": the purpose of YHWH and the actions of his agents are closely aligned (cf. Isa 10:5). "Your survivors": Hebrew *ʾaḥ^a^rîṯ*, "posterity." They escape only to fall by the sword or be devoured by fire. **23:28.** "I will deliver you into the hands of those whom you hate": paradoxically, those who had been her lovers, from whom she had turned in disgust. **23:31.** "You have gone the way of your sister": cf. v. 13. "Therefore I will give her cup into your hand": the recompense appropriate to her similar actions. The "cup" (Heb. *kôs*) of judgement and punishment is a widespread motif (cf. Isa 51:17–23; Jer 25:15–29; Hab 2:15–17; see Seidl 2001). **23:33.** "The cup of your sister Samaria": it is perhaps surprising that the name "Oholah" is not used here. Verses 32–34 manifest some features of poetry and could be a quotation from an earlier source. If this were so, the use of "Samaria" here would be less surprising. **23:34.** "Gnaw its sherds": this sounds like obsessive masochistic behaviour; one is reminded of the perverse wish to be punished articulated by Ezekiel's audience in the paradoxical words of 18:19. "Tear out your breasts": a further indication of desperate self-harming. Reference to the breasts takes us back to the very of start of the story (v. 3). This observation and also the extreme nature of the images of this verse tip the balance of judgement against the hypothesis that vv. 32–34 quotes a pre-existing poem. **23:35.** "Because you have forgotten me and cast me behind your back": the complaint of the spurned husband, YHWH. "Therefore": as before, introducing judgement; cf. vv. 9, 22, 31.

23:36. "Will you judge?…then declare to them their abominable deeds": the renewed reference to Oholah, not in focus since v. 10 (cf. vv. 31–33), indicates that this verse represents the beginning of a summation of the judgement. Affinities with 22:2 (cf. 20:4), however, suggest an address to Jerusalem as its fall looms. In such a context it is perhaps surprising that, although the northern kingdom is long gone, reference is made here to Oholah. This could be driven by the literary imperative to see through the allegory of the two sisters, or it could have in view the ongoing population in the north that would become the Samaritan community. **23:37.** "Offered up to them for food the children whom they had borne to me": see on 20:26; cf. 16:20–21. **23:38.** "Moreover this they have done to me": signals the weightiness of the charge that is about to be made. "They have defiled my sanctuary": cf. ch. 8. **23:39.** "On the same day they came into my sanctuary to profane it": reminiscent of the eighth-century prophetic polemic against the juxtaposition of social and cultic sin (e.g. Isa 1:12–17).

23:40. "They even sent for men to come from far away": cf. v. 16. **23:41.** "My incense and my oil": cf. 16:18, and the emphasis there on the fact that YHWH is the source of the precious things that are being misused. **23:42.** This elaboration of the scene of debauchery is a respect in which at this late point in the chapter the clarity of the original allegory is becoming somewhat diffuse; but there are no conclusive grounds for judging this material secondary. **23:43–44.** "She is worn out with adulteries, but they carry on their sexual acts with her": she is now passively abused; none the less, Oholah and Oholibah are still judged "wanton women." **23:45.** "Righteous judges shall declare them guilty": male judges, of course; in fact, the Hebrew reads *ʾănāšîm*, "men," rather than "judges." Van Dijk-Hemmes (1993:169) observes that this leaves the way open for many readers to identify with the righteous judges rather than with the sisters who actually represent the Hebrew kingdoms. Similarly, the words of the previous verse, "For they have gone in to her, as one goes in to a whore," might well seduce male readers into an identification that would undermine the purpose of the allegory and mark a further stage in its disintegration.

23:46. "Bring up an assembly against them": initially this sounds like a judicial gathering, but the brutality of the following words, "make them an object of terror and of plunder," takes us beyond the language of legal process. **23:47.** "The assembly shall stone them": cf. 16:40; Lev 20:10; Deut 22:21, 24. "They shall kill their sons and their daughters, and burn up their houses": reminiscent of the communal punishment of Achan, with his family, tent and all his belongings, in Josh 7:24–26. **23:48.** "Thus will I put an end to lewdness in the land, so that all women may take warning and not commit lewdness as you have done": here the metaphorical language breaks down completely, because instead of the Hebrew kingdoms (led, of course, by men) being judged under the guise of two sisters, the polemic is now addressed to actual women. Van Dijk-Hemmes (1993:169) described this as a case of reader response incorporated into the text.

CHAPTER 24

The long section of the book constituted by chs. 4–24 here reaches its climax. On ch. 24 as a whole, see Fuhs 1986b.

24:1. "In the ninth year, in the tenth month, on the tenth day of the month": 15th January 588. The same date is given for the start of the siege in 2 Kgs 25:1 and Jer 52:4, though in those verses the date is designated in relation to the length of Zedekiah's reign, whereas Ezekiel's dates are presented in terms of the length of Jehoiachin's exile (cf. 1:2; cf. 33:21). **24:2.** "Write down the name of this day": the act of writing underlines the importance of this and also provides a witness for the future (cf. Isa 30:8). "This very day": twice this phrase underscores "this day" (cf. vv. 26–27). Ezekiel is presented as learning this information by divine revelation, whereas news of the fall of the city will reach him through the report of a refugee (v. 26; 33:21). The siege would last for over a year and a half.

24:3–14. The Allegory of the Pot. For more detailed studies, see Kelso 1945; Allen 1987; Block 1991. **24:3.** "Utter an allegory": Hebrew *mᵉšōl māšāl*; as we have seen, Ezekiel is a "maker of allegories" (Heb. *mᵉmaššēl mᵉšālîm*, 20:49 [Heb. 21:5]). "The rebellious house": see on 2:3, 5. A "pot" allegory featured earlier, in 11:2–12; the two passages employ the same Hebrew word for "pot," *sîr*. In ch. 11, the "pot" represents the city, within which the leaders of Jerusalem imagine themselves secure; they will "be taken out of it" and the city will not provide them with the security they seek (11:7). The present passage falls into two parts, vv. 3–5 and 6–14. Verses 3–5 comprise mainly a staccato series of commands, giving instructions to "set on the pot" (v. 3) and "put in it the pieces" (v. 4). **24:5.** "Take the choicest one of the flock": representing the elite among those left in Jerusalem in 597. "Logs": Hebrew has *ʿᵃṣāmîm*, "bones," but may be amended in the light of v. 10 (MT *ʿēṣîm*, "logs") and also LXX. "Boil its pieces": MT has "boil its boilings," which gives tolerable sense. "Seethe…its bones": MT has "its bones seethe," and here too there is no need to amend. Block takes vv. 3–5 positively, the "pot" providing security for those within it as in ch.11, and writes that a "Jerusalem audience would have undoubtedly received this song with great enthusiasm and interpreted it positively" (Block 1997:776); he sees these words as rejected in vv. 6–14, in the manner of a "disputation speech." However, vv. 3–5 could equally well be read as an image of judgement by boiling and cooking; all, including the good and indeed the "choicest" (vv. 4–5), will be included (cf. 21:3–4 [Heb. vv. 8–9]). Given the ambiguity of these verses in this regard, they are probably best understood as setting the scene for the judgement of vv. 6–14, introduced unmistakably with the word "therefore" (Heb. *lāḵēn*) in v. 6.

24:6. "Woe to the bloody city": Hebrew *ʿîr haddāmîm*; cf. v. 9 and also 22:2, where the same phrase is used. The bloody city is equated with "the pot whose rust is in it," and the passage develops the image of the burning out of rust, representing "lewdness" and "filth" (v. 13). The instruction is given to "empty it piece by piece." "Making no choice at all": Hebrew reads *lōʾ-nāp̄al ʿālêhā gôrāl*, "No lot has fallen on it"; this could be taken to mean (as in NRSV) that the pieces will be removed indiscriminately, but it is better understood to mean "its luck has run out." **24:7.** "For the blood she shed is inside it": the contents of the pot are ritually unclean. The reference to bloodshed also suggests some similarity with ch. 11, where, in a development of that "pot" metaphor, the prophet contends that the leaders are cooking their victims within the "pot" that is the city (11:7). "She placed it on a bare rock": this reference to "bare rock" must be a metaphorical usage, conditioned by the contrast with blood properly poured out on the ground and covered with earth, as prescribed in the Holiness Code, at Lev 17:10–16 (cf. Deut 12:16, 24; 15:23). The image conveys flagrant disregard for propriety. The phrase "bare rock" is used of Tyre in 26:4, 14; this forms part of the case made by Davis for the paralleling of fates of Jerusalem and Tyre and the other nations (Davis 1999:227). **24:8.** "To rouse my wrath, to take vengeance": in the light of what follows, YHWH seems to be the subject of the verbs here. "I have placed the blood she shed on a bare rock, so that it may not be covered": YHWH appropriates the sinful action as part of his punishment of the city's crimes; in this respect this verse is strangely reminiscent of 20:25–26.

24:9. "Therefore": cf. v. 6; with this second "therefore" the judgement is escalated. "Woe to the bloody city!": cf. v. 6; 22:2. **24:10.** "Heap up the logs, kindle the fire…": cf. the staccato series of commands of vv. 3–5. This reinforces the sense of the unity of passage as a whole (vv. 3–14), within which vv. 3–5 set the scene for vv. 6–14. **24:11.** "Stand it empty upon the coals, so that it may become hot…its rust be consumed": cf. the smelting image of 22:17–22. **24:12.** "In vain I have wearied myself": the meaning of the Hebrew is uncertain; dittography of the final words of v. 11 may have occurred. "To the fire with its rust": the point is probably that further purging is necessary, because "its thick rust does not depart." **24:13.** "You shall not again be cleansed until I have satisfied my fury upon you": there will no resolution before the definitive judgement comes. **24:14.** "The time is coming": reminiscent of the eschatological urgency of 7:2–4; in this chapter we have learned that the final act, the siege of Jerusalem, is now under way. "I will not spare… According to your ways and your doings I will judge you": this language is typical of the sustained message of judgement found in chs. 4–24.

24:15–24. Oracle on the death of Ezekiel's wife. On these verses, see Odell 2000. **24:16.** "I am about to take away from you the delight of your eyes": v. 18

confirms that the reference is to the death of the prophet's wife; vv. 15–18 should be read as focusing exclusively on this loss, without yet introducing any other theme. "With one blow": Hebrew *b^e^maggēpâ*; AV reads "with a stroke." The phrase conveys divine agency and should not be made the basis for any speculation about the medical cause of death. "Yet you shall not mourn or weep": Ezekiel is denied the customary rites of mourning. **24:17.** "Sigh, but not aloud...": allusions to various mourning rituals may be found in, for example, Jer 16:5–9; Mic 1:8 (cf. Bloch-Smith 1992 on Judahite burial practices). "Eat the bread of mourners": MT, here and at v. 22, has *leḥem ʾ^a^nāšîm*, "the bread of men," which makes poor sense in this context. NRSV plausibly amends *ʾ^a^nāšîm*, "men," to *ʾônîm*, "mourners" (cf. Targum and Vulgate). **24:18.** "So I spoke to the people in the morning": presumably reporting this oracle. "And at evening my wife died": she is given no name. "And on the next morning I did as I was commanded": in other words, he abstained from the standard mourning rituals.

This episode affords a rare glimpse into the personal life of Ezekiel, for we learn only here that Ezekiel was married. Marriage was overwhelmingly the norm in Judahite society. Jeremiah is told, "You shall not take a wife, nor shall you have sons or daughters in this place," but this illustrates the extremity of the times (Jer 16:2); even the Rechabites, the ascetical group whose faithfulness Jeremiah commends in 35:18–19, practised marriage. Among other prophets, Hosea (1:2–3) and Isaiah (8:3) are reported to have been married (cf. 2 Kgs 4:1). Nothing is known of Ezekiel's wife, though Stiebert explores the theme through both historical enquiry and imagination (Stiebert 2005). It is increasingly recognized that the books of the prophets are by no means straightforward reports by the prophets of their personal experiences, and we should not be naïve about recovering the Ezekiel of history. Ezekiel was a historical person but he is also a literary character within a book (cf. de Moor 2001). Zimmerli acknowledged that "Difficulties are just as much present in the symbolic actions of Ezekiel as they are in the reconstruction of the 'biography' of Hosea in the history of his marriage" (Zimmerli 1979a:18), while Herrmann wrote that "Ezekiel is as near and as far from us in his book as is the historical Jesus in the gospel of John" (Herrmann 1965:281–82). Halperin, in his psychoanalytical study of Ezekiel, postulates a person dominated by a pathological dread of female sexuality, and sees this manifested in Ezekiel's failure to mourn his wife's death: "His inability to mourn her death points to some paralyzing ambivalence... Ezekiel's guilt over his wife's death will be intelligible only if we suppose that he had unconsciously wished for it" (Halperin 1993:180–81). However, the scant personal details found in this ancient text are an insufficient basis for a project as bold as psychoanalysis (cf. Joyce 1995b). We must not, like Halperin, fail to engage with the theology of this image. It is vital to see that this episode is recounted precisely because of the theological point that is to be made here, as is spelled in the verses that follow.

24:19. Then the people said to me, "Will you not tell us what these things mean for us...?": cf. 12:9. **24:21.** "Thus says the Lord GOD: 'I will profane my sanctuary'": the fall of the Jerusalem temple to the Babylonians is described as YHWH's act of defiling (Heb. root *ḥll*) his own "sanctuary" or "holy place" (Heb. *miqdāš*). This is a profoundly paradoxical statement that nonetheless coheres with the narrative of the departure of the divine glory in chs. 10–11. Only now is the analogy with the death of the prophet's wife articulated explicitly. Note that after the reference to "my sanctuary," the subsequent descriptions of the temple are couched in terms of "your" (plural), rather than "my." It is as though YHWH is already detached from the sanctuary that means so much to the Judahites. We have learned that he is to become a "sanctuary (albeit in small measure)" (Heb. *miqdāš meʿaṭ*) to the exiles (11:16). "The delight of your eyes" (Heb. *maḥmaḏ ʿênêḵem*): a direct parallel with the phrase of v. 16, except that now the possessive suffix is plural, referring to the people of Israel. "And your sons and your daughters whom you left behind": those offspring who remained in Jerusalem in 597. This is a rare reminder of the intimate familial and social links between the exiles and those still in Jerusalem; compare the polarized contrast between the two communities evidenced in material such as 11:14–21 and 33:23–29 (cf. Rom-Shiloni 2005b). **24:22.** "And you shall do as I have done": the exiles are not to mourn for the fall of the city (cf. vv. 16, 24). "The bread of mourners": see on v. 17. **24:23.** "Your turbans shall be on your…": the phrases of v. 17 are echoed. "You shall pine away in your iniquities and groan to one another": like the sighing "but not aloud" of v. 17; compare also the motif of self-loathing (e.g. 6:9). **24:24.** "Ezekiel": one of only two references to the prophet's personal name, the other being at the start of the book, at 1:3. This *inclusio* may be further evidence of the importance of the present passage within the book as a whole, closing the major section that concludes with ch. 24. "A sign": Hebrew *môp̄ēṯ*; cf. v. 27; and see on 4:3. Hebrew *môp̄ēṯ* is used also at 12:6, 11, where Ezekiel performs a comparable sign-action representing the deportation of those still in Jerusalem. It is appropriate, given all the sign-actions that Ezekiel himself performs, that he himself should be said to be a "sign." "You shall do just as he has done": cf. Ezekiel's command in v. 22. "When this comes, then you shall know that I am the Lord GOD": these words constitute another link between chs. 24 and 33, for ch. 33 ends with words that pick up the role of Ezekiel as a "sign": "When this comes—and come it will!—then they shall know that a prophet has been among them" (33:33).

What is the theme of non-mourning about? First, it is important that the command not to mourn is bad news rather than good. Te Stroete argued that the exiles are not to mourn "because they know that a new era is dawning through the catastrophe. The messenger of doom who has managed to escape from the city turns into a messenger of joy who announces a new season" (te Stroete 1977). But this interpretation is mistaken, not least in that it fails to acknowledge the valuable and therapeutic nature of appropriate mourning. The non-mourning motif rather performs two functions. First, it conveys that the punishment is fully warranted and that the nation deserves no sympathy, much as Jeremiah is instructed not to mourn the many who are to die in the judgement (Jer 16:5–8). And second, the refusal to allow proper mourning compounds the punishment of sin, making the trauma of the end of the nation even harder to bear.

This interpretation is presented on the understanding that this chapter refers to mourning after death. But attention should be given to a recent alternative interpretation of the whole passage. Lipton (2006) notes striking parallels to 2 Sam 12:13–23, where the mourning described is not posthumous but rather petitionary mourning, in which rituals are undertaken before a death or disaster in the hope of averting it (cf. Olyan 2004:62–96). Lipton interprets 24:15–24 as a divine attempt to block prophetic intercession: the deity is determined to destroy the temple and prohibits Ezekiel and, by extension, Israel, from undertaking petitionary mourning rituals that might have persuaded him to change his mind. One attraction of this challenging suggestion is that it would cohere with Wilson's interpretation of the dumbness motif as amounting to a denial to Ezekiel of the role of intercessor (see on 3:26–27).

24:25. "On the day when I take from them their stronghold, their joy and glory, the delight of their eyes and their heart's affection": cf. vv. 16 and 21. The phrase "the delight of their eyes" (with only the possessive suffix varying) has now occurred three times, like a refrain through the chapter (vv. 16, 21, 25). Poignantly, the positive language of this verse reminds one of the effusive devotion of the Psalms of Zion (e.g. Ps 48:2 [Heb. v. 3]). Note that here the reference is to the loss of "their," and not "your," let alone "my," special things; it is as though the loss is now even further distanced from YHWH himself. "And also": the Hebrew lacks "and also" before the reference to sons and daughters (unlike in v. 21, where there is a conjunction), but there is no reason to think that this whole verse should therefore be referred exclusively to the loss of sons and daughters. **24:26.** "On that day": cf. v. 25; repeated in v. 27 for further emphasis (cf. v. 2). In fact, the messenger arrives from Jerusalem some months later than the actual fall of the city; see on 33:21–22. The imminence of the end is a theme at the start, middle and end of this chapter (vv. 1–2, 14, 25–27). "One who has escaped": Hebrew *happālîṭ*, "the fugitive." "To report to you the news": Hebrew *lᵉhašmāʿûṯ ʾoznāyim*, literally, "to cause the ears to hear"; cf. 21:7 (Heb. v. 12). **24:27.** "On that day your mouth shall be opened to the one who has escaped": on the dumbness motif, see on 3:26–27 (and also Glazov 2001:220–74). "And you shall speak and no longer be silent": cf. 33:22. "So you shall be a sign to them": as in v. 24. "And they shall know that I am the LORD": it is appropriate that the "sign" should be related to the "Recognition Formula" (cf. v. 24), and especially so as the long major section comprising chs. 4–24 draws to a close.

CHAPTER 25

Oracles addressed to nations other than Israel and Judah are a recurrent feature of the prophetic literature (e.g. Isa 13–23; Jer 46–51; Amos 1–2). Within Ezekiel, ch. 25 contains short oracles against four small neighbouring nations (Ammon, Moab, Edom and Philistia), and then the following chapters feature two unusually extended sequences, chs. 26–28 (against Tyre) and chs. 29–32 (against Egypt). Chapters 35–36 return to the theme of Edom, while chs. 38–39 address the mysterious Gog of Magog.

How is the role of the nations in Ezekiel to be viewed? Reventlow (1959) attempted to show that the "I am YHWH" formula is to be associated with a hope that the nations will turn to YHWH. But there is no clear evidence of this. There are no cases of this "Recognition Formula" used in connection with the deliverance of the nations and in the very few cases where it is said that the nations will know YHWH when he delivers Israel there is no indication of a positive interest in the nations for their own sake. Another important formula that Reventlow considered in this connection was the phrase "in the sight of the nations" or "in their sight" (together with the closely related expressions "among the nations" and "among them"). Characteristically, these phrases are used of YHWH himself as witnessed by the nations; some texts speak of the profanation of the divine name in the sight of the nations (20:9, 14, 22), while others look forward to his self-vindication in their sight (36:23). Contrary to Reventlow, reference to the nations in these cases too is very bare and gives no indication of any positive interest in their response for its own sake. The concern is not with the nations knowing or witnessing YHWH so much as with YHWH being known and witnessed. In short, the usage of Ezekiel in this area lends no support to the view that there is an expectation that the nations will turn in allegiance to the God of Israel; rather, reference to the nations seems to be a mere backdrop to the central concern of the promised vindication of YHWH. (For further discussion, see Wong 2003:231.)

How, then, should we understand the oracles against the nations in Ezekiel? Brownlee (1983) argued that Ezekiel visited all the places he condemned, but this is unnecessary (just as ch. 8 or ch. 12 do not require Ezekiel to have been in Jerusalem after 597 B.C.E.). Even if it were thought necessary for him to confront the nations he addresses face-to-face, Ezekiel may not have needed to travel, for some at least of the nations referred to would have been represented in the self-contained ghettos of deportees in Babylonia. Moreover, there is reason to believe that Ezekiel's concern is not as exclusively focused on the nations addressed as might at first seem. It is noteworthy that Babylon, the great enemy of Israel in the age of Ezekiel, is not found among his oracles (whereas Babylon is treated at length in Jer 50–51, and even in Isa 13–14). Some have interpreted "Magog" in chs. 38–39 as a cryptic reference to Babylon, but this is unlikely. Notwithstanding Babylon's role as instrument of YHWH's purposes, the absence of an oracle against this nation is contrary to what might be expected if the focus were on the nations themselves, and may give a clue as to the primary purpose of these oracles in Ezekiel. Davis has pointed out that Tyre and Egypt were at the time allies rather than enemies of Israel and has argued persuasively that the extensive oracles against them are presented as object lessons to Judah: "In confronting the nationalistic absolutism of the foreign nations, Ezekiel is obliquely challenging Israelite absolutism" (Davis 1999:226–27). Davis highlights the "pivotal function that the oracles against the nations serve in Ezekiel, a function to which their present placement contributes," arguing that "the oracles against the nations, dated to the year of Jerusalem's fall, mark the transition out of Israel's own idolatrous past into a possible future." She continues: "Rendering an accurate judgement on the false perception of reality embedded in foreign mythologies is the necessary prerequisite for the renewal of Israel's life (ch. 37) under the dominion of its God" (Davis 1999:227–28).

Many foreign nation oracles in the Hebrew Bible are closely related to the prospect of deliverance for the people of YHWH, with Israel's fortunes rising as those of the nations decline, rather in the manner of a "seesaw" or "teeter-totter" (e.g. Isa 14:1–23; Jer 50:33–34). But this does not characterize Ezekiel, at least not before chs. 35–36. The oracles of ch. 25 condemn the minor nations for speaking of and acting towards the people of YHWH inappropriately and v. 14 refers to punishment of Edom through the agency of Israel, but there is no reference to deliverance for Israel. Within the Tyre and Egypt sections, there are just two cases of positive reference to Israel's future: 28:24–26 is a section at the end of the Tyre cycle promising restoration for Israel, while 29:21 is a brief messianic oracle in the midst of the Egypt sequence; both seem to be additions in their present context, not integrated with the Tyre or Egypt material. It is not until chs. 35–36 that we find an integrated combination of condemnation of foreigners with promises to Israel. I shall argue later that 33:1–20 recapitulates themes of chs. 1–24, bringing the pre-587 phase of Ezekiel's ministry to a climax before the fall of the final blow is reported in 33:21–22. This coheres with the spotlight remaining on the challenge to Israel through the foreign nations section of chs. 25–32. Moreover, it is of interest that whereas in some other prophetic collections (notably Isa 13–23 and Jer 46–51) there is reason to believe that many oracles may be secondary, the foreign nations oracles in Ezekiel, closely related to the prophet's first task of announcing divine judgement on his own people, seem for the most part to be primary in provenance.

The rapid survey of minor neighbouring nations in ch. 25 is reminiscent of Amos 1–2; the four territories treated here appear in that longer sequence. Moreover, if Davis is right in arguing that Ezekiel's Tyre and Egypt oracles obliquely challenge Israel, then this feature too would be to some extent analogous with Amos 1–2, where the sequence leads up to the judgement on Israel in 2:6–8. The oracles of Ezek 25 share some features with each other, including the "because…therefore" pattern, common in judgement oracles; the placing of quotations on the lips of interlocutors, one of Ezekiel's favourite techniques (vv. 3 and 8); and the "Recognition Formula" (vv. 5, 7, 11, 17; cf. 14). The latter is noteworthy in that it has been argued that the "Recognition Formula" originated in the context of foreign nation oracles (cf. Strong 1995).

25:1–7. The oracle against Ammon is much the longest in the chapter, and the only one presented in second-person address to the nation. Compare the brief Ammon oracle in 21:28–29 (Heb. vv. 33–34). **25:2.** "Set your face": see on 4:3. "The Ammonites": a Semitic people, living to the east of the river Jordan. According to Gen 19:36–38, the Ammonites were descended from Lot, Abraham's nephew. **25:3.** "Aha!": the briefest quotation in Ezekiel (cf. 26:2; 36:2). "Over my sanctuary when it was profaned": it is as though it is YHWH's reputation that is at stake (cf. 36:20). "The land of Israel…the house of Judah": the territory of Judah and the Davidic dynasty. "When it went into exile": gloating over the fate of Judah (cf. v. 6) is more commonly associated with the particularly hated Edomites (see on v. 12), though Jer 49:1 suggests that Ammonites seized Israelite territory. **25:4.** "The people of the east": probably refers to desert tribes (cf. Isa 11:14), to which Ammon was particularly vulnerable. **25:5.** "Rabbah": the Ammonites' capital, later Philadelphia, one of the Decapolis cities; it was on the site of modern Amman, which reflects the name of Ammon. **25:7.** "I will destroy you": although the initial reference to the stealing of fruit and milk sounded tame (v. 4), complete obliteration is now threatened.

25:8–11: The oracle against Moab, another Semitic people, living to the east of the Dead Sea. According to Gen 19:36–38, the Moabites were descended from Lot, Abraham's nephew. This and the following oracles in this chapter are couched in the third person. **25:8.** "Because Moab": so LXX and Old Latin; MT has also "and Seir"; this is surprising, since Seir is more commonly associated with Edom; but perceptions of the location of Seir may have varied (see on 35:2). "The house of Judah is like all the other nations": this amounts to an insult to YHWH (cf. 36:20). **25:9.** "From the towns": MT has "from the towns from its towns," which perhaps conveys the extent of the losses by repetition. **25:10.** "The people of the east": again desert tribes, as in v. 4. "Thus Ammon shall be remembered no more among the nations": it is surprising that Ammon, already treated at length, comes in again; this may represent a redactional summary of vv. 1–11.

25:12–14. The oracle against Edom, a further Semitic people, living to the south-east of Judah, a traditional enemy generally perceived as the descendents of Jacob's brother Esau (though this association should not always be assumed;

cf. Davies 1979:99). Chapters 35–36 return to the theme of Edom. **25:12.** "Because Edom acted revengefully against the house of Judah": in line with Edom's general reputation for treachery at the time of Judah's greatest need, when conquered by the Babylonians; cf. Obad vv. 12–15; Ps 137:7; Lam 4:21–22. Bartlett has argued that the portrait of treachery painted by such texts is much exaggerated (Bartlett 1982; 1989:150), a case countered to some degree by Dicou (1994:174, 182). Assis (2006) suggests that relations between Edom and Israel were influenced by ideological and theological factors relating to the struggle between their forefathers, Esau and Jacob (Gen 25–28; 32–33). Edom's aspiration to occupy areas in Israel may have been interpreted as a wish to restore the election and the birthright to Esau. According to Assis, the anti-Edomite oracles were meant to reassure the Judahites that they are still the chosen people and that the sins of Edom will not remain unpunished. **25:13.** "From Teman even to Dedan": though even Ezekiel's geography may be somewhat vague here, this rhetorical phrase means "all Edom, from south to north, and beyond." **25:14.** "I will lay my vengeance": picks up and reverses the motif of vengeance of v. 12. "Upon Edom by the hand of my people Israel": Israel is to act as YHWH's instrument in punishing Edom. No positive reference to Israel's restoration is made, though the phrase "my people" may hint at a better future. "According to my anger and according to my wrath": language often used against Israel (e.g. 5:13; 22:21).

25:15–17. The oracle against the Philistines, an uncircumcised, non-Semitic people, living on the Mediterranean coast to the south-west, having migrated from Europe (cf. Gen 10:14). **25:15.** "With unending hostilities": this had certainly been a long-standing enmity (cf. Judg 3:31; 13:1). **25:16.** "The Cherethites": associated elsewhere with the Philistines (e.g. Zeph 2:5), and possibly originally Cretan. With the Pelethites, they are often mentioned in the context of David's entourage, presumably as mercenaries (e.g. 2 Sam 8:18). **25:17.** "I will execute great vengeance on them with wrathful punishments. Then they shall know that I am the LORD, when I lay my vengeance on them": an unusual twist to the "Recognition Formula," to end the chapter and indeed to summarize the whole. This grim verse provided the recurrent refrain of Quentin Tarantino's 1994 film *Pulp Fiction*.

Chapter 26

Three chapters (26:1–28:19) are devoted to a series of oracles against Tyre, the thriving Phoenician city-state that commanded an extensive maritime trading empire. Van Dijk (1968) and Corral (2002) offer a detailed treatment of Ezekiel's oracles against Tyre. Also to be noted is an influential essay on the Tyre sequence by Newsom (1984). See also Strong 1993, 1997; Geyer 2004a.

26:1. "In the eleventh year, on the first day of the month": the month is not specified. Half of the dates in the book appear in the oracles against the nations section (chs. 25–32). I have noted that these dates are generally close to the period of the collapse of Jerusalem, which should probably be dated in August 587 (see on 33:21). This is of a piece with Davis' view that (particularly in the case of the Tyre and Egypt material) these oracles present object lessons for Israel (Davis 1999). The Tyre and Egypt sequences appear in the "wrong" order, at least on the basis of the dates in 26:1 (the "eleventh year," or indeed "twelfth year" according to LXX) and 29:1 (the "tenth year"); see further on 29:1. **26:2.** "Because Tyre said…": such quotation continues to be a feature here in the Tyre sequence (vv. 17–18; 27:3, 32; 28:2). "Aha": cf. 25:3; 36:2. **26:3.** "Thus says the Lord GOD": this formula introduces new sections of the extended oracle that fills the whole chapter, here and also in vv. 7, 15, 19. "I am against you": cf. 28:22. **26:4.** "A bare rock": Hebrew *ṣᵉḥîaḥ sālaʿ*. The phrase "bare rock" is used in connection with Jerusalem in 24:7, 8 (taken by Davis as part of the evidence for the paralleling of the fates of Tyre and Jerusalem). There is probably also here a play on the Hebrew word for Tyre (*ṣōr*), very like another Hebrew word for "rock" (*ṣûr*). **26:5.** "In the midst of the sea": Tyre was based on an island just off the coast of what is today known as southern Lebanon. **26:6.** "Its daughter-towns ": a line of suburbs on the mainland constituted Tyre's second urban centre (Ushu or Palaetyrus).

26:7. "I will bring against Tyre…King Nebuchadrezzar of Babylon": a thirteen-year siege of Tyre by the Babylonians began in 586, not long after the fall of Jerusalem. **26:10.** "When he enters your gates": the proverbially impregnable fortress will yield to the Babylonian conqueror. **26:14.** "I will make you a bare rock…": Ezekiel's powerful rhetoric, picking up the language of vv. 4–5, anticipates that Nebuchadrezzar will eventually destroy Tyre completely. In fact, the Babylonians were unsuccessful and ended their siege sometime around 573 (see further Ezek 29:17–20).

26:15. "Shall not the coastlands shake…?": a reference to Tyre's mainland suburbs (see on v. 6). **26:16.** "Then all the princes of the sea shall step down from their thrones": what follows ("shall be appalled at you") implies a distinction between Tyre and these "princes of the sea"; the latter are probably cities in trading relationships with Tyre. **26:17.** "And they shall raise a lamentation over you": cf. 27:2; 28:12; vv. 17–18 are cast in verse (in the *qînâ*, "lament," metre). "How you have vanished": so LXX, Old Latin and Aquila; MT continues *nôšeḇeṯ*, "O inhabited one." "O city renowned, once mighty on the sea": cf. Lam 1:1.

26:19. "When I bring up the deep over you, and the great waters cover you": a fitting punishment for the great maritime power, evoking mythological ideas of the primordial deep (cf. Gen 1:2); cf. 27:25b–36. **26:20.** "I will thrust you down with those who descend into the Pit": the "Pit" (Heb. *bôr*) is the same as "Sheol," the abode of the dead; cf. 28:8; 31:15–18; 32:17–32 (Day 1996:231–37). "Or have a place": so LXX; MT has *w^{e}nāṯattî ṣ^{e}ḇî*, which is best read as an archaic second person feminine form, giving the sense "or radiate splendour" (cf. Van Dijk 1968:46).

Chapter 27

27:2. "Raise a lamentation": cf. 26:17–18. Within the present chapter, it is vv. 25b–36 that take up the lament. **27:3.** "Tyre, which sits at the entrance to the sea": so different from Israelites, for the most part land-locked and not greatly given to sea travel. "I am perfect in beauty": Tyre's hubristic arrogance; cf. 28:1–10. **27:4.** At first, in vv. 4–25a, the specialness of Tyre is affirmed (cf. 28:3–5), under the guise of a great ship. The ship, here wonderfully described, is the perfect symbol for the paradigmatic sea-faring nation of the ancient world. Geyer speaks also of the mythological dimensions of the "Cosmic Ship" (Geyer 1993, 2004a). "In the heart of the seas": a recurrent motif (vv. 25–27; 28:2, 8). **27:5.** "They made all your planks of fir trees from Senir": Senir is Mount Hermon (cf. Deut 3:9). **27:7.** "Purple": Hebrew *ʾargāmān* (cf. v. 16); Tyre's reputation owed much to the trade in "purple," a highly prized dye made from a marine snail. **27:8.** "Sidon": see on 28:21. "Arvad": an island city 120 miles north of Tyre. **27:9.** "Gebal": Byblos, 70 miles north of Tyre. **27:10.** "Lud and Put": see on 30:5.

27:12. The chapter turns from the ship itself to its wares, continuing positively to celebrate Tyre as a merchant success. Verses 12–25a are in distinctive prose and seem to be a trade document or cargo list; this could be a secondary addition or it could, more likely, reflect the adaptation of such a document by Ezekiel. Liverani (1991) sees it as offering us a map of the trade network of Tyre. The section begins and ends with "Tarshish" (vv. 12, 25), in the manner of an *inclusio*. This was perhaps Tarsus in Turkey or, more likely, the proverbially remote Tartessos in Spain (cf. Jon 1:3). "Silver, iron, tin, and lead": cf. 22:17–22 (on metals in the Bible, see Singer 1980). Corral's (2002) monograph includes study of economic aspects of the Tyre oracles. "They exchanged for your wares…": a recurrent phrase here. **27:13.** "Tubal and Meshech": associated with Gog at 38:2–3; 39:1; cf. also 32:26. "They exchanged human beings": apparently regarded as goods like any other in this context. **27:15.** "Ivory tusks and ebony": an indication of the geographical range of Tyre's indirect trade. **27:17.** "Judah and the land of Israel": listed like any other nations, a further indication that this material is probably from a pre-existing source. **27:19.** "Vedan and Javan": Hebrew *wᵉdān weᵉyāwān*. Better *wᵉdannê yayin*, "and casks of wine" (Millard 1962). "Uzal": probably iron-exporting Izalla, in Anatolia (cf. Elat 1983). **27:24.** "Choice garments": Hebrew *maklulîm*; this *hapax legomenon* denotes specially crafted clothing of some kind (cf. Görg 1982).

27:25b. We move back to verse, and indeed the theme changes from celebration to a gloating account of catastrophe, which continues to the end of the chapter. This is the real lament section (cf. v. 2). **27:26.** "The east wind": cf. 17:10; 19:12. "Wrecked you in the heart of the seas": an ironic allusion to the positive v. 4. **27:28.** "The countryside shakes": an allusion to the region around Tyre's mainland suburbs; cf. 26:6. **27:31.** "They make themselves bald for you, and put on sackcloth": cf. Bloch-Smith (1992) on mourning rites. **27:32.** "In their wailing they raise a lamentation for you": cf. v. 2. "Destroyed": NRSV follows the Targum and Vulgate; but MT has *k*ᵉ*ḏumâ*, "like silence," which makes some sense. **27:33.** The "when…now" pattern constituted by this and the following verse is like a microcosm of the chapter and is typical of biblical lament. **27:34.** "You are wrecked by the seas": poetic justice indeed.

CHAPTER 28

Both of the final parts of the Tyre sequence (vv. 1–10 and vv. 11–19) challenge the king of Tyre's hubristic aspirations, but they do so in significantly different ways.

28:2. "The prince": cf. v. 12, "the king." In spite of the difference in terminology here, the reference is to the same figure. "Because your heart is proud": cf. 27:3. "I am a god; I sit in the seat of the gods": pride leads to self-deification, the worst form of idolatry. "You compare your mind with the mind of a god": the word used for "mind" here and in v. 6 is *lēḇ*, "heart." **28:3.** "You are indeed…": as in 27:4–25a, so here in 28:3–5 there is first acknowledgement of due honour; compare the dialectic between proper human dignity and its limits in Ps 8. "Wiser than Daniel": cf. 14:14, 20, where Daniel is cited as an example of righteousness. As there, the name may here be read "Danʾel"; in the Ugaritic story of Danʾel, the hero is the wise judge of widows and orphans. The king of Tyre is like those "wise in their own eyes," criticized by Isaiah (5:21). **28:7.** "Therefore, I will bring strangers against you, the most terrible of the nations": the Babylonians are in mind here (cf. 26:7; 30:11); comparable language is used of Gog in chs. 38–39. "They shall draw their swords against the beauty of your wisdom and defile your splendour": Hebrew verb *ḥll*, "defile, desecrate," is used here and in vv. 9, 16, 18; it is as though Tyre's commercial wealth is her "temple" (Davis 1999:232–33). **28:8.** "They shall thrust you down to the Pit": cf. 26:20; 31:14, 16; 32:17–32. Whereas these other verses employ the Hebrew word *bôr* for "Pit," the present verse uses Hebrew *šaḥaṯ*. "You shall die a violent death in the heart of the seas": as in ch. 27, so in this chapter we move from a positive use of the phrase "in the heart of the seas" (v. 2) to a negative one (v. 8). **28:9.** "Will you still say, 'I am a god,' in the presence of those who kill you, though you are but a mortal, and no god…": cf. Ps 82:6–7. **28:10.** "You shall die the death of the uncircumcised": cf. 31:18; 32:17–32. Like most other peoples of the ancient Near East, the Phoenicians did in fact practise circumcision; so Ezekiel is using the term "uncircumcised" metaphorically, to signal uncleanness and cultural inferiority.

28:11–19. These verses provide the closest parallel in ancient literature to Gen 2–3: the main character is placed in the garden of Eden (v. 13; cf. Gen 2:8, 10, 15; 3:23–24); though he was originally perfect, sin is later exposed (v. 15; cf. Gen 3:11); he is driven out (v. 16; cf. Gen 3:23–24); and there is reference to a cherub (vv. 14, 16; cf. Gen 3:24). There are differences, of course (e.g. Eden is set on a mountain in Ezek 28:14, 16, which is unattested in Gen 2–3, as are the precious stones of v. 13). Nonetheless, the similarities are striking, especially with Gen 3:22–24. **28:12.** "Raise a lamentation": cf. 27:2. "The signet of perfection": Hebrew *ḥôṯēm toḵnîṯ*. Callender (2000b:180–89) argues that MT should be amended to *ḥôṯām taḇnîṯ*, "a seal, a likeness," and that this may be considered equivalent to the terms *ṣelem*, "image," and *d^emûṯ*, "likeness," in Gen 1:26. Miller (1993:500), on the other hand, amends to *ḥayyaṯ maṯkunîṯ*, "a being of propriety," as a reference to a covering cherub who preserves propriety in a cultic setting. Both Callender and Miller thus interpret this phrase in a way that coheres with their different answers to the key crux of this passage, namely the identity of the main character (see on v. 14). **28:13.** "You were in Eden, the garden of God": cf. 31:9, 16, 18; 36:35. "Every precious stone was your covering…": cf. the stones in the priestly "breastpiece of judgement" (Exod 28:17–20; 39:10–13). "Beryl": Hebrew *taršîš*; cf. 1:16; 10:9. "Sapphire" (or "lapis lazuli"): Hebrew *sappîr*; cf. 1:26; 10:1. Wilson argues that 28:11–19 is an oblique oracle against Israel itself, representing an indictment of the Israelite priesthood (Wilson 1987); this would cohere with the thesis of Davis that the Tyre and Egypt oracles are primarily an object lesson for Israel (Davis 1999:226–27; see on ch. 25). **28:14.** "With an anointed cherub as guardian": MT *ʾat-k^erûḇ mimšaḥ hassôḵēḵ*. NRSV depends on reading Hebrew *ʾeṯ-*, "with," following LXX and the Syriac (so Zimmerli 1983:85; Day 2000:176–78; Callender 2000b:178). Stordalen argues that the MT here represents a late stage of the tradition (Stordalen 2000:347–48). If one in this way takes the original meaning to be "*with* a cherub," this passage would seem to be about a "primal human being"; indeed it may be that an old tradition related to Ezek 28:11–19 played a part in the construction of the Genesis narrative. Arbel (2005) fascinatingly extends such discussion to explore feminine aspects of a "primal figure" in Ezek 28:11–19 in the light of *Genesis Rabbah*. On a "primal human being" interpretation, the oracles of vv. 1–10 and vv. 11–19 are rather similar, even though the second is more explicitly mythological. However, Barr (1992) persuasively defends MT *ʾat-*,"you"; he argues that it is easier to understand how this rare second person singular masculine pronoun was misunderstood as *ʾeṯ-*, "with," than the reverse. On such a reading the king of Tyre is addressed as a cherub (similarly Miller 1993; Greenberg 1997:583–84). Barr contends that one should not connect Ezek 28:11–19 and Gen 2–3, except in so far as the reading of Genesis has been distorted by ideas from Ezek 28:11–19. The notion of an expelled cherub would be comparable to the fallen "Day Star" of Isa 14:12–15. This Isaiah passage is often, with good reason, likened to other verses in the Tyre sequence (Ezek 27:3; 28:2); but the present passage (on a "cherub" interpretation) is the one to which it is closest (for an alternative view, see Day 2000:175–78). Kaiser argues that the Isaiah verses are post-exilic and indebted to Ezekiel (Kaiser 1974:29–32). "You were on the holy mountain of God": in Ugaritic mythology the divine dwelling place was Mount Zaphon, modern Jebel el-Aqraʿ, north of Ugarit (cf. Clifford 1972). "You walked among the stones of fire": these may echo the coals on the altar of the temple (Wilson 1987:216). **28:15.** "You were blameless in your ways from the day that you were created": not claimed of the "primal human being" in Gen 2–3, which favours Barr's alternative interpretation of the present passage. "Until iniquity was found in you": compare ch. 16 (where note especially v. 15). **28:16.** "The guardian cherub drove you out": cf. Gen 3:24. On the view that interprets v. 14 as "with a cherub," this verse is usually taken (as NRSV) to mean "the guardian cherub drove you out" (again with support from LXX; e.g. Zimmerli 1983:86). But Barr persuasively argues that it should be taken to refer to the banishment of the cherub (so Jerome and AV, taking "cherub" as a vocative), which would fit the corresponding interpretation of v. 14. **28:17.** "I exposed you before kings, to feast their eyes on you": compare the language of humiliation used of women in chs. 16 and 23. **28:18.** "By the multitude of your iniquities, in the unrighteousness of your trade": cf. the reference to violence in v. 16; there is here a critique of economic injustice reminiscent of the eighth-century prophets. "So I brought out fire from within you": perhaps a reference to the "stones of fire" (v. 14) flaring up and consuming the cherub (Block 1998:117). **28:19.** "All who know you among the peoples are appalled at you": a recurrent motif (e.g. 27:36). "You have come to a dreadful end": the Tyre sequence is over and this is signalled by the use of the same words as were used in the final verse of both chs. 26 and 27, "dreadful end" (Heb. *ballāhôṯ*) and also "shall be no more" (Heb. *ʾênᵉḵā*).

28:21. "Set your face toward Sidon": to the north of Tyre, and mentioned in Ezekiel at 27:8 and 32:30. Tyre had been founded by Sidon, and they are sometimes mentioned as a pair elsewhere (e.g. Jer 47:4; Zech 9:2). **28:22.** "I am against you": cf. 26:3. "Manifest my holiness": cf. 20:41; 36:23. The "Recognition Formula" did not occur in the Tyre sequence after its one appearance in 26:6; now it is found twice in this short Sidon oracle, and twice more before the end of the chapter (cf. Strong 1995).

28:24–26. These verses constitute one of only two references to restoration for Israel in chs. 25–32 (the other being 29:21). Both seem additional in their contexts and unintegrated with the surrounding material. **28:24.** "The house of Israel shall no longer find a pricking brier or a piercing thorn among all their neighbours": an isolated verse, followed by a fresh introduction in v. 25. The thought is reminiscent of Num 33:55, but the Hebrew is dissimilar. **28:25.** The final two verses of the chapter look like a systematizing summary of Ezekiel's theology (cf. 39:21–29), possibly secondary. "When I gather the house of Israel…and manifest my holiness…then they shall settle on their own soil": much of the language of chs. 34–37 is found here.

CHAPTER 29

Four chapters are devoted to Egypt (chs. 29–32); see Boadt 1980; also Strong 1993; Geyer 2004a.

29:1. "In the tenth year, in the tenth month, on the twelfth day of the month": 7th January 587. The first of no less than six dates found within the oracle sequence against Egypt. The date given here is earlier than that given at the start of the preceding Tyre section (see on 26:1), but the placing of the Egypt sequence after that about Tyre could be explained by the fact that the Egypt section contains later dates, including in 29:17. **29:2.** "Set your face": see on 4:3. "Pharaoh": currently Hophra (589–570); as with the Tyre sequence, the leader represents his people. "Egypt": the great and ancient power in north-east Africa, which frequently played a role in the foreign policy of Judah. As in the time of Isaiah (e.g. Isa 30:1–7), so during that of Ezekiel, alliances with Egypt against a Mesopotamian power were a constant temptation and often the cause of trouble. **29:3.** "I am against you": cf. 26:3; 28:22. "The great dragon": the reference to the "dragon" (Heb. *tannîn*; cf. 32:2) alludes to the crocodile, but more importantly to the myth of the chaos monster (cf. Day 1985). Using another of the names of this mythical beast, Isaiah called ineffectual Egypt "Rahab who sits still" (Isa 30:7). "Its channels": the many branches of the Nile, in the Delta region. "My Nile is my own; I made it for myself": Pharaoh has pretensions to deity, as did the king of Tyre (28:2); in the case of Egypt this charge has particular potency in the light of developed Egyptian notions of divine kingship (cf. Isa 31:3). The Nile is the great river of north Africa, and the focus of the life of Egypt. **29:4.** "I will put hooks in your jaws": the fate to befall kings of Judah and also Gog (cf. 19:4, 9; 38:4). **29:5.** "I will fling you into the wilderness": the antithesis of the dragon's watery home; cf. 32:4; similar to the fate of Shebna in Isa 22:17–18. **29:6.** "Staff of reed": Hebrew *miš*ʿ*ene*ṯ *qāneh*. Egypt was a notoriously unreliable ally for Judah; cf. Isa 36:6. **29:8.** "I will bring a sword upon you": the recurrent motif of ch. 21. "Cut off from you human being and animal": one of Ezekiel's inclusive formulae; cf. 14:13, 17. **29:10.** "From Migdol to Syene": that is, north to south, another inclusive formula. "Ethiopia": Hebrew *kûš*: a territory to the south of Egypt, possibly "Nubia." **29:11.** "It shall be uninhabited forty years": the reference to "forty years" here and in v. 12 recalls the wilderness wanderings of Israel (Num 14:33–34), which is ironic given the link between that episode and the Exodus from Egypt. Compare also Ezek 4:6, of the years of Judah's exile. **29:12.** "I will scatter the

Egyptians among the nations…": using language usually elsewhere used of Israel's exile. **29:13.** "At the end of forty years I will gather the Egyptians…": a surprising turn, not paralleled in the Tyre sequence; again employing language usually used of Israel; see further on 32:31. **29:14.** "Restore the fortunes of Egypt": cf. the restoration of Sodom and Samaria in 16:53, 55. See also Isa 19:16–25. Vogels (1972) goes so far as to speak of universalism here. "Pathros": upper (southern) Egypt, presented here as the "land of their origin." **29:15.** "It shall be the most lowly of the kingdoms": a corrective to Egypt's hubris, its characteristic sin in the past, as in v. 3. **29:16.** "Never again…the reliance of the house of Israel": Egypt will no longer be in a position to tempt Israel into ill-advised alliances. "They will recall their iniquity, when they turned to them for aid": the subject, recalling and turning, is Israel; but the subject of the closing "Recognition Formula" could be either Israel or Egypt.

29:17. "In the twenty-seventh year, in the first month, on the first day of the month": 26th April 571; this is the latest date in the book, leaving aside the much debated 1:1. These verses refer to the fact that Tyre had not in fact fallen to Nebuchadrezzar of Babylon and represent a correction of 26:7–21, which anticipated the fall of Tyre. After a thirteen-year siege, there was a negotiated settlement, and Tyre remained unconquered until its fall to Alexander in 332 B.C.E. These verses could have been added by Ezekiel himself when older, as Greenberg argues (1997:618), or by his redactors (cf. Fishbane 1985:467–74). **29:20.** "I have given him the land of Egypt as his payment for which he laboured": compensation for the fruitless years of siege at Tyre. "They worked for me": explicit confirmation that Nebuchadrezzar had been acting as agent for YHWH. As matters turned out, Nebuchadrezzar made significant incursions into north Africa but never conquered Egypt in the decisive way that the Assyrians had or that the Persians would. That this oracle is not further updated confirms other indications that the book of Ezekiel reached closure early.

29:21. Isolated here in the midst of the oracles against Egypt, this is a verse of "messianic" hope. Note especially the introductory eschatological formula "On that day" and also the use of the words "horn" (Heb. *qeren*) and "sprout up" (Hiphil of Heb. verb *ṣmḥ*) (cf. Ps 132:17). This is one of only two references to restoration for Israel in chs. 25–32 (the other being 28:24–26). Both seem additional in their contexts and unintegrated with the surrounding material. "I will open your lips among them": the Hebrew phrase *piṯḥôn peh* is the equivalent of the Akkadian *pit pi*, used of the dedication of sacred images for liturgical use, after which the image becomes the source of oracles. Here the point seems to be that YHWH works in and through a human agent and not an object (Kennedy 1991; cf. Glazov 2001:351, 380–81).

CHAPTER 30

30:2. "Alas for the day!": the eschatological tone of this chapter is reminiscent of ch. 7. The absence of a date notice (here alone in the Egyptian sequence) is among factors leading some scholars to doubt the originality of vv. 1–19 (e.g. Cooke 1936:331). However, it would be awkward to have a dating formula alongside reference to an indeterminate eschatological day. **30:3.** "The day of the LORD is near": see on 7:7; cf. Amos 5:18–20. "A time of doom for the nations": NRSV unnecessarily supplies "of doom"; the point may indeed be that Egypt's allies will suffer with her (cf. vv. 5–9), or alternatively the reference could be to the nations plundering Egypt. **30:4.** "A sword shall come upon Egypt": cf. ch. 21. **30:5.** "Put and Lud": among Tyre's mercenaries at 27:10; "Lud" is Lydia in Asia Minor; "Put" is "Libya," though NRSV (following LXX, Syriac, Vulgate) gives "Libya" at the end of the list of specific nations, where MT has the obscure *kûḇ* (possibly a corruption of Heb. *lûḇ*, "Libya"). The list seems intended to include reference to several neighbouring peoples in north Africa. "The people of the allied land": Hebrew *bᵉnê ʾereṣ habbᵉrîṯ*, literally "the people of the land of the covenant"; NRSV implies Egypt's allies, but an alternative is reference to Jewish mercenaries. **30:7.** "They shall be desolated among other desolated countries…": cf. 29:12. **30:9.** "On that day": an eschatological formula. "Messengers shall go out from me in ships to terrify the unsuspecting Ethiopians": the wording seems indebted to Isa 18:2. "Anguish shall come upon them on the day of Egypt's doom": as in v. 3, NRSV again supplies "doom," this time more appropriately.

30:10. "I will put an end to the hordes of Egypt": "hordes" represents Hebrew *hāmôn*, "multitude," a characteristic word within the Egypt cycle, where it is used eleven times. **30:11.** "The most terrible of the nations": the Babylonians; cf. 28:7. **30:12.** "I will dry up the channels": the worst imaginable disaster for Egypt, whose life was so dependent on the Nile. **30:13.** "Memphis": Hebrew *nōp̱*; the ancient capital of lower (northern) Egypt; cf. v. 16. "There shall no longer be a prince": as in his critique of Judahite monarchy (e.g. 21:25 [Heb. v. 30]), Ezekiel provocatively employs the term "prince" (Heb. *nāśîʾ*) to rob a sovereign of his pretensions. **30:14.** "Zoan" (Tanis), "Pelusium" (Heb. *sîn*; vv. 15–16), "On" (Heb. *ʾāwen*; Heliopolis; v. 17), "Pi-beseth" (Bubastis; v. 17) and "Tehaphnehes" (Tahpanhes; v. 18) were all towns in or near the Delta region, an area already accommodating a significant Jewish community, as is reflected in the book of Jeremiah (e.g. Jer 43–44). "Thebes": Hebrew *nōʾ*; the major city of upper (southern) Egypt, now Karnak. **30:16.** "Face adversaries by day": Hebrew *ṣārê yômām*. Though a range of emendations have been offered (e.g. Albrektson 1995; Porter 1997), NRSV gives a good rendering of the elliptical Hebrew text. **30:17.** "Shall go into captivity": cf. vv. 23, 26; 29:12. **30:18.** "The day shall be dark": cf. 32:7–8; also Amos 5:18–20. "Covered by a cloud": cf. v. 3. "Its daughter-towns": dependent settlements; cf. 26:6, 8. **30:19.** "Thus I will execute acts of judgement on Egypt. Then they shall know that I am the LORD": the "Recognition Formula" occurs nine times in the Egypt sequence (cf. Strong 1995). It is interesting, in the light of this Egyptian context, to note that one view links the origin of the formula to the Exodus narrative (e.g. Exod 7:17; 11:7; cf. Fohrer 1961:310; 1970:104).

30:20. "In the eleventh year, in the first month, on the seventh day of the month": 29th April 587. The chapter ends with a section in prose, opened by the third of the six dates found in the Egyptian cycle. **30:21.** "I have broken the arm of Pharaoh king of Egypt": this reference may be to Hophra's unsuccessful attack against Nebuchadrezzar in the spring of 588, when he failed to relieve Jerusalem (cf. Jer 37:5–7). **30:22.** "I…will break his arms, both the strong arm and the one that was broken": more humiliation is to come. **30:23.** "I will scatter the Egyptians among the nations, and disperse them throughout the lands": cf. vv. 17, 26; 29:12; language normally reserved for Israel's exile. This time there is no reference to restoration for Egypt (cf. 29:13–16). **30:24.** "I will strengthen the arms of the king of Babylon": in contrast to those of Pharaoh. The effective arm of YHWH is a recurrent motif in the Exodus narrative (e.g. Exod 6:6: cf. Ezek 20:33–34).

CHAPTER 31

Pohlmann (1989; 1992:185–97) discusses this chapter as among the oldest texts in the book. **31:1.** "In the eleventh year, in the third month, on the first day of the month": 21st June 587, shortly before Jerusalem fell. **31:2.** "Whom are you like in your greatness?": Pharaoh is addressed (cf. 29:2). **31:3.** "Consider Assyria": a remarkable comparison of two great nations; Assyria, centred in northern Mesopotamia, had been the major world power for several centuries, but had recently been humbled and eclipsed by the re-emergence of Babylonia as an imperial force. Assyria's fate is to provide an object lesson for Egypt (over which it had exercised sway before its cataclysmic fall). The MT, *ʾaššûr*, "Assyria," has the unanimous support of the versions and should be retained, rather than emended in favour of *tᵉʾaššûr*, "cypress" (as it is by Zimmerli 1983:141, and many others). "A cedar of Lebanon": cf. 27:5. There is further reference to Lebanon, the mountainous territory immediately to the north of Israel, in vv. 15–16. The allegory seems to be based on a complex web of ancient Near Eastern mythology (see Geyer 2004a on the "Cosmic Tree"), which has also influenced apocalyptic literature, cf. Dan 4:10–12 (Heb. vv. 7–9). Though the myth does not fit well the vegetation of Egypt, it provides an excellent vehicle for challenging her hubris. **31:4.** "The deep made it grow tall": Hebrew *tᵉhôm* is the primeval deep (cf. Gen 1:2); there could here be a mythological allusion to Tiamat, the chaos monster, helping the great tree to reach for the divine realm, but in this still positive context the reference is probably only to ample irrigation; see further on v. 15. "Making its rivers flow…sending forth its streams": cf. Ps 46:4 (Heb. v. 5). **31:6.** "All the birds of the air made their nests in its boughs; under its branches all the animals of the field gave birth to their young; and in its shade all great nations lived": a universal vision of inclusion. We may compare the eschatological and mythological overtones of 17:22–24; see also on 34:25 for the notion of a "cosmic covenant." **31:8.** "No tree in the garden of God was like it in beauty": the garden of God is mentioned twice here, and also in v. 9, where it is equated with "Eden" (cf. vv. 16, 18). The intention is probably to picture the great tree as being within the garden; see further on v. 16. **31:9.** "I made it beautiful…": YHWH is the creator of this magnificent tree. The image is entirely positive up to this point; but we know from Ezekiel that pride comes before a fall (cf. chs. 16, 27, 28).

31:10. "Therefore thus says the Lord GOD": these words signal the beginning of the declaration of judgement. "Towered high…and its heart was proud of its height": hubris, as in the Tower of Babel narrative of Gen 11; cf. Isa 2:12–17. **31:11.** "I gave it into the hand…": YHWH's agency is affirmed. "Prince": Hebrew *ʾayil*, a "ram," used of leaders also at 17:13; presumably here the king of Babylon. **31:12.** "The most terrible of the nations": cf. 28:7; 30:11; 32:12; confirmation that Babylon is intended. "Cut it down and left it": cf. Dan 4:14 (Heb. v. 11). There may be an allusion here to the battle of Carchemish (605 B.C.E.), where the combined forces of Egypt and Assyria were decisively defeated by the Babylonians. **31:13.** "On its fallen trunk settle all the birds of the air…": cf. v. 6. **31:14.** "All this is in order that no trees by the waters may grow to lofty height…": a rather pedestrian spelling out of the moral; somewhat reminiscent of 23:48.

"For all of them are handed over to death, to the world below; along with all mortals, with those who go down to the Pit": the first introduction here of a theme that will dominate the remainder of the chapter and indeed much of the next. On ideas of the afterlife in ancient Israel, see Day 1996. "Pit": Hebrew *bôr*; cf. 26:20; 28:8; 32:17–32. **31:15.** "Sheol": Hebrew *šᵉʾôl*; cf. 32:21, 27. "The deep": Hebrew *tᵉhôm*; here, as at 26:19, there is definitely a mythological echo of Tiamat, the chaos monster, in the image of the deep closing over the tree; importantly, however, it remains the case that YHWH is the agent of this judgement. "I restrained its rivers, and its mighty waters were checked": the judgement involves the reversal of the ample provision of v. 4. **31:16.** "I made the nations quake at the sound of its fall": cf. 28:19; 32:10. "All the trees of Eden, the choice and best of Lebanon": Ezekiel seems to identify Eden and Lebanon. We may compare 28:11–19, where Eden is on a mountain; see Clifford 1972 on the cosmic mountain in Canaanite mythology. (Note also Ps 80:10 [Heb. v. 11], the "cedars of God" [NRSV, "the mighty cedars"]; Ps 104:16, the "cedars of Lebanon that he [YHWH] planted.") The idea that the garden of Eden (or "garden of God," 31:8–9) was in Lebanon differs from that in Gen 2, which implies a location adjacent to Mesopotamia (note especially Gen 2:14). According to NRSV, the "trees of Eden" (vv. 16, 18) "were consoled" (Heb. *wayyinnāḥᵃmû*) when they observed the fate of the great cedar; but vv. 17–18 suggest that they share the same fate, and so a more likely interpretation is that that they "repented" (cf. Davis 1999 on 32:31). "The world below": Hebrew *ʾereṣ taḥtîṯ*; v. 18 also; cf. 32:18. **31:17.** "They also went down to Sheol with it, to those killed by the sword": as in v. 18, this refers to the ignominious fate of those who are executed or who die violent or untimely deaths (cf. 32:17–32). "Along with its allies": Hebrew *ûzᵉrōʿô*, "and its arm"; an unspecific reference to the sword-wielding arm (cf. Block 1998:193). "Those who lived in its shade among the nations": the tree image is still in play; cf. v. 6. **31:18.** "Which among the trees of Eden was like you in glory and in greatness?": this question recalls v. 2. "You shall lie among the uncircumcised": see on 32:17–32. "This is Pharaoh and all his horde": as the chapter ends, we come full circle (cf. v. 2) and are reminded that this chapter, which has virtually no specific allusion to matters Egyptian, serves as a further critique of the hubris of Pharaoh.

Chapter 32

The fourth and last chapter of the Egypt cycle. **32:1.** "In the twelfth year, in the twelfth month, on the first day of the month": 3rd March 585. **32:2–16:** A lamentation over Pharaoh (cf. 29:2). **32:2.** "Raise a lamentation": cf. 19:1; 26:17; 27:2, 32; 28:12. "You consider yourself a lion among the nations": cf. 19:1–9, of Judah; the theme of hubris features yet again; perhaps the image of the sphinx is in mind. "But you are like a dragon in the seas": this reference, together with 29:3, forms an *inclusio* around the bulk of the Egypt oracles. "You thrash about in your streams": the Nile and its channels. "Foul your streams": cf. 34:18–19. **32:3.** "I will throw my net over you": cf. the fate of kings of Judah, in 12:13; 17:20; 19:8. **32:4.** "I will throw you… I will fling you": cf. 29:5. "Will cause all the birds of the air to settle on you": cf. 31:13. "I will let the wild animals of the whole earth gorge themselves with you": cf. 29:5. **32:5.** "I will strew your flesh on the mountains, and fill the valleys with your carcass": for the word translated "carcass" by NRSV, MT has the unique word *rāmûṯeḵā*, literally "your height," best translated, with Greenberg (1997:652) as "your bulk." One is reminded of the Babylonian epic of *Enuma Elish*, in which the god Marduk slays Tiamat and then disposes of her remains. **32:7.** "I will cover the sun with a cloud": as though eclipsing the Pharaoh, who was regarded as the light of Egypt; cf. Joel 2:10, 31. **32:8.** "Put darkness on your land": cf. the plague of darkness in Exod 10:21–22. The language of the "day of YHWH" is evoked, as in chs. 7 and 30. **32:9.** "Carry you captive": NRSV follows LXX; Hebrew has *bahᵃḇîʾî šiḇrᵉḵā*, "bring your destruction," which makes acceptable sense. **32:10.** "I will make many peoples appalled at you": cf. 27:35. "Their kings shall shudder because of you": cf. 31:16. "When I brandish my sword before them": the recurrent theme of ch. 21; cf. also 30:25. This is reminiscent of portrayals of Baal. **32:12.** "Most terrible among the nations": used of Babylon elsewhere; cf. 28:7; 30:11; 31:12. **32:14.** "Then I will make their waters clear": this signals bad news, namely the absence of living things. **32:16.** "This is a lamentation": forming an *inclusio* with v. 2. "The women of the nations": probably women as professional mourners (cf. Jer 9:17–18 [Heb. vv. 16–17]).

32:17–32: The final section of the Egypt sequence, picking up and developing the underworld themes already introduced (26:20; 28:8; and, within the Egypt chapters, 31:14–18). Nobile (1986) discusses the relationship between 32:17–32 and the Gog material of chs. 38–39 in the light of the final redaction of the book. **32:17.** "In the twelfth year, in the first month, on the fifteenth day of the month":

the last of the six dates in the Egypt cycle. The MT lacks "in the first month," which NRSV supplies from LXX. This would be 27th April 586, more than ten months earlier than the date in v. 1. **32:18.** "Wail": continuing the lamenting theme of vv. 1–16. "The world below": Hebrew *ʾereṣ taḥtîṯ*; cf. 31:16, 18. "The Pit": see on 31:14. **32:19.** "Whom do you surpass in beauty?": one of a number of such rhetorical questions in these oracles; cf. 31:2, 18. "The uncircumcised": Hebrew *ʿarēlîm*. The Egyptians did in fact practise circumcision; so, as in 28:10, Ezekiel is using the term "uncircumcised" metaphorically, to signal uncleanness and cultural inferiority. **32:20.** "Those who are killed by the sword": Hebrew *ḥalᵉlê-ḥereḇ*. This refers to those who are executed or who die violent or untimely deaths; cf. 31:17–18. The Egyptians will go to the area of the underworld set aside for the dishonourable, in contrast to the honoured war-dead, who were properly buried (cf. v. 27). Verse 20b constitutes one of the cases (and indeed v. 21b another) where Allen (1990b) argues that a cluster of marginal annotations and glosses have mistakenly been taken together and then incorporated into the text. As in the other examples he cites, the context here is an eschatological one, which may account for the particular intensity of the postulated glossing. **32:21.** "The mighty chiefs shall speak of them, with their helpers, out of the midst of Sheol": cf. Isa 14:9–11. On Sheol, see Day 1996:231–37.

At v. 22 we move into a review of the nations in Sheol, a natural sequel to v. 18. There is much repetition of formulaic language, including the metaphorical use of the word "uncircumcised" (of the nations listed here, the Edomites and the Sidonians practised physical circumcision). **32:22.** "Assyria is there": for Assyria, see on 31:3. Babylon is conspicuous by her absence, though it is possible that here Assyria stands for the Mesopotamian powers in a generic way. **32:24.** "Elam is there": a people located in what is now Iran, with their capital in Susa; cf. Jer 49:35–39. **32:25.** Dittography is the most likely explanation of the substantial repetition of v. 24. **32:26.** "Meshech and Tubal": these traded with Tyre (27:13); Gog is said to be "chief prince of Meshech and Tubal" (e.g. 38:2). **32:27.** "They do not lie with the fallen warriors": the reference seems to be to the honoured war-dead, who were properly buried. "Of long ago": MT has *mēʿarēlîm*, "of the uncircumcised," but it is better (like NRSV) to follow LXX and the Old Latin and read Hebrew *mēʿôlām*, "of old." "Whose shields": MT has *ʿawōnōṯām*, "their iniquities," but this makes no sense; NRSV is based on a plausible emendation to *ṣinnôṯām*, "their shields." **32:29.** "Edom": cf. 25:12–14 and 35:1–36:7. "For all their might": a reminder of the contrast between former worldly power and this humiliating fate. **32:30.** "The princes of the north": a general reference to leaders of Phoenicia and Syria. "And all the Sidonians": cf. 28:20–23. **32:31.** "When Pharaoh sees them": though it has taken in many other territories, the passage now ends, as it began, with Egypt (cf. 31:18). "He will be consoled" (Heb. *wᵉniḥam*): so NRSV; similarly NEB, NJPS. Smend (1880) called this "biting mockery," and it is certainly difficult to make sense of in any straightforward way. Davis argues, boldly and yet persuasively, that the meaning of the Niphal of the verb *nḥm* here is that Pharaoh "will change his mind" (cf. Isa 57:6; Jer 8:6; 18:8, 10; Amos 7:3, 6). Pharaoh, she contends, will "repent" (a similar meaning can be defended at 14:22 and 31:16). This would amount to nothing less than the conversion of Israel's oldest enemy—Pharaoh's heart at last no longer hardened (Davis 1999:234–35). The powerful motif of the repentance of the most unlikely sinner is found elsewhere too, as in the case of Manasseh (2 Chr 33:13; Prayer of Manasseh). We may also compare Egypt's modest restoration in Ezek 29:13–16.

CHAPTER 33

The tone of this chapter is largely one of judgement, but it contains, in vv. 21–22, what proves to be the turning-point of the book. For, once the news that the city of Jerusalem has fallen reaches the prophet, the book shifts by stages from the minor key to the major, and themes of promise and restoration begin to come to the fore. As I have noted, the book of Ezekiel is characterized by a greater degree of systematic organization than any other prophetic book. The report of the fall of Jerusalem represents the transition between the preceding material, which is overwhelmingly concerned with judgement (both upon Israel and upon the nations), and that which follows, which is devoted largely to promises of favour for Israel. For the most part, this pattern has a consistency that suggests that at some point a deliberate editorial systematization has been imposed upon the book.

The chapter is, however, also in significant part retrospective. It shares features with several earlier chapters, notably chs. 3, 18 and 24. Rather than inaugurating a new period of the prophet's ministry suited to the situation after 587 (Zimmerli 1983:189–90), 33:1–20 recapitulates themes of chs. 1–24, bringing the pre-587 phase of Ezekiel's ministry to a climax before the blow falls, serving as a prelude to the announcement of the final judgement that follows in 33:21–22 (cf. Greenberg 1997:680, 692). Coherent with this is that the foreign nations material of chs. 25–32 continues the judgement upon Israel, as we have seen, so that ch. 33 stands more in continuity with chs. 1–24 than might be assumed.

33:1–9. These verses reintroduce the motif of the "sentinel" or "watchman" (Heb. *ṣōp̄eh*), which first occurs in 3:16–21. It is important to note that the two sentinel passages form "bookends" around the pre-587 ministry of Ezekiel. This material only superficially appears to refer to an open call to repentance, as we have seen (see on 3:16–21 and also the "Theological Themes" section, above). The metaphor seems to be that of the lookout who blows the trumpet, so that the warning can be acted upon, to fight off thieves, wild animals or impending military threat. But what is actually said through the sentinel is "You shall surely die" (33:8; cf. 3:18). This is not the call of a sentinel but rather a term from the context of law, indeed, nothing other than the formal declaration of the sentence of death. As we saw, Wilson correctly argued that the prophetic task here is not to call the people to repentance, but "to deliver to the accused a legal decision which YHWH has already given" (Wilson 1972:96). **33:2.** "If I bring the sword upon a land": priestly case law format, very similar to 14:13. "The people of the land": not a technical term here (see on 22:29); the meaning is simply "the people." In vv. 1–6 the sentinel theme is introduced in general terms, only to be applied specifically to Ezekiel in vv. 7–9. But the implications for Ezekiel's situation and role are clear throughout. **33:5.** "They heard the sound of the trumpet and did not take warning; their blood shall be upon themselves": these words summarize the actual situation of the nation in 587 in a nutshell (cf. 3:19). "But if they had taken warning, they would have saved their lives": the case of the wicked turning and avoiding death appears overtly only here within the two sentinel passages (3:21 states that if the righteous stays faithful he will live, but we never in 3:16–21 have the case of the wicked turning and avoiding death). It is striking, though, that even here the positive case is only mentioned briefly and, significantly, the reference is retrospective, to an opportunity missed and now passed. **33:7.** "So you, mortal": the general role becomes here a personal commissioning (on vv. 7–9, see Simian-Yofre 1982). "I have made a sentinel for the house of Israel": cf. 3:17. **33:8.** "You shall surely die": cf. 3:18; 18:13. "Their blood I will require at your hand": as in 3:16–21, a major concern here is the awesome responsibility of the prophet to fulfil his task (cf. v. 6). **33:9.** "If you warn the wicked to turn from their ways, and they do not turn from their ways": it is noteworthy that within these verses personalizing the task of sentinel as Ezekiel's (vv. 7–9) there is no reference either to the righteous staying faithful and living (cf. 3:21) or to the wicked turning from their ways and saving their lives (cf. 33:5).

33:10–20. These verses pick up themes from 18:21–32. On vv. 10–20 in relation to ch. 18, see Schenker 1981. **33:10.** "Thus you have said…": as often before, words are ascribed to Ezekiel's audience; this could be a proverb or popular saying. "Our transgressions and our sins weigh upon us, and we waste away because of them; how then can we live?": most scholars have taken the words of the people here as an admission of responsibility (e.g. Greenberg 1983a:341; 1997:673–77; Mein 2001a:207–8). This might seem the most natural interpretation of these words read in isolation; however, vv. 17 and 20, denying the justice of God, indicate that the prophet's audience has still not accepted responsibility. Perhaps therefore Hebrew *pᵉšāʿênû wᵉḥaṭṭōʾṯênû* in v. 10 should be taken to refer not to (acknowledged) sins but rather to (undeserved) punishments. This is possible in the light of usage elsewhere (cf. Dan 8:12, 13; 9:24; Zech 14:19). The words of 33:10 would then amount to the same as the "sour grapes" proverb of 18:2, and constitute a denial of responsibility. If this is correct, 33:10–20, though less carefully argued, is in fact very similar to ch. 18 (with which it in any case shares so much language). This would cohere with 33:1–20 belonging with what goes before it in chs. 1–32. **33:11.** "As I live": a divine oath, emphasizing what follows. "I have no pleasure in the death of the wicked, but that the wicked turn from their ways and live; turn back, turn back from your evil ways; for why will you die, O house of Israel?": cf. 18:23, 30–32; 14:6. As in those other contexts, Ezekiel's repentance language demands careful interpretation, given that repentance can obviously not avert the judgement and also will never in Ezekiel be the condition of national restoration. This language anticipates a time when YHWH will grant a new beginning, in which "life" will consist in the fullness of relationship with him, freely enabled by his gift of obedience (cf. 36:26–27); also, more immediately, the language of repentance represents a concern that the exiles should conduct their lives in accordance with God's will. As in 18:21–32, there is a strong emphasis here on the future not being limited by the past; and as there we find here no particular concern for the individual (indeed recurrent reference is made to the "house of Israel," in vv. 10, 11, 20). But the most immediate function of the repentance motif here, as the judgement falls, is to highlight the nation's unqualified responsibility for the just fate that is befalling her. Every chance has been given, but the trumpet has been ignored and the nation has no one to blame but herself (see the "Theological Themes" section, above). **33:12.** "The righteousness of the righteous shall not save them when they transgress": cf. 18:24, 26. "As for the wickedness of the wicked, it shall not make them stumble when they turn from their wickedness": cf. 18:21–22, 27–28. As in ch. 18, in this respect YHWH is more generous than is the practice of criminal law, within which the past offences of the penitent are by no means discounted. "The righteous shall not be able to live by their righteousness when they sin": the verse ends, as it began, with this theme, which again v. 13 reinforces. **33:13.** "They shall surely live": Hebrew *ḥāyō yiḥyeh*; cf. 3:21; 18:9, 17, 19, 21, 28; 33:15, 16. **33:14.** "Again, though I say to the wicked, 'You shall surely die,' yet if they turn from their sin and do what is lawful and right…": this is a remarkable sequence within this context. It employs the death sentence formula, "You shall surely die" (Heb. *môṯ tāmûṯ*; cf. 3:18; 18:13), but then—speaking of the same people—goes on to hold out the prospect of life (vv. 15–16, "they shall surely live"). Yet this comes as the nation is breathing her last, and only a few verses before the announcement that the final blow has fallen (in vv. 21–22). In a profound way this verse looks beyond the absolute judgement to the new future that YHWH will inaugurate and enable. **33:15.** "If the wicked restore the pledge, give back what they have taken by robbery, and walk in the statutes of life, committing no iniquity": cf. vv. 25–26 and also the sin lists of chs. 18 and 22. **33:17.** "Yet…": this verse indicates the reality that actually confronts Ezekiel, as does more especially the final verse of the section, v. 20. "Your people say": it is telling that YHWH does not refer to "my people." "'The way of the Lord is not just,' when it is their own way that is not just": cf. 18:25, 29 (in ch. 18, NRSV reads "fair," rather than "just," but the Hebrew is the same, employing the verb *tkn*). Ezekiel's audience are still questioning the divine justice, which goes hand-in-hand with their denial of their own responsibility. **33:18.** "When the righteous turn from their righteousness, and commit iniquity, they shall die for it": this verse and the next reiterate the twofold theme, negative and then positive, that the future is not bound by the past in the dealings of YHWH with his people. **33:20.** "Yet you say, 'The way of the Lord is not just'": the people have still not relinquished the last vestiges of their illusion that it is YHWH and not they who are unjust. "All of you according to your ways!":

Hebrew *ʾîš kiḏrāḵāyw*; as in 18:30, these words are not to be understood to imply that YHWH will punish individuals in isolation from their contemporaries. Rather, they constitute a reference to the legal principle (enunciated in 18:4, 20) whereby in law it is the guilty party who is to be punished. Applied to the question at issue, this means that the present generation of the house of Israel is being punished for its own sins alone. This is a final reinforcement of the prophet's central concern, to establish the absolute justice of the judgement that is imminent—indeed, that has now at last definitively arrived.

33:21. "In the twelfth year…in the tenth month, on the fifth day of the month": some amend to the "eleventh" year, with the Syriac and some Hebrew manuscripts, since the "twelfth" year gives an implausibly long time-gap before the arrival of the news (so Howie 1950; Taylor 1969). "Of our exile": spelled out on this occasion; cf. 1:2. News of the fall of Jerusalem reaches Ezekiel; the date, reading "eleventh" rather than "twelfth," would be 19th January 586, two years later than the date of 24:1 and about five months after the fall of the city, if we date that event to August 587 (Kutsch 1974; Cazelles 1983; cf. 2 Kgs 25:8; Jer 52:12). "Someone who had escaped": Hebrew *happālîṭ*, "the fugitive." "The city has fallen": cf. 24:1–2, 25–27. **33:22.** "My mouth was opened, and I was no longer unable to speak": on the dumbness motif, see on 3:26–27.

33:23–29. Rival claims to the land. **33:24.** "Mortal, the inhabitants of these waste places in the land of Israel": this unit is very like 11:14–21, reflecting the polarized and alienated nature of the relationship between the exiles and those back in the homeland (cf. Rom-Shiloni 2005b). "Abraham was only one man, yet he got possession of the land; but we are many; the land is surely given us to possess": still the non-exiles make hubristic claims. The object is a decidedly materialistic one, namely possession of land. This is the only reference to Abraham in Ezekiel (cf. Isa 51:2, where similar sentiments are expressed as a legitimate hope by the anonymous prophet). Along similar lines, Ezek 28:25 and 37:25 speak of the restored people settling on the land given to Jacob. Whereas a strong case was made for the pre-587 dating of 11:14–21, the present passage seems to reflect a post-587 situation, in three respects. First, whereas 11:15 still referred to "the inhabitants of Jerusalem," 33:24 speaks of "the inhabitants of these waste places in the land of Israel." Second, while 33:23–29 certainly bears witness to the continuing pretensions of the non-exiles, gone is the mocking derision of the deportees found in 11:15 ("They have gone far from the LORD; to us this land is given for a possession"). Third, the self-sufficient arrogance on the part of the Jerusalemites in 11:15 has here given way to a more dependent appeal to the promises to Abraham. It is likely therefore that this unit reflects a situation after 587. This would, of course, fit with its placement after vv. 21–22. **33:25.** "Therefore": introduces the declaration of judgement. "You eat flesh with the blood…": cf. the sin lists of chs. 18 and 22, and also v. 15 here. "Shall you then possess the land?": a rhetorical question. **33:26.** "You depend on your swords…shall you then possess the land?": the pattern is repeated, with more offences listed, followed again by the rhetorical question. **33:27.** "Those who are in the waste places...": cf. v. 24. "The sword...wild animals...pestilence": cf. threefold punishment in 5:2, 12; 6:11–12. The sword and pestilence feature in those and other contexts; for punishment by animals, cf. 5:17; 14:15, 21. Given the historical context, it is surprising that famine does not feature here. While the book generally contrasts the periods before and after 587 in a schematic way, this chapter reflects the more complex historical reality. Judgement continues upon the sinners in the land; there was in fact to be a third deportation by the Babylonians in 581. **33:28.** "Its proud might shall come to an end": contrast the hubristic statement of v. 24. "The mountains of Israel shall be...desolate": contrast ch. 36, with its reversal of the judgement upon the mountains enunciated in ch. 6. **33:29.** "Then they shall know that I am the LORD": the last occasion in the book when the "Recognition Formula" is used in connection with the prospective punishment of Israelites.

33:30. "Your people": YHWH does not speak of them as "my" people (cf. v. 17). "Who talk together about you...at the doors of the houses": the place of gossip. "Come and hear what the word is that comes from the LORD": this sounds respectful so far. **33:31.** "They come to you as people come": in context, this must be a positive statement. "They sit before you as my people": the reference to "my people" appears inconsistent with the "your people" of v. 30; but, as we shall see, this is only because they are not as they seem. "And they hear your words": so far, so good; in three phrases the verse has built up a positive expectation. "But": the reality is different, for "they will not obey them." "Flattery": Hebrew *ᶜᵃg̱āḇāh*, here in the plural, can mean "lust," as in 23:11; but the context calls for a positive interpretation of the word here, for example, as in v. 32, "love." "Their lips, but their heart": a familiar contrast between external appearance and inner reality; see on 11:19, and compare also the "heart of stone" of 36:26. "Gain": Hebrew *beṣaᶜ*; cf. Harland 2000. Verse 31b constitutes one of the cases where Allen argues that a cluster of marginal annotations have mistakenly been taken together and then incorporated into the text (Allen 1990b). **33:32.** "A singer of love songs": Hebrew *šîr ᶜᵃg̱āḇîm*, "a song of love"; cf. Isa 5:1. Hebrew *ᶜᵃg̱āḇîm* is the same word as is translated "flattery" in v. 31. Compare the designation of Ezekiel at 20:49 (Heb. 21:5): "a maker of allegories." "One who has a beautiful voice and plays well on an instrument": cf. David in 1 Sam 16:18. The overall point seems to be that the people dismiss Ezekiel's performance as a matter of ephemeral entertainment. "They hear what you say, but they will not do it": as in the contrast of v. 31. **33:33.** "When this comes—and come it will!—then they shall know that a prophet has been among them": cf. 2:5; 24:24.

CHAPTER 34

Chapters 34–37 paint a vivid picture of hope for the future. The exiles will return to the land (34:13; 36:24; 37:12), cities will be rebuilt (36:10, 33), nature itself will be renewed (34:25–29; 36:8–9, 29–30). Judah and Israel will be united again (37:15–22), there will be a restored Davidic monarchy (34:23–24; 37:22, 24–25) and YHWH will set his sanctuary in the midst of his people for evermore (37:26–27).

Can this really be from Ezekiel? Herrmann contended that the deliverance oracles in the book are to be attributed to redactors active later in the exilic period. For him, the hopeful nature of this material is itself an indication that it does not derive from Ezekiel (Herrmann 1965:266–75). However, such a position tends to beg the question of the content of the prophet's teaching. While Clements is right to acknowledge that elaboration of prophetic books generally seems more evident in their hopeful sections (Clements 1986:286), any assumption that restoration material is secondary should be resisted. In fact, two telling theological arguments can be advanced in favour of attributing a message of hope to Ezekiel himself. The theme of restoration is characterized by the emphasis on the need for YHWH to vindicate his "name" (see especially 36:20–23), a feature rooted in the soil of Ezekiel's theology of judgement (cf. 20:9, 14, 22). This suggests that the restoration theme itself is integral rather than extraneous. Raitt offers another theological argument, based on the presence of strikingly rigorous elements within the oracles of restoration in Ezekiel (e.g. 36:22–23, 31–32; 37:23). He notes a "remarkable combination of unconditional promises of deliverance together with a vivid awareness of the validity and profoundly serious implications of the judgment" (Raitt 1977:126). This interpenetration of grace and rigour is most reasonably accounted for on the hypothesis that the themes of judgement and hope come from the one prophet, wrestling to "make sense of the movement of God's initiative toward salvation without ignoring the reality and justice of the judgment God brought on Judah" (Raitt 1977:126).

Theological arguments call for care, however, if circularity is to be avoided, and they are best not advanced in isolation from other criteria. Certain stylistic aspects of chs. 34–37 do in fact suggest authorship by Ezekiel. The vocabulary and motifs of the chapter exhibit numerous features characteristic of what appears to be "primary" material in the book. For example, the address "mortal" (Heb. *ben-ʾāḏām*) (e.g. 34:2; 35:2; 36:17; 37:11), reference to YHWH's wrath (Heb. *ḥēmâ*) and jealousy (Heb. *qinʾâ*) (36:5–6, 18; cf. 5:13; 8:18), and the placing of words in the mouths of interlocutors (35:10; 36:20, 35; 37:11; cf. 12:22; 18:2). These stylistic features, taken with the two theological considerations mentioned above, would seem to constitute a strong case for the primary provenance of chs. 34–37. The matter is not quite so simple, of course, for to demonstrate continuity of thought and style is not to prove that one has isolated the *ipsissima verba* of the prophet. We have seen that even where features originate with the prophet they may subsequently become the common currency of the redactional tradition. So an element of redactional elaboration, closely aligned to the thought and the style of the prophet himself, cannot be ruled out. But we can be confident that in these restoration chapters we are dealing with a new message of Ezekiel, couched in language forged by the prophet himself.

Having become familiar with Ezekiel's recurrent themes of judgement, it is indeed remarkable to move onto these sunny uplands of hope, and yet to hear the recognizable voice of Ezekiel. Ezekiel's first message had been fully vindicated in the final collapse of the city. Ezekiel's holy God had acted decisively to punish wickedness and to remove himself from his defiled temple. Now he initiates a new act, but it is again one that springs from his deep and consistent nature as the holy and powerful God who must make himself known. As we shall see, he restores Israel both to vindicate his reputation and also to forestall any danger that the nation will again defile his name.

Mein, drawing upon sociological studies of so-called millenarian groups, speaks of restoration promises as in part a "strategy for survival" in exile, for hopes for the future are often largely concerned with the present, providing strength and common purpose and defining and preserving the community (Mein 2001a:216–33).

Chapter 34 features a sustained polemic against the "shepherds" of Israel. Both the context here and usage elsewhere (e.g. 2 Sam 5:2; Isa 44:28) indicate that this is a reference to royal leaders. In the prophet's explanation of the national disaster, judgement on the royal rulers of Judah plays a central part (Duguid 1994:10–57; Joyce 1998). An important model for the shepherd image is found in the language of Jeremiah (notably ch. 23). Influence upon later texts is extensive, including Zech 13:7, the *Apocryphon of Ezekiel* (fragment 5; cf. Mueller 1994), Matt 25:31–33 and John 10. Willmes argued for a source-critical distinction between two texts now combined in the final form of the chapter, but the grounds for this are insufficient (Willmes 1984, 1986).

34:2. "Prophesy against the shepherds of Israel": the scathing critique of the "shepherds" opens with the charge of "feeding yourselves," literally "shepherding yourselves." Such play with the Hebrew verb *rʿh*, "to shepherd, pasture, feed" is a recurrent feature of this chapter. **34:3.** "You eat the fat, you clothe yourselves with the wool, you slaughter the fatlings": cf. the sin lists of 18:5–18; 22:6–12, 25–29; 33:15, 25–26. We should resist detailed allegorization, but references to self-indulgence and abusive violence are obvious. **34:4.** "You have not strengthened the weak…you have not sought the lost": this is a beautiful expression of pastoral care (cf. v. 16), rather untypical of Ezekiel. **34:5.** "So they were scattered": cf. Jer 10:21; an allusion to exile. **34:6.** "My sheep": the use of the possessive "my" anticipates the divine initiative of vv. 10–22. "Wandered over all the mountains and on every high hill": cf. Jer 50:6–7.

34:7. "Therefore, you shepherds": for the first time they are addressed directly. **34:8.** "As I live": a divine oath, a measure of the gravity of the judgement. **34:10.** "I am against the shepherds": after the long build-up of vv. 7–9 comes this uncompromising declaration. Somewhat surprising is that (the emphasis being on rescuing the sheep) the punishment of the shepherds is nowhere referred to; perhaps this is because for Ezekiel's audience the fate of the deposed kings was accomplished and obvious. **34:11.** "I myself will search": as the shepherds had not (v. 8). The Hebrew for "search" in these cases (*drš*) is the same word as that used for "demand" in v. 10. **34:13.** "I will bring them out from the peoples…and will bring them into their own land": the reference to restoration from exile becomes overt; cf. Jer 31:10. "On the mountains of Israel": cf. chs. 6 and 36. **34:14.** "I will feed them with good pasture…": this and the following verse share features with Ps 23. **34:15.** "I myself will be the shepherd of my sheep": the most explicit statement of this promise (cf. Isa 40:11). Since the polemic is against the failings of Davidic monarchy, implied also is that YHWH will reign as king. Only at 20:33 is the Hebrew root *mlk* ("to reign," or "to be king") used of YHWH in the book. The notion that YHWH is the true king of Israel is found in, among other places, Judg 8:23, 1 Sam 8:7 and the Psalms of Divine Kingship (e.g. Pss 93; 95–99), and it seems very likely that this theme was reinforced if not initiated in the wake of the disaster of 587 B.C.E.

34:16. "But the fat and the strong I will destroy": in vv. 16–22 the judgement theme is developed to take in divine judgement between animals. The "fat and the strong" who "butted at all the weak animals" (v. 21) seems to be another metaphor for the cruel and exploitative leaders. **34:17.** "Rams and goats": the range of animals is broadened. **34:18.** "Foul…with your feet": there may be some play here on the sense of "your feet" (Heb. *raglêḵem*) as a euphemism for genitals. **34:20.** "Therefore": introduces the judgement. "I myself will judge": the role of judge is by no means incompatible with YHWH's role as shepherd. The image of the shepherd caring for his sheep can seem an idyllic one; but Mein has recently drawn attention to the harsher practical and economic realities of sheep rearing in ancient Israel, and the implications of this for the present metaphor (Mein 2007). The polemical distinction between the "fat sheep" and "my flock" in these verses is in part reminiscent of 20:33–38, which features both shepherding imagery and also judgement within the community. Like that passage, it is untypical of Ezekiel's characteristic emphasis on the people as a whole, both in judgement and in promise; the fat sheep will clearly not form part of the restored community. This is best explained by observing that "fat sheep" is another way of speaking of the cruel and exploitative leaders whose time has come to an end. **34:21.** "You scattered them far and wide": another echo of exile. **34:22.** "I will save my flock ": cf. 36:38, "so shall the ruined towns be filled with flocks of people. Then they shall know that I am the LORD."

34:23. "I will set up over them one shepherd": the passage at this point moves from divine shepherding to royal shepherding, under God; cf. Jer 3:15. Unity under the "one" leader is an important element (cf. 37:24), though we do not find here the concern with the unification of the southern and northern territories that is promised in 37:15–28. "My servant": servant language was often used of kings (e.g. 2 Sam 3:18). "David": the first reference to David in the book (cf. 37:24–25); a ruler of the Davidic line is in view, rather than David himself returned. Aytoun excised all references to future human rule in ch. 34 as post-exilic glosses (Aytoun 1920:28–29). But this is unnecessary. It would be surprising if there were not speculation about the future of the monarchy in the wake of its demise, and there are sixth-century parallels (e.g. Jer 23:5–6). Moreover, it is not at all unusual in Ezekiel or other prophetic books for themes to develop within a passage; compare the way the object of the polemic earlier in the present chapter moves from bad shepherds to bad sheep. **34:24.** "I, the LORD, will be their God, and my servant David shall be prince among them": the Davidic prince here is like a viceroy to a king—so, in a way, the divine shepherding image of vv. 10–22 is maintained rather than abandoned. The "I…my servant" pattern reflects the so-called "covenant formula," on which see v. 30. With the exception of the book of Numbers, the Hebrew word *nāśîʾ*, "prince," is used more times in Ezekiel than in any other book of the Hebrew Bible. It seems likely that this word *nāśîʾ* represents a downgrading of royal language and that Ezekiel's use of it is a deliberate archaizing, an echo of the leadership patterns of pre-monarchic Israel, as pictured in Numbers (e.g. Num 2:3; 13:2). This appears to be so not only in the critique of past and present (cf. 12:10, 12; 21:25 [Heb. v. 30]) but also in looking ahead to the future (here and in 37:25). And we see this trend continued in the limited role assigned to the *nāśîʾ*, "prince," in chs. 40–48. In the use of *nāśîʾ* in Ezekiel's future expectation we encounter a dialectical critique of monarchy, allowing it a place within the divinely ordained polity, but only when radically subordinated to the will of God and to the real needs and interests of the community of the people of God (see further Joyce 1998).

34:25. "I will make": Hebrew verb *krt*, "to cut." The oldest Hebrew term for covenant making (cf. Gen 15:18; also used in Jer 31:31–34). "A covenant of peace": Hebrew *bᵉrîṯ šālôm*. Compare 37:26, which features both a "covenant of peace" and an "everlasting covenant" (Heb. *bᵉrîṯ ʿôlām*), the latter phrase also occurring at 16:60. Nicholson (1986) has shown that theological covenant language was particularly characteristic of the seventh and sixth centuries. The word "peace," Hebrew *šālôm*, suits the present context particularly well. "Banish wild animals": cf. Lev 26:6 and v. 28 here; this is part of the reversal of the former situation, for wild animals had been a mode of judgement (cf. 5:17; 14:15, 21; 33:27; and, in the present chapter, vv. 5, 8). "So that they may live in the wild and sleep in the woods securely": a theme continued in vv. 27–28; cf. Isa 11:6–9. Murray has used the term "cosmic covenant" for this and similar conceptions in the Hebrew Bible (Murray 1992). With the present passage we may compare also accounts of blessedness in classical antiquity (e.g. Homer, *Odyssey*, xix.109–14, where under a just ruler the crops grow more abundantly; Horace, *Epodes*, xvi.41–56, where the wild animals are no longer a threat). **34:26.** "I will make them and the region around my hill a blessing": the use of "hill" (Heb. *giḇʿâ*) is unusual, but the reference is clearly to Jerusalem. "I will send down the showers in their season; they shall be showers of blessing": cf. Gen 8:22; Joel 2:23–24. **34:27.** "The trees of the field shall yield their fruit, and the earth shall yield its increase": cf. Amos 9:13–14. "They shall know that I am the LORD": the "Recognition Formula"; this refers to the people of YHWH, in the context now of blessing. "When I break the bars of their yoke, and save them from the hands of those who enslaved them": second Exodus language, as in 20:33–38 (in the context of royal language used of YHWH at v. 33) and Jer 23:7–8 (alongside the Davidic promise of vv. 5–6). **34:29.** "They shall no more be consumed with hunger in the land": reversing the former scourge of famine (e.g. 5:12, 16–17; 6:11–12; 7:15; 14:13). The vegetation is described as "splendid" (Heb. *lᵉšēm*, "deserving of its reputation"). "No longer suffer the insults of the nations": cf. 36:20. **34:30.** "They shall know that I, the LORD their God, am with them": an adapted version of the familiar "Recognition Formula." "And that they, the house of Israel, are my people": continuation in this way means that the verse as a whole constitutes a case of the so-called "covenant formula" (cf. v. 24); similar words occur elsewhere in Ezekiel at 11:20; 14:11; 36:28; 37:23, 27. In the Hebrew Bible as a whole, this formula frequently occurs in the same context as the word *bᵉrîṯ* ("covenant"), as in Exod 6:7; Lev 26:12; Deut 29:13 (Heb. v. 12); Jer 11:4; 31:33; 32:38 (cf. Rendtorff 1998). Within Ezekiel, we find these words juxtaposed to *bᵉrîṯ* also at 37:23, 27. Commenting on this formula, von Rad wrote: "This puts it beyond all doubt that Ezekiel is speaking of a saving appointment of Yahweh analogous to the making of the old covenant" (von Rad 1962–65:2.235). **34:31.** "You are my sheep, the sheep of my pasture": cf. Ps 100:3. After the word for "pasture," the MT has *ʾāḏām ʾattem*, "you are people" or "you are human," an unnecessary reminder (quite possibly redactional) that the language of the chapter is metaphorical. NRSV follows LXX and the Old Latin, which lack these words. "I am your God": this verse too resembles the "covenant formula." It is telling that after the David references (vv. 23–24), the chapter culminates here in v. 31 with the formulation "You are my sheep…and I am your God," picking up the divine shepherding motif of vv. 10–22. This motif seems to be given primacy over renewed Davidic "shepherding," in keeping with the radical theocentricity of Ezekiel. We sense that for Ezekiel there is ultimately to be no central role for royal mediators; the function of kings is melting away, overwhelmed—it would seem—by the emphasis on the holy God.

Chapter 35

Chapter 35 returns to the foreign nations theme of chs. 25–32. Judgement upon Edom is the focus of the chapter and indeed this issue continues through 36:1–7. Concerning Edom, see on 25:12–14. With regard to chs. 6, 35 and 36 (three interrelated chapters, featuring the recurrent theme of the "mountains of Israel"), see Simian 1974 and Gosse 1989. Mathews (1995) argues that Ezek 35–36 exercised a literary influence upon Isa 34–35. Among the features that Ezek 35–36 and Isa 34–35 share is the "seesaw"/"teeter-totter" phenomenon with Israel's fortunes rising as those of the nations decline; whereas we observed that the oracles against the nations in chs. 25–32 feature very little anticipation of Israel's restoration, in the case of chs. 35–36 Edom's condemnation goes hand-in-hand with the revival of Israel's circumstances. This coheres with this material's placement within the latter part of the book, after 33:21–22.

35:2. "Set your face": see on 4:3. "Mount Seir": its location is disputed; possibly somewhere in the southern Negev (cf. Bartlett 1969; Davies 1979:97–100). It may be a later biblical view that, as here (v. 15), places Seir in Edom (Williamson 1982:297). **35:3.** Verses 3–4 could be a fragment of quoted poetry. "I am against you, Mount Seir": direct address. **35:4.** "You shall know that I am the LORD": the "Recognition Formula" (also here at vv. 9 and 15, with a variation in v. 12). **35:5.** "Because you cherished an ancient enmity": this may be an allusion to the rivalry between Esau and Jacob (Assis 2006; cf. Gen 25–28; 32–33). See further on 25:12–14. "Gave over the people of Israel to the power of the sword at the time of their calamity": an allusion to events of the early sixth century, when Edom occupied part of southern Judah (cf. Jer 49:7–22). Edom is criticized for participating in YHWH's chastisement of his people, much as Assyria is rebuked in Isa 10:12–19. **35:7.** "I will cut off from it all who come and go": in other words, all people; cf. 21:3–4 (Heb. vv. 8–9). **35:8.** "Its mountains": an appropriate designation, partly because of the mountainous terrain of Edom and also corresponding to the abused "mountains of Israel" in v. 12.

35:10. "Because you said…": Ezekiel's typical placing of words on the lips of others is found here and at v. 12. "These two nations and these two countries shall be mine": Israel and Judah; cf. 37:15–28. "We will take possession of them": note the comparable words of the Jerusalemites in 11:15; 33:24. "Although the LORD was there": as in 36:20, events have been misinterpreted by the nations at YHWH's expense. Compare 48:35, where the name of the restored city is to be "The LORD is There." **35:11.** "I will make myself known among you": so LXX; MT has "among them." **35:12.** "The mountains of Israel": see on 36:1. "They are laid desolate, they are given us to devour": again, cf. 11:15; 33:24. **35:14.** "As the whole earth rejoices, I will make you desolate": the following verse exploits the irony that Edom had rejoiced over Israel's downfall, employing the same Hebrew word *śmḥ*. **35:15.** "Desolate…desolate": play on the Hebrew root *šmm*, "to be desolate, appalled." The punishment fits the crime of Edom (cf. also v. 6), an entirely appropriate response wherein sin and judgement correspond closely (cf. Miller 1982:69–74).

CHAPTER 36

36:1–15. A prophecy to the "mountains of Israel," picking up that theme from ch. 35 (v. 12) and reversing the condemnation of the mountains enunciated in ch. 6. This reversal reflects the broader architecture of the book. **36:1.** "The mountains of Israel": on the principle of "the part for the whole," the reference is to all Israel. **36:2.** "The enemy": probably more general than Edom (mentioned only in v. 5), whose role here is in part representative of the nations. "Aha!": declared previously by Ammon (25:3) and Tyre (26:2). **36:3.** "An object of gossip and slander among the people": cf. vv. 4–6, 15 and especially v. 20. **36:4.** "The desolate wastes and the deserted towns": cf. 33:24. **36:5.** "Against the rest of the nations": at first a general reference, as in v. 2, only then followed by a more specific mention of Edom (see on 25:12–14). "Took my land": YHWH's land, for which he is jealous. **36:6.** "The land of Israel": Hebrew *ʾaḏmaṯ yiśrāʾēl*, a characteristic formulation of Ezekiel, used both in contexts of judgement (e.g. 7:2; 20:38) and of blessing (e.g. 11:17; 20:42); its "earthiness" (the word *ʾaḏāmâ* means "ground" as well as "land") seems particularly appropriate and evocative now that return to the land is anticipated. "I am speaking in my jealous wrath": now Israel is to be the beneficiary of the divine jealousy and wrath, so often mentioned in the context of judgement upon the nation throughout the first half of the book (e.g. 5:13; 8:18). **36:7.** "I swear that the nations that are all around you shall themselves suffer insults": those who have insulted YHWH and his people (vv. 3–6) will get their recompense; as before, the punishment fits the crime (cf. Miller 1982:69–74).

36:8. "But you, O mountains of Israel": a clear case of the aforementioned "see-saw" phenomenon, with Israel's fortunes now rising as those of the nations decline. "Shall shoot out your branches, and yield your fruit to my people Israel": famine was a feature of the judgement upon the mountains of Israel in 6:11–12; but now (cf. also vv. 9, 11, 29–30, 34–35) fertility and fecundity are to be renewed (as in 34:25–31). "For they shall soon come home": although the word "home" is not in the Hebrew, this is a very explicit promise of restoration. **36:9.** "See now, I am for you": the positive promise of favour continues; cf. Jer 31:16–17. "I will turn to you": employs the Hebrew verb *pānâ* ("to turn"), to which the Hebrew noun *pānîm*, "face," is related; this is reminiscent of the so-called Priestly Blessing of Num 6:24–26, "The LORD make his face to shine upon you, and be gracious to you; the LORD lift up his countenance upon you, and give you peace." **36:10.** "I will multiply your population…the towns shall be inhabited": repopulation is a recurrent theme here; cf. vv. 11–12, 33–38. The impression given is that the land had been denuded of people during the exile, a similar picture to that painted in 2 Kgs 24–25, but several scholars have emphasized the ongoing nature of life in the land during these years, writing indeed of the "myth of the empty land" (Carroll 1992; Barstad 1996). **36:11.** "I will multiply human beings and animals upon you. They shall increase and be fruitful": cf. Gen 1:28; a new creation indeed, as is suggested also by the reference to "Eden" in v. 35; the animals here are domestic animals (with regard to wild animals, see on 34:25). "Will do more good to you than ever before": a grandiose promise, in the spirit of Isa 40–55 (e.g. Isa 42:9; 43:19; 48:6–7; cf. also Jer 24:6; 32:39–42). **36:12.** "I will lead people upon you": evoking the great acts of salvation history, above all the conquest. "My people Israel": perhaps an explanatory gloss. "No longer shall you bereave them of children": a remarkable statement to the personified mountains. The reference could be to famine or wild animals (cf. 5:17; 14:13–15), or possibly to human sacrifice (see on 20:26; it is noteworthy that at Lev 20:3 human sacrifice is linked closely with the profanation of YHWH's holy name, an important theme here in Ezek 36). **36:13.** "Because they say to you": this verse in part renders into a quotation what we have already learned in another mode in v. 12. This is typical of Ezekiel's repetitive style. "Devour people": cf. Num 13:32. **36:14.** "You shall no longer…": this implies that the charge of the quotation was accurate. "Your nation": the retrospective use of the distant term "nation" (Heb. *gôy*) of Israel reflects the old times that are now passing away, to be replaced by an era of blessing, represented by the use of the relational term "my people" (Heb. *ʿammî*) in v. 12. **36:15.** "Bear the disgrace of the peoples": this amounts to the same as the preceding phrase, "hear the insults of the nations." "No longer shall you cause your nation to stumble": this makes it more likely that the preceding verses include reference to Israel's sinning, and perhaps especially to human sacrifice.

36:16–32. With v. 16 a new section begins, cast in narrative form, first reviewing the past and then looking to the imminent future. YHWH is to renew his people (cf. Ohnesorge 1991; Renz 1999a). Rendtorff compares this passage with ch. 20, in the context of discussing the composition of the book (Rendtorff 1986). **36:17.** "When the house of Israel lived on their own soil, they defiled it": for example, through the abominations recounted in ch. 8. "Like the uncleanness of a woman in her menstrual period": Ezekiel's analogy reflects his priestly preoccupation with cultic purity. **36:18.** "The blood that they had shed…the idols with which they had defiled it": both ethical and cultic sins are identified as the cause of the judgement. **36:19.** "In accordance with their conduct and their deeds I judged them": a retrospective summary of Ezekiel's judgement theology, in the manner of Isa 42:24. **36:20.** "When they came to the nations, wherever they came": the *idem per idem* technique; see on 12:25 (cf. Ogden 1992:115; Greenberg 1997:728). "They profaned my holy name": YHWH's essential nature is thereby contradicted (see the "Theological Themes" section, above). "These are the people of the LORD, and yet they had to go out of his land": yet another quotation and in this case a remarkable one: it sounds like a Yahwist statement on the lips of the nations—but then it is, of course, an imaginative projection by the prophet. **36:21.** "But I had concern for my holy name": cf. 20:9, 14, 22; also Isa 48:9–11. **36:22.** "I am about to act": Hebrew *ʾanî ʿōśeh*; at this point, the focus of the passage shifts to the prospect of a new divine initiative. "Not for your sake…but for the sake of my holy name" (cf. v. 32); this is the antithesis of "according to your ways," the principle upon which the judgement had been enacted (cf. v. 19). **36:23.** "I will sanctify my great name": the divine name is "great" as well as holy; this coheres with the fact that the quotation of v. 20 questions the power of YHWH; he acts now to ensure that this cannot be doubted. "When through you I display my holiness before their eyes": YHWH will vindicate his holiness as well as his power through restoring his people and making them holy. **36:24.** "I will take you from the nations…and bring you into your own land": an explicit promise of return, as in v. 8. **36:25.** "I will sprinkle clean water upon you, and you shall be clean from all your uncleannesses": cf. Exod 30:17–21.

36:26–27. "A new heart I will give you, and a new spirit I will put within you; and I will remove from your body the heart of stone and give you a heart of flesh": see on 11:19, where a survey was presented of use of the key terms "heart" (Heb. *lēḇ*) and "spirit" (Heb. *rûaḥ*). In the light of that survey it was noted that here in 36:26 two important senses of *lēḇ* converge, the heart as the locus of the moral will and as the symbol of inner reality as distinct from mere outward appearance. The "new spirit" (*rûah ḥᵃḏāšâ*) in v. 26 refers to the renewal of "the moral will." The words of v. 27, "I will put my spirit within you" (cf. 37:14; 39:29), employ *rûaḥ* the sense of the dynamic power of YHWH, which inspires judges, kings and prophets, and also evoke the eschatological outpouring of that *rûaḥ* of YHWH (e.g. Joel 2:28 [Heb. 3:1]; cf. Isa 61:1). However, these senses converge, since the two expressions "a new spirit I will put within you" and "I will put my spirit within you" are quite clearly intended to refer to the same reality, namely the renewal of the moral will of the house of Israel by the outpouring of the dynamic power of YHWH. This is the more likely in view of the words that follow the promise in v. 27: "I will…make you follow my statutes and be careful to observe my ordinances." Although obedience is never the condition of restoration, right behaviour is an integral part of the renewal. YHWH will now enable that of which Israel had shown herself to be incapable. Mein helpfully highlights "the way that this theological shift from responsibility to passivity mirrors the social experience of the exiles…a shift from positions of social responsibility and power to a new world in which there is far less scope for influential decision making and action" (Mein 2001a:240). It is probably unwise to attempt to distinguish between the aspects of obedient moral response represented by the "new heart" and the "new spirit" as does Wolff, who relates the former to "the pure guidings of the conscience" and the latter to "the steadfast power of the will to act accordingly" (Wolff 1974:38, 54).

We should rather regard the two expressions as essentially synonymous, each conveying both these aspects of the promised renewal. The theme of the "new" has a significant place in exilic prophecy (cf. Jer 31:31; Isa 42:9; 43:19; Wolff 1978).

As with 11:19, some have sought to interpret the promise of a "new heart" and a "new spirit" here in ch. 36 in a particularly individualistic way. Thus Eichrodt argued for "a direct connection between the covenant God and every single member of his people," claiming that here "we see the new importance of the individual member of the people" (Eichrodt 1970:500–501). However, the text of Ezekiel itself gives little justification for such an individualistic reading. First, the audience is both referred to and addressed as the "house of Israel" (vv. 17, 21, 22, 32). Second, it is important that "heart," "spirit" and "body" (Heb. *bāśār*) are all terms used of aspects of the human being; thus the giving of a new heart and new spirit and the replacement of the heart within the body are decidedly "corporate" images. Third, the covenant formula "you shall be my people, and I will be your God" (v. 28) underlines the essentially collective nature of the promise. This is not to interpret the renewal merely in terms of "the outward regulation of obedient conduct" (Eichrodt 1970:501) and nor is it to deny that particular individuals are involved in the renewal of the nation. But distortion by anachronistic individualizing interpretation must be rejected.

The divine gift of a "new heart" and a "new spirit" in Ezekiel shares affinities with other material of the exilic age, much of which evidences deuteronomistic features: Jer 24:7; 31:31–34; 32:38–40; Deut 30:6; Ps 51:10 (Heb. v. 12). But Ezekiel does make his distinctive contribution. The word "heart" (Heb. *lēḇ*; *lēḇāḇ*) is characteristic of deuteronomistic material (e.g. Deut 6:5; Josh 24:28; 1 Kgs 2:4), but the same can certainly not be said of "spirit" (Heb. *rûaḥ*), which is conspicuously rare in Deuteronomy (where it occurs just twice, at 2:30 and 34:9) and also in Jeremiah (just one relevant case, at Jer 51:11). By contrast, it occurs frequently in Ezekiel (41 times, excluding references to "wind"). A second distinctive feature is the radical theocentricity that we have seen to characterize Ezekiel. YHWH restores his undeserving people in order to demonstrate his power and thereby vindicate his profaned "name." The moral renewal of Israel is primarily a means of protecting the "name" of YHWH from ever again being profaned (cf. vv. 20–22). The extent to which in Ezekiel this initiative focuses upon YHWH's own nature stands out clearly in comparison with the more "affectionate" account of the "circumcision of the heart" in Deut 30:1–10, which speaks of YHWH "having compassion" (Heb. root *rḥm*) upon his people (v. 3) and "taking delight" (Heb. root *śwś*) in prospering them (v. 9).

There is an important text-critical issue to acknowledge here. There is a significant lacuna (or "minus") in the earliest Greek text, P. 967, when compared with MT, beginning at v. 23c and extending to the end of the chapter. Lust contends that this Greek text represents a more primitive witness than MT and regards the final section of ch. 36 as secondary (Lust 1981a; 1986a:12–15; cf. Irwin 1943:62–64; Bogaert 1978). This possibility is intriguing but ultimately not persuasive. Long ago Filson argued that the evidence of P. 967 could satisfactorily be explained on the grounds of accidental damage to the text at an early stage (Filson 1943:27–32; cf. Spottorno 1982). This line was followed also by Wevers (1969:273), in spite of his positive attitude to LXX Ezekiel. Moreover, it is noteworthy that the lacuna of P. 967 is evident in no extant Hebrew text (including the Masada manuscript of 35:11–38:14; cf. Talmon 1999). Ultimately, there are no compelling text-critical grounds to believe that the entire section vv. 23c–38 was missing from an original Hebrew text. There are also literary and theological arguments against this: the account of the vindication of YHWH's "name" is far from complete at v. 23b, and moreover the *inclusio* formed by v. 22 and v. 32 is striking.

36:28. "Then you shall live in the land that I gave to your ancestors": the people had lost the land and understandably looked to the traditions that claimed that it had been promised to their ancestors (cf. 28:25; 33:24; 37:25). "You shall be my people, and I will be your God": the "covenant formula"; see on 34:30. Although the word "covenant" (Heb. *b^erîṯ*) is not found in this passage, renewal of the covenant is in view, as it is in 11:20 (cf. Jer 31:31–33; 32:36–41). The verses that follow give further details of the restoration, particularly its more physical aspects. **36:29.** "I will save you from all your uncleannesses": cf. v. 25; in the present verse we encounter a noteworthy combination of cultic and soteriological language. "I will summon the grain and make it abundant": vv. 29–30, 34–35 emphasize the return of fertility; see on v. 8. **36:31.** "You shall loathe yourselves for your iniquities and your abominable deeds": a recurrent motif in Ezekiel; see on 6:9. This reinforces that restoration is undeserved, and provides a good example of the interpenetration of blessing and rigour highlighted by Raitt (1977:126). **36:32.** "It is not for your sake that I will act": cf. v. 22. This underlines the fact that it is in spite of rather than because of Israel's behaviour that all this is to happen. "Be ashamed and dismayed for your ways": see on 6:9 and also the "Theological Themes" section, above. Van Grol argues that this verse provides the "text" for the exegetical "sermon" in Ezra 9:6–9, which he describes as a realization of Ezekiel's call to shame (Van Grol 1998:61).

Two shorter sections, each with its own introductory formula, fill out the picture (vv. 33–36 and 37–38). These two sections could be secondary elaborations, but conclusive evidence of this is lacking. **36:33.** "I will cause the towns to be inhabited": see on v. 10. **36:34.** "The land that was desolate shall be tilled": the opposite of the situation described in Lamentations (cf. 1:1, 4; 5:18). "In the sight of all who passed by": cf. Lam 1:12; 2:15. **36:35.** "Like the garden of Eden": cf. Gen 2–3; Ezek 28:13; 31:9, 16, 18. The quotation given in this verse represents an important acknowledgement that the misconception expressed by the nations in v. 20 will be corrected by the powerful initiative of the holy God YHWH. **36:36.** "Shall know that I, the LORD, have rebuilt…I, the LORD, have spoken, and I will do it": a complex adaptation of the "Recognition Formula." "Replanted that which was desolate": cf. Jer 31:28. **36:37.** "I will also let the house of Israel ask me to do this for them: to increase their population": whereas YHWH refused to be consulted in 14:3 and 20:3, he will now let Israel ask things of him; the same Hebrew verb (*drš*, "to ask, seek, enquire, consult") is employed. **36:38.** "Like the flock for sacrifices": Hebrew *ṣōʾn qoḏāšîm*, "flock of holy things." The phrase hints at the holiness of the renewed people, while it also likens them to sheep, as in ch. 34. The particular image is that of the many animals assembled for sacrifice at festival time in Jerusalem. In the present context, the image must be a positive one of burgeoning crowds, and is not to be pressed for any darker threat!

CHAPTER 37

This sequence of restoration passages is brought to a climax with a pair of sections, one on the valley of the dry bones and the other on the reunification of Judah and Israel. Barth (1977) argued for the unity of the entire chapter, but it is best divided into vv. 1–14 and vv. 15–28, which constitute largely self-contained sections, even though they share the theme of restoration (explicitly at vv. 12 and 21).

37:1–14. The Valley of the Dry Bones. This justly famous passage has a brief model in the macabre passage of judgement in Jer 8:1–3, which speaks of the bones of the kings of Judah and other inhabitants of Jerusalem spread before "the sun and the moon and all the host of heaven." Among specialist studies of vv. 1–14 not referred to below, we may note Nobile 1984 and Wahl 1999. **37:1.** "The hand of the LORD came upon me…by the spirit of the LORD": two formulae for prophetic inspiration. "Set me down in the middle of a valley": MT actually has the definite article, hence "the valley," as in 3:22–23 and 8:4, but the location is unknown (see on 3:22). "It was full of bones": we might expect Ezekiel to protest (cf. 4:14), because human remains were judged ritually unclean according to priestly rules (cf. Num 19:16; Ezek 39:11–12; 44:25–26), but he does not. Lang suggested that this was because in Zoroastrian thought (which he took as the key to understanding this passage) dry bones, in contrast to dead bodies, were no longer unclean (Lang 1986:310). More likely is that the visionary nature of this experience overshadows such considerations. **37:2.** "He led me all around them": cf. 8:7, 14, 16; 40:3–4, 17, 24. "There were very many…and they were very dry": this image sums up well the situation of the exiles, who are here represented. **37:3.** "'Can these bones live?'…'O Lord GOD, you know'": compare the dialogue of 9:8–9, though strikingly here YHWH asks the question. The prophet's answer is typical of his radical theocentricity, and unusually presents YHWH as the subject of the knowing to which the "Recognition Formula" in different ways calls both Israel and the nations. **37:4.** "O dry bones, hear the word of the LORD": the personification of the bones reflects the fact that they represent the exiles. **37:5.** "I will cause breath to enter you, and you shall live": the multiple senses of the Hebrew word *rûaḥ* ("breath," "wind," "spirit") are a key feature of this passage; see on 11:19. **37:6.** "I will lay sinews on you, and will cause flesh to come upon you, and cover you with skin": the different aspects here are best not allegorized; their role is to help build up the overall picture. "Put breath in you, and you shall live": so far this is all instruction as to what is to happen, characteristically repetitive and not to be trimmed.

37:7. "As I prophesied, suddenly there was a noise, a rattling…": this dramatic action is in response to Ezekiel's prophesying, but before the summoning of the breath (v. 9). This visionary report is the only one of Ezekiel's where the prophet's activity has a direct and explicit effect on what transpires (the death of Pelatiah in 11:13 is not a clear exception). **37:8.** "I looked, and there were sinews on them…but there was no breath in them": the account affirms the remarkable developments but also indicates the incomplete nature of the revival. The two phases of restoration here in vv. 7–10 are like the two stages of Gen 2:7, that is, forming and inspiration (even though the Genesis verse uses the Hebrew word *nᵉšāmâ* for "breath," and not *rûaḥ*). **37:9.** "Come from the four winds, O breath": symbolizing the whole world; cf. fourfoldness elsewhere in Ezekiel (e.g. 1:6, 17; 10:9; 14:21). "Breathe upon these slain, that they may live": the first indication that the bones are those of the "slain"; the reference is to the nation, fallen to the Babylonians. **37:10.** "They lived, and stood on their feet, a vast multitude": an amazing image. On the basis of formal inconsistencies, Höffken (1981) and Bartelmus (1985) both argue for secondary elaboration within vv. 1–10; but they anachronistically impose modern assumptions of literary consistency. Fox (1980) and Allen (1993a) argue persuasively for the rhetorical coherence of vv. 1–14.

37:11. "Mortal, these bones are the whole house of Israel": an interpretation is given, as in 12:10–16; 17:12–21. Verse 11 plays a pivotal role, both spelling out the meaning of what has been seen and introducing the dialogue that follows. Ezekiel identifies the dead bones with his living contemporaries (of whom the phrase "house of Israel" is frequently used), thereby excluding any notion of a literal resurrection from the dead. "Our bones are dried up, and our hope is lost; we are cut off completely": this could be a line of a popular dirge. The words are comparable to those of 18:2 and 33:10; but, unlike in those cases, there is no suggestion here that the people deny their responsibility for what has happened; the remaining problem now is despondency in the wake of the judgement. **37:12.** "I am going to open your graves, and bring you up from your graves": the image of dry bones scattered about the valley is followed here by a scene of resurrected bodies emerging from graves. Lang argues that vv. 12–13 contain a later gloss, assimilating the Persian custom of exposing dead bodies to the Jewish practice of burying the dead (Lang 1986:312); but the inconsistency is adequately explained as part of the visionary mode of the passage. "O my people": the people of YHWH are now being renewed (as stressed by Ohnesorge 1991). "I will bring you back to the land of Israel": an explicit statement of the meaning of the vision. **37:13.** This verse represents a classic case of the "Recognition Formula" used in connection with blessing upon Israel. **37:14.** "I will put my spirit within you": cf. 36:27; 39:29. "And you shall live": cf. vv. 6, 9; and compare the positive declarations of 18:9, 17, 19. "I will place you on your own soil": the Hebrew employs the evocative word *ʾᵃḏāmâ* for "soil"; see on 36:6.

Lang contends that Ezekiel intends actual bodily resurrection and that this belief was appropriated by Ezekiel in Babylonia, from the Zoroastrian religion of the Persians (Lang 1986:309). But while Persian influence may well have played its part in the development of Israel's thinking in this area in later times, here in Ezekiel we have a metaphor for national restoration after exile. Personal resurrection is not intended and comes rather later (Dan 12:2 and, arguably, Isa 26:19). Day observes that Hos 5–6 and 13–14 had already in the eighth century used death and resurrection imagery to denote Israel's exile and restoration (Day 1996:240–48). Although Ezek 37 is similarly metaphorical, the development of the hope of personal resurrection within post-exilic Judaism probably owes something to Ezekiel's expression of the hope of national restoration in this powerful vision, which spurred the imagination in ancient times as it does in modern.

37:15–28. A new section: Judah and Israel are to be reunited. **37:16.** "Take a stick and write on it": the words written sound like a motto (cf. Isa 28:16; 30:8). This passage may have influenced Zech 11:7–14. "For Judah, and the Israelites associated with it": Israelites in the broad sense of the people of YHWH. The reference could be to people of Simeon and Benjamin, though the social reality of Israel would have been much more complex than the stylized twelve-tribe model suggests. "For Joseph (the stick of Ephraim)": descendants of Joseph's younger son Ephraim, politically more important than those of his brother Manasseh (as is reflected in Gen 48:19). "And all the house of Israel associated with it": again, Israel in the broad sense of the people of YHWH, but in this case also an echo of the northern political unit; the reference is to Manasseh and the other tribes of the north. **37:17.** "Join them together": a prophetic sign-action; cf. the commentary on ch. 4. **37:18.** "Will you not show us what you mean by these?": cf. 12:9. **37:19.** An interpretation is given, as in v. 11 above. "I am about to take the stick of Joseph…and I will put the stick of Judah upon it": in the latter clause the Hebrew has simply "I will put them upon it"; this suggests a Judahite perspective, as might be expected, but the overall picture is an egalitarian one. **37:21.** "I will take the people of Israel": that is, the whole people of YHWH. "Gather them from every quarter": Hebrew *missāḇîḇ*, "from round about." "Bring them to their own land": cf. v. 12; restoration from exile is what both sections of the chapter are about.

37:22. "I will make them one nation in the land": this is the main emphasis in this second half of the chapter. "On the mountains of Israel": continuing the theme of 36:1, 8. "One king shall be king over them all": it is conceivable that rule by God as king is intended here in v. 22, but since the root *mlk* is only otherwise used of YHWH at 20:33 this is unlikely. Unity under one human ruler is probably intended, as with the one shepherd of 34:23; cf. Hos 1:11. But the issue of the restoration of monarchy is overshadowed here by the affirmation of renewed unity. Perhaps this is why Hebrew *meleḵ*, "king," is used, rather than the more considered word *nāśîʾ*, "prince" (see on v. 25). "Never again shall they be divided into two kingdoms": a reference to the many years of divided monarchy that followed the end of the United Monarchy on the death of Solomon. There were aspirations to reunification with the north under Josiah, just a generation before Ezekiel's time (2 Kgs 22–23); moreover, it is possible that the "one heart" of 11:19 may reflect related hopes. **37:23.** "They shall never again defile themselves with their idols": 4Q Florilegium 1.16–17 probably refers to these words, though the text is damaged (see Lust 1986c:92; Brooke 1985:116–18). "Their detestable things…any of their transgressions": note that the element of rigour remains, even in this rather utopian context. "I will save them from all the apostasies into which they have fallen": NRSV "apostasies" is based on a plausible emendation of MT *môšᵉḇōṯêhem*, "their settlements," with the support of the LXX. "And will cleanse them": cf. 36:25, 29. "Then they shall be my people, and I will be their God": the "covenant formula"; see on 34:30.

37:24. "My servant David shall be king over them": as in 34:23–24, the reference is to a member of the Davidic house rather than to David himself returned. "They shall all have one shepherd": cf. the one shepherd of 34:23. "They shall follow my ordinances and be careful to observe my statutes": cf. 36:27. **37:25.** "They shall live in the land that I gave to my servant Jacob, in which your ancestors lived": cf. 28:25; 33:24; 36:28. "They and their children and their children's children shall live there forever": progeny in the land is still the summation of the ideal future, rather than personal resurrection. "My servant David shall be their prince": as in 34:24, Hebrew *nāśîʾ*, "prince," represents a downgrading of royal language. In the present chapter, at vv. 22 and 24, Hebrew *meleḵ*, "king," is also employed, unlike in ch. 34, where *nāśîʾ* alone is used.

37:26. The final verses of the chapter (vv. 26–28) envisage the restored community gathered around the sanctuary (cf. 20:40–44). "I will make a covenant of peace with them; it shall be an everlasting covenant with them": the Hebrew terms *bᵉrîṯ šālôm*, "covenant of peace," and *bᵉrîṯ ʿôlām*, "everlasting covenant," provide further evidence of the significant place that covenant theology has in Ezekiel; see on 34:25, 30. "I will bless them": NRSV follows the Targum; but MT *ûnᵉṯattîm* makes reasonable sense (cf. AV, "I will place them"). "Multiply them": repopulation is a recurrent theme in these restoration chapters; cf. 36:10. "Set my sanctuary among them forevermore": reference to the sanctuary (Heb. *miqdāš*) recalls 11:16; whereas YHWH had himself been a *miqdāš mᵉʿaṭ*, "a sanctuary (albeit in small measure)," to his people in exile, he now promises the full restoration of his sanctuary as the focus of restored life in the land. **37:27.** "My dwelling place shall be with them": the term employed for "dwelling place" (Heb. *miškān*, used in this sense only on this one occasion in Ezekiel) is frequently associated with the "tent of meeting" in the Priestly account of the wilderness wanderings (e.g. Exod 39:40; Num 4:31). "I will be their God, and they shall be my people": the "covenant formula"; cf. v. 23; see on 34:30. **37:28.** "Then the nations shall know that I the LORD sanctify Israel": a variation of the "Recognition Formula." On God's holy people, see Wells 2000. "When my sanctuary is among them forevermore": this final passage of the chapter, like chs. 34 and 36, echoes Lev 26, the important closing chapter of the Holiness Code, with which Ezekiel shares much.

Ezekiel 37 continues the collective emphasis of the hopeful sections of the book as a whole. Thus, for example, the "dry bones" are said to be "the whole house of Israel" (v. 11), and the promise of new life is addressed by YHWH to "my people" (vv. 12, 13). I have noted that vv. 1–14 refer not to individual resurrection but to the corporate renewal of Israel. Verses 15–28 look forward to the reunification of Judah and Israel; v. 22 emphasizes that they shall no longer be two nations but "one nation" under "one king," while v. 24 speaks of the promised king as "one shepherd" over the people. And the final verses of the chapter, vv. 26–28, envisage the restored community gathered around the sanctuary.

Several scholars have observed that the last section of ch. 37 arguably serves as a more fitting introduction to chs. 40–48 than does ch. 39 (e.g. Lemke 1984; Blenkinsopp 1990:180). One may note, for example, in 37:26, "I will set my sanctuary in the midst of them forevermore" (cf. v. 28). Moreover, in v. 25 we find reference to a *nāśîʾ*), "prince," to be an important theme in chs. 40–48 (44:3; 45:7–22; 46:2–18; 48:21–22). In other ways too, the thought and language of these final verses of ch. 37 share much with chs. 40–48. There is a case on these grounds alone for speculating that they once formed the prelude to ch. 40, without the intervention of chs. 38–39. This is the more plausible given the relative independence of chs. 38–39 and also the affinity between chs. 38–39 and another self-contained, proto-apocalyptic block of material, namely Isa 24–27. It is possible that a late addition of chs. 38–39 has separated ch. 37 from chs. 40–48.

Text-critical issues too are relevant here. The earliest Greek text of Ezekiel, P. 967, moves straight from ch. 37 to ch. 40 (with chs. 38–39 preceding ch. 37). Lust argues that this Greek chapter sequence is more primitive than that of the MT, and that 36:23c–38 (not represented in the Greek of P. 967) was a late insertion to form a bridge between ch. 36 and a newly transposed ch. 37 (Lust 1981a; see the commentary on ch. 36). This possibility is intriguing but ultimately not persuasive. Long ago Filson argued that the arrangement of P. 967 could satisfactorily be explained on the grounds of accidental damage to the text at an early stage (Filson 1943; cf. Spottorno 1982), and it is interesting that no extant Hebrew text (including the Masada manuscript of 35:11–38:14; cf. Talmon 1999) features the chapter sequence of P. 967. Yet, although Lust's proposal is not to be followed, there is heuristic value in considering how chs. 40–48 might look if preceded by ch. 37 (and indeed the implications for reading ch. 37 if it were followed immediately by ch. 40). The similarities and differences between the Greek sequence and that of the Hebrew are worthy of comparison in their own right, for one can benefit simply from exploring these as different reading options, even though the Hebrew sequence seems historically the more original.

CHAPTER 38

Chapters 38–39 form a pair and tell of the assault of Gog of Magog upon the people of Israel and of his eventual defeat.

These chapters exemplify certain proto-apocalyptic features: radical eschatology, a strong emphasis on divine agency, and dualism, not only between present and future but also between good and evil. They also exercise a significant influence on later apocalyptic tradition (see, e.g., Bøe 2001, with regard to Rev 19:17–21 and 20:7–10). Proto-apocalyptic sections are found in several of the prophetic books, for example, Isa 24–27 and Zech 9–14. The relative independence of chs. 38–39 and also their affinity with such comparable blocks of material in other books raise the question as to whether they come from Ezekiel himself or not. I have observed that the last section of ch. 37 (vv. 24–28) might, in some respects, serve as a more fitting introduction to chs. 40–48 than does ch. 39 and that there is a case for speculating that it once formed the prelude to ch. 40, without the intervention of chs. 38–39. Thus, it is possible that chs. 38–39 represent a late addition to the book. Among those who judge chs. 38–39 to be such an addition are Cooke (1936:407–8) and Eichrodt (1970:519). However, these chapters manifest many features and themes that characterize primary Ezekiel material, such as the address to "Mortal" (Heb. *ben-ʾāḏām*; 38:2, 14; 39:1, 17), quotations (38:11, 13), the "Recognition Formula" (38:23; 39:6–7, 22–23, 28) and the motif of divine holiness (38:16, 23; 39:27). While these could just be examples of the phenomenon whereby the Ezekiel tradition exhibits a strong family resemblance to its founder (see the "Unity, Authorship and Redaction" section, above), there are other reasons to link the chapters with Ezekiel himself. In particular, the situation anticipated is that of a newly restored community, which shows much continuity with the promises of chs. 34–37. Zimmerli (1983:302–4) argued for an original kernel, and among those regarding them as substantially primary are Allen (1990a:204) and Block (1998:426–27).

Ezekiel 38–39 not only manifests proto-apocalyptic elements, but also priestly themes such as a preoccupation with divine holiness (e.g. 38:23) and cultic purity (e.g. 39:14). Cook has argued for the hand of "central priests" in producing Ezek 38–39, as part of his challenge to the widely held hypothesis, associated especially with Plöger (1962) and Hanson (1979), that apocalyptic literature emerged from marginal circles far removed from the priests who exercised power at the centre of society (Cook 1995a:85–121; see also the valuable discussion in Mein 2001a:224–33). The book of Ezekiel has always fitted poorly with the polar theory of Plöger and Hanson, and so it is not surprising that these chapters should loom large in an important challenge to it. Similarly, Gillingham observes that "the Gog of Magog oracles in Ezek 38–39 occur immediately after the promise that God would set his sanctuary in the midst of his people for evermore (37:26–28), and before the long section concerning the vision of the restored Temple (chapters 40–48)" (Gillingham 1996:147). In Ezekiel, priestly and visionary features are found alongside each other, and indeed often interleaved.

We have noted several times the absence of Babylon, the arch-enemy of Ezekiel's day, from the foreign nation oracles. Some have sought to remedy this by finding in the letters of the word "Magog" a cryptic reference to Babylon (e.g. Cooke 1936:480). The foe from the north (cf. 38:6, 15; 39:2) was certainly Babylon in 26:7, as in Jer 25:9. But the case for identifying Gog with Babylon is weak. I have argued that the foreign nation oracles in Ezekiel are primarily intended to provide object lessons for Israel, and so one need not search endlessly for a Babylon oracle. Moreover, Babylon is consistently the instrument of YHWH's purposes in Ezekiel, rather than his enemy. Gog is to be seen more as an early example of the personification of the nations in opposition to YHWH's people that became normative in apocalyptic literature.

38:1–9. Invasion by Gog. **38:2.** "Gog, of the land of Magog": neither Gog nor Magog has ever been satisfactorily identified, in spite of numerous attempts, and they may indeed be literary creations. For a review of the many specific proposals, see Block (1998:433–35). "Chief prince": Hebrew *n*^{e}*śîʾ rōʾš*. "Meshech and Tubal": these traded with Tyre (27:13) and would languish in Sheol (32:26). Like "Gomer" and "Beth-togarmah" (v. 6), they were in what is now Turkey, which fits in with the references to the "north" (vv. 6, 15; 39:2). **38:3.** "I am against you": this phrase (like "set your face" in v. 2; see on 4:3) is a feature of the foreign nation oracles (cf. 26:3; 28:22; 29:3, 10), and amounts to a clear statement of YHWH's opposition to Gog; in what follows, however, an element of ambiguity about this is found. **38:4.** "I will turn you around and put hooks into your jaws": cf. 19:4, 9; 29:4. **38:5.** "Ethiopia": see on 29:10. "Put": see on 30:5. **38:6.** "From the remotest parts of the north": cf. v. 15; 39:2; and see on 1:4 for the symbolic and mythological dimensions of reference to the "north." That many of the places here that can be identified are northern (see on v. 2) coheres with this, geography reinforcing symbolism. **38:8.** "After many days…in the latter years": eschatological formulae (cf. Hos 3:5; Jer 30:24). "You shall be mustered…you shall go against…": here, in vv. 7–9, it seems that YHWH summons and directs the onslaught by Gog (see also on v. 16), even though YHWH's overall opposition to Gog is indicated (v. 3). This ambiguity is reminiscent of Isa 10, where Assyria is YHWH's "rod" (v. 5) and yet is subsequently condemned for its hubris (vv. 7–19). But there is also a sense of YHWH being behind everything that happens (an old theme in the Hebrew Bible—see Exod 9:12; Isa 6:9–10; Ezek 20:25–26). "A land where people were gathered from many nations on the mountains of Israel": this sounds like the returned Israelite exiles and that becomes clearer in what follows (e.g. v. 12). **38:9.** "You shall be like a cloud covering the land": cf. Joel 2:2.

38:10–23. The Plot Doomed to Defeat. From here, by stages, it becomes quite clear that the attack will fail. **38:10.** "Thoughts will come into your mind, and you will devise an evil scheme": this motif distances Gog's expedition from the purposes of YHWH. **38:11.** "I will fall upon the quiet people": idealized and vulnerable Israelites. "Who live in safety": cf. vv. 8, 14; 28:26; 34:25, 28. **38:12.** "To assail the waste places that are now inhabited": formerly deserted (cf. 33:24), but now repopulated (cf. 36:10–12, 33–38). "Who live at the centre of the earth": Hebrew *ṭabbûr hāʾāreṣ*, literally the "navel of the earth"; see on 5:5; one is reminded also of language used in other ancient cultures of great centres such as Babylon and Rome (cf. Vermeylen 2007). **38:13.** "Sheba": probably in south-west Arabia, rather than the traditional location in Ethiopia; cf. 27:22. "Dedan": probably in west central Arabia, and not the place referred to in the Edomite context in 25:13. "Tarshish": see on 27:12. "Its young warriors": Hebrew *kᵉpirêhā*, literally "its young lions." **38:14.** "Therefore… Thus says the Lord GOD": the decisive turn to judgement. "You will rouse yourself": NRSV follows LXX; MT has *hᵃlôʾ tēḏāʿ*, "will you not know?" **38:16.** "I will bring you against my land": remarkably, even though judgement has been signalled, the theme of YHWH's agency continues. Though these two chapters are rightly seen as anticipating later dualism, this aspect is very much in tension with a strong sense of divine control. "So that the nations may know me": a radically theocentric rationale, in a phrase related to the "Recognition Formula." "When through you, O Gog, I display my holiness before their eyes": that is, in defeating Gog. Interestingly, these are nations other than Gog and his hordes (cf. v. 13), even though Gog to some degree represents the nations of the world. With the divine holiness theme in these chapters, compare also 20:41; 28:22, 25; 36:23. **38:17.** "Are you he of whom I spoke in former days by my servants the prophets of Israel, who in those days prophesied for years that I would bring you against them?": a crucial verse for the understanding of chs. 38–39, but its implications are far from clear. Most hold that the question invites a positive answer, and that Gog is understood as fulfilling hitherto unfulfilled prophecies (e.g. Zimmerli 1983:299–304; cf. Fishbane 1985:467–77). However, Block persuasively argues that the answer to the question of v. 17 is "no" (Block 1992; cf. Odell 1988:122). This verse is not about unfulfilled prophecy, but about earlier prophecies illegitimately appropriated. Gog is not commissioned to serve as an agent of punishment (the subject of the earlier prophecies)—Babylon has already fulfilled that role for Ezekiel's age. Rather, Gog is raised up only to manifest YHWH's holiness. **38:18.** "When Gog comes against the land of Israel…my wrath shall be aroused": Gog has no commission to devastate YHWH's people. **38:19.** "There shall be a great shaking in the land of Israel": earthquake imagery (cf. Amos, e.g. 9:5–6); the emphasis is on the manifestation of YHWH's power. **38:20.** "The fish of the sea, and the birds of the air…": an inclusive summary of the created order that evokes the language of Gen 1. "Shall quake at my presence": cf. 26:15; 31:16. **38:22.** "Hailstones, fire and sulphur": all the forces of nature are employed against Gog, as in the judgement upon Sodom in Gen 19:24. **38:23.** "So I will display my greatness and my holiness and make myself known in the eyes of many nations": the real purpose of the Gog episode; cf. 36:22–23.

Chapter 39

39:1–20. Gog's Armies Defeated. **39:1.** Rather than picking up where ch. 38 left off, the first verses of this chapter reprise much of the early part of the previous one. But then, as this chapter develops, it majors on the aftermath of the defeat of the forces of Gog. **39:6.** "I will send fire on…": a recurrent motif in Amos 1–2. "Those who live securely": the familiar motif of attack on those who are living securely (38:8, 14) is here transferred to Gog's associates. **39:7.** "My holy name I will make known among my people Israel; and I will not let my holy name be profaned any more": cf. 20:9, 14, 22; 36:20–23. In this context, both Israel and the nations are to know YHWH (cf. also vv. 22–23), though this is ultimately for the vindication of YHWH. "The Holy One in Israel": similar to the divine title "the Holy One of Israel," which is so characteristic of the book of Isaiah (e.g. 1:4; 41:14; 60:14). Williamson (2001) shows that the title comes into its own within Isaiah only in chs. 40–55. The possibility should be considered that the prominence of the motif of divine holiness in Ezekiel may have provided a spur to Deutero-Isaiah to develop the title, found but rarely in primary material in Isa 1–39. **39:8.** "It has come! It has happened": compare the eschatological language of ch. 7 (especially vv. 2, 5, 10). "This is the day of which I have spoken": the reference is to oracles such as 36:22–23; this affirmative phrase may well be intended to stand in deliberate contrast to 38:17 (whose question invited the answer "no").

39:9. "Then those who live in the towns of Israel will go out and make fires of the weapons": cf. the eschatological motif of "beating swords into ploughshares" in Isa 2:4 and Mic 4:3. "For seven years": the massive quantity of weapons is stressed so as to highlight the magnitude of YHWH's victory. **39:10.** "They will despoil those who despoiled them, and plunder those who plundered them": poetic justice (cf. Barton 1979; Miller 1982). **39:11.** "I will give to Gog a place for burial in Israel": as a witness to the vindication of YHWH's holiness. "The Valley of the Travellers": Hebrew *gê hāʿōḇᵉrîm*. An alternative reading is "of Abarim," a place name of unknown location; Block offers the attractive translation "the valley of those who have passed on" (Block 1998:469). The Hebrew word *ʿōḇᵉrîm* occurs several times in this passage, translated by NRSV variously as "travellers" (v. 11), "to pass through" (v. 14, cf. v. 15), "invaders" (v. 14) and "searchers" (v. 15). One may compare, in a similar eschatological context, Joel's "Valley of Jehoshaphat," a place of judgement of the nations (Joel 3:2, 12 [Heb. 4:2, 12]). "East of the sea": if this were the Dead Sea it would contradict "in Israel," and so, although unusual, the reference seems to be to the Mediterranean. "The Valley of Hamon-gog": the valley of the horde or multitude of Gog; see also v. 16. **39:12.** "Seven months": the long period spent burying the dead and searching (v. 14) echoes the seven years of burning weapons in v. 9. "In order to cleanse the land": human remains were judged ritually unclean according to priestly rules (cf. Num 19:16; Ezek 44:25–26; see also on 37:1). **39:13.** "On the day that I show my glory": central to the concerns of the Gog material; cf. the eschatological "Day of YHWH" (see on 7:7). **39:16.** "A city Hamonah is there also": possibly just a marginal annotation, giving an aetiology for a town whose name means "The Horde" (cf. Allen 1990a). But Odell (1994) helpfully explores the association of the Hebrew word *hāmôn*, "horde, multitude," with Jerusalem in three earlier judgement oracles (5:7; 7:12–14; 23:40–42); the once tumultuous city of Jerusalem, Odell argues, is to be transformed in this new age.

39:17. "Sacrificial feast": Hebrew *zeḇaḥ*, here a communion meal, celebrating the victory and the glory of YHWH (cf. Zeph 1:7; Isa 34:6–8). "You shall eat flesh and drink blood": contrast the cup of judgement (see on 23:31). Irwin (1995) argues that vv. 17–20 draw upon the features of a *marzēaḥ* banquet (see on 8:10), to describe the birds and animals feasting on the bodies of Gog's soldiers, and this is supported by McLaughlin (2001:196–213). **39:18.** "Bashan": an area of northern Transjordan, famed for its cattle (cf. Amos 4:1). **39:20.** "Charioteers": Hebrew *reḵeḇ*, "chariot"; best understood to refer to "chariot horses" (Zimmerli 1983:294). With this scene of feasting the Gog material ends.

39:21–29. Israel Restored to the Land. This concluding summary section contains much that is familiar in ideas and language, but also rounds out the theology of Ezekiel with a symmetry and completeness that the prophet himself may never have achieved. Like 28:25–26, it is probably an example of classic "house style" developed by redactors. But it is not very late, for, while one must make allowances for hyperbole ("they all fell by the sword," v. 23), the expectation that "I will leave none of them behind" (v. 28) was proved erroneous long before the end of the sixth century. **39:21.** "I will display my glory among the nations; and all the nations shall see my judgement that I have executed": cf. 5:8. **39:22.** "The house of Israel shall know…": both Israel and the nations are described as knowing, a systematizing element here. **39:23.** "And the nations shall know that the house of Israel went into captivity for their iniquity": cf. 36:20. "So I hid my face from them": the motif of the "hiding of the face" occurs three times in Ezekiel, all in this passage, twice negatively (here and v. 24), and once positively (v. 29) (cf. Balentine 1983). **39:26.** "They shall forget their shame": MT is actually pointed *wᵉnāśû*, "they shall bear," and Zimmerli (1983:295; cf. Lust 1986b) defends this. But the more unusual reading *wᵉnāšû*, "they shall forget," fits the emphasis of this passage in terms of symmetry and resolution, and is more probable here. However, this in turn, being an untypical—indeed unique—idea in Ezekiel, provides yet another argument for the secondary nature of vv. 21–29. On the motif of shame in Ezekiel, see 16:52, 54, 61, 63; 36:32 (cf. 7:18; 43:10–11; 44:13). **39:28.** "I sent them into exile among the nations, and then gathered them into their own land": in this symmetrical emphasis on exile and restoration we have another systematizing element. **39:29.** "I will never again...": cf. Gen 9:15; Isa 54:9–10, both also probably exilic. "When I pour out my spirit upon the house of Israel": cf. 36:27; 37:10. In the earliest Greek text, P. 967, ch. 37 fittingly follows on at this very point. But the Hebrew sequence has its own logic. Niditch (1986) persuasively argues that the battle scenes of chs. 38–39 provide the natural prelude to chs. 40–48, in keeping with a familiar ancient Near Eastern mythic sequence of victory followed enthronement of the deity, a pattern that appears, with variations, in both the Babylonian *Enuma Elish* and the Ugaritic epic of Baal and Anat. On the mythological dimensions of chs. 38–39, see also Fitzpatrick 2004.

CHAPTERS 40–48

Studies of Ezek 40–48 cover the spectrum from the stratifying (Gese 1957) to the holistic (Greenberg 1984). Gese saw chs. 40–48 as a confusing structure, with many layers of redaction. His detailed examination of the tradition history of these chapters has dominated their interpretation to a marked extent for fifty years, whereas study of redaction in chs. 1–39 has seen much more flux over the same period. Gese's approach is followed through in detail by Zimmerli (1983; cf. Zimmerli 1968). Rudnig in many ways represents the latest phase of the stratifying method (Rudnig 2000; Pohlmann [with Rudnig] 2001). Others favour a more holistic approach, above all Greenberg (1984), with Niditch (1986) providing another, less thoroughgoing, example of this trend. Greenberg writes of the final long section of Ezekiel that "it is the product of a single mind (and hand)...carrying forward ideas and values found in the preceding prophecies, it may reasonably be attributed to their author, the priest-prophet Ezekiel" (Greenberg 1984:181). This rests both on the view that chs. 1–39 derive from the prophet himself and on a particular judgement about the degree of continuity between chs. 1–39 and chs. 40–48.

So, scholarship is somewhat polarized on the question of the authorship of Ezek 40–48. If Greenberg fails to engage with the diachronic dimension, it has to be said that Rudnig's refined stratification attempts to demonstrate more than could ever be known about the undoubtedly complex history of the book's redaction. On the issue of authorship and redaction within chs. 40–48, the most appropriate stance is one of responsible agnosticism. This is not to commend a casual approach, but rather a rigorous dialectic between what we may reasonably claim and that which is beyond our knowing. As we have seen, the fact that the "house style" of Ezekiel is so homogeneous makes it difficult to distinguish between primary and secondary material (Joyce 1995a; cf. Niditch 1986:211); but there are cases where redactional expansion seems particularly likely (e.g. in the more polemical pro-Zadokite verses, 44:15–31 and 48:11).

Whether or not it is all from Ezekiel, several factors favour a sixth-century date for Ezek 40–48 as a whole. There is nothing that unambiguously refers to events after the sixth century. This is to apply a principle that Clements (1986) employs effectively in his treatment of chs. 1–24. Moreover, the fact that Ezekiel's vision is so divergent from the restoration reality strongly suggests that it predates it (Collins 1993:96). If the second temple had already been inaugurated, it would have been difficult to write in this way; the account would surely have been accommodated to the new reality. This is not an absolutely necessary conclusion (we should not forget the freedom with which the Dead Sea Scrolls and also the Mishnah work with temple themes). Nevertheless, it must be acknowledged as persuasive.

Much discussion of the dating of chs. 40–48 involves comparative work of one kind or another, and yet so much is unknown to us. Given that we do not know what priestly writings or oral traditions existed prior to Ezekiel, it is impossible to judge the implications of divergences between Ezek 40–48 and the priestly sections of the Torah. Also, we do not know precisely what changes had taken place in Solomon's temple by late pre-exilic times (e.g. in the days of Manasseh or of Josiah) and so it is hard to weigh apparent differences between the account of Solomon's temple and Ezekiel's. Moreover, it is difficult to know what conclusions, if any, to draw from "silences" in the Ezekiel account (e.g. with regard to the virtual absence of reference to the contents of Ezekiel's temple).

Approaches to the question of the overall purpose of these chapters cover the range from the realistic (Cooke 1936; Wevers 1969) through to the eschatological (Eichrodt 1970) and the utopian (Kasher 1998a; cf. Liss 2006). Further complexity may be hinted at. Scholars often argue or assume that realistic details are a sign of secondary elaboration of an original vision (e.g. Zimmerli 1983). And they interpret diverse redactional layers (as they perceive them) very differently. For example, Tuell (1996) offers a decidedly non-realistic interpretation of what he takes to be the original vision of chs. 40–42, but presents a very realistic reading of the final revision of Ezek 40–48, as providing nothing less than a political constitution for Jewish life under the Persians, with the *nāśîʾ*, "prince," interpreted as none other than the Persian governor (Tuell 1992).

The interweaving of the richly visionary and the precisely mathematical in these chapters is striking. This apparently future-oriented combination of profound theological questions and minute practical detail can be compared with another text from the exilic age, namely Lamentations, where a retrospective exploration of the tragedy of loss is expounded in meticulously crafted acrostic form. Much in Ezek 40–48 exemplifies the concerns and style of the priests (cf. Jenson 1992; Gorman 1990); it is clear that both the broad ideological framework of chs. 40–48 and their attention to detail reflect the priestly tradition within which Ezekiel stood. At the same time, this section stands in continuity with Ezekiel's prophetic heritage. As we have seen, the priest-prophet Ezekiel confounds any simple dichotomy between the visionary and the priestly, such as that once popularized by Plöger (1962) and Hanson (1979). The tension between dream and reality is explored with profundity in this final section of the book (see further Joyce 2005).

Ezekiel's temple has been understood in many different ways. Some have interpreted it as based in part on a preserved description or even blueprint of the first, Solomonic temple. There are elements of this in Cooke: "We can imagine him poring over architectural plans…"; "in chs. 40–42 he describes its ground-plan, which is based partly on the lines of Solomon's temple…" (Cooke 1936:425). Others have read it as first and foremost a plan for a restoration temple; so, for example, Clements: "Ezekiel 40–48 is not just a vision of a new and restored Israel but a practical 'renewal program' for national reorganization" (Clements 1996a:178). And others again have seen it as primarily an eschatological temple; thus, for example, Eichrodt: "they provide a picture of the temple, land and people in the time of fulfilment," referring to the "land and the people in the time of salvation" (Eichrodt 1970:530).

In the long run, Ezek 40–48 would certainly be read both in the context of an actual restoration after return from exile and also in terms of eschatological hope, but what of the genesis of these chapters? The view that they are to be seen as reflecting a visionary ascent to the heavenly temple, championed especially by Tuell (1996), deserves more attention than it has so far received. Indeed, there are good grounds for believing that chs. 40–42, though now accommodated within a developed literary work, were based in the first instance on a vision of the heavenly temple seen by Ezekiel himself during the exile (a view presented in detail in Joyce 2007). This was an early "Heavenly Ascent" account, some centuries older than *1 Enoch* 14, enhancing Ezekiel's role as a key figure at the beginning of a trajectory of mystical experience and interpretation, fundamental within both Judaism and Christianity alike.

It can be difficult to see the wood for the trees when reading Ezek 40–48, such is the wealth of detail; and so in what follows a deliberate attempt is made to foreground and highlight matters of particular theological importance.

Chapter 40

The chapter opens with the last of the sequence of dates in Ezekiel, although the references in 29:17 ("the twenty-seventh year") and 1:1 (the obscure "thirtieth year") apparently give later dates. "The twenty-fifth year of our exile, at the beginning of the year, on the tenth day of the month, in the fourteenth year after the city was struck down": probably 28th April 573. There is widespread agreement that the number twenty-five is significant, being half a Jubilee period, but scholars divide between those such as Van Goudoever (1986) who date the exile itself as beginning halfway through a Jubilee period and so place this vision at the beginning of a Jubilee year, and the majority, led by Zimmerli, who favour the more likely view that halfway through a Jubilee period Ezekiel is here granted a foretaste of the anticipated release, the end of exile, which will itself come in a Jubilee year (cf. Lev 25:10; Zimmerli 1983:346). It is interesting to reflect that the Jubilee shares with Ezekiel's temple the question of whether it was intended as a realistic provision or was only ever a utopian aspiration. Opinions also vary on whether "at the beginning of the year" reckons with an autumn or, as seems more probable in the light of 45:21, a spring new year. But there is growing support for the view that the phrase "at the beginning of the year, on the tenth day of the month" is the first hint of the relevance of the Babylonian New Year festival to what follows (e.g. Stevenson 1996:51–53).

In v. 2 we read, "He brought me, in visions of God, to the land of Israel": cf. 8:3, where the prophet is similarly "brought…in visions of God to Jerusalem." It is important to take seriously the visionary nature of both references (8:1–3; 40:1–2), neither of which gives grounds for a view that Ezekiel actually exercised a ministry in Jerusalem. As we have seen, 40:1–2 shares with 1:1–3 and 8:1–3 a range of features, a signal that these three visionary contexts stand in close relation to each other (cf. Parunak 1980). The prophet is not named in these nine chapters; like the book as a whole, they are couched in autobiographical style, with Ezekiel as the presumed first-person speaker. "He set me down upon a very high mountain, on which was a structure like a city to the south": Jerusalem is not named as such anywhere in chs. 40–48 (nor Zion, which is never used anywhere in the book), but there can be no doubt that Jerusalem is intended by this reference to a city (much as it is clear that "the place that the Lord your God will choose" in Deut 12:5 refers to Jerusalem). Note, though, that in what follows the temple is not in the city, which is located, as here, away to the south. This may simply reflect the location of Solomon's temple, which was to the north of the city of David. "A very high mountain": Sinai is surely in mind, as well as Zion (so Levenson 1976:37–49); "the law of the temple" is referred to in 43:12 and could be seen as confirming a Sinai allusion here. But there are also resonances of the cosmic mountain of ancient Near Eastern mythology (Clifford 1972), echoes of which are picked up later in the account of the river in ch. 47.

"A man was there" (v. 3): an angelic guide (compare the "man clothed in linen," featured in chs. 9–10). "Mortal" (v. 4): it is usually YHWH himself who addresses Ezekiel in this way; but this confirms the impression that this "man" is an angelic representative. He leads Ezekiel on a tour, the account of which is most sustained in chs. 40–42 but is resumed at various points thereafter. He instructs Ezekiel to pay close attention so that he can declare what he sees to the house of Israel (a motif that recurs, for example, in 43:10). As for the geography of the tour, Block is particularly helpful (see especially Figs. 1 and 2, Block 1998:508–9); and Stevenson (1996) is instructive on what she calls the "territorial rhetoric" of these chapters. "Now there was a wall all around the outside of the temple area" (v. 5): this is the first reference to the temple in chs. 40–48, and it is a remarkably low-key one, taking the temple itself for granted. Significantly, this wall is mentioned again at the end of ch. 42 (v. 20); this *inclusio* is one of several features that mark chs. 40–42 aside as a distinct unit (cf. Tuell 1996).

Most of ch. 40 is devoted to an account of the temple area, the gates and the outer and inner courts, with the "man" taking measurements with his measuring reed. Verses 38–43 refer to a chamber where the burnt offering was to be washed, and tables on which the various offerings were to be slaughtered, and then v. 47 reports that "the altar was in front of the temple," this being the stone altar of burnt sacrifice (cf. 43:13–27). Before the chapter ends, there commences a presentation of the tripartite structure of the temple (Heb. *habbayiṯ*, the "house") itself. At v. 48 we have the *ʾulām*, "vestibule." This section extends from 40:48 to the end of ch. 41, and so will be treated with the next chapter.

CHAPTER 41

This chapter features a presentation of the tripartite structure of the temple (Heb. *habbayiṯ*, the "house"). The section actually commenced at 40:48 and extends to the end of ch. 41. The basic structure of the temple, as it is described, follows the pattern familiar to us from 1 Kgs 6–8 and indeed from the archaeology of the ancient Near East (cf. Hurowitz 1992, 2005). At 40:48 we have the *ʾulām* or "vestibule," at 41:1 the *hêḵāl* or "nave," and then in 41:3 the *pᵉnîmâ* or "inner room." The word *dᵉḇîr* is not used for the inner room in Ezekiel (as it is in 1 Kgs 8:6), but importantly, in 41:4, Ezekiel's guide declares that this (the inner room) is *qōḏeš haqqᵒḏāšîm*, "the most holy place" (NRSV) or "the holy of holies," employing the phrase used for the inner room elsewhere in the Hebrew Bible (including 1 Kgs 8:6).

Much, then, about the new temple envisaged in Ezek 40–48 is in continuity with what we read of Solomon's temple as presented in 1 Kings. But there are discontinuities too. For example, Ezekiel's temple appears to be all but empty. Virtually all the furnishings of the Solomonic temple, and indeed the desert tabernacle, go unmentioned. The only interior furniture referred to is the "altar of wood" (Heb. *hammizbēaḥ ʿēṣ*) in front of the "holy place" (Heb. *haqqōḏeš*), the inner room (41:21–22; also described as "the table that stands before the LORD"). This is distinct from the stone altar of burnt sacrifice that stands outside the temple itself (40:47 and 43:13–27). Most notable among the omissions is the Ark of the Covenant. Why is Ezekiel's temple apparently all but empty, and in particular why no Ark?

Various attempts have been made to explain the omissions. Greenberg has argued that the implications of the gaps must remain obscure. He writes, "In subsequent divisions of Ezekiel's program...omissions cannot serve as a warrant for negative conclusions—unmentioned therefore absent" (Greenberg 1984:193). Haran grounds the omission of the various items on historical accidents that had befallen the Solomonic temple. He has in view here, in particular, his hypothesis that the Ark was removed by Manasseh, king of Judah, in the seventh century, in connection with the setting up of an image of Asherah in the Holy of Holies (Haran 1978:276–88). But, even if that particular theory of the fate of the Ark were correct, which is doubtful (cf. Day 2005a:256–58), why should Ezekiel's vision be constrained by such historical accidents? After all, the whole temple was razed to the ground by the Babylonians and yet Ezekiel is able to envisage its restoration. Alternatively, it might be argued that the Ark, being more intimately associated with YHWH than anything else in the temple, was felt to be unique and for this reason irreplaceable. This may indeed be the reason the Ark was not in fact replaced after its destruction with the temple in 587 B.C.E., but, again, a *vision* of restoration such as Ezek 40–48 need not be so constrained, particularly when it is so bold in other respects. Kasher helps us towards an answer when he persuasively argues that the particularly anthropomorphic conception of God in Ezekiel is the key to the omission of various objects from Ezekiel's temple (Kasher 1998a:192–98). For when we read in 43:5 that "the glory of the LORD filled the temple," we are to understand this as implying that the divine presence filled up the space, and thereby rendered the Ark of the Covenant and other cultic paraphernalia redundant. Kasher's insight is not unrelated to the radical theocentricity that we have repeatedly encountered in Ezekiel. Such is Ezekiel's focus on YHWH himself that much else is simply eclipsed (see further Joyce 2005:150–52).

Verses 17–20 describe the decorations on the walls in the inner room and the nave, an alternating pattern of cherubim and palm trees. There is an echo here of the cherubim of ch. 10 (cf. the "living creatures" of ch. 1). We read in vv. 18–19 that "Each cherub had two faces, a human face turned toward the palm tree on the one side, and the face of a young lion turned toward the palm tree on the other side," with which may be compared the four faces of 10:14 (cf. 1:10).

CHAPTER 42

The bulk of ch. 42 is devoted to an account of the priests' chambers. In them, according to vv. 13–14, the priests were to store their share of the sacrifices (44:28–31; cf. Lev 2:1–10; 7:7–10), eat their portion of the holy offerings, and deposit the garments they wore for the services before putting on other clothes to enter the less sacred space of the outer court. In the latter part of ch. 40 we found mention of a chamber where the burnt offering was to be washed and of tables on which the various offerings were to be slaughtered (40:38–43), and we also encountered reference to "the altar…in front of the temple," the stone altar of burnt sacrifice (40:47). Animal sacrifice is, then, to be a feature of Ezekiel's new temple. There has been much discussion about what actually happened on the ruined site of the temple during the years of exile (cf. Jones 1963; Albertz 2001; Middlemas 2005, 2007), but these verses move beyond that situation to envisage a full restoration of the sacrificial system. This may not seem surprising within a priestly context, but is nonetheless worthy of note when one thinks of the long-standing prophetic critique of the sacrificial system (cf. Isa 1:10–17; Hos 6:6; Amos 5:21–25; Mic 6:6–8) and also of the spiritualizing tendency found in, for example, the bulk of Ps 51 (itself probably exilic). Moreover, within Ezekiel there is the motif in 11:16 of YHWH himself becoming a *miqdāš mᵉʿaṭ*, a "sanctuary in some measure," to the exiles, in many ways a radical accommodation to the loss of the temple. But, for all this, Ezekiel's new temple will indeed feature the slaughtering of animals and the offering of sacrifices.

The interweaving of the richly visionary and the precisely mathematical in chs. 40–48 is striking. This combination of profound theological questions and minute practical detail is well exemplified in the present chapter with its characteristic cases of specific measurement, for example "The length of the building that was on the north side was one hundred cubits, and the width fifty cubits" (v. 2). Both the broad ideological framework of this material and its attention to detail reflect the concerns and style of the priestly tradition within which Ezekiel stood (cf. Gorman 1990; Jenson 1992; Milgrom forthcoming).

I observed earlier that v. 20, the last verse of the present chapter, forms an *inclusio* with 40:5 (with the reference to the wall around the outside of the temple area). This signals the end of the initial tour of the temple and of the first section of chs. 40–48. Another feature that highlights the key role of this verse is the programmatic statement that the purpose of this wall was "to make a separation between the holy (*qōḏeš*) and the common (*ḥōl*)" (cf. 44:23). This priestly emphasis on separation (employing the Hebrew verb *bdl*, in the Hiphil) is determinative for Ezek 40–48. Division, gradation, order, degree, access: these are priorities central to the priestly world-view.

CHAPTER 43

Chapter 43 begins with a powerful scene, the return of YHWH to his sanctuary. Ezekiel is taken to the outer eastern gate of the temple compound: "And there the glory of the God of Israel was coming from the east" (v. 2). Just as Ezekiel witnessed the deity's departure from his sanctuary in ch. 11, so now he sees his return. There is at v. 3 an explicit (if perhaps editorial) cross-reference to ch. 1 as well as to chs. 8–11: "The vision I saw was like the vision I had seen when he came to destroy the city, and like the vision that I had seen by the river Chebar." Bodi has helpfully highlighted the importance of the Akkadian *Poem of Erra* for the motif of the absence of the deity (Bodi 1991:183–218), while Stevenson is among those who have elaborated certain parallels with the Babylonian New Year festival, and in particular the Akitu element, featuring the return of the god to his sanctuary (Stevenson 1996:52–53). This is a persuasive case, though a significant divergence is that in Ezekiel the deity is not brought back by a king. More generally, there has been much valuable discussion of the absence and presence of God in Ezekiel (see, e.g., Block 2000b; Kutsko 2000a; Tuell 2000a).

The culmination of the account of YHWH's return reads: "The glory of the LORD filled the temple" (v. 5). This echoes the words of both Exod 40:34 and 1 Kgs 8:11. The passage that follows is particularly important for Ezekiel's understanding of the divine presence. Verse 6 reports that "While the man was standing beside me, I heard someone speaking to me out of the temple." This is a device to highlight the fact that in v. 7 it is YHWH himself who speaks: "This is the place of my throne and the place for the soles of my feet, where I will reside among the people of Israel forever." This verse strongly affirms the divine presence within the sanctuary, and it does so echoing imagery (of throne and footstool) used elsewhere in association with the Ark of the Covenant (cf. 1 Sam 4:4; 2 Sam 6:2; Ps 132:7; 1 Chr 28:2), language that is here reapplied and transformed in a new context, precisely because the Ark itself no longer has a place. Such reworking and reapplication of language is characteristic of Ezekiel. A comparable example is proposed by Hurowitz, who suggests that the great metal "sea" of 1 Kgs 7:23 is reworked symbolically and theologically in Ezek 40–48 to become the river flowing from the temple in ch. 47 (Hurowitz 2005:80–81). The similarity between Ezek 43:7 and Jer 3:15–18 is significant: 43:7 speaks of the temple being the place of the divine throne, while Jer 3:17 comparably says (precisely in the context of an explicit statement that the Ark will be no more) that "Jerusalem shall be called the throne of the LORD." It is intriguing to note in this Jeremiah pericope (3:15–18) several other affinities with Ezekiel (including shepherds, as in Ezek 34, and the reunification of Judah and Israel, as in Ezek 37). If T. Collins is right that the book of Ezekiel reached its final form well before the book of Jeremiah (Collins 1993:96–97), one wonders whether this Jeremiah passage may reflect the influence of Ezekiel.

The return of YHWH to his sanctuary is one of many satisfying symmetries that the book of Ezekiel features. The book opens with the great vision of ch. 1, where the divine throne is witnessed in far-off Babylonia. YHWH is with his people in exile, no longer tied to the land of Israel. The word used for the "throne" in ch. 1 is the same as in 43:7 (Heb. *kissēʾ*). And when, in the vision of chs. 8–11, the divine throne is seen again, leaving the temple, it is striking that the term "cherubim" (Heb. *kᵉrub̲îm*), intimately connected with the Ark tradition, is associated with Ezekiel's motif of the free and mobile deity. Just as remarkably, we read in 11:16 that YHWH has himself become a *miqdāš mᵉʿaṭ* to his people; that is, he himself is to be their sanctuary "in some measure" (Joyce 1996). And now here, in the final section of the book, comes this grand return of the deity to his shrine.

A pleasing symmetry, and yet is it not also a disappointment that Ezek 43 brings back the deity and shuts him up again in his temple? Is this return not an undoing of one of the most profound contributions of Ezekiel, whereby the limitations of place are transcended? One might regard the *miqdāš mᵉʿaṭ* theme of 11:16 as one of the pinnacles of the book, an insight that was to help equip generations of Jews for millennia of diaspora life. Is it possible that, while the "throne chariot" vision of ch. 1, the departure of the glory in ch. 11 and indeed the *miqdāš mᵉʿaṭ* theme are all from Ezekiel, the return of YHWH in ch. 43 is from a secondary hand, possibly representing a timid retrenchment on the part of priests lacking the boldness of Ezekiel himself? No; while there is doubtless redactional elaboration within chs. 40–48, the theme of the return of the deity cannot be dealt with so easily. Vogt, for example, advances a persuasive case for the primary nature of Ezek 43:4–7a (Vogt 1981). In the absence of clear evidence that material is secondary, the integrity of the work that is before us must be respected. The "throne chariot" vision of ch. 1, the departure of the glory in ch. 11 and indeed the *miqdāš mᵉʿaṭ* motif: all of this needs to be borne in mind when in ch. 43 the glory of YHWH returns from the east and fills the temple. This return does not undo or erase the motif of the "throne chariot" or indeed that of the *miqdāš mᵉʿaṭ* (as argued earlier, *mᵉʿaṭ* in 11:16 is not to be understood in a temporal sense, "for a while"). Rather, the affirmation of 43:7 that "This is the place of my throne and the place of the soles of my feet" stands within the context of that overarching theology of the freedom of YHWH. Having abandoned his sanctuary for a time, YHWH now commits himself to dwell there permanently. But this commitment remains, within the grand architecture of the book of Ezekiel, in tension with the affirmation of the divine presence with his people in their dispersion, for whom he will himself indeed remain a "sanctuary in some measure." "Forever" (v. 7; Heb. *lᵉʿôlām*) is an important exilic theme: cf. Gen 9:8–17; Isa 54:9–10; Ezek 37:24–28.

We read in 43:7b: "The house of Israel shall no more defile my holy name, neither they nor their kings, by their whoring, and by the corpses of their kings at their death." Although archaeological evidence is lacking, the most natural interpretation of these words is to relate them to the inappropriate location of royal tombs, encroaching upon the temple. Odell (2004) offers a challenging alternative interpretation. She argues that vv. 7b–9 afford a clear reference to cult statues. Although this text is not usually discussed in connection with ch. 8, a number of clues suggest that it is to be read as its counterpart. As has been noted, 43:3 explicitly links this context to that of chs. 8–11. More particularly, both 43:7–9 and 8:3–6 revolve around themes of drawing near and distancing. What the people had done in 8:3–6 to draw near to the deity had prompted his departure, while in 43:7–9 the deity's return involves a reversal of those earlier conditions. Furthermore, argues Odell, both visions refer to the offensive presence of cult statues. In 8:3–6, the statue in question had been the "image of jealousy," while in 43:7b–9, the offensive objects are described as Hebrew *pigrê malkêhem*. This Hebrew phrase is rendered in the NRSV as "the corpses of their kings" (43:7b, 9), but Odell argues that it should rather be understood to refer to statues commemorating offerings to the deity, and more specifically *mlk*-offerings, child sacrifices of the kind proposed by Eissfeldt long ago (Eissfeldt 1935). Without necessarily following Odell in her specific interpretation of the phrase of 43:7b, 9, it cannot be denied that the general parallel with ch. 8 is persuasive.

Verses 10–12 constitute an important section for the understanding of the overall purpose of chs. 40–48. Here Ezekiel is told to describe the pattern of the temple to the people of Israel, "so that they may observe and follow the entire plan" (v. 11). The key Hebrew words used in vv. 10–11 are rare: *toknît*, "pattern" (as in Ezek 28:12), *ṣûrâ*, "plan," and *tᵉkûnâ*, "arrangement." One is reminded of the Exodus narrative, notably Exod 25:9, 40 (cf. 1 Chr 28:11–12), which uses the fairly common word *tabnît*, for "pattern" or "form" (indeed, perhaps unsurprisingly, some wish to emend *toknît* in Ezek 43:10 to conform to that). The phrase "so that they may observe and follow the entire plan" (v. 11) seems to imply a definite expectation that the envisaged restoration of the temple will actually happen and moreover that it will be based on the pattern given to Ezekiel in his vision.

The verse that rounds off this section, namely v. 12, is signalled as especially important since it both begins and ends with the words "This is the law of the temple." It could be that this declaration refers back to the preceding verses, focusing on the pattern of the temple. But another explanation is more likely. For between the two occurrences of the refrain, which feature like "bookends" within v. 12, we read, "The whole territory on the top of the mountain all around shall be most holy." The fact that these words are sandwiched between the double "This is the law of the temple" would seem to point to this as the immediate referent. The phrase used for "most holy" is *qōdeš qodāšîm*. Here we come to another distinctive feature of Ezek 40–48 that demands special attention, namely the diffusion of the realm of the most holy. When the three-fold structure of the temple was presented, the inner room (*pᵉnîma*) was also called in 41:4 *qōdeš haqqᵒdāšîm*, "the holy of holies," as elsewhere in the Hebrew Bible (e.g. 1 Kgs 8:6). It is interesting, then, to find that this same phrase (but without the definite article) is used in chs. 40–48 of special areas of holiness in a more general sense. Ezekiel 43:12 of course affirms the holiness of the mountain top, but there is another point here too. The words "whole" and "all around" emphasize the breadth of the area of holiness, as though to diffuse the holiness that pertains not so much to the place as to the deity who dwells there. Elsewhere too we find this generalizing or spreading of the realm of the most holy, which seems surprising in a priestly context where one expects a very sharp focus upon the defined holy place. Another case is found in 48:12, where the whole special portion of land assigned to the Zadokites is described as "a most holy place," *qōḏeš qoḏāšîm*, without the article. A further possible case is at 45:3, where we read that a section of the holy district, containing the sanctuary (*hammiqdāš*), is to be measured off. This verse is commonly taken to refer to "the sanctuary, the most holy place of all" (e.g. Block 1998:648), but the absence of the article in the phrase *qōḏeš qoḏāšîm* suggests that it could be the area as a whole that is described as "a most holy place." (Incidentally, it should be noted that in the above verses the English versions tend to supply the English definite article or not, according to context, frequently obscuring the particularities of the Hebrew usage.) Kasher writes: "This conception of the supreme sanctity of the temple and its environs is unique to Ezekiel; nowhere else in biblical literature do we find the term "holy of holies" as a designation for an area outside the temple proper" (Kasher 1998a:201–2).

Does this recurrent feature represent a casual attitude to the extent of holiness in Ezek 40–48? No, far from it. It is to be seen in the light of Ezekiel's version of the priestly concept of "graded holiness." Ezekiel 40–48 is passionately concerned with the proper separation between holy and common, as we see in 42:20 and 44:23. A key part of this is the notion of degrees of holiness. But in Ezekiel the whole concept is given an added dimension by the radical theocentricity of this tradition. The use of *qōḏeš qoḏāšîm*, without the article, in the above contexts takes the absolute and exclusive emphasis off the inner room of the temple as the locus of YHWH's holy presence and this is all of a piece with the fact that it is holy God himself who is the focus rather than any particular institution.

There follow in vv. 13–27 the ordinances for the stone altar of burnt offering, which is located in front of the temple itself (cf. 40:47) and is to be distinguished from the smaller altar of wood, the table standing before the entrance to the inner room (41:22). The stone altar of burnt offering is in many ways the primary focus of active worship. Stevenson, in her exploration of Ezekiel's "territorial rhetoric," notes that within Ezekiel's temple design there are twin focuses. One is the inner room, the symbolic dwelling place of YHWH; the other is the stone altar, the place of purgation and, significantly, the exact centrepiece of the temple complex (Stevenson 1996: esp. 40–41). Her observations reinforce the comments made earlier about the diffusion of the realm of the most holy in these chapters. Dijkstra (1992) explores what is said here about the construction of the altar in relation to traditions elsewhere, including in the Mishnah. The account of the arrangements for the consecration of the stone altar culminates with the simple but powerful words of v. 27, couched in classic priestly language: "I will accept you, says the Lord GOD."

Chapter 44

The chapter begins with the announcement that when the prophet was brought back to the outer eastward-facing gate of the sanctuary, "it was shut." He is told in v. 2 that it is to remain shut because the God of Israel has entered by it. This is a reference back to the return of the deity by the gate facing east in 43:4. There is, of course, no suggestion that, having returned to the temple, YHWH is in any sense now shut up in his house. The point is that the gate is hallowed because the deity has passed through it to return to the place of his special abode. The word translated by the NRSV as "has entered" (v. 2) is Hebrew *bāʾ*. This is most naturally taken as a perfect tense, which fits the reference back to 43:4; however, it could be read as a participle and various interpreters (e.g. LXX and Rashi) have preferred to construe the word with a future reference, which would fit an eschatological interpretation relating to the future return of the deity. Jerome, however, understood it with past reference, consistent with his own christological understanding. This motif of the "shut gate" has had an important place in Christian tradition, as a scriptural authority for the doctrine of the virginity of Mary the mother of Jesus, a reading facilitated in various ways by Jerome's Latin rendition. (I am grateful to have been given access to an as yet unpublished paper by J. F. A. Sawyer including discussion of this theme.)

We read in v. 3 that "Only the prince, because he is a prince" may sit in the gate. Just as the move to "prince" (Heb. *nāśîʾ*) as a title for the future royal leader of Israel in 34:24 and 37:25 represented a downgrading of royal language, so we see this process continued in the limited role assigned to the "prince" in chs. 40–48, where he is essentially the chief patron of the liturgy, responsible for supplying the materials required for the sacrificial system of worship (45:17, 22; 46:12). Indeed, he might be described as a functionary of the worshipping community. Tuell (1992) overstates the role of the prince in seeing him as the Persian governor. Nonetheless, the prince does enjoy certain privileges (45:7; 48:21), of which that described here is one (see further Joyce 1998:330–32).

In v. 5 Ezekiel is told to "Mark well those who may be admitted to the temple and those who are to be excluded from the sanctuary." The following verses articulate a rigorous attitude to the exclusion of foreigners from the sanctuary. They are described as "uncircumcised in heart and flesh" (vv. 7, 9); the metaphorical sense of "uncircumcised" was noted earlier, in various of the foreign nation oracles of Ezekiel (e.g. 28:10; 32:21). The concern here is the typically priestly one of preserving holiness and proper separation, a theme highlighted later in this chapter in the priestly task of teaching the people the difference between the holy (*qōdeš*) and the common (*ḥōl*), the unclean (*ṭāmēʾ*) and the clean (*ṭāhôr*) (44:23; cf. 42:20). Relations with foreigners constitute a recurrent theme in the Hebrew Bible. Schaper discusses this text in relation to two other important passages, Deut 23:2–9 and Isa 56:1–8 (Schaper 2004). The rigour of these Ezekiel verses invites speculation as to the particular circumstances behind them. Galambush (2004b) proposes that an Egyptian text concerning a tour of Palestine by Pharaoh Psammeticus II in c. 592 B.C.E. may help explain the background; she suggests that during this tour some of the Pharaoh's entourage were permitted entrance into the Jerusalem temple. The exclusive tone of the present verses might appear to stand in some tension with the inclusive emphasis in 47:21–23, where aliens are to receive their share in the allotment of territory ("They shall be to you as citizens of Israel," v. 22). But the concern there seems to be with pious proselytes and with land tenure, whereas here the concern is with sinful pagans and admission to the sanctuary.

Chapter 44 is best known as a classic text in discussion of the history of the priesthood. Several verses earlier in chs. 40–48 refer to the descendants of Zadok coming near YHWH to minister to him (40:46; 43:19). But it is the present chapter that develops the theme of the special status of the Zadokites over against the Levites. We read in v. 10 that the Levites went astray after their idols when Israel went astray, and so "they shall bear their punishment" (Heb. *wᵉnāśᵉʾû ʿᵃwōnām*). The Levites are to be permitted to serve in the temple (vv. 11, 14), but it is the descendants of Zadok alone who shall enter the sanctuary itself and approach the table, since they have been faithful (vv. 15–16). Famously, Wellhausen (1883, Eng. Tr. 1957:121–67) regarded this chapter as a key turning-point in the history of the priesthood, establishing the special status of the Zadokites, with the Priestly work being dated later. This has been the consensus view, broadly shared by, for example, Cody (1969, 1984) and Duguid (1994). But this position has not gone unchallenged. Critical alternatives include Haran's argument for the Priestly work preceding Ezek 40–48 (Haran 1978:147), Cook's proposal that ch. 44 does not refer to a historical development but is an interpretation of Korah's rebellion in Num 16–18 (Cook 1995b), and Stevenson's thesis that the passage is a text of "political geography" dealing with matters of access but not taking a punitive attitude towards the Levites (Stevenson 1996:66–78). Others dissenting from Wellhausen have included Abba (1978), McConville (1983) and Duke (1988).

The description of the Levites in ch. 44 is ambiguous; they hold responsibilities of some honour (vv. 11 and 14) and some statements about them are more positive than the Wellhausen theory can readily account for. Nevertheless, the most natural reading remains that the Levites are seriously criticized and indeed in some sense demoted. It could well be that, whereas the distinction between Zadokites and other priests goes back to Ezekiel himself (40:46; 43:18–27), the more polemical references to Zadokite pre-eminence (44:15–31; 48:11) may come from redactional elaboration, as is argued even by Niditch, who is generally reluctant to entertain the possibility of secondary addition (Niditch 1986:210).

Interestingly, this temple appears to lack a High Priest (Rooke 2000:116–19). It is difficult to weigh the significance of this absence; it is possibly a case in which we should not make too much of silence, but Kasher has persuasively presented this as a further example of the all-sufficiency of YHWH rendering many institutions redundant (Kasher 1998a:197).

Chapter 45

Significant parts of the latter sections of chs. 40–48 are devoted to the boundaries of the land, the allocation of territory and related matters. This material is focused in chs. 45 and 48 and could be described as an exercise in theological geography, a map whose heart and focus is the temple and the worship of the God of Israel. Verses 1–8 concern the distribution of land, a theme that is continued in 47:13–48:35 (indeed 45:1–8 could be a late insertion under the influence of ch. 48; see further, on ch. 48). The presentation is highly schematized and idealistic, but this is not to say that it was not hoped that it would be put into effect (cf. 43:11). The "holy district" (v. 1; Heb. *qōḏeš*) is divided into two sections, the northern section for the Levites and the southern for the Zadokite priests (cf. 44:10–16); the latter includes a section for the temple area (see further, on ch. 48). To the south of the "holy district" is an area of property for the city (v. 6), while the "prince" holds land to the east and west (v. 7; cf. on 44:3). All of this falls between the tribal holdings of Judah, to the north, and Benjamin, to the south (cf. 48:8, 23).

It was noted earlier that sometimes in chs. 40–48 there is a certain diffusion of the realm of the most holy. I proposed that this might reflect Ezekiel's preoccupation with the holiness of YHWH, above and beyond that attaching to related places or institutions. It is possible that 45:3 provides a further example of this phenomenon (see the discussion on 43:12).

Reference to the allocation of land to the "prince" (v. 7) leads on to a critique of the behaviour of "my princes," in the plural: "My princes shall no longer oppress my people" (v. 8). This is both a promise to the people and a warning to the princes. It could either be a reference to the succession of holders of the one office or more probably a general reference to the leadership (cf. 21:12; 22:6, 25). But the critique is in any case similar to that directed to the "prince" in the singular at 46:18. Verse 8 continues, "They shall let the house of Israel have the land according to their tribes": the land allocation arrangements of chs. 45 and 48 depend in significant part upon such yielding of former privilege. In v. 9 the language takes a yet more polemical turn: "Enough, O princes of Israel! Put away violence and oppression." The concern of v. 10 is related and reminiscent of the eighth-century prophets: "You shall have honest balances."

Festival regulations are found in the latter part of ch. 45. Passover (vv. 18–24) and, probably, Booths (v. 25) feature, but not Weeks or the Day of Atonement. A spring New Year seems to be assumed (v. 21; cf. on 40:1). (For important recent contributions on these and related questions, see Wagenaar 2005a, 2005b.)

CHAPTER 46

Chapter 46 features the most extended treatment of the "prince" (Heb. *nāśîʾ*). See also on 34:24; 44:3 and 45:7–8. He has a significant role in worship, with both duties and privileges, and these are spelled out in detail in this chapter. So, for example, he is able to enter by the gate of the inner court that faces east on special days (46:1–2; cf. v. 12). He makes special offerings but he has to provide them himself (46:4–7, 13–14). He is constrained by regulation with regard to his giving of gifts (v. 17). The prince is more a functionary of the worshipping community than its focus. And it is striking what a robustly critical tone v. 18 adopts: "The prince shall not take any of the inheritance of the people, thrusting them out of their holding." One is reminded of Elijah's critique of Ahab's injustice in seizing Naboth's vineyard (1 Kgs 21), and of the so-called "law of the king" in Deut 17. The prince is well and truly kept in his place within the polity envisaged in these last nine chapters of the book, and the circumscribed figure described here is a mere shadow of the old Davidic hopes. In the most characteristic formulations of the future in Ezekiel there is no ultimately significant role for royal mediators; their importance is melting away, overwhelmed by the emphasis on the holy God. As Block puts it, "The issue is not the return of David, but the presence of Yahweh," or again Aytoun, "Instead of a kingdom of David, a kingdom of God" (Block 1995:187; Aytoun 1920:29; see further Joyce 1998:330–37).

"The people of the land" (v. 3): Hebrew *ʿam-hāʾāreṣ*; a much-debated phrase that has a range of senses in Hebrew literature (Würthwein 1936). Commonly in Ezekiel (e.g. 7:27; 22:29) it refers to a group of powerful figures in Jerusalem, with close ties to the Davidic house (Duguid 1994:119–121). But within chs. 40–48 it seems to have the more general sense of the people gathered for worship (cf. 45:16, 22; 46:9). "On the day of the new moon he shall offer a young bull without blemish, and six lambs and a ram, which shall be without blemish" (v. 6): this is one of the famous cases of problematic divergence between Ezekiel and Torah (cf. Num 28:11), and v. 7 is another (cf. Num 15:6, 9; 28:12). The question of inconsistency with the Torah is best seen as an "inner-canonical" issue: had it not been for an already established sense that the book of Ezekiel was inspired scripture, inconsistencies between Ezekiel and the Torah would not have troubled the rabbis (see further the "Place in the Canon" section, above). "Then he brought me through the entrance" (v. 19): Ezekiel's angelic guide, the "man" introduced at 40:3, is still active. Though the motif was especially consistent in chs. 40–42, it has persisted, albeit sporadically, through the intervening chapters, and will reach its fullest development in the next chapter.

CHAPTER 47

This penultimate chapter falls into two very different parts, vv. 1–12 presenting the dramatic picture of the sacred river and vv. 13–23 returning to the theme of the meticulous disposition of the land (cf. 45:1–8).

Verses 1–12 present a striking scene of a river flowing from the temple, the place of the divine throne (43:7), and down through the desert to bring life to the Dead Sea. Though the popular phrase "River of Life" is not actually used here (as indeed "Chariot" is not used in ch. 1), this justly famous passage has made a rich contribution to later tradition (e.g. Joel 3:18 [Heb. 4:18]; Zech 14:8; John 4:14; Rev 22:1–2). Of particular importance is its indebtedness to "sacred river" mythology, which was a feature of both Canaanite and Mesopotamian culture; and there are similarities with other Hebrew Bible material bearing that influence (e.g. Ps 46:4 [Heb. v. 5]). Tuell highlights affinities with Eden, notably the rivers of paradise in Gen 2:10–14 (Tuell 2000b), while Hurowitz suggests that the great metal "sea" of 1 Kgs 7:23 is here reworked symbolically and theologically (Hurowitz 2005:80–81). But though the canvas is broad, even cosmic in some ways, nevertheless we encounter measurement even here (vv. 3–5), and moreover the limits of the vision are those of the land of Israel, as Darr (1987) has shown.

There is a close similarity in tone to the restoration oracles of chs. 34–37, not least the "valley of dry bones" vision in 37:1–14, where that which was dead is brought to life. In many ways this great passage seems like the crown and culmination of Ezekiel. Eichrodt wrote of 47:1–12: "What follows, however, agrees so strikingly with the former description given by the prophet of the miraculous change in Israel's fortunes, and brings it to a conclusion so characteristic of him, that one would need to have very convincing reasons before one could treat it as being on the same level as the regulations found in ch. 40–48" (Eichrodt 1970:582). It is not difficult to share Eichrodt's enthusiasm, but one should remain self-critically aware of the ways in which this passage appeals to some modern tastes and one should resist the notion that the surrounding regulations of chs. 40–48 would be any less important to the priest-prophet Ezekiel.

Ezekiel's guide here is the "man" (v. 3), the angelic figure introduced at 40:3; indeed, his role is most prominent of all in this passage, in which he measures with a "cord" (v. 3; mentioned in 40:3 alongside the "reed"), leads Ezekiel through the waters (vv. 3–5) and also speaks (v. 6). They leave the temple by way of the north gate (v. 2), because the east gate was barred (cf. 44:1–2).

Ezekiel's guide measures one thousand cubits four times as they head eastwards and each time the waters get deeper—ankle-deep, knee-deep, waist-deep, and then too deep to ford. The river has become so deep that it cannot be crossed on foot; but this is a measure of the abundance of life-giving water, very different from the waters of destruction and judgement mentioned in 13:13 (cf. Gen 6–9). In v. 6, the "man" speaks: "Mortal, have you seen this?" This recalls similar questions in the distinct context of the inspection of the abominations in the temple (8:15, 17). This may be a deliberate echo, highlighting the extent to which YHWH has effected resolution and transformation. With this they turn back and head upstream, towards the temple, and Ezekiel sees on both banks of the river a great many trees (v. 7). This is evidence of the fructifying effects of the water but also evokes the mythological notion of the tree of life, in keeping with Tuell's paradise analogy (Tuell 2000b). The water goes down into the "Arabah" (v. 8), which is the valley of the Dead Sea. "Wherever the river goes" (v. 9): NRSV, like the versions, translates "river" in the singular; but the MT reads *naḥ^{a}layim*, "the two rivers"; this dual form could possibly have been influenced by the reference to two rivers at Zech 14:8; moreover, there may be another echo of mythology here, for at Ugarit the home of El was at the source of two rivers. "Everything will live where the river goes": the revitalizing of the Dead Sea will allow fishing even in that most inhospitable of environments, which will become like the Great Sea, that is the Mediterranean. "En-gedi" (v. 10) is an oasis half way down the western shore of the Dead Sea; the location of "En-eglaim" is less clear, but it may have been on the opposite shore. The swamps and marshes are to be left for salt (v. 11), a splendidly pragmatic acknowledgement that the needs of life are many, for salt was an absolute essential. At the end of the passage, more is said about the trees, which will provide both for food and for healing (v. 12). It is reported that they will "bear fresh fruit every month" (Heb. *loḥ^{o}ḏāšāyw y^{e}ḇakkēr*). The trees will consistently yield produce of the quality of early fruit; whether the implication is that they will do this every month or simply each according to its due season is unclear. There is a final reminder of the source of all this blessing: "because the water for them flows from the sanctuary" (v. 12).

At 47:13 and indeed effectively for the remainder of the book, the reader is thrown back into the minute detail of precise theological geography, including the boundaries of the land (vv. 15–20) and a note about the place of aliens (vv. 22–23), followed in the final chapter by details of the tribal territorial allocations, the special areas in the middle of the land and the city gates. Verses 13–14 here refer to the division of the land among the twelve tribes of Israel, anticipating the presentation of 48:1–7, 23–29. It is noted that Joseph is to have two tribal portions (v. 13), one each for Ephraim and Manasseh (48:4–5). In order to accommodate this it is Levi who will receive no regular tribal territory in ch. 48. As elsewhere in the Hebrew Bible (cf. Gen 49:1–28), the number twelve is maintained as the number of tribal units, even when the particulars change. The land is to be divided equally (v. 14). The Hebrew words translated "equally" by NRSV are *ʾîš k^{e}ʾāḥîw*, literally, "a man like his brother." There is a marked egalitarian emphasis here, to be noted also at 45:8; compare the modest role given to the "prince" (*nāśîʾ*) in these chapters. "I swore to give it to your ancestors" (v. 14). That patriarch language reappears in the exilic age is not surprising, since the people had lost the land and looked to the traditions that claimed that it had been promised to their ancestors. Ezekiel features reference to the promises to Abraham (33:24), Jacob (28:25; 37:25) and, as here, unspecified "ancestors" (Heb. *ʾāḇôṯ*) (20:42; 36:28).

What vv. 15–20 gives are the boundaries of the land of Israel as a whole, without reference to tribes (even though vv. 13 and 21 emphasize division among the tribes, presumably in anticipation of ch. 48). The perimeter is delineated tracing the northern, eastern, southern, and western boundaries in turn. These are relatively modest boundaries (contrast the grandiose sweep of Gen 15:18–21). That this should be so, in spite of the utopian elements in the presentation of chs. 40–48, indicates a significant degree of pragmatic realism. Particularly noteworthy is the statement in v. 18 that the boundary will run "along the Jordan between Gilead and the land of Israel"; in other words, there is no claim laid here to territory in Transjordan.

The chapter concludes with a note (vv. 22–23) about the situation of the "aliens" (Heb. *gērîm*). The positive statement that the land is to be allotted as an inheritance "for yourselves and for the aliens who reside among you" is surpassed with the words "They shall be to you as citizens." The Hebrew here uses the word *ʾezrāḥ*, a "native," hence "like a native." Verse 23 adds: "In whatever tribe aliens reside, there you shall assign them their inheritance." This sounds remarkably generous, utopian indeed, but it is consistent with the generally humane attitude to the resident alien within the Hebrew Bible (e.g. Lev 19:33–34; Jer 22:3). The inclusive tone here appears to stand in tension with the passage in 44:5–9, which emphasized the exclusion of foreigners from the sanctuary. But the contexts are different: the issue there was about sinful pagans and admission to the sanctuary, whereas here the concern is with properly regulated proselytes and land tenure.

Chapter 48

This final chapter details the allocations of tribal lands (vv. 1–7, 23–29), the special areas in the middle of the land (vv. 8–22) and the city gates (vv. 30–34). See also on 45:1–8 and 47:13–23.

I have noted that, whereas Joseph has two tribal portions (47:13), one each for Ephraim and Manasseh (48:4–5), Levi receives no regular tribal territory. However, special territory in the heart of the land is allocated to the Zadokites on the one hand (called the "consecrated priests, the descendants of Zadok" at v. 11; cf. 45:4) and the Levites on the other (v. 13; cf. 45:5). Note also in this context 44:28, where YHWH is presented as saying with reference to the Zadokites (introduced as "the levitical priests, the descendants of Zadok" at v. 15): "I am their inheritance; and you shall give them no holding in Israel; I am their holding"; the reference here is clearly to their having no regular tribal territory.

The chapter moves straight into the list of tribal areas at v. 1. First, within vv. 1–7 are given the northern seven (including, interestingly, Judah) and then, after the discussion of the special territories in the middle of the land (vv. 8–22), the southern five (vv. 23–29). Verse 1 picks up the reference to the northern boundary of the land as a whole from 47:15, 17. Then, in a stylized manner, the tribal territories are given, as lateral strips, stretching from east to west. The sequence of the first group of tribes is, from north to south, Dan, Asher, Naphthali, Manasseh, Ephraim, Reuben and Judah. Once the list is properly underway, a standard formulaic pattern is followed in the Hebrew (vv. 2–7), literally "Adjoining the territory of Tribe X, from the east side to the west, Tribe Y, one." That Judah appears to the north is intriguing; it is likely that this is to neutralize the old north/south regional loyalties—which would cohere with the aspirations to reunification expressed in 37:15–28.

Verses 8–22 deal with the special areas in the middle of the land. Zimmerli suggested that 45:1–8 is an excerpt from the present chapter (Zimmerli 1983:467), whereas Block more plausibly sees the material here as representing an expansion of 45:1–8 (Block 1998:650). In the middle of the land a special "portion" (Heb. *tᵉrûmâ*) is set apart (v. 8). We may compare 45:1, where it is also called a "holy district" (Heb. *qōḏeš*); here, at v. 10, the conflate phrase "holy portion" (Heb. *tᵉrûmaṯ-haqqōḏeš*) occurs. The "portion" is divided into two main sections, one for the Zadokite priests (vv. 10–12; cf. 45:4), to include also the temple area (48:10; cf. 45:4), and another for the Levites (v. 13; cf. 45:5). It is not made clear, either in ch. 45 or here, precisely how the territories of the Zadokites and the Levites stood geographically in relation to each other. The

Zadokites are mentioned before the Levites in both contexts because of their higher status. However, Allen is probably right to judge that the territory of the Levites is envisaged as standing to the north of that of the Zadokites (Allen 1990a:284). To the south of the "portion" was an area of property for the city (vv. 15–20; cf. 45:6), while the "prince" held land to the east and west of the "portion" (vv. 21–22; cf. 45:7–8).

I argued earlier that sometimes in chs. 40–48 there is a certain diffusion of the realm of the most holy, proposing that this might reflect Ezekiel's preoccupation with the holiness of YHWH, above and beyond that attaching to related places or institutions. It is possible that v. 12 here provides a further example of this phenomenon (see the discussion on 43:12).

It is important that vv. 8–22 stand at the heart of this chapter, because those verses are central thematically as well as geographically. But now vv. 23–29 pick up the task left off at the end of v. 7, namely the presentation of the tribal areas. The standard pattern established earlier is followed, giving five further names (Benjamin, Simeon, Issachar, Zebulun and Gad), thereby bringing the total number to the standard twelve. Verse 28 describes the southern boundary of the land as a whole in words that pick up those of 47:19, before v. 29 gives a typical concluding summary.

Verses 30–34 present the exits (Heb. *tôṣeʾōṯ*) of the city. There are three gates (Heb. *šeʿārîm*) on each of the four sides of the city, and each gate bears the name of a tribe. The presentation shares some formal features with that of the tribal territories, the typical formula here being, literally "gate of Tribe X, one." However, whereas the tribal list counted Ephraim and Manasseh separately but excluded Levi, here the names of the gates include Levi, but Joseph is counted as one unit. The explanation for this may be that here, unlike when presenting the territorial arrangements, Ezekiel does not have the opportunity to accommodate Levi by other means.

It is typical of chs. 40–48 that the last verse of this long section (48:35) should combine both specific mathematical measurement ("The circumference of the city shall be eighteen thousand cubits") and weighty theological statement. The gates having been named, the city itself receives a name. The word "Zion" is never used in Ezekiel, and this is no doubt deliberate. As Renz puts it, this "mutes any suggestion of an inherent sanctity of this place" (Renz 1999b:95). Ezekiel certainly draws freely on the Zion tradition for images and vocabulary. Jerusalem has a special place of honour (cf. 5:5; 38:12) and its infringement constitutes a serious ground for the judgement (ch. 8). But both Ezekiel and his God "sit loose" to the site itself, exhibiting a remarkable degree of detachment. YHWH shows himself in alien Babylonia (ch. 1). In ch. 11, we see YHWH withdraw from the temple (vv. 22–23), and also declare himself "a sanctuary in some measure" to the exiles (v. 16). At 24:21 it is YHWH himself who profanes his sanctuary. When the book turns to the future and to restoration, the prophet again draws upon the Zion tradition, including the "very high mountain" of Ezek 40:2 (cf. Levenson 1976:7–24). But while YHWH returns to his temple in ch. 43, the place itself never provides the theological basis for the restoration. The Zion tradition in itself guarantees nothing, and so it is appropriate that here at the end of the book the name of the city is not Zion.

The book ends on a profound note: "The name of the city from that time on shall be, The LORD is There (Heb. *yhwh šāmmâ*)." A magnificently theocentric note for this most God-centred of biblical books to end on! "The Lord is There." Where? Not the temple, in this case. A name normally sums up the person or place named, and so it is unlikely that the Hebrew word *šāmmâ* is here intended to point away from the city to the temple, which is to the north of the city according to Ezekiel's theological geography (40:2; cf. 45:1–6; 48:8–20). The reference is then to the city itself. Central though the temple is within chs. 40–48, there is here affirmed the presence of YHWH in the city, whose setting was earlier in the chapter described as "ordinary" or "unconsecrated" (v. 15; Heb. *ḥōl*). This is a final striking case of Ezekiel both emphasizing the location of the holy, but also diffusing or spreading it—all within, of course, a highly ordered theocentric system. For what matters ultimately for Ezekiel is not the place, be it city or temple, but the holy God who dwells in the midst of his people—"The LORD is There."

Bibliography

Works are cited in the text by author's name and year of publication. In the Bibliography items by a single author are listed in chronological order; in cases in which more than one work by a single author appeared in the same year, these are indicated by use of "a," "b," "c." Original versions are normally given first in the bibliography, with details of English translations given subsequently. Where extensive use has been made of the English translation, however, the English publication details are given first.

A thorough annotated bibliography of Ezekiel publications between 1969 and 2004 may be found in Pohlmann 2006.

Commentaries

Allen, L. C. 1990a. *Ezekiel 20–48*. WBC 29. Dallas: Word.

———. 1994. *Ezekiel 1–19*. WBC 28. Dallas: Word.

Becker, J. 1971. *Der priesterliche Prophet. Das Buch Ezechiel*. 2 vols. Stuttgarter Kleiner Kommentar, Altes Testament, 12/1–2. Stuttgart: Katholisches Bibelwerk.

Bertholet, A. 1897. *Das Buch Hesekiel erklärt*. KHAT 12. Freiburg: Mohr.

——— (with K. Galling). 1936. *Hesekiel*. HAT 13. Tübingen: Mohr (Siebeck).

Biggs, C. R. 1996. *The Book of Ezekiel*. Epworth Commentaries. London: Epworth.

Blenkinsopp, J. 1990. *Ezekiel*. Interpretation Commentary. Louisville, Ky.: John Knox.

Block, D. I. 1997. *The Book of Ezekiel: Chapters 1–24*. NICOT. Grand Rapids: Eerdmans.

———. 1998. *The Book of Ezekiel: Chapters 25–48*. NICOT. Grand Rapids: Eerdmans.

Boadt, L. 1990a. Ezekiel. Pages 305–28 in *The New Jerome Bible Commentary*. Edited by R. E. Brown, J. A. Fitzmyer and R. E. Murphy. 2d ed. London: Chapman.

Bowen, N. R. 2009. *Ezekiel*. Abingdon Old Testament Commentary Series. Nashville: Abingdon.

Brownlee, W. H. 1986. *Ezekiel 1–19*. WBC 28. Waco, Tex.: Word.

Brunner, R. 1969. *Ezechiel*. Zürcher Bibelkommentare. 2 vols. 2d ed. Zurich: Zwingli.

Calvin, J. 1849–50. *Commentaries on the First Twenty Chapters of the Book of the Prophet Ezekiel*. 2 vols. Edinburgh: Calvin Translation Society.

———. 1994. *Ezekiel I: Chapters 1–12*. Rev. ed. Calvin's Old Testament Commentaries: The Rutherford House Translation 18. Grand Rapids: Eerdmans. Carlisle: Paternoster. Translated from posthumous first edition of 1565: *Ioannis Calvini in viginti prima Ezechielis Prophetae capita Praelectiones*. Ioannis Budaei et Caroli Ionvillaei labore et industria exceptae. Genevae: Ex officina Francisci Perrini.

Carley, K. W. 1974. *The Book of the Prophet Ezekiel*. CBC. London: Cambridge University Press.

Carvalho, C. L. Forthcoming. *Ezekiel*. Collegeville Bible Commentary. Collegeville, Minn.: Liturgical Press.

———. In preparation. *Ezekiel 25–48*. HCOT. Leuven: Peeters.
Clements, R. E. 1996a. *Ezekiel*. Westminster Bible Companion. Louisville, Ky.: Westminster John Knox.
Cody, A. 1984. *Ezekiel, with an Excursus on Old Testament Priesthood*. Old Testament Message: A Biblical-Theological Commentary 11. Wilmington, Del.: Michael Glazier.
Cook, S. L. 2009a. Ezekiel. Pages 241–56 in *Theological Bible Commentary*. Edited by G. R. O'Day and D. L. Petersen. Louisville, Ky.: Westminster John Knox.
Cooke, G. A. 1936. *A Critical and Exegetical Commentary on the Book of Ezekiel*. ICC. Edinburgh: T. & T. Clark.
Cooper, L. E., Sr. 1994. *Ezekiel*. NAC 17. Nashville: Broadman & Holman.
Cornill, C. H. 1886. *Das Buch des Propheten Ezechiel*. Leipzig: Hinrichs.
Craigie, P. C. 1983. *Ezekiel*. Daily Study Bible. Edinburgh: Saint Andrew. Philadelphia: Westminster.
Darr, K. P. 1992. Ezekiel. Pages 183–90 in *The Women's Bible Commentary*. Edited by C. A. Newsom and S. H. Ringe. Louisville, Ky.: Westminster John Knox.
———. 2001. Ezekiel. *NIB* 6:1073–1607.
Davidson, A. B. 1892. *The Book of the Prophet Ezekiel*. The Cambridge Bible for Schools and Colleges. Cambridge: Cambridge University Press.
Dijkstra, M. 1986. *Ezechiël*. 2 vols. Kampen: Kok.
Duguid, I. 1999. *Ezekiel*. New International Version Application Commentary. Grand Rapids: Zondervan.
Eichrodt, W. 1970. *Ezekiel*. OTL. London: SCM. Eng. trans. of the German original: *Der Prophet Hesekiel*. 3d ed. ATD 22. Göttingen: Vandenhoeck & Ruprecht, 1968.
Ellison, H. L. 1956. *Ezekiel: The Man and His Message*. London: Paternoster.
Feinberg, C. L. 1969. *The Prophecy of Ezekiel: The Glory of the Lord*. Chicago: Moody.
Fisch, S. 1950. *Ezekiel: Hebrew Text and English Translation with an Introduction and Commentary*. Soncino Books of the Bible. London: Soncino.
Fohrer, G. (with K. Galling). 1955. *Ezechiel*. HAT 13. Tübingen: Mohr (Siebeck).
Fuhs, H. F. 1986a. *Ezechiel 1–24*. Die Neue Echter Bibel 7. Würzburg: Echter.
———. 1988. *Ezechiel 25–48*. Die Neue Echter Bibel 22. Würzburg: Echter.
Galambush, J. 2001. Ezekiel. Pages 533–62 in *The Oxford Bible Commentary*. Edited by J. Barton and J. Muddiman. Oxford: Oxford University Press.
Goldingay, J. A. 2003. Ezekiel. Pages 623–64 in *Eerdmans Commentary on the Bible*. Edited by J. D. G. Dunn and J. W. Rogerson. Grand Rapids: Eerdmans.
Gowan, D. E. 1985. *Ezekiel*. Atlanta: John Knox.
Greenberg, M. 1983a. *Ezekiel 1–20*. AB 22. Garden City, NY: Doubleday.
———. 1997. *Ezekiel 21–37*. AB 22A. New York: Doubleday.
Henderson, E. 1870. *The Book of the Prophet Ezekiel*. Andover: Draper.
Hengstenberg, E. 1869. *The Prophecies of the Prophet Ezekiel Elucidated*. Edinburgh: T. & T. Clark.
Herrmann, J. 1924. *Ezechiel, übersetzt und erklärt*. KAT 11. Leipzig: A. Deichert.
Hitzig, F. 1847. *Der Prophet Ezechiel*. KeH 8. Leipzig: Weidmann.
Hornsby, T. J. 2006. Ezekiel. Pages 412–26 in *The Queer Bible Commentary*. Edited by D. Guest, R. E. Goss, M. West and T. Bohache. London: SCM.
Howie, C. G. 1961. *The Book of Ezekiel / The Book of Daniel*. Layman's Bible Commentary. Atlanta: John Knox.
Huey, F. B., Jr. 1983. *Ezekiel, Daniel*. Layman's Bible Commentary 12. Nashville: Broadman.
Jahn, G. 1905. *Das Buch Ezechiel auf Grund der Septuaginta hergestellt, übersetzt und kritisch erklärt*. Leipzig: Pfeiffer.
Jenson, R. W. 2009. *Ezekiel*. Theological Commentary on the Bible Series. Wheaton, Ill.: Brazos; London: SCM.

Kasher, R. 2004. *Ezekiel*. 2 vols. Tel Aviv: Am Oved. [Hebrew]
Keil, C. F. 1868. *Biblischer Commentar über den Propheten Ezechiel*. Biblischer Commentur über das Alte Test. 3/3. Leipzig. Eng. trans. *Ezekiel*. 2 vols. Grand Rapids: Eerdmans, 1988.
Konkel, M. In preparation. *Ezekiel 38–48*. Herders Theologischer Kommentar zum Alten Testament.
Kraetzschmar, R. 1900. *Das Buch Ezechiel*. HKAT. Göttingen: Vandenhoeck & Ruprecht.
Lamparter, H. 1968. *Zum Wächter bestellt: Der Prophet Hesekiel*. Die Botschaft des Alten Testaments 21. Stuttgart: Calwer.
Lapsley, J. E. In preparation. *Ezekiel: A Commentary*. OTL. Louisville, Ky.: Westminster John Knox.
Lind, M. C. 1996. *Ezekiel*. Believer's Church Bible Commentary. Scottdale, Pa: Herald.
Lofthouse, W. F. n.d. (1909?). *Ezekiel*. The Century Bible. Edinburgh: T. C. & E. C. Jack.
Lucas, E., 2002. *Ezekiel*. The People's Bible Commentary. Oxford: Bible Reading Fellowship.
Maarsingh, B. 1985–91. *Ezechiël*. 3 vols. De Prediking van het Oude Testament. Nijkerk: Callenbach.
May, H. G. (Introduction and Exegesis) and E. L. Allen (Exposition). 1956. The Book of Ezekiel. *IB* 6:39–338.
Mays, J. L. 1978. *Ezekiel, Second Isaiah*. Philadelphia: Fortress.
Mein, A. In preparation. *Ezekiel through the Centuries*. Blackwell Bible Commentary. Oxford: Blackwell.
Milgrom, J. Forthcoming. *Ezekiel 38–48*. Anchor Yale Bible Commentary 22B. New Haven, Conn.: Yale University Press.
Mosis, R. 1978. *Das Buch Ezechiel. Teil I. Kap. 1:1–20:44*. Geistliche Schriftlesung 8/1. Düsseldorf: Patmos.
Muilenburg, J. 1962a. Ezekiel. Pages 568–90 in *Peake's Commentary on the Bible*. Edited by M. Black and H. H. Rowley. London: Nelson.
———. 1962b. Holiness. Pages 616–23 in *The Interpreter's Dictionary of the Bible*. Edited by G. A. Buttrick. Nashville: Abingdon.
Odell, M. S. 2005. *Ezekiel*. Smyth and Helwys Bible Commentary. Macon, Ga.: Smyth & Helwys.
Olley, J. W. 2009. *Ezekiel: A Commentary based on Iezekiel in Codex Vaticanus*. Septuagint Commentary Series. Leiden: Brill.
Orelli, C. von. 1896. *Das Buch Ezechiel*. Kurzgefasster Kommentar zu den heiligen Schriften Alten und Neuen Testaments 5/1. Munich: Beck.
Petersen, D. L. 2000. Ezekiel. In *HarperCollins Bible Commentary: Revised Edition*. Edited by J. L. Mays. San Francisco: HarperSanFrancisco, 2000.
Pohlmann, K.-F. 1996. *Das Buch Hesekiel (Ezechiel). Kapitel 1–19*. ATD 22/1. Göttingen: Vandenhoeck & Ruprecht.
——— (mit einem Beitrag von T.A. Rudnig). 2001. *Das Buch Hesekiel (Ezechiel). Kapitel 20–48*. ATD 22/2. Göttingen: Vandenhoeck & Ruprecht.
Redpath, H. A. 1907. *The Book of the Prophet Ezekiel*. Westminster Series. London: Methuen.
Ruiz, J. A. 1998. Ezekiel. Pages 1050–84 in *The International Bible Commentary: A Catholic and Ecumenical Commentary for the Twenty-First Century*. Edited by W. R. Farmer. Collegeville, Minn.: Liturgical Press.
Sedlmeier, F. 2002. *Das Buch Ezechiel*. Neuer Stuttgarter Kommentar 21. Stuttgart: Katholisches Bibelwerk.
Skinner, J. 1895. *The Book of Ezekiel*. The Expositor's Bible. New York: A. C. Armstrong & Son.
Smend, R. 1880. *Der Prophet Ezechiel*. 2d ed. KeH 8. Leipzig: Hirzel.
Stalker, D. M. G. 1968. *Ezekiel*. Torch. London: SCM Press.

Stevenson, K., and M. Glerup, eds. 2008. *Ezekiel, Daniel.* Ancient Christian Commentary on Scripture, Old Testament 13. Downers Grove, Ill.: Inter-Varsity Press.

Stuart, D. 1989. *Ezekiel.* The Communicator's Commentary, Old Testament Series 18. Dallas: Word.

Sweeney, M. A. In preparation. *Ezekiel.* Reading the Old Testament Commentary Series. Macon, Ga.: Smyth & Helwys.

Taylor, J. B. 1969. *Ezekiel.* TOTC. London: Inter-Varsity Press.

Toy, C. H. 1899. *The Book of the Prophet Ezekiel.* New York: Dodd, Mead.

Tuell, S. S. 2009. *Ezekiel.* New International Bible Commentary 15. Peabody, Mass.: Hendrickson.

Van Rooy, H. F. In preparation. *Ezekiel 1–24.* HCOT. Leuven: Peeters.

Vawter, B. and L. J. Hoppe. 1991. *A New Heart: A Commentary on the Book of Ezekiel.* International Theological Commentary. Grand Rapids: Eerdmans. Edinburgh: Handsel.

Wevers, J. W. 1969. *Ezekiel.* NCB. London: Nelson.

Wilson, R. R. 1988. Ezekiel. Pages 652–94 in *Harper's Bible Commentary.* Edited by J. L. Mays. San Francisco: Harper.

Wright, C. J. H. 2001. *The Message of Ezekiel: A New Heart and a New Spirit.* The Bible Speaks Today: Old Testament Series. Leicester: Inter-Varsity Press.

Zimmerli, W. 1979a, 1983. *Ezekiel.* Hermeneia. 2 vols. Philadelphia: Fortress. Eng. trans. of the German original: *Ezechiel.* BKAT 13. 2 vols. Neukirchen–Vluyn: Neukirchener, 1969. [2d ed. 1979.]

Special Studies, Texts and Other Books

Ackerman, S. 1992. *Under Every Green Tree: Popular Religion in Sixth-Century Judah.* HSM 46. Atlanta: Scholars Press.

Ackroyd, P. R. 1968. *Exile and Restoration: A Study of Hebrew Thought of the Sixth Century BC.* London: SCM.

Ahn, J. J., and S. L. Cook, eds. 2009. *Thus Says the Lord: Essays on the Former and Latter Prophets in Honor of Robert R. Wilson.* LHBOTS. New York: T&T Clark International.

Albertz, R. 1992. *Religionsgeschichte Israels in alttestamentlicher Zeit.* Das Alte Testament Deutsch Ergänzungsreihe 8/1–2. Göttingen: Vandenhoeck & Ruprecht. Eng. trans. *A History of Israelite Religion in the Old Testament Period.* 2 vols. London: SCM Press, 1994.

———. 2001. *Die Exilszeit: 6 Jahrhundert v. Chr.* Biblische Enzyklopädie 7. Stuttgart: Kohlhammer. Eng. trans. *Israel in Exile: The History and Literature of the Sixth Century BCE.* Studies in Biblical Literature 3. Atlanta: Society of Biblical Literature, 2003.

Anderson, G. W. 1967. *Prophetic Contemporaries: A Study of Jeremiah and Ezekiel.* London: Epworth.

Andrew, M. E. 1985. *Responsibility and Restoration: The Course of the Book of Ezekiel.* Dunedin: University of Otago Press.

Auffarth, C. 1991. *Der drohende Untergang: "schöpfung" in Mythos und Ritual im Alten Orient und in Griechenland am Beispiel der Odyssee und des Ezechielbuches.* Religionsgeschichtliche Versuche und Vorarbeiten 39. Berlin: de Gruyter.

Baker, J. A. 1970. *The Foolishness of God.* London: Darton, Longman & Todd.

Balentine, S. E. 1983. *The Hidden God: The Hiding of the Face of God in the Old Testament.* OTM. Oxford: Oxford University Press.

Balla, E. 1958. *Die Botschaft der Propheten.* Tübingen: Mohr (Siebeck).

Baltzer, D. 1971. *Ezechiel und Deuterojesaja: Berührungen in der Heilserwartung der beiden grossen Exilspropheten.* BZAW 121. Berlin: de Gruyter.

Barstad, H. M. 1996. *The Myth of the Empty Land: A Study in the History and Archaeology of Judah during the "Exilic" Period.* Symbolae Osloenses, Fasc. Suppl. 28. Oslo: Scandinavian University Press.

Barthélemy, D., et al., eds. 1980. *Preliminary and Interim Report on the Hebrew Old Testament Text Project.* Vol. 5, *Prophetical Books II.* New York: United Bible Societies.

———. 1992. *Critique textuelle de l'Ancien Testament.* Vol. 3, *Ézéchiel, Daniel et les 12 Prophètes.* OBO 50/3. Fribourg, Suisse: Editions Universitaires. Göttingen: Vandenhoeck & Ruprecht.

Bartlett, J. R. 1989. *Edom and the Edomites.* JSOTSup 77. Sheffield: JSOT.

Barton, J. 1986. *Oracles of God: Perceptions of Ancient Prophecy in Israel after the Exile.* London: Darton, Longman & Todd.

———. 1997. *The Spirit and the Letter: Studies in the Biblical Canon.* London: SPCK.

Barton, J., and D. J. Reimer, eds. 1996. *After the Exile: Essays in Honour of Rex Mason.* Macon, Ga.: Mercer University Press.

Baumgärtel, F. 1932. *Die Eigenart der alttestamentlichen Frömmigkeit.* Schwerin: Bahn.

Beale, G. K. 2004. *The Temple and the Church's Mission: A Biblical Theology of the Dwelling Place of God.* New Studies in Biblical Theology 17. Downers Grove, Ill.: Apollos/ InterVarsity.

Becking, B., and M. Dijkstra, eds. 1996. *On Reading Prophetic Texts: Gender-Specific and Related Studies in Memory of Fokkelien van Dijk-Hemmes.* Leiden: Brill.

Becking, B., and M. C. A. Korpel, eds. 1999. *The Crisis of Israelite Religion: Transformation of Religious Tradition in Exilic and Post-Exilic Times.* OtSt 42. Leiden: Brill.

Beckwith, R. 1985. *The Old Testament Canon of the New Testament Church.* London: SPCK.

Berquist, J. L. 1993. *Surprises by the River: The Prophecy of Ezekiel.* St Louis: Chalice.

Berrigan, D., and T. Lewis-Borbely. 1997. *Ezekiel: Vision in the Dust.* Maryknoll, N.Y.: Orbis.

Bettenzoli, G. 1979. *Geist der Heiligkeit. Traditionsgeschichtliche Untersuchung des QDŠ-Begriffes im Buch Ezechiel.* Quaderni di Semitistica 8. Florence: Instituto di Linguistica e di Lingue Orientali.

Betts, T. J. 2005. *Ezekiel the Priest: A Custodian of Tôrâ.* Studies in Biblical Literature 74. New York: Lang.

Bloch-Smith, E. 1992. *Judahite Burial Practices and Beliefs about the Dead.* JSOTSup 123. ASORMS 7. Sheffield: JSOT Press.

Block, D. I. 2000a. *The Gods of the Nations: Studies in Ancient Near Eastern National Theology.* 2d ed. Evangelical Theological Society Studies. Grand Rapids: Baker Academic. Leicester: Apollos.

Boadt, L. 1980. *Ezekiel's Oracles against Egypt: A Literary and Philological Study of Ezekiel 29–32.* BibOr 37. Rome: Pontifical Biblical Institute.

Boardman, J., et al., eds. 1991. *The Assyrian and Babylonian Empires and Other States of the Near East, from the Eighth to the Sixth Centuries BC*, vol. 3, Part 2. 2d ed. The Cambridge Ancient History. Cambridge: Cambridge University Press.

Boccaccini, G. 2001. *Roots of Rabbinic Judaism: An Intellectual History, from Ezekiel to Daniel.* Grand Rapids: Eerdmans.

Bodendorfer, G. 1997. *Der Drama des Bundes: Ezechiel 16 in rabbinischer Perspektive.* Freiburg: Herder.

Bodi, D. 1991. *The Book of Ezekiel and the Poem of Erra.* OBO 104. Fribourg, Suisse: Universitätsverlag. Göttingen: Vandenhoeck & Ruprecht.

Bøe, S. 2001. *Gog and Magog: Ezekiel 38–39 as Pre-text for Revelation 19, 17–21 and 20, 7–10.* WUNT 2/135. Tübingen: Mohr Siebeck.

Brenner, A. ed. 2001. *Prophets and Daniel.* A Feminist Companion to the Bible, Second Series. London: Sheffield Academic Press.

Brettler, M. Z. 1989. *God is King: Understanding an Israelite Metaphor*. JSOTSup 76. Sheffield: JSOT.

Brockington, L. H. 1973. *The Hebrew Text of the Old Testament: The Readings Adopted by the Translators of the New English Bible*. Cambridge: Cambridge University Press.

Brooke, G. J. 1985. *Exegesis at Qumran: 4QFlorilegium in its Jewish Context*. JSOTSup 29. Sheffield: JSOT.

Browne, L. E. 1952. *Ezekiel and Alexander*. London: SPCK.

Brueggemann, W. 1986. *Hopeful Imagination: Prophetic Voices in Exile*. Philadelphia: Fortress.

———. 1997. *Cadences of Home: Preaching among Exiles*. Louisville, Ky: Westminster John Knox.

———. 2002. *Ichabod Toward Home: The Journey of God's Glory*. Grand Rapids: Eerdmans.

Burrows, M. 1925. *The Literary Relations of Ezekiel*. Philadelphia.

Cahinga, J. 2003. *O Fim da iniquidade, esperança de uma nova era: Uma leitura apocalíptica de Ez 7*. Rome: N. Domenici Pécheux.

Callender, D. E., Jr. 2000a. *Adam in Myth and History: Ancient Israelite Perspectives on the Primal Human*. HSS 48. Winona Lake, Ind.: Eisenbrauns.

Carley, K. W. 1975. *Ezekiel among the Prophets*. SBT 2/31. London: SCM.

Carroll, R. P. 1979. *When Prophecy Failed: Reactions and Responses to Failure in the Old Testament Prophetic Traditions*. London: SCM.

———. 1981. *From Chaos to Covenant: Uses of Prophecy in the Book of Jeremiah*. London: SCM.

Carson, D. A., and H. G. M. Williamson, eds. 1988. *It Is Written: Scripture Citing Scripture*. Cambridge: Cambridge University Press.

Causse, A. 1937. *Du groupe ethnique à la communauté réligieuse: le problème sociologique de la réligion d'Israël*. Paris: Jouve/F. Alcan.

Charlesworth, J. H., ed. 1983–85. *The Old Testament Pseudepigrapha*. 2 vols. Garden City, N.Y.: Doubleday.

Childs, B. S. 1979. *Introduction to the Old Testament as Scripture*. London: SCM Press.

Christman, A. R. 2005. *"What Did Ezekiel See?": Christian Exegesis of Ezekiel's Vision of the Chariot from Irenaeus to Gregory the Great*. The Bible in Ancient Christianity 4. Leiden: Brill.

Clements, R. E. 1996b. *Old Testament Prophecy: From Oracles to Canon*. Louisville, Ky.: Westminster John Knox.

Clifford, R. J. 1972. *The Cosmic Mountain in Canaan and the Old Testament*. HSM 4. Cambridge, Mass.: Harvard University Press.

Cody, A. 1969. *A History of Old Testament Priesthood*. Rome: Pontifical Biblical Institute.

Cogan, M., B. L. Eichler and J. H. Tigay, eds. 1997. *Tehillah le-Moshe: Biblical and Judaic Studies in Honor of Moshe Greenberg*. Winona Lake, Ind.: Eisenbrauns.

Cogan, M., and I. Eph'al, eds. 1991. *Ah, Assyria... Studies in Assyrian History and Ancient Near Eastern Historiography Presented to Hayim Tadmor*. Scripta Hierosolymitana 33. Jerusalem: Magnes.

Cohen, R. 1997. *Global Diasporas: An Introduction*. London: UCL.

Collins, T. 1993. *The Mantle of Elijah: The Redaction Criticism of the Prophetical Books*. The Biblical Seminar 20. Sheffield: JSOT.

Cook, S. L. 1995a. *Prophecy and Apocalypticism: The Postexilic Social Setting*. Minneapolis: Fortress.

Cook, S. L., and C. L. Patton, eds. 2004. *Ezekiel's Hierarchical World: Wrestling with a Tiered Reality*. SBL Symposium Series 31. Atlanta: SBL.

Corral, M. A. 2002. *Ezekiel's Oracles Against Tyre: Historical Reality and Motivations*. BibOr 46. Rome: Editrice Pontificio Istituto Biblico.

Cox, C. E., ed. 1987. *VI Congress of the International Organization for Septuagint and Cognate Studies: Jerusalem 1986*. SBLSCS 23. Atlanta: Scholars Press.
Crane, A. S. 2008. *Israel's Restoration: A Textual-Comparative Exploration of Ezekiel 36–39*. VTSup 122. Leiden: Brill.
Däniken, E. von. 1969. *Chariots of the Gods? Unsolved Mysteries of the Past*. London: Souvenir.
Daube, D. 1947. *Studies in Biblical Law*. Cambridge: Cambridge University Press.
Davidson, A. B. 1904. *The Theology of the Old Testament*. Edinburgh: T. & T. Clark.
Davies, P. R. ed., 1996. *The Prophets: A Sheffield Reader*. The Biblical Seminar 42. Sheffield: Sheffield Academic Press.
Davies, P. R., and D. J. A. Clines, eds. 1993. *Among the Prophets: Language, Image and Structure in the Prophetic Writings*. JSOTSup 144. Sheffield: Sheffield Academic Press.
Davis, E. F. 1989a. *Swallowing the Scroll: Textuality and the Dynamics of Discourse in Ezekiel's Prophecy*. JSOTSup 78. Bible and Literature Series 21. Sheffield: Almond.
Day, J. 1985. *God's Conflict with the Dragon and the Sea: Echoes of a Canaanite Myth in the Old Testament*. UCOP 35. Cambridge: Cambridge University Press.
———. 1989. *Molech: A God of Human Sacrifice in the Old Testament*. UCOP 41. Cambridge: Cambridge University Press.
———. 2000. *Yahweh and the Gods and Goddesses of Canaan*. JSOTSup 265. Sheffield: Sheffield Academic Press.
———. ed. 2005b. *Temple and Worship in Biblical Israel: Proceedings of the Oxford Old Testament Seminar*. LHBOTS 422. London: T&T Clark International.
De Boer, E. A. 2004. *John Calvin on the Visions of Ezekiel: Historical and Hermeneutical Studies in John Calvin's "sermons inédits", Especially on Ezek. 36–48*. Kerkhistorische Bijdragen 21. Leiden: Brill.
Dempsey, C. J. 2000. *Hope Amid the Ruins: The Ethics of Israel's Prophets*. St Louis: Chalice.
Dhorme, E. 1963. *L'emploi métaphorique des noms de parties du corps en hébreu et en akkadien* (Edition anastatique d'un ouvrage publié en 1923). Paris: Geuthner.
Dicou, B. 1994. *Edom, Israel's Brother and Antagonist: The Role of Edom in Biblical Prophecy and Story*. JSOTSup 169. Sheffield: Sheffield Academic Press.
Diestel, A. A. 2006. *"Ich bin Jahwe": Der Aufstieg der Ich-bin-Jahwe-Aussage zum Schlüsselwort des alttestamentlichen Monotheismus*. WMANT 110. Neukirchen–Vluyn: Neukirchener.
Donner, H., R. Hanhart and R. Smend, eds. 1977. *Beiträge zur alttestamentlichen Theologie. Festschrift für W. Zimmerli zum 70 Geburtstag*. Göttingen: Vandenhoeck & Ruprecht.
Driver, S. R. 1913. *An Introduction to the Literature of the Old Testament*. 9th ed. Edinburgh: T. & T. Clark.
Duguid, I. M. 1994. *Ezekiel and the Leaders of Israel*. VTSup 56. Leiden: Brill.
Duhm, B. 1892. *Das Buch Jesaja*. HKAT. Göttingen: Vandenhoeck & Ruprecht.
———. 1901. *Das Buch Jeremia*. KHAT. Tübingen: Mohr.
Dupont-Sommer, A. 1961. *The Essene Writings from Qumran*. Oxford: Blackwell.
Dürr, L. 1923. *Die Stellung des Propheten Ezechiel in der israelitisch-jüdischen Apokalyptik*. AA 9/1. Münster: Aschendorff.
Durlesser, J. A. 2006. *The Metaphorical Narratives in the Book of Ezekiel*. Lewiston, N.Y.: Edwin Mellen.
Dus, R. A. 2003. *Las Parábolas del Reino de Judá: Lingüística textual y comunicación (Ez 17; 19; 21)*. Estudios Universitarios 1. Paraná-Entre Ríos: Pontificia Universidad Católica Argentina.
Edinger, E. F. 2000. *Ego and Self: The Old Testament Prophets, from Isaiah to Malachi*. Studies in Jungian Psychology by Jungian Analysts. Toronto: Inner City Books.

Eichrodt, W. 1933–39. *Theologie des Alten Testaments*. 3 vols. Stuttgart: Ehrenfried Klotz Verlag. Eng. trans. *Theology of the Old Testament*. OTL. 2 vols. London: SCM, 1961–67.

Eissfeldt, O. 1913. *Der Maschal im Alten Testament*. BZAW 24. Giessen: Töpelmann.

———. 1934. *Einleitung in das Alte Testament*. Tübingen: Mohr. [3d ed. 1964]. Eng. trans. *The Old Testament: An Introduction*. Oxford: Blackwell, 1965.

———. 1935. *Molk als Opferbegriff im Punischen und Hebräischen und das Ende das Gottes Moloch*. Halle: Max Niemeyer.

Elior, R. 2004. *The Three Temples: On the Emergence of Jewish Mysticism*. Oxford: Littman Library of Jewish Civilization.

Ellens, J. H., and W. G. Rollins, eds. 2004. *Psychology and the Bible: A New Way to Read the Scriptures*. Vol. 2, *From Genesis to Apocalyptic Vision*. Westport, Conn.: Praeger.

Elliger, K., and W. Rudolph, eds. 1967/1977. *Biblia Hebraica Stuttgartensia*. Stuttgart: Württembergische Bibelanstalt.

Exum, J. C., ed. 1989. *Signs and Wonders: Biblical Texts in Literary Focus*. Semeia Studies. Atlanta: Scholars Press.

Fechter, F. 1992. *Bewältigung der Katastrophe. Untersuchungen zu ausgewählten Fremdvölkersprüchen im Ezechielbuch*. BZAW 208. Berlin: de Gruyter.

Feist, U. 1995. *Ezechiel: Das literarische Problem des Buches forschungsgeschichtlich betrachtet*. BWANT 138. Stuttgart: Kohlhammer.

Finley, T. J., ed. 1999. *Bilingual Concordance to the Targum of the Prophets: Ezekiel*. 3 vols. Leiden: Brill.

Fishbane, M. 1985. *Biblical Interpretation in Ancient Israel*. Oxford: Oxford University Press.

Fitzmyer, J. A. 1990. *The Dead Sea Scrolls: Major Publications and Tools for Study*. Rev. ed. SBLRBS 20. Atlanta: Scholars Press.

Fitzpatrick, P. E. 2004. *The Disarmament of God: Ezekiel 38–39 in Its Mythic Context* CBQMS 37. Washington, D.C.: Catholic Biblical Association of America.

Fohrer, G. 1952. *Die Hauptprobleme des Buches Ezechiel*. BZAW 72. Berlin: Töpelmann.

———. 1953. *Die symbolischen Handlungen der Propheten*. ATANT 25. Zurich: Zwingli.

———. 1970. *Introduction to the Old Testament*. London: SPCK. Eng. trans. of the German original: *Einleitung in das Alte Testament*. 10th rev. ed. of the work by E. Sellin, first published 1910. Heidelberg: Quelle & Meyer, 1965.

Fontaine, C. R. 1982. *Traditional Sayings in the Old Testament: A Contextual Study*. Bible and Literature Series 5. Sheffield: Almond.

Freedy, K. S. 1969. The Literary Relations of Ezekiel. A Historical Study of Chapters 1–24. Ph.D. diss., University of Toronto.

Friebel, K. G. 1999. *Jeremiah's and Ezekiel's Sign-Acts: Rhetorical Nonverbal Communication*. JSOTSup 283. Sheffield: Sheffield Academic Press.

Friedman, R. E. 1981. *The Exile and Biblical Narrative: The Formation of the Deuteronomistic and Priestly Works*. HSM 22. Chico, Calif.: Scholars Press.

Galambush, J. 1992. *Jerusalem in the Book of Ezekiel: The City as Yahweh's Wife*. SBLDS 130. Atlanta: Scholars Press.

García Martínez, F., and M. Vervenne, eds. 2005. *Interpreting Translation: Studies on the LXX and Ezekiel in Honour of Johan Lust*. BETL 192. Leuven: Leuven University Press / Peeters.

Garscha, J. 1974. *Studien zum Ezechielbuch: Eine redaktionskritische Untersuchung von Ez 1–39*. Europäische Hochschulschriften 23. Bern: Herbert Lang. Frankfurt: Peter Lang.

Gese, H. 1957. *Der Verfassungsentwurf des Ezechiel (Kap. 40–48) traditionsgeschichtlich untersucht*. Beiträge zur historischen Theologie 25. Tübingen: Mohr.

Geyer, J. B. 2004b. *Mythology and Lament: Studies in the Oracles About the Nations*. SOTS Monographs. Aldershot: Ashgate.

Gibson, A. 1981. *Biblical Semantic Logic: A Preliminary Analysis*. Oxford: Blackwell.

Gindin, T. E. 2007. *The Early Judaeo-Persian Tafsîrs of Ezekiel: Text, Translation, Commentary*. vol. 1, *Text*; vol 2, *Translation*. Philosophisch-historische Klasse, Sitzungsberichte, 763 and 766; Veröffentlichungen zur Iranistik, 40 and 44; Vienna: Verlag der Österreichischen Akademie der Wissenschaften.

Glazov, G. Y. 2001. *The Bridling of the Tongue and the Opening of the Mouth in Biblical Prophecy*. JSOTSup 311. Sheffield: Sheffield Academic Press.

Good, E. M. 1981. *Irony in the Old Testament*. 2d ed. Bible and Literature Series 3. Sheffield: Almond.

Gordon, R. P., ed. 1995. *The Place Is Too Small for Us: The Israelite Prophets in Recent Scholarship*. Sources for Biblical and Theological Study 5. Winona Lake, Ind.: Eisenbrauns.

Gorman, F. H., Jr. 1990. *The Ideology of Ritual: Space, Time and Status in the Priestly Theology*. JSOTSup 91. Sheffield: JSOT Press.

Goshen-Gottstein, M. H., and S. Talmon, eds. 2004. *The Book of Ezekiel*. The Hebrew University Bible. Jerusalem: Hebrew University/Magnes.

Gottwald, N. K. 1979. *The Tribes of Yahweh*. Maryknoll, N.Y.: Orbis.

Goudoever, J. Van. 1961. *Biblical Calendars*. 2d ed. Leiden: Brill.

Grabbe, L. L., ed. 1998. *Leading Captivity Captive: "The Exile" as History and Ideology*. JSOTSup 278. European Seminar in Historical Methodology 2. Sheffield: Sheffield Academic Press.

Grabbe, L. L., and Alice Ogden Bellis, eds. 2004. *The Priests in the Prophets: The Portrayal of Priests, Prophets, and Other Religious Specialists in the Latter Prophets*. JSOTSup 408. London: T&T Clark International.

Grabbe, L. L., and R. D. Haak, eds. 2003. *Knowing the End from the Beginning: The Prophetic, the Apocalyptic and Their Relationships*. JSPSup 46. London: T&T Clark International.

Graf, K. H. 1866. *Die geschichtlichen Bücher des Alten Testaments*. Leipzig: T.O. Weigel.

Graffy, A. 1984. *A Prophet Confronts his People: The Disputation Speech in the Prophets*. AnBib 104. Rome: Biblical Institute Press.

Gray, G. B. 1913. *A Critical Introduction to the Old Testament*. London: Duckworth.

Grayson, A.K. 1975. *Assyrian and Babylonian Chronicles*. Texts from Cuneiform Sources 5. Locust Valley, N.Y.: J. J. Augustin.

Gruenwald, I. 1980. *Apocalyptic and Merkavah Mysticism*. Arbeiten zur Geschichte des antiken Judentums und des Urchristentums 14. Leiden: Brill.

Haag, H. 1943. *Was lehrt die literarische Untersuchung des Ezechiel-Textes? Eine philologisch-theologische Studie*. Fribourg, Suisse: Universitätsbuchhandlung.

Habel, N. C. ed. 2001. *The Earth Story in the Psalms and the Prophets*. The Earth Bible 4. Sheffield: Sheffield Academic Press. Cleveland, Ohio: Pilgrim.

Hall, H. R. 1928. *Babylonian and Assyrian Sculpture in the British Museum*. Paris and Brussels: Van Oest.

Halperin, D. J. 1980. *The Merkabah in Rabbinic Literature*. American Oriental Series 62. New Haven, Conn.: American Oriental Society.

———. 1988. *The Faces of the Chariot: Early Jewish Responses to Ezekiel's Vision*. Texte und Studien zum antiken Judentum 16. Tübingen: J. C. B. Mohr (Paul Siebeck).

———. 1993. *Seeking Ezekiel: Text and Psychology*. University Park, Pa.: Pennsylvania State University Press.

Hals, R. M. 1989. *Ezekiel*. FOTL 19. Grand Rapids: Eerdmans.

Hanson, P. D. 1979. *The Dawn of Apocalyptic: The Historical and Sociological Roots of Jewish Apocalyptic Eschatology*. Philadelphia: Fortress. Rev. ed. of 1975 original.

Haran, M. 1978. *Temples and Temple-Service in Ancient Israel: An Inquiry into the Character of Cult Phenomena and the Historical Setting of the Priestly School*. Oxford: Clarendon.
Harford, J. Battersby. 1935. *Studies in the Book of Ezekiel*. Cambridge: Cambridge University Press.
Harl, M., G. Dorival and O. Munnich. 1994. *La Bible Grecque des Septante: Du judaïsme hellénistique au christianisme ancient*. 2d ed. Initiations au christianisme ancien. Paris: Cerf / C.N.R.S.
Hartberger, B. 1986. *"An den Wassern von Babylon...": Psalm 137 auf dem Hintergrund von Jeremia 51, der biblischen Edom-Traditionen und babylonischer Originalquellen*. Bonner Biblische Beiträge 63. Frankfurt am Mein: Peter Hanstein.
Hauser, A., ed. 2008. *Recent Research on the Major Prophets*. Recent Research in Biblical Studies 1. Sheffield: Sheffield Phoenix.
Hayes, J. H., and P. K. Hooker. 1988. *A New Chronology for the Kings of Israel and Judah*. Atlanta: John Knox.
Hays, R. B. 1989. *Echoes of Scripture in the Letters of Paul*. New Haven, Conn.: Yale University Press.
Heaton, E. W. 1977. *The Old Testament Prophets*. Rev. ed. London: Darton, Longman & Todd.
Heider, G. C. 1985. *The Cult of Molek: A Reassessment*. JSOTSup 43. Sheffield: JSOT.
Hempel, J. 1964. *Das Ethos des Alten Testaments*. 2d ed. BZAW 67. Berlin: Töpelmann.
Hermisson, H.-J. 1965. *Sprache und Ritus im altisraelitischen Kult*. WMANT 19. Neukirchen–Vluyn: Kreis Moers, Neukirchener.
Herntrich, V. 1933. *Ezechielprobleme*. BZAW 61. Giessen: Töpelmann.
Herrmann, J. 1908. *Ezechielstudien*. BWANT 2. Leipzig: Hinrichs.
Herrmann, S. 1965. *Die prophetischen Heilserwartungen im Alten Testament: Ursprung und Gestaltwandel*. BWANT 85. Stuttgart: Kohlhammer.
———. 1973. *Geschichte Israels in alttestamentlicher Zeit*. Munich: Kaiser. Eng. trans. *A History of Israel in Old Testament Times*. 2d ed. London: SCM, 1981.
Himmelfarb, M. 1993. *Ascent to Heaven in Jewish and Christian Apocalypses*. New York: Oxford University Press.
Hölscher, G. 1914. *Die Profeten*. Leipzig: Hinrichs.
———. 1924. *Hesekiel, der Dichter und das Buch: Eine literarkritische Untersuchung*. BZAW 39. Giessen: Töpelmann.
Hoffman, Y., and H. Reventlow, eds. 1992. *Justice and Righteousness: Biblical Themes and Their Influence*. JSOTSup 137. Sheffield: JSOT Press.
Hossfeld, F. L. 1977. *Untersuchungen zu Komposition und Theologie des Ezechielbuches*. FB 20. Würzburg: Echter. 2d ed., 1983.
Howie, C. G. 1950. *The Date and Composition of Ezekiel*. JBL Monograph Series 4. Philadelphia: Society of Biblical Literature.
Hunter, A. Vanlier. 1982. *Seek the Lord! A Study of the Meaning and Function of the Exhortations in Amos, Hosea, Isaiah, Micah, and Zephaniah*. Baltimore, Md.: St Mary's Seminary and University Press.
Hurowitz, V. A. 1992. *I Have Built You and Exalted House: Temple Building in the Bible in Light of Mesopotamian and North-West Semitic Writings*. JSOT/ASOR Monograph Series 5; JSOTSup 115. Sheffield: JSOT Press.
Hurvitz, A. 1982. *A Linguistic Study of the Relationship between the Priestly Source and the Book of Ezekiel: A New Approach to an Old Problem*. Cahiers de la Revue Biblique 20. Paris: Gabalda.
Irwin, W. A. 1943. *The Problem of Ezekiel: An Inductive Study*. Chicago: University of Chicago Press.
Jahn, P. L. G. 1972. *Der griechische Text des Buches Ezechiel*. Bonn: R. Habelt.

Janssen, E. 1956. *Juda in der Exilszeit: Ein Beitrag zur Frage der Entstehung des Judentums*. FRLANT 69. Göttingen: Vandenhoeck & Ruprecht.

Jenson, P. P. 1992. *Graded Holiness: A Key to the Priestly Conception of the World*. JSOTSup 106. Sheffield: JSOT Press.

Johnson, A. C., H. S. Gehman and J. E. H. Kase, eds. 1938. *The John H. Scheide Biblical Papyri: Ezekiel*. Princeton University Studies in Papyrology 3. Princeton: Princeton University Press.

Johnson, A. R. 1949. *The Vitality of the Individual in the Thought of Ancient* Israel. Cardiff: University of Wales Press.

———. 1961. *The One and the Many in the Israelite Conception of God*. 2d ed. Cardiff: University of Wales Press.

Joosten, J. 1996. *People and Land in the Holiness Code: An Exegetical Study of the Ideational Framework of the Law in Leviticus 17–26*. VTSup 67. Leiden: Brill.

Joyce, P. M. 1989. *Divine Initiative and Human Response in Ezekiel*. JSOTSup 51. Sheffield: JSOT Press.

Kaiser, O. 1970. *Einleitung in das Alte Testament*. 2d ed. Gütersloh: Gütersloher Verlagshaus, Gerd Mohn. Eng. trans. *Introduction to the Old Testament: A Presentation of its Results and Problems*. Oxford: Blackwell, 1975.

———. 1974. *Isaiah 13–39*. OTL. London: SCM. Eng. trans. of the German original: *Das Buch des Propheten Jesaja 13–39*. ATD 18. Göttingen: Vandenhoeck & Ruprecht, 1973.

Kaminsky, J. S. 1995. *Corporate Responsibility in the Hebrew Bible*. JSOTSup 196. Sheffield: Sheffield Academic Press.

Kamionkowski, S. T. 2003. *Gender Reversal and Cosmic Chaos: A Study on the Book of Ezekiel*. JSOTSup 368. London: Sheffield Academic Press.

Kaufmann, Y. 1961. *The Religion of Israel: From its Beginnings to the Babylonian Exile* Translated by M. Greenberg. London: Allen & Unwin.

Keel, O. 1977. *Yahwe-Visionen und Siegelkunst: eine neue Deutung der Majestätsschilderungen in Jes 6, Ez 1 und 10 und Sach 4*. Stuttgarter Bibelstudien 84/85. Stuttgart: Katholisches Bibelwerk.

Kelle, B. E., and Megan Bishop Moore, eds. 2006. *Israel's Prophets and Israel's Past: Essays on the Relationship of Prophetic Texts and Israelite History in Honor of John H. Hayes*. LHBOTS 446. New York: T&T Clark International.

Kennett, R. H. 1928. *Old Testament Essays*. Cambridge: Cambridge University Press.

Kenyon, F. G. 1937. *The Chester Beatty Biblical Papyri: Descriptions and Texts of Twelve Manuscripts on Papyrus of the Greek Bible. Fasc. 7: Ezekiel, Daniel, Esther*. London: Emery Walker.

Kessler, W. 1926. *Die innere Einheitlichkeit des Buches Ezechiel*. Berichte des theologischen Seminars der Brüdergemeine 11. Herrnhut: Verlag der Missionsbuchhandlung.

Kiefer, J. 2005. *Exil und Diaspora: Begrifflichkeit und Deutungen im antiken Judentum und in der Hebräischen Bibel*. Arbeiten zur Bibel und ihrer Geschichte 19. Leipzig: Evangelische Verlagsanstalt.

Klein, A. 2008. *Schriftauslegung im Ezechielbuch: redaktionsgeschichtliche Untersuchungen zu Ez 34–39*. BZAW 391. Berlin: de Gruyter.

Klein, R. W. 1979. *Israel in Exile: A Theological Interpretation*. OBT. Philadelphia: Fortress.

———. 1988. *Ezekiel: The Prophet and his Message*. Studies on Personalities of the Old Testament. Columbia: University of South Carolina Press.

Knohl, I. 1995. *The Sanctuary of Silence: The Priestly Torah and the Holiness School*. Philadelphia: Fortress.

Koch, K. ed. 1972. *Um das Prinzip der Vergeltung in Religion und Recht des Alten Testaments*. Wege der Forschung 125. Darmstadt: Wissenschaftliche Buchgesellschaft.

Königs, K. 2000. *St Maria und St Clemens Schwarzrheindorf.* Bonn: Katholische Pfarrgemeinde Schwarzrheindorf.

Konkel, M. 2001. *Architektonik des Heiligen: Studien zur zweiten Tempelvision Ezechiels (Ez 40–48).* Bonner Biblische Beiträge 129. Berlin: Philo.

Kowalski, B. 2004. *Die Rezeption des Propheten Ezechiel in der Offenbarung des Johannes.* Stuttgarter Biblische Beiträge 52. Stuttgart: Katholisches Bibelwerk.

Kraeling, C. H. 1956. *The Synagogue.* The Yale University Excavations at Dura-Europos, Final Report 8/1. New Haven, Conn.: Yale University Press.

Krispenz, J. 2001. *Literarkritik und Stilstatistik im Alten Testament: Eine Studie zur literarkritischen Methode, durchgeführt an Texten aus den Büchern Jeremia, Ezechiel und 1 Könige.* BZAW 307. Berlin: de Gruyter.

Krüger, T. 1989. *Geschichtskonzepte im Ezechielbuch* BZAW 180. Berlin/NewYork: de Gruyter.

Kutsch, E. 1985. *Die chronologischen Daten des Ezechielbuches* OBO 62. Fribourg, Suisse: Universitätsverlag. Göttingen: Vandenhoeck & Ruprecht.

Kutsko, J. F. 2000a. *Between Heaven and Earth: Divine Presence and Absence in the Book of Ezekiel.* Biblical and Judaic Studies from the University of California, San Diego 7. Winona Lake, Ind.: Eisenbrauns.

Laato, A. 1992. *Josiah and David Redivivus: The Historical Josiah and the Messianic Expectations of Exilic and Postexilic Times.* ConBibOT 33. Stockholm: Almqvist & Wiksell International.

Lanfranchi, P. 2006. *L'*Exagoge *d'Ezéchiel le Tragique: Introduction, texte, traduction et commentaire.* Studia in Veteris Testamenti Pseudepigrapha 21. Leiden: Brill.

Lang, B. 1981a. *Kein Aufstand in Jerusalem: Die Politik des Propheten Ezechiel.* Stuttgarter Biblische Beiträge. 2d ed. Stuttgart: Katholisches Bibelwerk.

———. 1981b. *Ezechiel: Der Prophet und das Buch.* Erträge der Forschung 153. Darmstadt: Wissenschaftliche Buchgesellschaft.

———. 1983a. *Monotheism and the Prophetic Minority: An Essay in Biblical History and Sociology.* Social World of Biblical Antiquity 1. Sheffield: Almond.

Lange, A. 2002. *Vom prophetischen Wort zur prophetischen Tradition: Studien zur Traditions- und Redaktionsgeschichte innerprophetischer Konflikte in der Hebräischen Bibel.* Forschungen zum Alten Testament 34. Tübingen: Mohr Siebeck.

Lange, N. R. M. de. 1996. *Greek Jewish Texts from the Cairo Genizah.* Texte und Studien zum antiken Judentum 51. Tübingen: Mohr.

Lapsley, J. E. 2000a. *Can These Bones Live? The Problem of the Moral Self in the Book of Ezekiel.* BZAW 301. Berlin: de Gruyter.

Lara, J. 2004. *City, Temple, Stage: Eschatological Architecture & Liturgical Theatrics in New Spain.* Notre Dame, Ind.: University of Notre Dame Press.

Lauha, R. 1983. *Psychophysischer Sprachgebrauch im alten Testament: Eine struktur-semantische Analyse von leb, nepes und ruah* Annales Academicae Scientiarum Fennicae, Dissertationes Humanarum Litterarum 35. Helsinki: Suomalainen Tiedeakatemia.

Launderville, D. F. 2007. *Spirit and Reason: The Embodied Character of Ezekiel's Symbolic Thinking.* Waco, Tex.: Baylor University Press.

Leiman, S. 1976. *The Canonization of Hebrew Scripture: The Talmudic and Midrashic Evidence.* Hamden, Conn.: Archon.

Levenson, J. D. 1976. *Theology of the Program of Restoration of Ezekiel 40–48.* HSM 10. Missoula, Mont.: Scholars Press.

Levey, S. H. 1987. *The Targum of Ezekiel: Translated, with a Critical Introduction, Apparatus and Notes.* The Aramaic Bible 13. Wilmington, Del.: Michael Glazier. Edinburgh: T. & T. Clark.

Levitt Kohn, R. 2002a. *A New Heart and a New Soul: Ezekiel, the Exile and the Torah* JSOTSup 358. London: Sheffield Academic Press.
Lieb, M. 1991. *The Visionary Mode: Biblical Prophecy, Hermeneutics and Cultural Change*. Ithaca, N.Y.: Cornell University Press.
———. 1998. *Children of Ezekiel: Aliens, UFOs, the Crisis of Race, and the Advent of End Time*. Durham, N.C.: Duke University Press.
Lindblom, J. 1962. *Prophecy in Ancient Israel*. Oxford: Blackwell.
Lipschits, O., and J. Blenkinsopp, eds. 2003. *Judah and the Judeans in the Neo-Babylonian Period*. Winona Lake, Ind.: Eisenbrauns.
———. 2005. *The Fall and Rise of Jerusalem: Judah Under Babylonian Rule*. Winona Lake, Ind.: Eisenbrauns.
Liwak, R. 1976. Überlieferungsgeschichtliche Probleme des Ezechielbuches. Eine Studie zu postezechielischen Interpretationen und Kompositionen. Ph.D. diss., Bochum.
Longman, T., III. 1991. *Fictional Akkadian Autobiography: A Generic and Comparative Study*. Winona Lake, Ind.: Eisenbrauns.
Lust, J. 1969. *Traditie, Redactie en Kerygma bij Ezechiel: Een Analyse van Ez., XX, 1-26*. Verhandelingen van de Koninklijke Vlaamse Academie voor Wetenschappen, Letteren en Schone Kunsten van België, Letteren 65. Brussels: Paleis der Academiën.
———. ed. 1986d. *Ezekiel and His Book: Textual and Literary Criticism and their Interrelation*. BETL 74. Leuven: Leuven University Press/Peeters.
Lyons, M. A. 2009. *From Law to Prophecy: Ezekiel's Use of the Holiness Code* LHBOTS 507. New York: T&T Clark International.
Lys, D. 1962. *Rûach. Le souffle dans l'Ancien Testament*. Études d'Histoire et de Philosophie Religieuse. Paris: Presses Universitaires de France.
Manning, G. T. Jr. 2004. *Echoes of a Prophet: The Use of Ezekiel in the Gospel of John and in Literature of the Second Temple Period*. JSNTSup 270. London: T&T Clark International.
Marks, J. H., and R. M. Good, eds. 1987. *Love and Death in the Ancient Near East: Essays in Honor of Marvin H. Pope*. Guilford, Conn.: Four Quarters.
Mathews, C. R. 1995. *Defending Zion: Edom's Desolation and Jacob's Restoration (Isaiah 34–35) in Context*. BZAW 236. Berlin: de Gruyter.
Matties, G. H. 1990. *Ezekiel 18 and the Rhetoric of Moral Discourse*. SBLDS 126. Atlanta: Scholars Press.
Mays, J. L., and P. J. Achtemeier, eds. 1987. *Interpreting the Prophets*. Philadelphia: Fortress.
McCarthy, D. J. 1973. *Old Testament Covenant*. Oxford: Blackwell.
McGregor, L. J. 1985. *The Greek Text of Ezekiel: An Examination of Its Homogeneity*. SBLSCS 18. Atlanta: Scholars Press.
McKeating, H. 1993. *Ezekiel*. Old Testament Guides. Sheffield: Sheffield Academic Press.
McKim, D. K., ed. 1998. *Historical Handbook of Major Biblical Interpreters*. Downers Grove, Ill.: InterVarsity.
McLaughlin, J. L. 2001. *The Marzeah in the Prophetic Literature: References and Allusions in Light of the Extra-Biblical Evidence*. VTSup 86. Leiden: Brill.
Mein, A. R. 2001a. *Ezekiel and the Ethics of Exile*. OTM. Oxford: Oxford University Press.
Mendenhall, G. E. 1973. *The Tenth Generation: The Origins of the Biblical Tradition*. Baltimore, Md.: The Johns Hopkins University Press.
Messel, N. 1945. *Ezechielfragen*. Oslo: Jacob Dybwad.
Mettinger, T. N. D. 1982. *The Dethronement of Sabaoth: Studies in the Shem and Kabod Theologies*. ConBibOT 18. Lund: C. W. K. Gleerup.
Middlemas, J. 2005. *The Troubles of Templeless Judah*. OTM. Oxford: Oxford University Press.

———. 2007. *The Templeless Age: An Introduction to the History, Literature, and Theology of the "Exile."* Louisville, Ky.: Westminster John Knox.
Milgrom, J. 1991. *Leviticus 1–16*. AB 3. New York: Doubleday.
Miller, J. W. 1955. *Das Verhältnis Jeremias und Hesekiels sprachlich und theologisch untersucht mit besonderer Berucksichtigung der Prosareden Jeremias*. Assen: van Gorcum.
Miller, P. D., Jr. 1982. *Sin and Judgment in the Prophets: A Stylistic and Theological Analysis*. SBLMS 27. Chico, Calif.: Scholars Press.
Mills, M. E. 2007. *Alterity, Pain and Suffering in Isaiah, Jeremiah, and Ezekiel*. LHBOTS 479. New York: T&T Clark International.
Mintz, A. 1984. *Hurban: Responses to Catastrophe in Hebrew Literature*. New York: Columbia University Press.
Moberly, R. W. L. 2006. *Prophecy and Discernment*. Cambridge Studies in Christian Doctrine 14. Cambridge: Cambridge University Press.
Moor, J. C. de, ed. 2001. *The Elusive Prophet: The Prophet as a Historical Person, Literary Character and Anonymous Artist*. OtSt 45. Leiden: Brill.
Morgan, D. F. 1981. *Wisdom in the Old Testament Traditions*. Atlanta: John Knox. Oxford: Blackwell.
Moughtin-Mumby, S. R. 2008. *Sexual and Marital Metaphors in Hosea, Jeremiah, Isaiah, and Ezekiel*. OTM. Oxford: Oxford University Press.
Mueller, J. R. 1994. *The Five Fragments of the Apocryphon of Ezekiel: A Critical Study*. JSPSup 5. Sheffield: Sheffield Academic Press.
Mulder, M. J., ed. 1985. *Ezekiel*. The Old Testament in Syriac According to the Peshitta Version 3/3. Leiden: Brill.
Murray, R. 1992. *The Cosmic Covenant: Biblical Themes of Justice, Peace and the Integrity of Creation*. Heythrop Monographs 7. London: Sheed & Ward.
Nay, R. 1999. *Jahwe im Dialog: Kommunikationsanalytische Untersuchung von Ez 14, 1-11 unter Berücksichtigung des dialogischen Rahmens in Ez 8–11 und Ez 20*. AnBib 141. Rome: Pontifical Biblical Institute.
Neuss, W. 1911. *Die Entwicklung der theologischen Auffassung des Buches Ezechiel zur Zeit der Fruhscholastik*. Bonn: n.p.
———. 1912. *Das Buch Ezechiel in Theologie und Kunst bis zum Ende des XII Jahrhunderts*. Beiträge zur Geschichte des Alten Mönchtums und des Benediktinerordens 1–2. Münster: Aschendorff.
Newsom, C. 1985. *Songs of the Sabbath Sacrifice: A Critical Edition*. HSS 27. Atlanta: Scholars Press.
Newsome, J. D. 1979. *By the Waters of Babylon: An Introduction to the History and Theology of Exile*. Edinburgh: T. & T. Clark.
Nicholson, E. W. 1967. *Deuteronomy and Tradition*. Oxford: Blackwell.
———. 1970. *Preaching to the Exiles: A Study of the Prose Tradition in the Book of Jeremiah*. Oxford: Blackwell.
———. 1986. *God and his People: Covenant and Theology in the Old Testament*. Oxford: Oxford University Press.
Nielsen, K. 1978. *Yahweh as Prosecutor and Judge: An Investigation of the Prophetic Lawsuit (Rîb Pattern)*. JSOTSup 9. Sheffield: JSOT.
Niemann, H. M., and M. Augustin, eds. 2006. *Stimulation from Leiden: Collected Communications to the XVIIIth Congress of the International Organization for the Study of the Old Testament, Leiden 2004*. BEATAJ 54. Frankfurt: Peter Lang.
Nissinen, M., with contributions by C. L. Seow and R. K. Ritner. 2003. *Prophets and Prophecy in the Ancient Near East*. SBL Writings from the Ancient World 12. Atlanta: Society of Biblical Literature.
Nobile, M. 1982. *Una lettura simbolico-strutturalistica di Ezechiele*. Rome: n.p.

Odell, M. S. 1988. "Are You He of Whom I Spoke by My Servants the Prophets?" Ezekiel 38–39 and the Problem of History in the Neobabylonian Context. Ph.D. diss., University of Pittsburgh.

Odell, M. S., and J. T. Strong, eds. 2000. *The Book of Ezekiel: Theological and Anthropological Perspectives*. SBL Symposium Series 9. Atlanta: SBL.

Oesterley, W. O. E., and T. H. Robinson. 1934. *An Introduction to the Books of the Old Testament*. London: SPCK.

Ohnesorge, S. 1991. *Jahwe gestaltet sein Volk neu: Zur Sicht der Zukunft Israels nach Ez 11,14–21; 20,1–44; 36,16–38; 37,1–14.15–28*. FB 64. Würzburg: Echter.

Olyan, S. M. 2004. *Biblical Mourning: Ritual and Social Dimensions*. Oxford and New York: Oxford University Press.

Origen. 1989. *Homelies sur Ezechiel*. Sources Chretiennes 352. Paris: Cerf.

Otto, R. 1923. *The Idea of the Holy: An Inquiry into the Non-Rational Factor in the Idea of the Divine and its Relation to the Rational*. London: Oxford University Press.

Pareira, B. A. 1975. *The Call to Conversion in Ezekiel: Exegesis and Biblical Theology*. Rome: Pontificia Universitas Gregoriana Facultas Theologiae.

Parker, R. A., and W. H. Dubberstein. 1956. *Babylonian Chronology, 626 B.C.–A.D. 45*. Brown University Studies 19. Providence, R.I.: Brown University Press.

Parker, T. H. L. 1986. *Calvin's Old Testament Commentaries*. Edinburgh: T. & T. Clark.

Parunak, H. Van Dyke. 1978. Structural Studies in Ezekiel. Ph.D. diss., Harvard University.

———. 1984. *Linguistic Density Plots in Ezekiel*. 2 vols. The Computer Bible 27. Wooton, Ohio: Biblical Research Associates.

Patrick, D. 1999. *The Rhetoric of Revelation in the Hebrew Bible*. OBT. Minneapolis: Fortress.

Perez Castro, F., ed. 1988. *Ezequiel*. El Códice de Profetas de el Cairo (Edición de su texto y masoras) 6. Textos y estudios "Cardenal Cisneros." Madrid: Instituto "Arias Montano."

Petersen, D. L. 1981. *The Roles of Israel's Prophets*. JSOTSup 17. Sheffield: JSOT.

———. 2002. *The Prophetic Literature: An Introduction*. Louisville, Ky.: Westminster John Knox.

Pfeiffer, R. H. 1941. *Introduction to the Old Testament*. 2d ed. New York: Harper.

Pikor, W. 2002. *La Comunicazione Profetica alla Luce di Ez 2–3*. Tesi Gregoriana, Serie Teologia 88. Rome: Editrice Pontificia Università Gregoriana.

Plöger, O. 1968. *Theocracy and Eschatology*. Oxford: Blackwell. Richmond, Va.: John Knox. Eng. trans. of the German original: *Theokratie und Eschatologie*. 2d ed. WMANT 2. Neukirchen–Vluyn: Kreis Moers, Neukirchener, 1962.

Pohlmann, K.-F. 1992. *Ezechielstudien: Zur Redaktionsgeschichte des Buches und zur Frage nach den ältesten Texten*. BZAW 202. Berlin: de Gruyter.

———. 2008. *Ezechiel: Der Stand der theologischen Diskussion*. Darmstadt: Wissenschaftliche Buchgesellschaft.

Porter, B. N. 1993. *Images, Power and Politics: Figurative Aspects of Esarhaddon's Babylonian Policy*. Philadelphia: American Philosophical Society.

Potter, G. R., and E. M. Simpson, eds. 1953–62. *The Sermons of John Donne*. Berkeley, Calif.: University of California Press.

Rad, G. von. 1962–65. *Old Testament Theology*. 2 vols. Edinburgh: Oliver & Boyd. Eng. trans. of the German original: *Theologie des Alten Testaments*. 2 vols. Munich: Kaiser, 1957–60.

Raitt, T. M. 1977. *A Theology of Exile: Judgment/Deliverance in Jeremiah and Ezekiel*. Philadelphia: Fortress.

Reimer, D. J. 1993. *Oracles Against Babylon in Jeremiah 50–51: A Horror Among the Nations*. San Francisco: Mellen Research University Press.

Rendtorff, R. 1998. *The Covenant Formula: An Exegetical and Theological Investigation*. Old Testament Studies. Edinburgh: T. & T. Clark. Eng. trans. of the German original: *Die Bundesformel*. Stuttgarter Bibelstudien. Stuttgart: Katholisches Bibelwerk, 1995.

Renz, T. 1999a. *The Rhetorical Function of the Book of Ezekiel*. VTSup 76. Leiden: Brill.

Reuchlin, J. 1517. *De arte cabalistica: On the Art of the Kabbalah*. Eng. translation with an Introduction by G. L. Jones. Lincoln: University of Nebraska Press, 1993.

Reventlow, H. G. 1961. *Das Heiligkeitsgesetz, formgeschichtlich untersucht*. WMANT 6. Neukirchen–Vluyn: Neukirchener.

———. 1962. *Wächter über Israel: Ezechiel und seine Tradition*. BZAW 82. Berlin: Töpelmann.

Robinson, H. W. 1948. *Two Hebrew Prophets: Studies in Hosea and Ezekiel*. London: Lutterworth.

Robson, J. 2006. *Word and Spirit in Ezekiel*. LHBOTS 447. New York: T&T Clark International.

Rom-Shiloni, D. In preparation. *God in Times of Destruction and Exiles: Tanakh (Hebrew Bible) Theology*. SBL Academia Biblica. Atlanta: SBL.

Rooke, D. W. 2000. *Zadok's Heirs: The Role and Development of the High Priesthood in Ancient Israel*. OTM. Oxford: Oxford University Press.

Rooker, M. F. 1990. *Biblical Hebrew in Transition: The Language of the Book of Ezekiel*. JSOTSup 90. Sheffield: JSOT Press.

Roth, C. ed., 1971. *Encyclopaedia Judaica*, vol. 6. Jerusalem: Keter. New York: Macmillan.

Rowland, C. C. 1975. The Influence of the First Chapter of Ezekiel on Judaism and Early Christianity. Ph.D. diss., Cambridge University.

———. 1982. *The Open Heaven: A Study of Apocalyptic in Judaism and Early Christianity*. London: SPCK.

Rudnig, T. A. 2000. *Heilig und Profan: Redaktionskritische Studien zu Ez 40–48*. BZAW 287. Berlin: de Gruyter.

Ruiz, J. P. 1989. *Ezekiel in the Apocalypse: The Transformation of Prophetic Language in Revelation 16,17–19,10*. European Studies 23/376. Bern: Herbert Lang. Frankfurt am Main: Peter Lang.

Ruppert, L., P. Weimar and E. Zenger, eds. 1982. *Künder des Wortes: Beiträge zur Theologie der Propheten—Joseph Schneider zum 60. Geburtstag*. Würzburg: Echter.

San Girolamo edition. 1978. *Liber Hiezechielis*. Biblia Sacra iuxta Latinam Vulgatam Versionem 15. Rome: Typis Polyglottis Vaticanis.

Sänger, D. ed. 2006. *Das Ezechielbuch in der Johannesoffenbarung*. Biblisch-theologische Studien 76. Neukirchen–Vluyn: Neukirchener.

Sanders, J. A. 1987. *From Sacred Story to Sacred Text*. Philadelphia: Fortress.

Satran, D. 1995. *Biblical Prophets in Byzantine Palestine: Reassessing the Lives of the Prophets*. Studia in Veteris Testamenti Pseudepigrapha 11. Leiden: Brill.

Sawyer, J. F. A. 1996. *The Fifth Gospel: Isaiah in the History of Christianity*. Cambridge: Cambridge University Press.

Schmidt, W. H. 1973. *Zukunftsgewissheit und Gegenwartskritik: Grundzüge prophetischer Verkündigung*. Biblische Studien 64. Neukirchen–Vluyn: Neukirchener.

Schnocks, J. 2009a. *Rettung und Neuschöpfung. Studien zur alttestamentlichen Grundlegung einer gesamtbiblischen Theologie der Auferstehung*. Bonner Biblische Beiträge 158. Göttingen: V&R Unipress / Bonn University Press.

Schöpflin, K. 2002. *Theologie als Biographie im Ezechielbuch: Ein Beitrag zur Konzeption alttestamentlicher Prophetie*. Forschungen zum Alten Testament 36. Tübingen: Mohr Siebeck.

Scholem, G. G. 1960. *Jewish Gnosticism, Merkabah Mysticism and the Talmudic Tradition*. New York: Jewish Theological Seminary of America.

———. 1961. *Major Trends in Jewish Mysticism*. New York: Schocken.
Schoors, A. 1973. *I am God Your Saviour: A Form-Critical Study of the Main Genres in Isaiah xl–lv*. VTSup 24. Leiden: Brill.
Schultz, R. L. 1999. *The Search for Quotation: Verbal Parallels in the Prophets*. JSOTSup 180. Sheffield: Sheffield Academic Press.
Schulz, H. 1969. *Das Todesrecht im Alten Testament: Studien zum Rechtsformen der Mot-Jumat-Sätze*. BZAW 114. Berlin: de Gruyter.
Schwemer, A. M. 1995–96. *Studien zu den frühjüdischen Prophetenlegenden* Vitae Prophetarum 49–50. Texte und Studien zum Antiken Judentum. 2 vols. Tübingen.
Scott, J. M., ed. 1997. *Exile: Old Testament, Jewish and Christian Conceptions*. Journal for the Study of Judaism: Supplement Series 56. Leiden: Brill.
Sedlmeier, F. 1990. *Studien zu Komposition und Theologie von Ezechiel 20*. SBB 21. Stuttgart: Katholisches Bibelwerk.
Seidl, T. 2001. *"Der Becher in der Hand des Herrn": Studie zu den prophetischen "Taumelbecher"-Texten*. Arbeiten zu Text und Sprache im Alten Testament 70. St Ottilien: Eos.
Seitz, C. R. 1989. *Theology in Conflict: Reactions to the Exile in the Book of Jeremiah* BZAW 176. Berlin: de Gruyter.
Simian, H. 1974. *Die theologische Nachgeschichte der Prophetie Ezechiels. Form- und traditions-kritische Untersuchung zu Ez. 6; 35; 36*. FB 14. Würzburg: Echter.
Singer, K. H. 1980. *Die Metalle Gold, Silber, Bronze, Kupfer und Eisen im Alten Testament und ihre Symbolik*. FB 43. Würzburg: Echter.
Sklar, J. 2005. *Sin, Impurity, Sacrifice, Atonement: The Priestly Conceptions*. Hebrew Bible Monographs 2. Sheffield: Sheffield Phoenix Press.
Smith, D. L. 1990. *The Religion of the Landless: The Social Context of the Babylonian Exile*. New York: Crossroad.
———. See also Smith-Christopher, D. L.
Smith, J. 1931. *The Book of the Prophet Ezekiel: A New Interpretation*. London: SPCK.
Smith-Christopher, D. L. 2002. *A Biblical Theology of Exile*. OBT. Minneapolis: Fortress.
Sparks, H. F. D. 1984. *The Apocryphal Old Testament*. Oxford: Clarendon.
Sperber, A., ed. 1962. *The Bible in Aramaic*. Vol. 3, *The Latter Prophets according to Targum Jonathan*. Reprinted 1992. Leiden: Brill.
Stacey, W. D. 1990. *Prophetic Drama in the Old Testament*. London: Epworth.
Stavrakopoulou, F. 2004. *King Manasseh and Child Sacrifice: Biblical Distortions of Historical Realities*. Berlin: de Gruyter.
Steinmann, J. 1953. *Le prophète Ézéchiel et les débuts de l'exil*. Lectio Divina 13. Paris: Cerf.
Stevenson, K. R. 1996. *The Vision of Transformation: The Territorial Rhetoric of Ezekiel 40–48*. SBLDS 154. Atlanta: Scholars Press.
Stiebert, J. 2002a. *The Construction of Shame in the Hebrew Bible: The Prophetic Contribution*. JSOTSup 346. Sheffield: Sheffield Academic Press.
———. 2005. *The Exile and the Prophet's Wife: Historic Events and Marginal Perspectives*. Interfaces. Collegeville, Minn.: Liturgical Press.
Stone, M. E., and T. A. Bergren, eds. 1998. *Biblical Figures Outside the Bible*. Harrisburg, Pa.: Trinity Press International.
Stone, M. E., B. G. Wright, and D. Satran, eds. 2000. *The Apocryphal Ezekiel*. Early Judaism and Its Literature Series 18. Atlanta: SBL.
Stordalen, T. 2000. *Echoes of Eden: Genesis 2–3 and Symbolism of the Garden in Biblical Hebrew Literature*. Contributions to Biblical Exegesis and Theology 25. Leuven: Peeters.
Strong, J. T. 1993. Ezekiel's Oracles against the Nations within the Context of his Message. Ph.D. diss., Union Theological Seminary in Virginia.
Stulman, L. and Hyun Chul Paul Kim. 2010. *You Are My People: An Introduction to Prophetic Literature*. Nashville, Tenn.: Abingdon.

Sundberg, A. C. 1964. *The Old Testament of the Early Church*. Harvard Theological Studies 20. Cambridge, Mass.: Harvard University Press.

Sweeney, M. A. 1996. *Isaiah 1–39, with an Introduction to Prophetic Literature*. FOTL 16. Grand Rapids: Eerdmans.

———. 2001. *Ezekiel: Zadokite Priest and Visionary Prophet of the Exile*. Occasional Papers of the Institute for Antiquity and Christianity 41. Claremont, Calif.: Institute for Antiquity and Christianity. Reprinted as pages 125–43 in Sweeney 2005a.

———. 2005a. *Form and Intertextuality in Prophetic and Apocalyptic Literature*. Forschungen zum Alten Testament 45. Tübingen: Mohr Siebeck.

———. 2005b. *The Prophetic Literature*. Interpreting Biblical Texts. Nashville: Abingdon.

Taylor, J. G. 1993. *Yahweh and the Sun: Biblical and Archaeological Evidence for Sun Worship in Ancient Israel*. JSOTSup 111. Sheffield: JSOT.

Thackeray, H. St. J. 1921. *The Septuagint and Jewish Worship: A Study in Origins*. The Schweich Lectures for 1920. London: Oxford University Press.

Tooman, W. A., and M. A. Lyons, eds. 2009. *Transforming Visions: Transformations of Text, Tradition, and Theology in Ezekiel*. Princeton Theological Monograph Series 127. Eugene, Oreg.: Pickwick.

Torrey, C. C. 1910. *Ezra Studies*. Chicago: University of Chicago Press. Reprinted and edited with a Prolegomenon by W. F. Stinespring; New York: Ktav, 1970.

———. 1930. *Pseudo-Ezekiel and the Original Prophecy*. Yale Oriental Series, Researches 18. New Haven: Yale University Press. Reprinted in the Library of Biblical Studies. New York: Ktav, 1970.

Torrey, C. C., et al. 1970. *Pseudo-Ezekiel and the Original Prophecy, and Critical Articles*. The Library of Biblical Studies. New York: Ktav.

Tov, E. 1997. *The Text-Critical Use of the Septuagint in Biblical Research*. 2d ed. Jerusalem Biblical Studies 8. Jerusalem: Simor.

———. 2001. *Textual Criticism of the Hebrew Bible*. 2d rev. ed. Minneapolis: Fortress. Assen: Royal Van Gorcum.

Tuell, S. S. 1992. *The Law of the Temple in Ezekiel 40–48*. HSM 49. Atlanta: Scholars Press.

Van der Toorn, K., B. Becking and P. W. van der Horst, eds. 1998. *Dictionary of Deities and Demons in the Bible*. 2d rev. ed. Leiden: Brill.

Van Dijk, H. J. 1968. *Ezekiel's Prophecy on Tyre (Ez 26,1–28,19): A New Approach*. BibOr 20. Rome: Editrice Pontificio Istituto Biblico.

Van Gemeren, W. A. 1974. The Exegesis of Ezekiel's "Chariot" Chapters in Twelfth-Century Hebrew Commentaries. Ph.D. diss., University of Wisconsin, Madison.

Vanderhooft, D. S. 1999. *The Neo-Babylonian Empire and Babylon in the Latter Prophets*. HSM 59. Atlanta: Scholars Press.

Vaughan, P. H. 1974. *The Meaning of* "bāmâ" *in the Old Testament: A Study of Etymological, Textual and Archaeological Evidence*. London: Cambridge University Press.

Verbeek, A. 1953. *Schwarzrheindorf: Die Doppelkirche und ihre Wandgemälde*. Düsseldorf: Schwann.

Vermes, G. 1997. *The Complete Dead Sea Scrolls in English*. London: Allen Lane, Penguin.

Vermeylen, J. 2007. *Jérusalem centre du monde: Développements et contestations d'une tradition biblique*. Lectio Divina. Paris: Cerf.

Vieweger, D. 1986. *Die Spezifik der Berufungsberichte Jeremias und Ezechiels im Umfeld ähnlicher Einheiten des Alten Testaments*. BEATAJ 6. Frankfurt am Main: Peter Lang.

———. 1993. *Die literarischen Beziehungen zwischen den Büchern Jeremia und Ezechiel*. BEATAJ 26. Frankfurt am Main: Peter Lang.

Vogt, E. 1981. *Untersuchungen zum Buch Ezechiel*. AnBib 95. Rome: Pontifical Biblical Institute.

Volz, P., F. Stummer and J. Hempel, eds. 1936. *Werden und Wesen des Alten Testaments.* BZAW 66. Berlin: Töpelmann.

Wacholder, B.-Z., and M. Abegg. 1995. *A Preliminary Edition of the Unpublished Dead Sea Scrolls: The Hebrew and Aramaic Texts from Cave Four.* Washington, D.C.: Biblical Archaeology Society.

Wagenaar, J. A. 2005a. *Origin and Transformation of the Ancient Israelite Festival Calendar.* BZAR 6. Wiesbaden: Harrassowitz.

Wagner, A. 2004. *Prophetie als Theologie: Die so spricht Jahwe-Formeln und das Grundverständnis alttestamentlicher Prophetie.* FRLANT 207. Göttingen: Vandenhoeck & Ruprecht.

Weber, R., et al., eds. 1994. *Biblia Sacra iuxta Vulgatam Versionem.* 4th ed. Stuttgart: Deutsche Bibelgesellschaft.

Weems, R. J. 1995. *Battered Love: Marriage, Sex, and Violence in the Hebrew Prophets.* OBT. Minneapolis: Fortress.

Weitzman, M. P. 1999. *The Syriac Version of the Old Testament: An Introduction* University of Cambridge Oriental Publications 56. Cambridge: Cambridge University Press.

Wellhausen, J. 1883. *Prolegomena zur Geschichte Israels.* Berlin: G. Reimer. Eng. trans. *Prolegomena to the History of Ancient Israel.* New York: Meridian, 1957.

Wells, J. Bailey. 2000. *God's Holy People: A Theme in Biblical Theology.* JSOTSup 305. Sheffield: Sheffield Academic Press.

Westermann, C. 1960. *Grundformen prophetischer Rede.* Munich: Kaiser. Eng. trans. *Basic Forms of Prophetic Speech.* Cambridge: Lutterworth. Louisville, Ky: Westminster John Knox, 1991.

———. 1987. *Prophetische Heilsworte im Alten Testament.* Göttingen: Vandenhoeck & Ruprecht. Eng. trans. *Prophetic Oracles of Salvation in the Old Testament.* Edinburgh: T. & T. Clark. Louisville, Ky: Westminster John Knox, 1991.

Wevers, J. W., and D. Fraenkel. 2003. *Studies in the Text Histories of Deuteronomy and Ezekiel.* Mitteilungen des Septuaginta-Unternehmens 26; Abhandlungen Akademie Göttingen, Phil.-Hist. Klasse, Series 3/256. Göttingen: Vandenhoeck & Ruprecht.

Whitley, C. F. 1957. *The Exilic Age.* London: Longmans, Green & Co.

Williamson, H. G. M. 1982. *1 and 2 Chronicles.* NCB. Grand Rapids: Eerdmans. London: Marshall, Morgan & Scott.

Willmes, B. 1984. *Die sogenannte Hirtenallegorie Ezekiel 34: Studien zum Bild des Hirten im AT.* Beiträge zur biblischen Exegese und Theologie 19. Frankfurt: Peter Lang.

Wilson, R. R. 1980. *Prophecy and Society in Ancient Israel.* Philadelphia: Fortress.

Wolff, H. W. 1937. *Das Zitat im Prophetenspruch.* BhEvTh 4. Munich: Kaiser. Reprinted as 36–129 in *Gesammelte Studien zum AT.* ThB 22. Munich: Kaiser, 1964.

———. 1964. *Gesammelte Studien zum AT.* ThB 22. Munich: Kaiser.

———. 1974. *Anthropology of the Old Testament.* London: SCM. Eng. trans. of the German original: *Anthropologie des Alten Testaments.* Munich: Kaiser, 1973.

Wolfson, E. R. 1994. *Through a Speculum that Shines: Vision and Imagination in Medieval Jewish Mysticism.* Princeton, N.J.: Princeton University Press.

Wong, K. L. 2001a. *The Idea of Retribution in the Book of Ezekiel.* VTSup 87. Leiden: Brill.

Würthwein, E. 1936. *Der ʿamm haʾarez im Alten Testament.* BWANT 4/17. Stuttgart: Kohlhammer.

———. 1995. *The Text of the Old Testament: An Introduction to the Biblia Hebraica.* 2d ed. Grand Rapids: Eerdmans. Based on 5th German ed., *Der Text des Alten Testaments.* Stuttgart, 1988.

Würthwein, E., and O. Kaiser, eds. 1963. *Tradition und Situation. Studien zur alttestamentlichen Prophetie A. Weiser zum 70. Geburtstag dargebracht.* Göttingen: Vandenhoeck & Ruprecht.

Yadin, Y. 1966. *Masada: Herod's Fortress and the Zealots' Last Stand*. London: Weidenfeld & Nicolson.
Young, F., and D. F. Ford. 1987. *Meaning and Truth in 2 Corinthians*. Biblical Foundations in Theology. London: SPCK.
Zadok, R. 1979. *The Jews in Babylonia during the Chaldean and Achaemenian Periods according to the Babylonian Sources*. Studies in the History of the Jewish People and the Land of Israel Monograph Series 3. Haifa: University of Haifa.
———. 2002. *The Earliest Diaspora: Israelites and Judaeans in Pre-Hellenistic Mesopotamia*. Tel Aviv: Diaspora Research Institute.
Ziegler, J. 1971. *Sylloge: Gesammelte Aufsätze zur Septuaginta* Mitteilungen des Septuaginta-Unternehmens 10. Göttingen: Vandenhoeck & Ruprecht.
———. 1977. *Ezechiel*. 2d ed., with addendum by D. Fraenkel. Septuaginta 16/1. Göttingen: Vandenhoeck & Ruprecht.
Zimmerli, W. 1954a. *Erkenntnis Gottes nach dem Buche Ezechiel. Eine theologische Studie*. ATANT 27. Zurich: Zwingli. Reprinted as pages 41–119 in *Gottes Offenbarung: Gesammelte Aufsätze I*. ThB 19. Munich: Chr. Kaiser Verlag, 1963b. Eng. trans. Knowledge of God According to the Book of Ezekiel, in Zimmerli 1982a, 29–98.
———. 1963b. *Gottes Offenbarung: Gesammelte Aufsätze I*. ThB 19. Munich: Kaiser.
———. 1968. *Der Mensch und seine Hoffnung im Alten Testament*. Kleine Vandenhoeck-Reihe 272. Göttingen: Vandenhoeck & Ruprecht. Eng. trans. *Man and his Hope in the Old Testament*. SBT 2/20. London: SCM, 1971.
———. 1972a. *Ezechiel. Gestalt und Botschaft*. Biblische Studien 62. Neukirchen–Vluyn: Neukirchener.
———. 1974b. *Studien zur alttestamentlichen Theologie und Prophetie: Gesammelte Aufsätze II*. ThB 51. Munich: Kaiser.
———. 1975. *Grundriss der alttestamentlichen Theologie*. 2d ed. Stuttgart: Kohlhammer. Eng. trans. *Old Testament Theology in Outline*. Edinburgh: T. & T. Clark, 1978.
———. 1982a. *I am Yahweh*. Edited by W. Brueggemann. Atlanta: John Knox.
———. 2003. *The Fiery Throne: The Prophets and Old Testament Theology*. Edited by K. C. Hanson. Fortress Classics in Biblical Studies. Minneapolis: Fortress.

Articles and Notes

In order to minimize unnecessary duplication, publication details for frequently cited multi-author volumes appear in the preceding books section.

Abba, R. 1978. Priests and Levites in Ezekiel. *VT* 28:1–9.
Aberbach, M. 1971. Ezekiel in the Aggadah. Pages 1095–96 in Roth 1971.
Abrams, D. 1996. Special Angelic Figures: The Career of the Beasts of the Throne-World in Hekhalot Literature, German Pietism and Early Kabbalistic Literature. *Revue des Etudes Juives* 155:363–86.
Ackerman, S. 1989. A *MARZĒAḤ* in Ezekiel 8:7–13? *HTR* 82:267–81.
Ackroyd, P. R. 1989. Ezekiel. Pages 319–32 in vol. 1 of *The Books of the Bible*. Edited by B. W. Anderson. New York: Charles Scribner's Sons.
Adler, J. J. 1990. The Symbolic Acts of Ezekiel (Chaps. 3–5). *JBQ* 19:120–22.
Albrektson, B. 1995. Ezekiel 30:16: A Conjecture. Pages 5–10 in *Texts and Contexts: Biblical Texts in Their Textual and Situational Contexts: Essays in Honor of Lars Hartman*. Oslo. Edited by T. Fornberg and D. Hellholm. Copenhagen: Scandinavian University Press.
Albright, W. F. 1932. The Seal of Eliakim and the Latest Preexilic History of Judah, With Some Observations on Ezekiel. *JBL* 51:77–106.
Allen, L. C. 1986. A Textual Torso in Ezekiel xxii.20. *JSS* 31:131–33.

———. 1987. Ezekiel 24:3–14: A Rhetorical Perspective. *CBQ* 49:404–14.
———. 1989. The Rejected Sceptre in Ezekiel xxi 15b, 18a. *VT* 39:67–71.
———. 1990b. Annotation Clusters in Ezekiel. *ZAW* 102:408–13.
———. 1992. The Structuring of Ezekiel's Revisionist History Lesson (Ezekiel 20:3–31). *CBQ* 54:448–62.
———. 1993a. Structure, Tradition and Redaction in Ezekiel's Death Valley Vision. Pages 127–42 in Davies and Clines 1993.
———. 1993b. The Structure and Intention of Ezekiel 1. *VT* 43:145–61.
Altschuler, E. L. 2002. Did Ezekiel Have Temporal Lobe Epilepsy? *Archives of General Psychiatry* 59:561.
Arbel, D. 2005. Questions About Eve's Iniquity, Beauty, and Fall: The "Primal Figure" in Ezekiel 28:11–19 and Genesis Rabbah Traditions of Eve. *JBL* 124:641–55.
Assis, E. 2006. Why Edom? On the Hostility Towards Jacob's Brother in Prophetic Sources. *VT* 56:1–20.
Astour, M. C. 1976. Ezekiel's Prophecy of Gog and the Cuthean Legend of Naram-Sin. *JBL* 95:567–79.
Auld, A. G. 1983. Prophets Through the Looking Glass: Between Writings and Moses, *JSOT* 27:3–23. Reprinted as pages 289–307 in Gordon 1995; pages 22–42 in Davies 1996; and pages of 45–59 in A. G. Auld, *Samuel at the Threshold: Selected Works of Graeme Auld*. SOTS Monographs. Aldershot: Ashgate, 2004.
Aytoun, W. R. 1920. The Rise and Fall of the "Messianic" Hope in the Sixth Century. *JBL* 39:24–43.
Bakon, S. 1991. Ezekiel: From Destruction to Redemption. *JBQ* 20:144–52.
Baltzer, D. 1986. Literarkritische und literarhistorische Anmerkungen zur Heilsprophetie im Ezechiel-Buch. Pages 166–81 in Lust 1986d.
Barr, J. 1969. The Symbolism of Names in the Old Testament. *BJRL* 52:11–29.
———. 1992. "Thou art the Cherub": Ezekiel 28.14 and the Post-Ezekiel Understanding of Genesis 2–3. Pages 213–23 in *Priests, Prophets and Scribes: Essays on the Formation and Heritage of Second Temple Judaism in Honour of Joseph Blenkinsopp*. Edited by E. Ulrich, J. W. Wright, R. P. Carroll, and P. R. Davies. JSOTSup 149. Sheffield: Sheffield Academic Press.
Bartelmus, R. 1985. Ez 37, 1–14, die Verbform *w^eqatal* und die Anfänge der Auferstehungshoffnung. *ZAW* 97:366–89.
———. 1993. Menschlicher Misserfolg und Jahwes Initiative. Beobachtungen zum Geschichtsbild des deuteronomistischen Rahmens im Richterbuch und zum geschichtstheologischen Entwurf in Ez 20. *BN* 70:28–47.
Barth, C. 1977. Ezechiel 37 als Einheit. Pages 39–52 in Donner, Hanhart, and Smend 1977.
Bartlett, J. R. 1969. The Land of Seir and the Brotherhood of Edom. *JTS* NS 20:1–20.
———. 1982. Edom and the Fall of Jerusalem, 587 B.C. *PEQ* 114:13–24.
Barton, J. 1979. Natural Law and Poetic Justice in the Old Testament. *JTS* NS 30:1–14.
———. 1987. Begründungsversuche der prophetischen Unheils-ankündigung im Alten Testament. *Evangelische Theologie* 47:427–35.
Batto, B. 1987. The Covenant of Peace: A Neglected Ancient Near Eastern Motif. *CBQ* 49:187–211.
Bauckham, R. 1992. A Quotation from *4Q Second Ezekiel* in the *Apocalypse of Peter*. *RevQ* 15:437–45.
———. 1996. The Parable of the Royal Wedding Feast (Matthew 22:1–14) and the Parable of the Lame Man and the Blind Man (*Apocryphon of Ezekiel*). *JBL* 115:471–88.
Beck, M. D., and W. Werbeck. 1962. Ezechielbuch—Das Ezechielbuch in der Kunst. Pages 850–51 in *Die Religion in Geschichte und Gegenwart*, vol. 2. 3d ed. Tübingen: Mohr Siebeck.

Becker, J. 1982. Erwägungen zur ezechielischen Frage. Pages 137–49 in Ruppert, Weimar and Zenger 1982.
———. 1986. Ez 8–11 als einheitliche Komposition in einem pseudepigraphischen Ezechielbuch. Pages 136–50 in Lust 1986d.
Beentjes, P. C. 1996. What a Lioness was your Mother: Reflections on Ezekiel 19. Pages 21–35 in Becking and Dijkstra 1996.
Begg, C. T. 1986a. *bᵉrît* in Ezekiel. Pages 77–84 in *Proceedings of the Ninth World Congress of Jewish Studies. Jerusalem, August 4–12, 1985. Division A: The Period of the Bible*. Jerusalem: World Union of Jewish Studies.
———. 1986b. The Non-mention of Ezekiel in the Deuteronomistic History, the Book of Jeremiah and the Chronistic History. Pages 340–43 in Lust 1986d.
———. 1988. The "Classical Prophets" in Josephus' *Antiquities*. *Louvain Studies* 13:341–57. Reprinted as pages 547–62 in Gordon 1995.
———. 1989. The Identity of the Princes in Ezekiel 19: Some Reflections. *ETL* 65:358–69.
———. 1993. Ezekiel, the Book of. Pages 217–19 in *The Oxford Companion to the Bible*. Edited by B. M. Metzger and M. D. Coogan. New York: Oxford University Press.
———. 1999. Exile in Ezekiel: Evaluating a Sociological Model. *NGTT* 40:133–39.
Begrich, J. 1936. Die priesterliche Tora. Pages 63–88 in Volz, Stummer and Hempel 1936.
Berry, G. R. 1930. Was Ezekiel in the Exile? *JBL* 49:83–93.
Bewer, J. A. 1953. Textual and Exegetical Notes on the Book of Ezekiel. *JBL* 72:158–68.
Biggs, C. R. 1983. The Role of *nāśîʾ* in the Programme for Restoration in Ezekiel 40–48. *Colloquium* 16:46–57.
Blenkinsopp, J. 1998. The Judaean Priesthood During the Neo-Babylonian and Achaemenid Periods: A Hypothetical Reconstruction. *CBQ* 60:25–43.
———. 2002. The Bible, Archaeology and Politics; or The Empty Land Revisited. *JSOT* 27:169–87.
Block, D. I. 1987. Gog and the Pouring Out of the Spirit: Reflections on Ezekiel xxxix 21–9. *VT* 37:257–70.
———. 1988. Text and Emotion: A Study in the "Corruptions" in Ezekiel's Inaugural Vision (Ezekiel 1.4–28). *CBQ* 50:418–39.
———. 1989. The Prophet of the Spirit: The Use of *RWḤ* in the Book of Ezekiel. *JETS* 32:27–49.
———. 1991. Ezekiel's Boiling Cauldron: A Form-critical Solution to Ezekiel xxiv 1–14. *VT* 41:12–37.
———. 1992. Gog in Prophetic Tradition: A New Look at Ezekiel xxxviii 17. *VT* 42:154–72.
———. 1995. Bringing David Back: Ezekiel's Messianic Hope. Pages 167–88 in *The Lord's Anointed: Interpretation of Old Testament Messianic Texts*. Edited by P. E. Satterthwaite, R. S. Hess and G. J. Wenham. Carlisle: Paternoster. Grand Rapids: Baker.
———. 2000b. Divine Abandonment: Ezekiel's Adaptation of an Ancient Near Eastern Motif. Pages 15–42 in Odell and Strong 2000.
———. 2004. In Search of Theological Meaning: Ezekiel Scholarship at the Turn of the Millennium. Pages 227–39 in Cook and Patton 2004.
Boadt, L. 1975. The A:B:B:A Chiasm of Identical Roots in Ezekiel. *VT* 25:693–99.
———. 1978. Textual Problems in Ezekiel and Poetic Analysis of Paired Words. *JBL* 97:489–99.
———. 1986. Rhetorical Strategies in Ezekiel's Oracles of Judgment. Pages 182–200 in Lust 1986d.
———. 1990b. The Function of the Salvation Oracles in Ezekiel 33–37. *HAR* 12:1–21.
———. 1992. Ezekiel, Book of. *ABD* 2:711–22.
———. 1999. A New Look at the Book of Ezekiel. *TBT* 37:4–9.
Bodi, D. 1993. Les *gillûlim* chez Ezéchiel et dans l'Ancien Testament, et les différentes pratiques cultuelles associées à ce terme. *RB* 100:481–510.

———. 2001. Le prophète critique la monarchie: Le term *nāśîʾ* chez Ezéchiel. Pages 249–57 in *Prophètes et rois: Bible et Proche-Orient*. Edited by A. Lemaire. Paris: Cerf, 2001.
Böckler, A. 1998. Ist *Gott* schuldig, wenn ein Gerechter stolpert? Zur Exegese von Ez. iii 20. *VT* 48:437–52.
Bogaert, P.-M. 1978. Le témoinage de la Vetus Latina dans l'étude de la tradition des Septante: Ézéchiel et Daniel dans le Papyrus 967. *Bib* 59:384–95.
———. 1983. Montagne sainte, jardin d'Eden et sanctuaire (hiérosolymitain) dans un oracle d'Ézéchiel contre le prince de Tyre (Ez. 28:11–19). *Homo Religiosus* 9:131–53.
———. 1986. Les deux rédactions conservées (LXX et TM) d'Ézéchiel 7. Pages 21–47 in Lust 1986d.
———. 1991. Le Chérub de Tyr (Ez 28,14–16) et l'hippocampe de ses monnaies. Pages 31–35 in *Prophetie und geschichtliche Wirklichkeit im alten Israel. Festschrift S. Herrmann*. Edited by R. Liwak and S. Wagner. Stuttgart: Kohlhammer.
———. 1993. Septante: Ézéchiel. Columns 642–45 in *Supplément au Dictionnaire de la Bible*. Edited by J. Briend and É. Cothenet. Fasc. 68/12. Paris: Letouzey & Ané.
———. 1995. Le Lieu de la Gloire dans le livre d'Ezéchiel et dans les Chroniques: De l'arche au char. *RTL* 26:281–98.
Bowen, N. R. 1999. The Daughters of Your People: Female Prophets in Ezekiel 13.17–23. *JBL* 118:417–33.
Bowker, J. W. 1971. "Merkavah" Visions and the Visions of Paul. *JSS* 16:157–73.
Bowman, J. 1957. Ezekiel and the Zadokite Priesthood. *Transactions of the Glasgow University Oriental Society* 16:1–14.
Brady, M. 2005. Biblical Interpretation in the "Pseudo-Ezekiel" Fragments (4Q383–391) from Cave Four. Pages 88–109 in *Biblical Interpretation at Qumran*. Edited by M. Henze. Studies in the Dead Sea Scrolls and Related Literature. Grand Rapids: Eerdmans.
Braulik, G. 2001. Ezechiel und Deuteronomium: Die "Sippenhaftung" in Ezechiel 18,20 und Deuteronomium 24,16 unter Berücksichtigung von Jeremia 31,29–30 und 2 Kön 14,6. Pages 171–201 in *Studien zum Deuteronomium und seiner Nachgeschichte*. Stuttgarter Biblische Aufsatzbände 33. Stuttgart: Katholisches Bibelwerk.
Brenner, A.1996. Pornoprophetics Revisited: Some Additional Reflections. *JSOT* 70:63–86. Reprinted as pages 252–75 in Davies 1996.
Brooke, G. J. 1992. Ezekiel in Some Qumran and New Testament Texts. Pages 317–37 in *The Madrid Qumran Congress: Proceedings of the International Congress on the Dead Sea Scrolls, Madrid 18–21 March, 1991*. Edited by J. Trebolle Barrera and L. Vegas Montaner. Studies on the Texts of the Desert of Judah 11/1. Leiden: Brill. Madrid: Editorial Complutense.
———. 1998. Parabiblical Prophetic Narratives. Pages 271–301 in *The Dead Sea Scrolls After Fifty Years: A Comprehensive Assessment*, vol. 1. Edited by P. W. Flint and J. C. VanderKam. Leiden: Brill.
Broome, E. C. 1946. Ezekiel's Abnormal Personality. *JBL* 65:277–92.
Brownlee, W. H. 1963. The Scroll of Ezekiel from the Eleventh Qumran Cave. *RevQ* 4:11–28.
———. 1978. Ezekiel's Parable of the Watchman and the Editing of Ezekiel. *VT* 28:392–408.
———. 1983. "Son of Man, Set Your Face": Ezekiel the Refugee Prophet. *HUCA* 54:83–110.
Brueggemann, W. 1979. Trajectories in Old Testament Literature and the Sociology of Ancient Israel. *JBL* 98:161–85.
Brummitt, M. 2004. Jeremiah to Ezekiel. Pages 97–101 in *Yours Faithfully: Virtual Letters from the Bible*. Edited by P. R. Davies. BibleWorld. London: Equinox.
Callender, D. E., Jr. 1998. The Primal Man in Ezekiel and the Image of God. Pages 606–25 in *Society of Biblical Literature 1998 Seminar Papers*. Atlanta: Scholars Press.
———. 2000b. The Primal Human in Ezekiel and the Image of God. Pages 175–93 in Odell and Strong 2000.
Caquot, A. 1964. Le Messianisme d'Ézéchiel. *Semitica* 14:5–23.

Carley, K. 2001. Ezekiel's Formula of Desolation: Harsh Justice for the Land/Earth. Pages 143–57 in Habel 2001.
———. 2004. From Harshness to Hope: The Implications for Earth of Hierarchy in Ezekiel. Pages 109–26 in Cook and Patton 2004.
Carroll, R. P. 1983. Poets not Prophets: A Response to "Prophets through the Looking Glass." *JSOT* 27:25–31. Reprinted as pages 43–49 in Davies 1996.
———. 1992. The Myth of the Empty Land. Pages 79–93 in *Ideological Criticism of Biblical Texts*. Edited by D. Jobling and T. Pippin. *Semeia* 59. Atlanta: Scholars Press.
———. 1995. Desire Under the Terebinths: On Pornographic Representation in the Prophets—A Response. Pages 275–307 in *A Feminist Companion to the Latter Prophets*. Edited by A. Brenner. The Feminist Companion to the Bible 8. Sheffield: Sheffield Academic Press.
———. 1996. Whorusalamin: A Tale of Three Cities as Three Sisters. Pages 67–82 in Becking and Dijkstra 1996.
———. 1997a. Razed Temples and Shattered Vessels: Continuities and Discontinuities in the Discourses of Exile in the Hebrew Bible. *JSOT* 75:93–106.
———. 1997b. Deportation and Diasporic Discourses in the Prophetic Literature. Pages 63–85 in Scott 1997.
Carvalho, C. L. 2009. Putting the Mother Back in the Center: Metaphor and Multivalence in Ezekiel 19. In Ahn and Cook 2009.
Cassem, N. H. 1973. Ezekiel's Psychotic Personality: Reservations on the Use of the Couch for Biblical Personalities. Pages 59–63 in *The Word in the World*. Edited by R. Clifford. Cambridge, Mass.: Weston College Press.
Cazelles, H. 1983. 587 ou 586? Pages 427–35 in *The Word of the Lord Shall Go Forth: Essays in Honor of David Noel Freedman in Celebration of His Sixtieth Birthday*. Edited by C. Meyers and M. O'Connor. Winona Lake, Ind: Eisenbrauns.
Christman, A. R. 1999. "What Did Ezekiel See?": Patristic Exegesis of Ezekiel 1 and Debates About God's Incomprehensibility. *Pro Ecclesia* 8:338–63.
Clements, R. E. 1977. Patterns in the Prophetic Canon. Pages 42–55 in *Canon and Authority*. Edited by G. W. Coats and B. O. Long. Philadelphia: Fortress. Reprinted in Clements 1996b.
———. 1982. The Ezekiel Tradition: Prophecy in a Time of Crisis. Pages 119–136 in *Israel's Prophetic Tradition: Essays in Honour of Peter R. Ackroyd*. Edited by R. Coggins, A. Phillips and M. Knibb. Cambridge: Cambridge University Press. Reprinted in Clements 1996b.
———. 1986. The Chronology of Redaction in Ezekiel 1–24. Pages 283–94 in Lust 1986d. Reprinted in Clements 1996b.
Coggins, R. 1993. A Future for the Commentary? Pages 163–75 in *The Open Text: New Directions for Biblical Studies?* Edited by F. Watson. London: SCM.
Collins, T. 1997. Deuteronomic Influence on the Prophetical Books. Pages 15–26 in *The Book of Jeremiah and Its Reception*. Edited by A. H. W. Curtis and T. Römer. BETL 128. Leuven: Leuven University Press/Peeters.
Conrad, E. W. 2003. "And it Happened" to Jonah and Ezekiel: Reading Ezekiel in the Light of Jonah. Pages 161–81 in *Reading the Latter Prophets: Toward a New Canonical Criticism*. JSOTSup 376. London: T&T Clark International.
Cook, S. L. 1995b. Innerbiblical Interpretation in Ezekiel 44 and the History of Israel's Priesthood. *JBL* 114:193–208.
———. 1996. Review of Mueller 1994. *JBL* 115:532–34.
———. 1999. Creation Archetypes and Mythogems in Ezekiel: Significance and Theological Ramifications. Pages 123–46 in *Society of Biblical Literature 1999 Seminar Papers*. Atlanta: SBL.

———. 2003. Mythical Discourse in Ezekiel and Daniel and the Rise of Apocalypticism in Israel. Pages 85–106 in Grabbe and Haak 2003.
———. 2004. Cosmos, *Kabod*, and Cherub: Ontological and Epistemological Hierarchy in Ezekiel. Pages 179–97 in Cook and Patton 2004.
———. 2009b. The Speechless Suppression of Grief in Ezekiel 24:15–27: The Death of Ezekiel's Wife and the Prophet's Abnormal Response. In Ahn and Cook 2009.
Cooke, G. A. 1924. Some Considerations on the Text and Teaching of Ezekiel 40–48. *ZAW* 42:105–15.
Dalley, S. 2000. Hebrew tahaš, Akkadian duḫšu, Faience and Beadwork. *JSS* 45:1–20.
Dandamaev, M. 1991. Neo-Babylonian Society and Economy. Pages 252–75 in Boardman et al. 1991.
Darr, K. P. 1987. The Wall Around Paradise: Ezekielian Ideas About the Future. *VT* 37:271–79.
———. 1989. Write or True? A Response to Ellen Frances Davis. Pages 239–47 in Exum 1989.
———. 1992. Ezekiel's Justifications of God: Teaching Troubling Texts. *JSOT* 55:97–117.
———. 1994. Ezekiel Among the Critics, in *Currents in Research: Biblical Studies* 2 (1994): 9–24. Reprinted as pages 249–59 in Hauser 2008.
———. 2004. Proverb Performance and Transgenerational Retribution in Ezekiel 18. Pages 199–223 in Cook and Patton 2004.
Dassmann, E. 1988. Hesekiel. *Reallexikon für Antike und Christentum* 14:1132–91.
Davies, G. I. 1979. The Significance of Deuteronomy 1.2 for the Location of Mount Horeb. *PEQ* 111:87–101.
———. 1994. An Archaeological Commentary on Ezekiel 13. Pages 108–25 in *Scripture and Other Artifacts: Essays on the Bible and Archaeology in Honor of Philip J. King*. Edited by M. D. Coogan, J. C. Exum, and L. E. Stager. Louisville, Ky.: Westminster John Knox.
Davies, P. R. 1998. Exile? What Exile? Whose Exile? Pages 128–38 in *Leading Captivity Captive: The Exile as History and Ideology*. Edited by L. L. Grabbe. JSOTSup 278 ; European Seminar in Historical Methodology 2. Sheffield: Sheffield Academic Press.
Davis, E. F. 1989b. Swallowing Hard: Reflections on Ezekiel's Dumbness. Pages 217–37 in Exum 1989.
———. 1999. "And Pharaoh will Change His Mind..." (Ezek. 32:31): Dismantling Mythical Discourse. Pages 224–39 in *Theological Exegesis: Essays in Honor of Brevard S. Childs*. Edited by C. Seitz and K. Greene-McCreight. Grand Rapids: Eerdmans.
Day, J. 1980. The Daniel of Ugarit and Ezekiel and the Hero of the Book of Daniel. *VT* 30:174–84.
———. 1988. Inner-Biblical Interpretation in the Prophets. Pages 39–55 in *It Is Written: Scripture Citing Scripture*. Edited by D. A. Carson and H. G. M. Williamson. Cambridge: Cambridge University Press. Reprinted as pages 230–46 in Gordon 1995.
———. 1996. The Development of Belief in Life After Death in Ancient Israel. Pages 231–57 in Barton and Reimer 1996.
———. 2005a. Whatever Happened to the Ark of the Covenant? In Day 2005b, 250–70.
Day, L. 2000. Rhetoric and Domestic Violence in Ezekiel 16. *BibInt* 8:205–30.
Day, P. L. 2000a. The Bitch had it Coming to Her: Rhetoric and Interpretation in Ezekiel 16. *BibInt* 8:231–54.
———. 2000b. Adulterous Jerusalem's Imagined Demise: Death of a Metaphor in Ezekiel xvi. *VT* 50:285–309.
Deeley, M. K. 1997. Ezekiel's Shepherd and John's Jesus: A Case Study in the Appropriation of Biblical Texts. Pages 252–64 in *Early Christian Interpretation of the Scriptures of Israel*. Edited by C. A. Evans and J. A. Sanders. Journal for the Study of the New Testament: Supplement Series 148; Studies in Scripture in Early Judaism and Christianity 5. Sheffield: Sheffield Academic Press.

Dempsey, C. J. 1998. The "Whore" of Ezekiel 16: The Impact and Ramifications of Gender-Specific Metaphors in Light of Biblical Law and Divine Judgment. Pages 57–78 in *Gender and Law in the Hebrew Bible and the Ancient Near East*. Edited by V. H. Matthews, B. M. Levinson and T. Frymer-Kensky. JSOTSup 262. Sheffield: Sheffield Academic Press.

Diakonoff, I. M. 1992. The Naval Power and Trade of Tyre. *IEJ* 42:168–93.

Dijkstra, M. 1986. The Glosses in Ezekiel Reconsidered: Aspects of Textual Transmission in Ezekiel 10. Pages 55–77 in Lust 1986d.

———. 1989. Legal Irrevocability (*lo' yāšūḇ*) in Ezekiel 7.13. *JSOT* 43:109–16.

———. 1992. The Altar of Ezekiel: Fact or Fiction? *VT* 42:22–36.

———. 1996. Goddess, Gods, Men and Women in Ezekiel 8. Pages 83–114 in Becking and Dijkstra 1996.

———. 1999. The Valley of Dry Bones: Coping with the Reality of the Exile in the Book of Ezekiel. Pages 114–33 in Becking and Korpel 1999.

Dimant, D. 1992. The Apocalyptic Interpretation of Ezekiel at Qumran. Pages 31–51 in *Messiah and Christos: Studies in the Jewish Origins of Christianity, Presented to David Flusser on the Occasion of His Seventy-Fifth Birthday*. Edited by I. Gruenwald, S. Shaked and G. G. Stroumsa. Tübingen: Mohr (Paul Siebeck).

———. 2001. Pseudo-Ezekiel, Principal Edition. Pages 7–88, and Plates i–iii in *Qumran Cave 4. XXI, Parabiblical Texts, Part 4: Pseudo-Prophetic Texts*. DJD 30. Oxford: Clarendon.

Dimant, D., and J. Strugnell. 1990. The Merkavah Vision in *Second Ezekiel* (4Q385 4). *RevQ* 14:331–48.

Dohmen, C. 1986. Das Problem der Gottesbeschreibung im Ezechielbuch. Pages 330–34 in Lust 1986d.

Dressler, H. H. P. 1979. The Identification of the Ugaritic Dnil with the Daniel of Ezekiel. *VT* 29:152–61.

Driver, G. R. 1938. Linguistic and Textual Problems: Ezekiel. *Bib* 19:60–69, 175–87.

———. 1954. Ezekiel: Linguistic and Textual Problems. *Bib* 35:145–59, 299–312.

Duguid, I. M. 2004. Putting Priests in Their Place: Ezekiel's Contribution to the History of the Old Testament Priesthood. Pages 43–59 in Cook and Patton 2004.

Duke, R. K. 1988. Punishment or Restoration? Another Look at the Levites of Ezekiel 44.6–16. *JSOT* 40:61–81.

Dutcher-Walls, P. 1991. The Social Location of the Deuteronomists: A Sociological Study of Factional Politics in Late Pre-exilic Judah. *JSOT* 52:77–94.

Eichrodt, W. 1963. Das prophetische Wächteramt. Zur Exegese von Ez. 33. Pages 31–41 in Würthwein and Kaiser 1963.

Eid, V. 1996. Ezechielvision 37, 1–14. Eine Reliefdarstellung aus dem 6. Jahrhundert in der Dara-Anastasioupolis, Türkisch-Nordmesopotamien. *BN* 83:22–34.

Elat, M. 1983. The Iron Export from Uzal (Ezekiel xxvii 19). *VT* 33:323–30.

Eph'al, I. 1978. The Western Minorities in Babylonia in the 6th–5th Centuries BC: Maintenance and Cohesion. *Orientalia* NS 47:74–90.

———. 1980. On the Political and Social Organization of the Jews in the Babylonian Exile. *ZDMG* Suppl. V:106–12.

Eshel, E. 1998. Songs of the Sabbath Sacrifice, Principal Edition. Pages 173–401, and Plates xvi–xxxi in *Qumran Cave 4. VI, Poetical and Liturgical Texts, Part 1*. DJD 11. Oxford: Clarendon.

Eslinger, L. 1998. Ezekiel 20 and the Metaphor of Historical Teleology: Concepts of Biblical History. *JSOT* 81:93–125.

Exum, J. C. 1995. The Ethics of Biblical Violence against Women. Pages 248–71 in *The Bible in Ethics: The Second Sheffield Colloquium*. Edited by J. W. Rogerson, M. Davies and M. D. Carroll R. JSOTSup 207. Sheffield: Sheffield Academic Press.

———. 1996. Prophetic Pornography. Pages 101–28 in *Plotted, Shot and Painted: Cultural Representations of Biblical Women*. JSOTSup 215. Gender, Culture, Theory 3. Sheffield: Sheffield Academic Press.

Farmer, W. R. 1956. The Geography of Ezekiel's River of Life. *The Biblical Archaeologist* 19:17–22. Reprinted as pages 284–89 in D. F. Freedman and G. E. Wright, eds. *The Biblical Archaeologist Reader*. Garden City, N.Y.: Doubleday, 1961.

Fechter, F. 2000. Priesthood in Exile According to the Book of Ezekiel. Pages 673–99 in *Society of Biblical Literature 2000 Seminar Papers*. Atlanta: SBL.

———. 2004. Priesthood in Exile According to the Book of Ezekiel. Pages 27–41 in Cook and Patton 2004.

Fensham, F. C. 1987. The Curse of the Dry Bones in Ezekiel 37:1–14 Changed to a Blessing of Resurrection. *JNSL* 13:59–60.

Fernández Galiano, M. 1971. Nuevas Paginás del Códice 967 del A.T. Griego (Ez 28,19–43,9) (P Matr. bibl. 1). *Studia Papyrologica* 10:9–76.

Filson, F. V. 1943. The Omission of Ezekiel 12 26–28 and 36 23b–38 in Codex 967. *JBL* 62:27–32.

Finegan, J. 1950. The Chronology of Ezekiel. *JBL* 69:61–66.

Fishbane, M. 1984. Sin and Judgment in the Prophecies of Ezekiel. *Interpretation* 38:131–50. Reprinted as pages 170–87 in Mays and Achtemeier 1987.

——— (with S. Talmon) 1975–76. The Structuring of Biblical Books. Studies in the Book of Ezekiel. *ASTI* 10:129–53.

Fohrer, G. 1951. Die Glossen im Buche Ezechiel. *ZAW* 63:33–53.

———. 1958. Das Symptomatische der Ezechielforschung. *ThLZ* 83:241–50.

———. 1961. Remarks on Modern Interpretation of the Prophets. *JBL* 80:309–19.

———. 1980. Neue Literatur zur alttestamentlichen Prophetie (1961–1970). *ThR* NF 45:121–29.

Foster, R. S. 1958. A Note on Ezekiel xvii 1–10 and 22–24. *VT* 8:374–79.

Fox, M. V. 1980. The Rhetoric of Ezekiel's Vision of the Valley of the Bones. *HUCA* 51:1–15. Reprinted as pages 176–90 of Gordon 1995.

Franke, C. 1999. Divine Pardon in Ezekiel. *TBT* 37:24–28.

Fredericks, D. C. 1998. Diglossia, Revelation, and Ezekiel's Inaugural Rite. *JETS* 41:189–99.

Freedy, K. S., and D. B. Redford. 1970. The Dates in Ezekiel in Relation to Biblical, Babylonian and Egyptian Sources, *JAOS* 90:462–85.

Fuhs, H. F. 1986b. Ez 24: Überlegungen zu Tradition und Redaktion des Ezechielbuches. Pages 266–82 in Lust 1986d.

Galambush, J. G. 1999a. Ezekiel, Book of. Pages 372–75 in *Dictionary of Biblical Interpretation*, vol. 1. Edited by J. H. Hayes. Nashville: Abingdon.

———. 1999b. Castles in the Air: Creation as Property in Ezekiel. Pages 147–72 in *Society of Biblical Literature 1999 Seminar Papers*. Atlanta: SBL.

———. 2004a. God's Land and Mine: Creation as Property in the Book of Ezekiel. Pages 91–108 in Cook and Patton 2004.

———. 2004b. The Northern Voyage of Psammeticus II and Its Implications for Ezekiel 44.7–9. Pages 65–78 in Grabbe and Ogden Bellis 2004.

———. 2006. Necessary Enemies: Nebuchadnezzar, YHWH, and Gog in Ezekiel 38–39. Pages 254–67 in Kelle and Moore 2006.

Ganzel, T. 2008. The Defilement and Desecration of the Temple in Ezekiel. *Bib* 89:369–79.

Garber, D. G., Jr. 2004. Traumatizing Ezekiel, the Exilic Prophet. Pages 215–35 in Ellens and Rollins 2004.

Gaster, T. H. 1941. Ezekiel and the Mysteries. *JBL* 60:421–37.

Gese, H. 1977. Ezechiel 20,25f. und die Erstgeburtsopfer. Pages 140–51 in Donner, Hanhart and Smend 1977.

Geyer, J. B. 1979. Ezekiel 18 and a Hittite Treaty of *Muršiliš* II. *JSOT* 12:31–46.

———. 1993. Ezekiel 27 and the Cosmic Ship. Pages 105–26 in Davies and Clines 1993. Reprinted (with additions) as pages 39–56 in Geyer 2004b.

———. 2004a. Ezekiel 31 and the Cosmic Tree. Pages 57–74 in Geyer 2004b.

Gillingham, S. 1996. Psalmody and Apocalyptic in the Hebrew Bible: Common Vision, Shared Experience? Pages 147–69 in Barton and Reimer 1996.

Görg, M. 1982. “Prachtgewänder” für Tyrus: Ein Hapax in Ez 27.24. *BN* 17:35–36.

Goshen-Gottstein, M. H. 1963. The Rise of the Tiberian Bible Text. Pages 79–122 in *Biblical and Other Studies*. Edited by A. Altmann. Cambridge, Mass.: Harvard University Press. Reprinted as pages 666–709 in *The Canon and Masorah of the Hebrew Bible: An Introductory Reader*. Edited by S. Z. Leiman. The Library of Biblical Studies. New York: Ktav, 1974.

———. 1967. Hebrew Biblical Manuscripts: Their History and Their Place in the Hebrew University Bible Project Edition. *Bib* 48:243–90.

———. 1972. Ezechiel und Ijob. Zur Problemgeschichte von Bundestheologie und Gott-Mensch-Verhältnis. Pages 155–70 in *Wort, Lied und Gottesspruch: Beiträge zu Psalmen und Propheten. Festschrift für Joseph Ziegler*. Edited by J. Schreiner. FB 2. Würzburg: Echter.

———. 1992. Editions of the Hebrew Bible–Past and Future. Pages 221–42 in *“Sha'arei Talmon”: Studies in the Bible, Qumran, and the Ancient Near East Presented to Shemaryahu Talmon*. Edited by M. Fishbane and E. Tov. Winona Lake, Ind.: Eisenbrauns.

Gosse, B. 1989. Ezéchiel 35–36,1–15 et Ezéchiel 6: La désolation de la montagne de Séir et le renouveau des montagnes d’Israël. *RB* 96:511–17.

———. 1990. L’emploie de *ʿwl(h)* dans le livre d’Ezéchiel, et quelques problèmes concernant la rédaction de ce livre. *BN* 53:23–25.

———. 1991. La nouvelle alliance et les promesses d’avenir se référant à David dans les livres de Jérémie, Ezéchiel et Isaïe. *VT* 41:419–28.

———. 1996. Le Temple dans le livre d’Ezéchiel en rapport à la rédaction des livres des Rois. *RB* 103:40–47.

———. 1997. La Réhabilitation des prophètes d’Israel en Ezéchiel 38:17–23. *OTE* 10:226–35.

———. 2003a. La rédaction du livre d’Ezéchiel en rapport avec celles du livre d’Isaïe. *Transeuphratène* 26:33–45.

———. 2003b. Etudes bibliques et préséance des textes: les rédactions du livre de Jérémie, le germe de David, Za 6 et Is 28–32, et l’influence de Ez 24–33 dans l’inclusion de Gn–2 R entre la perte de l’éden et celle de Jérusalem. *Transeuphratène* 26:87–104.

———. 2004a. La nouvelle alliance de Jérémie 31,31–34: Du livre d’Ezéchiel au livre de Jérémie. *ZAW* 116:568–80.

———. 2004b. Loi et sanctuaire à Jérusalem au retour de l’exil. *Transeuphratène* 28:91–115.

———. 2004c. Sabbath, Identity and Universalism Go Together After the Return from Exile. *OTE* 17:231–241. Reprinted in *JSOT* 29 (2005a):359–70.

———. 2005b. Le Psaume 80 dans le cadre du Psautier et Ezéchiel 17. *SJOT* 19:48–60.

———. 2005c. Le prophète Jérémie selon le Psautier et selon le livre d’Ezéchiel. *RB* 112:511–20.

Goudoever, J. Van. 1986. Ezekiel Sees in Exile a New Temple-City at the Beginning of a Jobel Year. Pages 344–49 in Lust 1986d.

Goulder, M. D. 1980–81. The Apocalypse as an Annual Cycle of Prophecies. *New Testament Studies* 27:342–67.

Grassi, J. 1964–65. Ezekiel xxxvii 1–14 and the New Testament. *New Testament Studies* 11:162–64.

Greenberg, M. 1957. Ezekiel 17 and the Policy of Psammetichus II. *JBL* 76:304–309.

———. 1958. On Ezekiel’s Dumbness. *JBL* 77:101–105.

———. 1968. Idealism and Practicality in Numbers 35:4–5 and Ezekiel 48. *JAOS* 88:59–66.

———. 1970. Prolegomenon. Pages xi–xxix in Torrey et al. 1970.

———. 1971. Ezekiel. Pages 1078–95 in Roth 1971.

———. 1978. The Use of the Ancient Versions for Interpreting the Hebrew Text: A Sampling from Ezekiel ii 1–iii 11. Pages 131–48 in *Congress Volume, Göttingen 1977*. VTSup 29. Leiden: Brill.
———. 1980a. The Vision of Jerusalem in Ezekiel 8–11: A Holistic Interpretation. Pages 143–64 in *The Divine Helmsman: Studies on God's Control of Human Events, Presented to Lou H. Silberman*. Edited by J. L. Crenshaw and S. Sandmel. New York: Ktav.
———. 1980b. The Meaning and Location of the "Lookout" Passage in Ezek. 3:16–21. *Proceedings of the American Academy for Jewish Research* 46/47:265–80.
———. 1983b. Ezekiel 17: A Holistic Interpretation. *JAOS* 3:149–54.
———. 1984. The Design and Themes of Ezekiel's Program of Restoration. *Interpretation* 38:181–208. Reprinted as pages 215–36 in Mays and Achtemeier 1987.
———. 1986. What Are Valid Criteria for Determining Inauthentic Matter in Ezekiel? In Lust 1986d, 123–35.
———. 1987. Ezekiel 16: A Panorama of Passions. Pages 143–50 in Marks and Good 1987.
———. 1991. Nebuchadnezzar and the Parting of the Ways: Ezek. 21:26–27. Pages 267–71 in Cogan and Eph'al 1991.
———. 1993. Notes on the Influence of Tradition on Ezekiel. *JANESCU* 22:29–37.
Greenfield, J. C. 1982. Two Biblical Passages in Light of Their Near Eastern Background—Ezekiel 16.30 and Malachi 3.17. *Eretz Israel* 16:56–61.
Gross, C. D. 1999. Ezekiel and Solomon's Temple. *BTrans* 50:207–14.
Gross, H. 1972. Umkehr im Alten Testament. In der Sicht der Propheten Jeremia und Ezechiel. Pages 19–28 in *Zeichen des Glaubens: Studien zu Taufe und Firmung. Balthasar Fischer zum 60. Geburtstag*. Edited by H. auf der Maur and B. Kleinheyer. Zurich: Benziger; Freiburg: Herder.
Gunkel, H. 1906. Die Israelitische Literatur. Pages 51–102 in *Die Kultur der Gegenwart*. Edited by P. Hinneberg. Berlin: Teubner.
Habel, N. C. 1967. Ezekiel 28 and the First Man. *Concordia Theological Monthly* 38:516–24.
———. 2004. The Silence of the Lands: The Ecojustice Implications of Ezekiel's Judgment Oracles. Pages 127–40 in Cook and Patton 2004.
Hahn, S. W., and J. S. Bergsma. 2004. What Laws Were "Not Good"? A Canonical Approach to the Theological Problem of Ezekiel 20:25–26. *JBL* 123:201–18.
Halperin, D. J. 1976. The Exegetical Character of Ezek x 9–17. *VT* 26:129–41.
———. 1981. Origen, Ezekiel's Merkabah, and the Ascension of Moses. *Cahiers d'histoire* 50:261–75.
Halpern, B. 1991. Jerusalem and the Lineages in the Seventh Century BCE: Kinship and the Rise of Individual Moral Liability. Pages 11–107 in *Law and Ideology in Monarchic Israel*. Edited by B. Halpern and D. W. Hobson. JSOTSup 124. Sheffield: Sheffield Academic Press.
Hammershaimb, E. 1953. Ezekiel's View of the Monarchy. Pages 130–40 in *Studia Orientalia, I. Pedersen Septuagenario Dicata*. Copenhagen: E. Munksgaard. Reprinted as pages 51–62 in E. Hammershaimb, *Some Aspects of Old Testament Prophecy*. Copenhagen: Rosenkilde og Bagger, 1966.
Hanson, P. D. 1987. Israelite Religion in the Early Postexilic Period. Pages 485–508 in *Ancient Israelite Religion: Essays in Honor of Frank Moore Cross*. Edited by P. D. Miller Jr., P. D. Hanson and S. D. McBride. Philadelphia: Fortress.
Haran, M. 1979. The Law-Code of Ezekiel XL–XLVIII and Its Relation to the Priestly School. *HUCA* 50:45–71.
———. 2008. Ezekiel, P, and the Priestly School. *VT* 58:211–18.
Hare, D. R. A. 1985. The Lives of the Prophets. *OTP* 2:379–99.
———. 1992. Prophets, Lives of the. *ABD* 5:502–503.
Harland, P. J. 1997. What Kind of "Violence" in Ezekiel 22. *ET* 108:111–14.

———. 1999. A Land Full of Violence: The Value of Human Life in the Book of the Prophet Ezekiel. Pages 113–27 in *New Heaven and New Earth: Prophecy and the Millennium; Essays in Honour of Anthony Gelston*. Edited by P. J. Harland and C. T. R. Hayward. VTSup 77. Leiden: Brill.

———. 2000. *bṣ*ʿ: Bribe, Extortion or Profit? *VT* 50:310–22.

Harvey, J. 1958. Collectivisme et Individualisme, Éz. 18:1–32 et Jér. 31:29. *Sciences Ecclésiastiques* 10:167–202.

Hawtrey, K. 1993. The Exile as a Crisis for Cultic Religion: Lamentations and Ezekiel. *Reformed Theological Review* 52:74–83.

Heider, G. C. 1988. A Further Turn on Ezekiel's Baroque Twist in Ezek. 20:25–26. *JBL* 107, no. 4:721–24.

Herbert, E. 1998. 11QEzek ("11Q4"), Principal Edition. Pages 15–28 and Plates ii and liv in *Qumran Cave 11: II*. DJD 23. Oxford: Clarendon.

Herrmann, S. 1971. Die konstruktive Restauration. Das Deuteronomium als Mitte biblischer Theologie. Pages 155–70 in *Probleme biblischer Theologie. Festschrift G. von Rad*. Edited by H. W. Wolff. Munich: Kaiser.

Himmelfarb, M. 1989. From Prophecy to Apocalypse: The *Book of the Watchers* and Tours of Heaven. Pages 145–65 in *Jewish Spirituality: From the Bible through the Middle Ages*. Edited by A. Green. World Spirituality. London: SCM Press.

———. 1991. The Temple and the Garden of Eden in Ezekiel, the Book of the Watchers, and the Wisdom of Ben Sira. Pages 63–78 in *Sacred Places and Profane Spaces: Essays in the Geographics of Judaism, Christianity and Islam*. Edited by J. S. Scott and P. Simpson-Horsley. Westport, Conn.: Greenwood.

Höffken, P. 1981. Beobachtungen zu Ezechiel 37, 1–10. *VT* 31:305–17.

Horst, F. 1953. Exilsgemeinde und Jerusalem in Ez 8–11: Eine literarische Untersuchung. *VT* 3:337–60.

Horst, P. W. van der. 1992a. "I gave them laws that were not good": Ezekiel 20:25 in Ancient Judaism and Early Christianity. Pages 94–118 in *Sacred History and Sacred Texts in Early Judaism: A Symposium in Honour of A. S. van der Woude*. Edited by J. N. Bremmer and F. García Martínez. Contributions to Biblical Exegesis and Theology 5. Kampen: Kok Pharos.

———. 1992b. Ezekiel the Tragedian. *ABD* 2:709.

Hossfeld, F. L. 1986. Die Tempelvision Ez 8–11 im Licht unterschiedlicher methodischer Zugänge. Pages 151–65 in Lust 1986d.

———. 1987. Probleme einer ganzheitlichen Lektüre der Schrift. Dargestellt am Beispiel Ez 9–10. *ThQ* 167:266–77.

Houk, C. B. 1981. A Statistical Linguistic Study of Ezekiel 1.4–3.11. *ZAW* 93:76–85.

Houston, W. 1993. What Did the Prophets Think They Were Doing? Speech Acts and Prophetic Discourse in the Old Testament. *BibInt* 1:167–88.

Hullinger, J. M. 1995. The Problem of Animal Sacrifices in Ezekiel 40–48. *BSac* 152:279–89.

Hunt, A. W. 2006. Ezekiel Spinning the Wheels of History. Pages 280–90 in Kelle and Moore 2006.

Hurowitz, V. A. 2005. YHWH's Exalted House: Aspects of the Design and Symbolism of Solomon's Temple. Pages 63–110 in Day 2005b.

Irwin, B. P. 1995. Molek Imagery and the Slaughter of Gog in Ezekiel 38 and 39. *JSOT* 65:93–112.

Jacobsen, T. 1962. Toward the Image of Tammuz. *History of Religions* 1:189–213.

Jaspers, K. 1947. Der Prophet Ezechiel: Eine pathographische Studie. Pages 77–85 in *Arbeiten zur Psychiatrie, Neurologie und ihren Grenzgebieten. Festschrift K. Schneider*. Edited by H. Kranz. Willsbach: Scherer.

Jeppesen, K. 1991. You Are a Cherub, But No God! *SJOT* 5:83–94.

Jobling, D. 2004. An Adequate Psychological Approach to the Book of Ezekiel. Pages 203–13 in Ellens and Rollins 2004.
Jones, D. R. 1963. The Cessation of Sacrifice After the Destruction of the Temple in 586 B.C. *JTS* NS 14:12–31.
Jones, G. Lloyd. 1968–69. Jewish Exegesis and the English Bible. *ASTI* 7:53–63.
Joyce, P. M. 1979. Individual Responsibility in Ezekiel 18? Pages 185–96 in *Studia Biblica 1978*. Vol. 1, *Papers on Old Testament and Related Themes*. Edited by E. A. Livingstone. JSOTSup 11. Sheffield: JSOT Press.
———. 1986. Ezekiel and Individual Responsibility. Pages 317–21 in Lust 1986d.
———. 1990. Ezekiel. Pages 228–29 in *A Dictionary of Biblical Interpretation*. Edited by R. J. Coggins and J. L. Houlden. London: SCM. Philadelphia: Trinity Press International.
———. 1991. Review of E. F. Davis, *Swallowing the Scroll*. *JTS* NS 42, no. 1:169–72.
———. 1995a. Synchronic and Diachronic Perspectives on Ezekiel. Pages 115–28 in *Synchronic or Diachronic? A Debate on Method in Old Testament Exegesis*. Edited by J. C. de Moor. OtSt 34. Leiden: Brill.
———. 1995b. Reading the Bible in the Public Domain. Pages 67–79 in *Dare We Speak of God in Public? The Cadbury Lectures for 1994*. Edited by F. M. Young. London: Mowbray.
———. 1996. Dislocation and Adaptation in the Exilic Age and After. Pages 45–58 in Barton and Reimer 1996.
———. 1998. King and Messiah in Ezekiel. Pages 323–37 in *King and Messiah in Israel and the Ancient Near East: Proceedings of the Oxford Old Testament Seminar*. Edited by J. Day. JSOTSup 270. Sheffield: Sheffield Academic Press.
———. 2005. Temple and Worship in Ezekiel 40–48. Pages 145–63 in Day 2005b.
———. 2006. Ezek. 20.32–38: A Problem Text for the Theology of Ezekiel. Pages 119–23 in Niemann and Augustin 2006.
———. 2007. Ezekiel 40–42: The Earliest "Heavenly Ascent" Narrative? Pages 17–41 in *The Book of Ezekiel and Its Influence*. Edited by H. J. de Jonge and J. Tromp. Aldershot: Ashgate.
———. 2009. Ezekiel and Moral Transformation. In Tooman and Lyons 2009.
———. 2010. The Prophets and Psychological Interpretation. In *Prophecy and the Prophets in Ancient Israel: Proceedings of the Oxford Old Testament Seminar*. Edited by J. Day. LHBOTS. New York: T&T Clark International.
———. Forthcoming. Ezekiel. In *The Oxford Handbook to the Reception History of the Bible*. Edited by M. Lieb, E. Mason and J. Roberts. Oxford: Oxford University Press.
Junker, H. 1963. Ein Kernstück der Predigt Ezechiels: Studie über Ez. 18. *BZ* NF 7:173–85.
Kaminsky, J. S. 1997. The Sins of the Fathers: A Theological Investigation of the Biblical Tension Between Corporate and Individualized Retribution. *Judaism* 46:319–32.
Kamionkowski, S. T. 2001a. Gender Reversal in Ezekiel 16. Pages 170–85 in Brenner 2001.
———. 2001b. The Savage Made Civilized: An Examination of Ezekiel 16.8. Pages 124–36 in *"Every City Shall Be Forsaken": Urbanism and Prophecy in Ancient Israel and the Near East*. Edited by L. L. Grabbe and R. D. Haak. JSOTSup 330. Sheffield: Sheffield Academic Press.
———. 2007. "In your Blood Live": A Reconsideration of Meir Malul's Adoption Formula. Pages 103–14 in *Bringing the Hidden to Light: The Process of Interpretation. Studies in Honor of Stephen A. Geller*. Edited by K. F. Kravitz and D. M. Sharon. Winona Lake, Ind.: Eisenbrauns.
Kasher, R. 1998a. Anthropomorphism, Holiness and Cult: A New Look at Ezek 40–48. *ZAW* 110:192–208.
———. 1998b. Ezekiel's Dumbness (Ezek 3:22–27): A New Approach. *Beth Mikra* 154–55:227–44.

———. 1998c. Remnant, Repentance, and Covenant in the Book of Ezekiel. *Beth Mikra* 156:15–34.

Katz, P. 1954. Zur Textgestaltung der Ezechiel-Septuaginta. *Bib* 35:29–39. Reprinted as pages 15–425 in J. Ziegler, *Sylloge: Gesammelte Aufsätze zur Septuaginta*. Mitteilungen des Septuaginta-Unternehmens 10. Göttingen: Vandenhoeck & Ruprecht, 1971.

Keller, B. 1975. La terre dans le livre d'Ezéchiel. *RHPR* 55:481–90.

Kelso, J. L. 1945. Ezekiel's Parable of the Corroded Copper Caldron. *JBL* 64:391–93.

Kennedy, J. M. 1991. Hebrew *pithon peh* in the Book of Ezekiel. *VT* 41:233–35.

Kister, M. 1990. Barnabas 12:1, 4:3 and 4Q Second Ezekiel. *RB* 97:63–67.

Kister, M., and E. Qimron. 1991–92. Observations on 4Q Second Ezekiel (4Q385 2–3). *RevQ* 15:595–602.

Klein, R. W. 2000. Introduction: Ezekiel at the Dawn of the Twenty-First Century. Pages 1–11 in Odell and Strong 2000.

Klostermann, A. 1877. Ezechiel: Ein Beitrag zu besserer Würdigung seiner Person und seiner Schrift. *Theologische Studien und Kritiken* 50:391–439.

———. 1893. Ezekiel und das Heiligkeitsgesetz. Pages 368–419 in *Der Pentateuch: Beiträge zu seinem Verständnis und seiner Entstehungsgeschichte*. Leipzig: Deichert.

Koch, K. 1955. Gibt es ein Vergeltungsdogma im Alten Testament? *ZThK* 52:1–42. Reprinted as pages 130–80 of Koch 1972. Eng. trans. "Is There a Doctrine of Retribution in the Old Testament?" Pages 57–87 in *Theodicy in the Old Testament*. Edited by J. L. Crenshaw. London: SPCK. Philadelphia: Fortress, 1983.

———. 1962. Der Spruch "Sein Blut bleibe auf seinem Haupt" und die israelitische Auffassung vom vergossenen Blut. *VT* 12:396–416. Reprinted as pages 396–416 in Koch 1972.

Konkel, M. 1998. Das Datum der zweiten Tempelvision Ezechiels (Ez 40:1). *BN* 92:55–70.

———. 2002. Die Gola von 597 und die Priester: Zu einem Buch von Thilo Alexander Rudnig. *Zeitschrift für Altorientalische und Biblische Rechtsgeschichte* 8:357–83.

Korpel, M. C. A. 1996. Avian Spirits in Ugarit and in Ezekiel 13. Pages 99–113 in *Ugarit, Religion and Culture*. Edited by N. Wyatt, W. G. E. Watson and J. B. Lloyd. UBL 12. Münster: Ugarit Verlag.

Kottsieper, I. 1993. "Was ist deine Mutter?" Eine Studie zu Ez 19,2–9. *ZAW* 105:444–61.

Krašovec, J. 1994. Is There a Doctrine of "Collective Retribution" in the Hebrew Bible? *HUCA* 65:35–89.

Kreuzer, S. 1997. Die Verwendung der Mächtigkeitsformel ausserhalb des Deuteronomiums. Literarische und theologische Linien zu Jer, Ez, dtrG und P. *ZAW* 109:369–84.

Kruger, P. A. 1984. The Hem of the Garment in Marriage: The Meaning of the Symbolic Gesture in Ruth 3:9 and Ezek. 16:8. *JNSL* 12:79–86.

Kuhl, C. 1933. Zur Geschichte der Hesekiel-Forschung. *ThR* NF 5:92–118.

———. 1952. Neuere Hesekielliteratur. *ThR* NF 20:1–26.

———. 1957–58. Zum Stand der Hesekiel-Forschung. *ThR* NF 24:1–53.

Kutsch, E. 1967. Gesetz und Gnade. Probleme des alttestamentliche Bundesbegriffs. *ZAW* 79:18–35.

———. 1974. Das Jahr der Katastrophe: 587 v.Chr. *Bib* 55:520–45.

Kutsko, J. F. 1998. Will the Real *ṣelem ᵓᵉlōhîm* Please Stand Up? The Image of God in the Book of Ezekiel. Pages 55–85 in *Society of Biblical Literature 1998 Seminar Papers*. Atlanta: Scholars Press.

———. 2000b. Ezekiel's Anthropology and Its Ethical Implications. Pages 119–41 in Odell and Strong 2000.

Lang, B. 1979. A Neglected Method in Ezekiel Research: Editorial Criticism. *VT* 29:39–44.

———. 1983b. Die erste und die letzte Vision des Propheten. Eine Überlegung zu Ezechiel 1–3. *Bib* 64:225–30.

———. 1986. Street Theater, Raising the Dead, and the Zoroastrian Connection in Ezekiel's Prophecy. Pages 297–316 in Lust 1986d.

Lapsley, J. E. 2000b. Shame and Self-Knowledge: The Positive Role of Shame in Ezekiel's View of the Moral Self. Pages 143–73 in Odell and Strong 2000.

———. 2005. Doors Thrown Open and Waters Gushing Forth: Mark, Ezekiel, and the Architecture of Hope. Pages 139–53 in *The Ending of Mark and the Ends of God: Essays in Memory of Donald Harrisville Juel*. Edited by B. R. Gaventa and P. D. Miller. Louisville, Ky.: Westminster John Knox.

———. 2007. A Feeling for God: Emotions and Moral Formation in Ezekiel 24:15–27. Pages 93–102 in *Character Ethics and the Old Testament: Moral Dimensions of Scripture*. Edited by M. D. Carroll R. and J. E. Lapsley. Louisville, Ky.: Westminster John Knox.

Launderville, D. 2003. Ezekiel's Cherub: A Promising Symbol or a Dangerous Idol? *CBQ* 65:165–83.

Leene, H. 1995. Unripe Fruit and Dull Teeth (Jer 31,29; Ez 18, 2). Pages 82–98 in *Narrative and Comment (FS W. Schneider)*. Edited by E. Talstra. Amsterdam: Societas Hebraica Amstelodamensis.

———. 2000. Jeremiah and Ezekiel: Promises of Inner Renewal in Diachronic Perspective. Pages 150–75 in *Past, Present, Future: The Deuteronomistic History and the Prophets*. Edited by J. C. de Moor and H. F. van Rooy. OtSt 44. Leiden: Brill.

———. 2001. Blowing the Same Shofar: An Intertextual Comparison of Representations of the Prophetic Role in Jeremiah and Ezekiel. Pages 175–98 in de Moor 2001.

Lemaire, A. 1986. Les formules de datation dans Ézéchiel à la lumière des données épigraphiques récentes. Pages 359–66 in Lust 1986d.

Lemke, W. E. 1984. Life in the Present and Hope for the Future. *Interpretation* 38:165–180. Reprinted as pages 200–14 in Mays and Achtemeier 1987.

Lenchak, T. A. 1999. Puzzling Passages: Ezekiel 4:4–5. *TBT* 37:387.

Levinson, B. M. 2003. "You must not add anything to what I command you": Paradoxes of Canon and Authorship in Ancient Israel. *Numen* 50:1–51.

Levitt Kohn, R. 1999. Ezekiel, the Exile and the Torah. Pages 501–26 in *Society of Biblical Literature 1999 Seminar Papers*. Atlanta: SBL.

———. 2002b. A Prophet like Moses? Rethinking Ezekiel's Relationship to the Torah. *ZAW* 114:236–254.

———. 2003. Ezekiel at the Turn of the Century. *Currents in Biblical Research* 2 (2003):9–31. Reprinted as pages 260–72 in Hauser 2008.

———. 2004. "With a Mighty Hand and an Outstretched Arm": The Prophet and the Torah in Ezekiel 20. Pages 159–68 in Cook and Patton 2004.

———. 2008. Ezekiel into the Twenty-First Century. Pages 273–77 in Hauser 2008.

Lieb, M. 1986. Children of Ezekiel: Biblical Prophecy, Madness and the Cult of the Modern. *Cithara* 26:3–22.

———. 1989. Ezekiel's Inaugural Vision as Jungian Archetype. *Thought* 64:116–29.

Lindars, B. 1965. Ezekiel and Individual Responsibility. *VT* 15:452–67.

Lipton, D. 2006. Early Mourning? Petitionary versus Posthumous Ritual in Ezekiel xxiv. *VT* 56:185–202.

Liss, H. 2006. "Describe the Temple to the House of Israel": Preliminary Remarks on the Temple Vision in the Book of Ezekiel and the Question of Fictionality in Priestly Literature. Pages 122–43 in *Utopia and Dystopia in Prophetic Literature*. Edited by E. Ben Zvi. Publications of the Finnish Exegetical Society 92. Göttingen: Vandenhoeck & Ruprecht.

Liverani, M. 1991. The Trade Network of Tyre according to Ezek. 27. Pages 65–79 in Cogan and Eph'al 1991.

Luc, A. 1983. A Theology of Ezekiel: God's Name and Israel's History. *JETS* 26:137–43.

Lust, J. 1967. Ezéchiel XX, 4–26: Une parodie de l'histoire religieuse d'Israël. *ETL* 43:488–527. Reprinted as "Ez 20:4–26: une parodie de l'histoire religieuse d'Israël." In *De Mari à Qumrân: l'Ancient Testament, son milieu, ses ecrits, ses relectures juives. Hommage à*

Mgr. J. Coppens. Edited by H. Cazelles. BETL 24. Gembloux: J. Duculot & P. Lethielleux, 1969.
———. 1968. "Mon Seigneur Jahweh" dans le texte hébreu d'Ézéchiel. *ETL* 44:482–88.
———. 1980. De samenhang van Ez. 36–40. Theologische relevantie van het ontbreken van Ez. 36,23c–38 in enkele handschriften. *Tijdschrift voor Theologie* 20:26–39.
———. 1981a. Ezekiel 36–40 in the Oldest Greek Manuscript. *CBQ* 43:517–33.
———. 1981b. "Gathering and Return" in Jeremiah and Ezekiel. Pages 119–42 in *Le livre de Jérémie: Le prophète et son milieu, les oracles et leur transmission*. Edited by P.-M. Bogaert. BETL 54. Leuven: Leuven University Press/Peeters.
———. 1981c. The Sequence of Ez 36–40 and the Omission of Ez 36,23c–38 in Pap. 967 and in Codex Wirceburgensis. *Bulletin of the International Organization of Septuagint and Cognate Studies* 14:45–46.
———. 1986a. The Use of Textual Witnesses for the Establishment of the Text. The Shorter and Longer Texts of Ezekiel: An Example: Ez 7. Pages 7–20 in Lust 1986d.
———. 1986b. The Final Text and Textual Criticism. Ez 39,28. Pages 48–54 in Lust 1986d.
———. 1986c. Ezekiel Manuscripts at Qumran. Preliminary Edition of 4Q Ez a and b. Pages 90–100 in Lust 1986d.
———. 1987a. Exegesis and Theology in the Septuagint of Ezekiel. The Longer "Pluses" and Ezekiel 43:1–9. Pages 201–32 in Cox 1987.
———. 1987b. Ezechiël en de zure druiven. *Collationes* 17:131–38.
———. 1996. Exodus 6, 2–8 and Ezekiel. Pages 209–24 in *Studies in the Book of Exodus: Redaction–Reception–Interpretation*. Edited by M. Vervenne. BETL 126. Leuven: Leuven University Press/Peeters.
———. 1997a. Ezekiel Salutes Isaiah: Ezekiel 20,32–44. Pages 367–82 in *Studies in the Book of Isaiah: Festschrift Willem A. M. Beuken*. Edited by J. Van Ruiten and M. Vervenne. BETL 132. Leuven: Leuven University Press/Peeters.
———. 1997b. The Vocabulary of LXX Ezekiel and Its Dependence upon the Pentateuch. Pages 529–46 in *Deuteronomy and Deuteronomic Literature: Festschrift C. H. W. Brekelmans*. Edited by M. Vervenne and J. Lust. BETL 133. Leuven: Leuven University Press/Peeters.
———. 2003. Major Divergences Between LXX and MT in Ezekiel. Pages 83–92 in *The Earliest Text of the Hebrew Bible: The Relationship Between the Masoretic Text and the Hebrew Base of the Septuagint Reconsidered*. Edited by A. Schenker. Septuagint and Cognate Studies 52. Atlanta: SBL.
———. 2006. An Introduction to the Hebrew Text of Ezekiel. Pages 153–67 in *Sôfer Mahîr: Essays in Honour of Adrian Schenker Offered by the Editors of Biblia Hebraica Quinta*. Edited by Y. A. P. Goldman, A. van der Kooij, and R.D. Weis. VTSup 110. Leiden: Brill.
Lutzky, H. C. 1996. On the "Image of Jealousy" (Ezekiel viii 3, 5). *VT* 46:121–24.
———. 1998. Shadday as a Goddess Epithet. *VT* 48:15–36.
Maarsingh, B. 1986. Das Schwertlied in Ez 21,13–22 und das Erra-Gedicht. Pages 350–58 in Lust 1986d.
MacKay, C. 1961. Ezekiel in the New Testament. *CQR* 162:4–16.
Malamat, A. 1997. New Mari Documents and the Prophecy of Ezekiel. Pages 71–76 in Cogan, Eichler and Tigay 1997.
Malul, M. 1990. Adoption of Foundlings in the Bible and Mesopotamian Documents: A Study of Some Legal Metaphors in Ezekiel 16.1–7. *JSOT* 46:97–126.
Marquis, G. 1987. Consistency of Lexical Equivalents as a Criterion for the Evaluation of Translation Technique as Exemplified in the LXX of Ezekiel. Pages 405–24 in Cox 1987.
May, H. G. 1961. Individual Responsibility and Retribution. *HUCA* 32:107–20.

———. 1962. The King in the Garden of Eden: A Study of Ezekiel 28:12–19. Pages 166–76 in *Israel's Prophetic Heritage: Essays in Honor of James Muilenburg*. Edited by B. W. Anderson and W. Harrelson. London: SCM. New York: Harper & Brothers.

McConville, J. G. 1983. Priests and Levites in Ezekiel: A Crux in the Interpretation of Israel's History. *Tyndale Bulletin* 34:3–31.

McKeating, H. 1994. Ezekiel the "Prophet Like Moses"? *JSOT* 61:97–109.

McKenzie, J. L. 1956. Mythological Allusions in Ezek 28:12–18. *JBL* 75:322–27.

Mein, A. 2001b. Ezekiel as a Priest in Exile. Pages 199–213 in de Moor 2001.

———. 2007. Profitable and Unprofitable Shepherds: Economic and Theological Perspectives on Ezekiel 34. *JSOT* 31:493–504.

Mendecki, N. 1994. Postdeuteronomische Redaktion von Ez 28,25–26? *BN* 73:66–73.

Mendenhall, G. E. 1960. The Relation of the Individual to Political Society in Ancient Israel. Pages 89–108 in *Biblical Studies in Memory of H. C. Alleman*. Edited by J. M. Myers et al. Locust Valley, N.Y.: Augustin.

———. 1962. The Hebrew Conquest of Palestine. *BA* 25:66–87.

Merx, A. 1883. Der Wert der Septuaginta für die Textkritik des Alten Testaments, am Ezechiel aufgezeigt. *Jahrbücher für protestantische Theologie* 9:65–77.

Middlemas, J. 2010. Exclusively Yahweh: Aniconism and Anthropomorphism in Ezekiel. In *Prophecy and the Prophets in Ancient Israel*. Edited by J. Day. LHBOTS. New York: T&T Clark International.

Milgrom, J. 1997. Leviticus 26 and Ezekiel. Pages 57–62 in *The Quest for Context and Meaning: Studies in Biblical Intertextuality in Honor of James A. Sanders*. Edited by C. A. Evans and S. Talmon. Leiden: Brill.

Millard A. R. 1962. Ezekiel 27:19: The Wine Trade of Damascus. *JSS* 7:201–3.

Miller, J. E. 1992. The 30th Year of Ezek. 1.1. *RB* 99:499–503.

———. 1993. The Mælæk of Tyre (Ezekiel 28,11–19). *ZAW* 105:497–501.

Mitchell, T. C. 1991a. Judah until the Fall of Jerusalem (c. 700–586 BC). Pages 371–409 in Boardman et al. 1991.

———. 1991b. The Babylonian Exile and the Restoration of the Jews in Palestine. Pages 410–60 in Boardman et al. 1991.

Monloubou, L. 1986. La signification du culte selon Ézéchiel. Pages 322–29 in Lust 1986d.

Mosis, R. 1975. Ez 14,1–11: Ein Ruf zur Umkehr. *BZ* 19:161–94.

Müller, H.-P. 1990. Parallelen zu Gen 2f. und Ez 28 aus dem Gilgamesch-Epos. *ZAH* 3:167–78.

Mueller, J. R., and S. E. Robinson. 1983. Apocryphon of Ezekiel. *OTP* 1:487–95.

———. 1992. Ezekiel, Apocryphon of. *ABD* 2:709–711.

Mulder, M. J. 1986, Die neue Peshitta-Ausgabe von Ezechiel. Pages 101–10 in Lust 1986d.

Mullo Weir, C. J. 1952. Aspects of the Book of Ezekiel. *VT* 2:97–112.

Murray, D. F. 1987. The Rhetoric of Disputation: Re-Examination of a Prophetic Genre. *JSOT* 38:95–121.

Newsom, C. A. 1984. A Maker of Metaphors: Ezekiel's Oracles Against Tyre. *Interpretation* 38:151–64. Reprinted as pages 188–99 in Mays and Achtemeier 1987, and pages 191–204 in Gordon 1995.

———. 1987. Merkabah Exegesis in the Qumran Sabbath Shirot. *JJS* 38:11–30.

———. 2006. Rhyme and Reason: The Historical Résumé in Israelite and Early Jewish Thought. Pages 215–33 in *Congress Volume: Leiden, 2004*. Edited by A. Lemaire. VTSup 109. Leiden: Brill.

Nicholson, O. 1985. Shall These Bones Live: A dakhma at Dara. *American Journal of Archaeology* 89:667–71.

Niditch, S. 1986. Ezekiel 40–48 in Visionary Context. *CBQ* 48:208–24.

Nobile, M. 1983. Lo sfondo cultuale di Ez 8–11. *Antonianum* 58:185–200.

———. 1984. Ez 37, 1–14. *Bib* 65:476–89.

———. 1986. Beziehung zwischen Ez 32,17–32 und der Gog-Perikope (Ez 38–39) im Lichte der Endredaktion. Pages 255–59 in Lust 1986d.
Noort, E. 1999. Gan-Eden in the Context of the Mythology of the Hebrew Bible. Pages 21–36 in *Paradise Interpreted*. Edited by G. P. Luttikhuizen. Leiden: Brill.
Noth, M. 1951. Noah, Daniel und Hiob in Ezechiel 14. *VT* 1:251–60.
———. 1953. La catastrophe de Jérusalem en l'an 587 avant Jésus-Christ et sa signification pour Israel. *RHPR* 33:82–102. Reprinted as: Die Katastrophe von Jerusalem im Jahre 587 v. Chr. und ihre Bedeutung für Israel. Pages 346–71 in *Gesammelte Studien zum Alten Testament*. 2d ed. Munich: Kaiser, 1960. Eng. trans, The Jerusalem Catastrophe of 587 BC and Its Significance for Israel. Pages 260–80 in *The Laws in the Pentateuch and Other Studies*. Edinburgh: Oliver & Boyd, 1966.
Odell, M. S. 1992. The Inversion of Shame and Forgiveness in Ezekiel 16.59–63. *JSOT* 56:101–12.
———. The City of Hamonah in Ezekiel 39:11–16: The Tumultuous City of Jerusalem. *CBQ* 56:479–89.
———. 1998a. You Are What You Eat: Ezekiel and the Scroll. *JBL* 117:229–48.
———. 1998b. The Particle and the Prophet: Observations on Ez. ii. 6. *VT* 48:425–31.
———. 1998c. Genre and Persona in Ezekiel 24:15–24. Pages 626–48 in *Society of Biblical Literature 1998 Seminar Papers*. Atlanta: Scholars Press.
———. 2000. Genre and Persona in Ezekiel 24:15–24. Pages 195–219 in Odell and Strong 2000.
———. 2003. Ezekiel Saw What He Said He Saw: Genres, Forms, and the Vision of Ezekiel 1. Pages 162–76 in *The Changing Face of Form Criticism for the Twenty-First Century*. Edited by M. A. Sweeney and E. Ben Zvi. Grand Rapids: Eerdmans.
———. 2004. What Was the Image of Jealousy in Ezekiel 8? In Grabbe and Ogden Bellis 2004, 134–48.
———. 2009. Creeping Things and Singing Stones: The Iconography of Ezekiel 8:7-13 in Light of Syro-Palestinian Seals and *The Songs of the Sabbath Sacrifice*. In *Prophecy and Iconography in the Ancient Eastern Mediterranean*. Edited by M. Nissinen and C. A. Carter. Mundus Orientis 1. Göttingen: Vandenhoeck & Ruprecht.
Ogden, G. S. 1992. Idem Per Idem: Its Use and Meaning. *JSOT* 53:107–20.
Olley, J. 2002. Paragraphing in the Greek text of Ezekiel in P967: With Particular Reference to the Cologne Portion. Pages 202–25 in *Studies in Scriptural Unit Division*. Edited by M. C. A. Korpel and J. M. Oesch. Pericope 3. Assen: Van Gorcum.
———. 2003. Trajectories in Paragraphing of the Book of Ezekiel. Pages 204–31 in *Unit Delimitation in Biblical Hebrew and Northwest Semitic Literature*. Edited by M. C. A. Korpel and J. M. Oesch. Pericope 4. Assen: Van Gorcum.
———. 2004. Divine Name and Paragraphing in Ezekiel: Highlighting Divine Speech in an Expanding Tradition. *Bulletin of the International Organization for Septuagint and Cognate Studies* 37:87–105.
———. 2009. Ezekiel LXX and Exodus Comparisons. *VT* 59:116–22.
Olyan, S. M. 2003. "We Are Utterly Cut Off": Some Possible Nuances of *nigzarnû lānû* in Ezek 37:11. *CBQ* 65:43–51
Parunak, H. Van Dyke. 1980. The Literary Architecture of Ezekiel's *marʾōṯ ʾĕlōhîm*. *JBL* 99:61–74.
Patmore, H. M. 2007. The Shorter and Longer Texts of Ezekiel: The Implications of the Manuscript Finds from Masada and Qumran. *JSOT* 32:231–42.
———. 2008. Did the Masoretes Get it Wrong? The Vocalization and Accentuation of Ezekiel 28:12–19. *VT* 58:245–57.
Patton, C. L. 1996. "I Myself Gave them Laws that Were Not Good": Ezekiel 20 and the Exodus Traditions. *JSOT* 69:73–90.
———. 1998a. Hugh and Andrew of St Victor. Pages 106–12 in McKim 1998.

———. 1998b. Nicholas of Lyra. Pages 116–22 in McKim 1998.

———. 1999. Pan-Deuteronomism and the Book of Ezekiel. Pages 201–21 in *Those Elusive Deuteronomists: The Phenomenon of Pan-Deuteronomism*. Edited by L. S. Schearing and S. L. McKenzie. JSOTSup 268. Sheffield: Sheffield Academic Press.

———. 2000a. "Should Our Sister be Treated Like a Whore?" A Response to Feminist Critiques of Ezekiel 23. Pages 221–38 in Odell and Strong 2000.

———. 2000b. Priest, Prophet and Exile: Ezekiel as a Literary Construct. Pages 700–27 in *Society of Biblical Literature 2000 Seminar Papers*. Atlanta: SBL.

———. 2004. Priest, Prophet, and Exile: Ezekiel as a Literary Construct. Pages 73–89 in Cook and Patton 2004.

Petersen, D. L. 1999. Creation in Ezekiel: Methodological Perspectives and Theological Prospects. Pages 490–500 in *Society of Biblical Literature 1999 Seminar Papers*. Atlanta: SBL.

———. 2004. Creation and Hierarchy in Ezekiel: Methodological Perspectives and Theological Prospects. Pages 169–78 in Cook and Patton 2004.

Phillips, A. 1982. Double for All Her Sins. *ZAW* 94:130–32.

Philonenko, M. 1994. De Qoumran à Doura-Europos: La vision des ossements desseches (Ezechiel 37, 1–4). *Revue d'Histoire et de Philosophie Religieuses* 74:1–12.

Phinney, D. N. 2009. Portraying Prophetic Experience and Tradition in Ezekiel. In Ahn and Cook 2009.

Pilch, J. J. 2005. Ezekiel: An Altered State of Consciousness Experience. The Call of Ezekiel: Ezekiel 1–3. Pages 208–22 in *Ancient Israel: The Old Testament in Its Social Context*. Edited by P. F. Esler. London: SCM.

Pohlmann, K.-F. 1989. Zur Frage nach den ältesten Texten im Ezechielbuch–Erwägungen zu Ez 17, 19 und 31. Pages 150–72 in *Prophet und Prophetenbuch, Festschrift für Otto Kaiser zum 65. Geburtstag*. Edited by V. Fritz, K.-F. Pohlmann and H.-C. Schmitt. BZAW 185. Berlin: de Gruyter.

———. 2006. Forschung am Ezechielbuch 1969–2004. *ThR* 71:60–90, 164–91, 265–309.

Polan, G. J. 1999. Ezekiel's Covenant of Peace. *TBT* 37:18–23.

Pons, J. 1986. Le vocabulaire d'Ezéchiel 20. Le prophète s'oppose à la vision deutéronomiste de l'histoire. Pages 214–33 in Lust 1986d.

———. 1991. Ezéchiel a-t-il été un prophète intercesseur? *ETR* 66:17–21.

Pope, M. H. 1995. Mixed Marriage Metaphor in Ezekiel 16. Pages 384–99 in *Fortunate the Eyes That See: Essays in Honor of David Noel Freedman in Celebration of His Seventieth Birthday*. Edited by A. B. Beck, et al. Grand Rapids: Eerdmans.

Porter, J. R. 1965. The Legal Aspects of the Concept of "Corporate Personality" in the Old Testament. *VT* 15:361–80.

———. 1997. Ezekiel xxx 16: A Suggestion. *VT* 47:128.

Propp, W. H. 1990. The Meaning of *Tapel* in Ezekiel. *ZAW* 102:404–8.

Puech, É. 1994. L'image de l'arbre en 4Q Deutéro-Ezéchiel (4Q385 2,9–10). *RevQ* 16:429–40.

Rabenau, K. von. 1955–56. Die Entstehung des Buches Ezechiel in formgeschichtlicher Sicht. *Wissenschaftliche Zeitschrift* 5:659–94.

———. 1961. Das prophetische Zukunftswort im Buch Hesekiel. Pages 61–80 in *Studien zur Theologie der alttestamentlichen Überlieferungen. Festschrift Gerhard von Rad*. Edited by R. Rendtorff and K. Koch. Neukirchen–Vluyn: Neukirchener.

Rad, G. von. 1950. "Gerechtigkeit" und "Leben" in der Kultsprache der Psalmen. Pages 418–37 in *Festschrift für Alfred Bertholet*. Edited by W. Baumgartner and O. Eissfeldt. Tübingen: Mohr. Eng. trans. "Righteousness" and "Life" in the Cultic Language of the Psalms. Pages 243–66 in *The Problem of the Hexateuch and Other Essays*. Edinburgh: Oliver & Boyd, 1966.

Raitt, T. M. 1971. The Prophetic Summons to Repentance. *ZAW* 83:30–49.

Raurell, F. 1986. The Polemical Role of the ΑΡΧΟΝΤΕΣ and ΑΦΗΓΟΥΜΕΝΟΙ in Ez LXX. Pages 85–89 in Lust 1986d.

Renaud, B. 1986, L'alliance éternelle d'Ez 16,59–63 et l'alliance nouvelle de Jér 31,31–34. Pages 335–39 in Lust 1986d.

Rendtorff, R. 1986. Ez 20 und 36,16ff im Rahmen der Komposition des Buches Ezechiel. Pages 260–65 in Lust 1986d. Eng. trans. "Ezekiel 20 and 36.16ff. in the Framework of the Composition of the Book." Pages 190–95 in *Canon and Theology*. OBT. Minneapolis: Fortress 1993.

Renz, T. 1999b. The Use of the Zion Tradition in the Book of Ezekiel. Pages 77–103 in *Zion: City of Our God*. Edited by R. S. Hess and G. J. Wenham. Grand Rapids: Eerdmans.

———. 2008. Ezekiel. Pages 226–35 in *Theological Interpretation of the Old Testament: A Book-by-Book Survey*. Edited by Kevin J. Vanhoozer. London: SPCK; Grand Rapids, Mich.: Baker.

Reventlow, H. G. 1959. Die Völker als Jahwes Zeugen bei Ezechiel. *ZAW* 71:33–43.

———. 1960. Sein Blut komme über sein Haupt. *VT* 10:311–27.

Robertson, R. G. 1985. Ezekiel the Tragedian. *OTP* 2:803–19.

Robinson, H. W. 1936. The Hebrew Conception of Corporate Personality. Pages 49–62 in Volz, Stummer and Hempel 1936. Reprinted in Robinson 1980.

———. 1937. The Group and the Individual in Israel. In *The Individual in East and West*. Edited by E. R. Hughes. London: Oxford University Press/H. Milford. Reprinted in Robinson 1980.

———. 1980. *Corporate Personality in Ancient Israel*. Philadelphia: Fortress (with an Introduction by G. M. Tucker). Edinburgh: T. & T. Clark, 1981 (with an Introduction by C. S. Rodd).

Rogerson, J. W. 1970. The Hebrew Conception of Corporate Personality: A Re-examination. *JTS* 21:1–16. Reprinted as pages 43–59 in B. Lang, ed. 1985. *Anthropological Approaches to the Old Testament*. Philadelphia: Fortress. London: SPCK.

Rom-Shiloni, D. 2005a. Facing Destruction and Exile: Inner-Biblical Exegesis in Jeremiah and Ezekiel. *ZAW* 117:189–205.

———. 2005b. Ezekiel as the Voice of the Exiles and Constructor of Exilic Ideology. *HUCA* 76:1–45.

———. 2008. Deuteronomic Concepts of Exile Interpreted in Jeremiah and Ezekiel. Pages 101–23 in *Birkat Shalom: Studies in the Bible, Ancient Near Eastern Literature, and Postbiblical Judaism Presented to Shalom M. Paul on the Occasion of his Seventieth Birthday*. 2 vols. Edited by C. Cohen et al. Winona Lake, Ind.: Eisenbrauns.

Rooker, M. F. 1990b. Ezekiel and the Typology of Biblical Hebrew. *HAR* 12:133–55.

———. 1998. The Use of the Old Testament in the Book of Ezekiel. *Faith and Mission* 15, no. 2:45–52.

Rosenberg, J. 1987. Jeremiah and Ezekiel. Pages 184–206 in *The Literary Guide to the Bible*. Edited by R. Alter and F. Kermode. London: Collins.

Roux, J. H. Le. 1987. The Book of Ezekiel. Pages 176–96 in *Dialogue With God: Preachers, Poets and Philosophers*. Edited by J. J. Burden and W. S. Prinsloo. The Literature of the Old Testament 3. Cape Town: Tafelberg.

Rowley, H. H. 1953. The Book of Ezekiel in Modern Study. *BJRL* 36:146–90.

Runions, E. 2001. Violence and the Economy of Desire in Ezekiel 16.1–45. Pages 156–69 in Brenner 2001.

Saggs, H. W. F. 1960. The Branch to the Nose. *JTS* NS 11:318–29.

Sakenfeld, K. D. 1978. Ezekiel 18:25–32. *Interpretation* 32:295–300.

Sanderson, J. E. 1997. "4QEzek[a]," "4QEzek[b]," "4QEzek[c]." Principal Edition. Pages 209–20 and Plates xxxviii–xxxix in *Qumran Cave 4: X*. DJD 15. Oxford: Clarendon.

Schaper, J. 2004. Rereading the Law: Inner-Biblical Exegesis of Divine Oracles in Ezekiel 44 and Isaiah 56. Pages 125–44 in *Recht und Ethik im Alten Testament*. Edited by B. M. Levinson and E. Otto. Altes Testament und Moderne 13. Münster: LIT.
Schenker, A. 1981. Saure Trauben ohne stumpfe Zähne. Bedeutung und Tragweite von Ez 18 und 33,10–20 oder ein Kapitel alttestamentlicher Moraltheologie. Pages 449–70 in *Mélanges Dominique Barthélemy*. Edited by P. Casetti, O. Keel and A. Schenker. OBO 38. Fribourg, Suisse: Editions Universitaires. Göttingen: Vandenhoeck & Ruprecht.
Schmitt, J. J. 2004. Psychoanalyzing Ezekiel. Pages 185–201 in Ellens and Rollins 2004.
Schnocks, J. 1996. Eine intertextuelle Verbindung zwischen Ezechiels Eifersuchtsbild und Sacharjas Frau in Efa. *BN* 84:59–63.
———. 2009b. “Und ich werde meinen Geist in euch geben” (Ez 37,14): Konzeptionen der Rede vom Geist in Ez 36–37. *Jahrbuch für Biblische Theologie* 24.
Schöpflin, K. 2006. The Destructive and Creative Word of the Prophet in the Book of Ezekiel. Pages 113–18 in Niemann and Augustin 2006.
Schoneveld, J. 1969. Ezekiel 14.1–8. *OTS* 15:193–204.
Schüngel-Straumann, H. 1996. *Rûaḥ* und Gender-Frage am Beispiel der Visionen beim Propheten Ezechiel. Pages 201–16 in Becking and Dijkstra 1996.
Schussman, A. 1998. The Prophet Ezekiel in Islamic Literature: Jewish Traces and Islamic Adaptations. Pages 316–39 in Stone and Bergren 1998.
Schwartz, B. J. 1994. Repentance and Determinism in Ezekiel. Pages 123–30 in *Proceedings of the Eleventh World Congress of Jewish Studies: The Bible and Its World*. Jerusalem: World Union of Jewish Studies.
———. 2000. Ezekiel’s Dim View of Israel’s Restoration. Pages 43–67 in Odell and Strong 2000.
———. 2004. A Priest Out of Place: Reconsidering Ezekiel’s Role in the History of the Israelite Priesthood. Pages 61–71 in Cook and Patton 2004.
Segert, S. 1958. Bis in das dritte und vierte Glied. *Communio Viatorum* 1:37–39.
Seidel, B. 1995. Ezechiel und die zu vermutenden Anfänge der Schriftreligion im Umkreis der unmittelbaren Vorexilszeit. Oder: Die Bitternis der Schriftrolle. *ZAW* 107:51–64.
Seitz, C. R. 1992. Ezekiel 37:1–14. *Interpretation* 46:53–56.
Setel, D. T. 1985. Prophets and Pornography: Female Sexual Imagery in Hosea. Pages 86–95 in *Feminist Interpretation of the Bible*. Edited by L. Russell. Philadelphia: Westminster.
Sharon, D. M. 1996. A Biblical Parallel to a Sumerian Temple Hymn? Ezekiel 40–48 and Gudea. *JANESCU* 24:99–109.
Sherlock, C. 1983. Ezekiel’s Dumbness. *ET* 94:296–98.
Shields, M. E. 1998a. Multiple Exposures: Body Rhetoric and Gender Characterization in Ezekiel 16. *Journal of Feminist Studies in Religion* 14:5–18. Reprinted as pages 137–53 in Brenner 2001.
———. 1998b. Gender and Violence in Ezekiel 23. Pages 86–105 in *Society of Biblical Literature 1998 Seminar Papers*. Atlanta: Scholars Press.
———. 2001a. An Abusive God? Identity and Power, Gender and Violence in Ezekiel 23. Pages 129–51 in *Postmodern Interpretations of the Bible: A Reader*. Edited by A. K. M. Adam. St. Louis: Chalice.
———. 2001b. Self-Response to “Multiple Exposures.” In Brenner 2001, 154–55.
Simian-Yofre, H. 1982. Wächter, Lehrer oder Interpret? Zum theologischen Hintergrund von Ez 33,7–9. Pages 151–62 in Ruppert, Weimar and Zenger 1982.
———. 1984. Ez 17,1–10 como enigma y parabola. *Bib* 65:27–43.
———. 1986. La métaphore d’Ézéchiel 15. Pages 234–47 in Lust 1986d.
Sinclair, L. A. 1989. A Qumran Biblical Fragment: 4QEzek[a] (Ezek. 10:17–11:11). *RevQ* 14:99–105.
Ska, J. L. 1979. La sortie d’Egypte (Ex 7–14) dans le récit sacerdotal (Pg) et la tradition prophétique. *Bib* 60:191–215.

Skehan, P. W. 1980. The Divine Name at Qumran, in the Masada Scroll, and in the Septuagint. *Bulletin of the International Society for Septuagint and Cognate Studies* 13:14–49.
Sloan, I. B. 1992. Ezekiel and the Covenant of Friendship. *BTB* 22:149–54.
Smith, M. S. 1998. The Heart and Innards in Israelite Emotional Expressions: Notes from Anthropology and Psychobiology. *JBL* 117:427–36.
Smith, Morton. 1975. The Veracity of Ezekiel, the Sins of Manasseh, and Jeremiah 44.18. *ZAW* 87:11–16.
Smith-Christopher, D. L. 1997. Reassessing the Historical and Sociological Impact of the Babylonian Exile (597/587–539 BCE). Pages 7–36 in Scott 1997.
———. 1999. Ezekiel on Fanon's Couch: A Postcolonial Dialogue with David Halperin's *Seeking Ezekiel*. Pages 108–44 in *Peace and Justice Shall Embrace: Power and Theopolitics in the Bible; Essays in Honor of Millard Lind*. Edited by T. Grimsrud and L. L. Johns. Telford, Pa.: Pandora.
———. 2004. Ezekiel in Abu Ghraib: Rereading Ezekiel 16:37–39 in the Context of Imperial Conquest. Pages 141–57 in Cook and Patton 2004.
Speiser, E. A. 1963. Background and Function of the Biblical *nāśîʾ*. *CBQ* 25:111–17.
Spiegel, S. 1931. Ezekiel or Pseudo-Ezekiel? *HTR* 24:245–321. Reprinted as pages 123–99 in Torrey et al. 1970.
———. 1945. Noah, Daniel and Job: Touching on Canaanite Relics in the Legends of the Jews. Pages 305–55 in *Louis Ginzberg Jubilee Volume*. New York: The American Academy for Jewish Research.
Spottorno, M. V. 1982. La Omisión de Ez. 36, 23b–38 y la transposición de capítulos en el papiro 967. *Emerita* 50:93–98.
———. 1986. Some Lexical Aspects in the Greek Text of Ezekiel. Pages 78–84 in Lust 1986d.
Sprinkle, P. 2007. Law and Life: Leviticus 18.5 in the Literary Framework of Ezekiel. *JSOT* 31:275–93.
Stevenson, K. R. 2001. If Earth Could Speak: The Case of the Mountains Against YHWH in Ezekiel 6; 35–36. Pages 158–71 in Habel 2001.
Stiebert, J. 2000. Shame and Prophecy: Approaches Past and Present. *BibInt* 8:255–75.
———. 2002b. Riches in Isaiah and Ezekiel: An Example of Prophetic Inversion. Pages 33–40 in *The Many Voices of the Bible*, *Concilium* 2002/1. Edited by S. Freyne and E. Van Wolde. London: SCM.
Stone, M. E. 2007. The City in 4 Ezra. *JBL* 126:402–7.
Stromberg, J. 2008. Observations on Inner-Scriptural Scribal Expansion in MT Ezekiel. *VT* 58:68–86.
Strong, J. T. 1995. Ezekiel's Use of the Recognition Formula in His Oracles Against the Nations. *Perspectives in Religious Studies* 22:115–33.
———. 1997. Tyre's Isolationist Policies in the Early Sixth Century BCE: Evidence from the Prophets. *VT* 47:207–19.
———. 2000. God's *Kāḇôḏ*: The Presence of Yahweh in the Book of Ezekiel. Pages 69–95 in Odell and Strong 2000.
Stroete, G. A. te. 1977. Ezekiel 24:15–27: The Meaning of a Symbolic Act. *Bijdragen: Tijdschrift voor Filosofie en Theologie* 38:163–75.
Strugnell, J., and D. Dimant. 1988. 4Q Second Ezekiel. *RevQ* 13:45–58.
Sulzbach, C. 2006. Nebuchadnezzar in Eden? Daniel 4 and Ezekiel 28. Pages 125–36 in Niemann and Augustin 2006.
Swanepoel, M. G. 1993. Ezekiel 16: Abandoned Child, Bride Adorned or Unfaithful Wife? In Davies and Clines 1993, 84–104.
Sweeney, M. A. 2000. Ezekiel: Zadokite Priest and Visionary Prophet of the Exile. Pages 728–51 in *Society of Biblical Literature 2000 Seminar Papers*. Atlanta: SBL.

———. 2003. The Priesthood and the Proto-Apocalyptic Reading of Prophetic and Pentateuchal Texts. Pages 167–78 in Grabbe and Haak 2003. Reprinted as pages 239–47 in Sweeney 2005a.

———. 2005c. The Destruction of Jerusalem as Purification in Ezekiel 8–11. Pages 144–55 in Sweeney 2005a.

———. 2005d. The Assertion of Divine Power in Ezekiel 33:21–39:29. Pages 156–72 in Sweeney 2005a.

———. 2006. The Royal Oracle in Ezekiel 37:15–28: Ezekiel's Reflection on Josiah's Reform. Pages 239–53 in Kelle and Moore 2006.

———. 2009. Ezekiel's Debate with Isaiah. In *IOSOT Congress Volume, Ljubljana 2007*. VTSup. Edited by A. Lemaire. Leiden: Brill.

Talmon, S. 1997. Fragments of an Ezekiel Scroll from Masada 1043–2220 (Ezekiel 35:11–38:14). Pages 53–69 in Cogan, Eichler, and Tigay 1997. [In Hebrew.]

———. 1999. Mas 1043–2220 (MasEzek) (Ezek. 35:11–38:14), Principal Edition. Pages 59–75 and Plate viii in *Masada VI: The Yigael Yadin Excavations 1963–1965, Final Reports*. Jerusalem: Israel Exploration Society/The Hebrew University of Jerusalem.

Talmon, S., and M. Fishbane. 1975–76. The Structuring of Biblical Books. Studies in the Book of Ezekiel. *ASTI* 10:129–53.

Tanner, P. J. 1996. Rethinking Ezekiel's Invasion by Gog. *JETS* 39:29–46.

Tarlin, W. T. 1997. Utopia and Pornography in Ezekiel. Pages 175–83 in *Reading Bibles, Writing Bodies: Identity and the Book*. Edited by B. Gunn. London: Routledge.

Thackeray, H. St. J. 1903. The Greek Translators of Ezekiel. *JTS* 4:398–411.

Thiel, W. 1969. Erwägungen zum Alter des Heiligkeitsgesetzes. *ZAW* 81:40–73.

Thomasson, J. de. 1992. Actes-Signes ou Actes Magiques?—Ez 2–5 et *šurpu*. *BN* 64:18–25.

Tiemeyer, L.-S. 2006a. God's Hidden Compassion. *Tyndale Bulletin* 57:239–61.

———. 2006b. The Question of Indirect Touch: Lam 4,14; Ezek 44,19 and Hag 2,12-13. *Bib* 87:64–74.

———. Forthcoming. Ezekiel—A Compromised Prophet in Reduced Circumstances. In *Constructs of Prophecy*. Edited by L. L. Grabbe and M. Nissinen. Atlanta, Ga.: SBL.

Tooman, W. A. 2009. Ezekiel's Radical Challenge to Inviolability. *ZAW* 121.

Tov, E. 1982. A Modern Textual Outlook Based on the Qumran Scrolls. *HUCA* 53:11–27.

———. 1986. Recensional Differences Between the MT and LXX of Ezekiel. *ETL* 62:89–101. Reprinted as pages 397–410 of *The Greek & Hebrew Bible: Collected Essays on the Septuagint*. VTSup 72. Leiden: Brill, 1999.

Tromp, N. J. The Paradox of Ezekiel's Prophetic Mission. Towards a Semiotic Approach to Ezekiel 3, 22–27. Pages 201–13 in Lust 1986d.

Tsevat, M. 1959, The Neo-Assyrian and Neo-Babylonian Vassal Oaths and the Prophet Ezekiel. *JBL* 78:199–204.

Tucker, G. M. 1966. Witnesses and Dates in Israelite Contracts. *CBQ* 28:42–45.

Tuell, S. S. 1982. The Temple Vision of Ezekiel 40–48: A Program for Restoration? *Proceedings of the Eastern Great Lakes Biblical Society* 2:96–103.

———. 1996. Ezekiel 40–42 as a Verbal Icon. *CBQ* 58:649–64.

———. 2000a. Divine Presence and Absence in Ezekiel's Prophecy. Pages 97–116 in Odell and Strong 2000.

———. 2000b. The Rivers of Paradise: Ezekiel 47.1–12 and Gen 2.10–14. Pages 171–89 in *God Who Creates: Essays in Honor of W. Sibley Towner*. Edited by W. P. Brown and S. Dean McBride Jr. Grand Rapids: Eerdmans.

———. 2000c. Haggai–Zechariah: Prophecy After the Manner of Ezekiel. Pages 263–86 in *Society of Biblical Literature 2000 Seminar Papers*. Atlanta: SBL. Reprinted as pages 273–91 in *Thematic Threads in the Book of the Twelve*. Edited by P. L. Redditt and A. Schart. BZAW 325. Berlin: de Gruyter, 2003.

———. 2004. Contemporary Studies of Ezekiel: A New Tide Rising. Pages 241–54 in Cook and Patton 2004.

———. 2005. The Priesthood of the "Foreigner": Evidence of Competing Polities in Ezekiel 44:1–14 and Isaiah 56:1–8. Pages 183–204 in *Constituting the Community: Studies on the Polity of Ancient Israel in Honor of S. Dean McBride Jr.* Edited by J. T. Strong and S. S. Tuell. Winona Lake, Ind.: Eisenbrauns.

Turner, N. 1956. The Greek Translators of Ezekiel. *JTS* NS 7:12–24.

Turner, P. D. M. 2001. The Translator(s) of Ezekiel Revisited: Idiosyncratic LXX Renderings as a Clue to Inner History. Pages 279–307 in *Helsinki Perspectives on the Translation Technique of the Septuagint*. Edited by R. Sollamo and S. Sipilä. The Finnish Exegetical Society in Helsinki. Göttingen: Vandenhoeck & Ruprecht.

Uffenheimer, B. 1992. Theodicy and Ethics in the Prophecy of Ezekiel. Pages 200–27 in Reventlow and Hoffman 1992.

Van Dijk-Hemmes, F. 1993. The Metaphorization of Woman in Prophetic Speech: An Analysis of Ezekiel xxiii. *VT* 43:162–70. Also in A. Brenner and F. Van Dijk-Hemmes, eds. *On Gendering Texts: Female and Male Voices in the Hebrew Bible* Biblical Interpretation Series 1. Leiden, 1993, 168–76; and reprinted in A. Brenner, ed. *A Feminist Companion to the Latter Prophets*. The Feminist Companion to the Bible 8. Sheffield: Sheffield Academic Press, 1995, 244–55.

Van Grol, H. W. M. 1998. Exegesis of the Exile: Exegesis of Scripture? Ezra 9.6–9. Pages 31–61 in *Intertextuality in Ugarit and in Israel*. Edited by J. C. de Moor. OtSt 40. Leiden: Brill.

Vanhoye, A. 1962. L'utilisation du Livre d'Ézéchiel dans l'Apocalypse. *Bib* 43:436–76.

Van Seters, J. 1999. In the Babylonian Exile with J: Between Judgment in Ezekiel and Salvation in Second Isaiah. Pages 71–89 in Becking and Korpel 1999.

Verdam, P. J. 1949. "On ne fera point mourir les enfants pour les pères" en droit biblique. *Revue Internationale des Droits de l'Antiquité* 3:393–416.

Verdegaal, C. M. L. 1986. The Jewish Influence on the Ezekiel Translation of the English and Dutch Authorized Versions. Pages 111–19 in Lust 1986d.

Vogels, W. 1972. Restauration de l'Égypte et universalisme en Ez 29:13–16. *Bib* 53:473–94.

Vogt, E. 1959. Textumdeutungen im Buch Ezechiel. *Sacra Pagina* 1:471–94.

———. 1970. Die Lähmung und Stummheit des Propheten Ezechiel. Pages 87–100 in *Wort–Gebot–Glaube: Beiträge zur Theologie des Alten Testaments. Walther Eichrodt zum 80. Geburtstag*. Edited by H. J. Stoebe, J. J. Stamm and E. Jenni. ATANT 59. Zurich: Zwingli.

Vries, S. de. 1962. Remembrance in Ezekiel: A Study of an Old Testament Theme. *Interpretation* 16:58–64.

Wacholder, B. Z. 1992. Ezekiel and Ezekielianism as Progenitors of Essenism. Pages 186–96 in *The Dead Sea Scrolls: Forty Years of Research*. Edited by D. Dimant and U. Rappaport. Jerusalem: Magnes. Leiden: Brill.

Wagenaar, J. A. 2005b. The Priestly Festival Calendar and the Babylonian New Year Festivals: Origin and Transformation of the Ancient Israelite Festival Year. Pages 218–52 in *The Old Testament in Its World: Papers Read at the Winter Meeting, January 2003, The Society for Old Testament Study and at the Joint Meeting, July 2003, The Society for Old Testament Study and Het Oudtestamentisch Werkgezelschap in Nederland en België*. Edited by R. P. Gordon and J. C. de Moor. OtSt 52. Leiden: Brill.

Wahl, H.-M. 1992. Noah, Daniel und Hiob in Ezechiel xiv 12–20 (21–3): Anmerkungen zum traditionsgeschichtlichen Hintergrund. *VT* 42:542–53.

———. 1999. "Tod und Leben": Zur Wiederherstellung Israels nach Ez. xxxvii 1–14. *VT* 49:218–39.

Waldman, N. W. 1984. A Note on Ezekiel 1.18. *JBL* 103:614–18.

Weinfeld, M. 1972. The Worship of Molech and the Queen of Heaven and Its Background. *UF* 4:133–54.
———. 1977. Ancient Near Eastern Patterns in Prophetic Literature. *VT* 27:178–95.
———. 1992. Justice and Righteousness: The Expression and Its Meaning. Pages 228–46 in Reventlow and Hoffman 1992.
Whitley, C. F. 1959. The "Thirtieth" Year in Ezekiel 1:1. *VT* 9:326–30.
Wiesel, E. 1987. Ezekiel. Pages 167–86 in *Congregation: Contemporary Writers Read the Jewish Bible*. Edited by D. Rosenberg. San Diego, Calif.: Harcourt Brace Jovanovich.
Williams, A. J. 1976. The Mythological Background of Ezekiel 28:12–19? *BTB* 6:49–61.
Williamson, H. G. M. 2001. Isaiah and the Holy One of Israel. Pages 22–38 in *Biblical Hebrew, Biblical Texts: Essays in Memory of Michael P. Weitzman*. Edited by A. Rapoport-Albert and G. Greenberg. JSOTSup 333. Sheffield: Sheffield Academic Press.
Willmes, B. 1986. Differenzierende Prophezeiungen in Ez 34. Pages 248–54 in Lust 1986d.
Wilson, R. R. 1972. An Interpretation of Ezekiel's Dumbness. *VT* 22:91–104.
———. 1984. Prophecy in Crisis: The Call of Ezekiel. *Interpretation* 38:117–30. Reprinted as pages 157–69 in Mays and Achtemeier 1987.
———. 1987. The Death of the King of Tyre: The Editorial History of Ezekiel 28. Pages 211–18 in Marks and Good 1987.
———. 1998. The Prophetic Books. Pages 212–25 in *The Cambridge Companion to Biblical Interpretation*. Edited by J. Barton. Cambridge: Cambridge University Press.
Winton Thomas, D. 1961. The Sixth Century B.C.: A Creative Epoch in the History of Israel. *JSS* 6:33–46.
Wiseman, D. J. 1991. Babylonia 605–539 BC. Pages 229–51 in Boardman et al. 1991.
Witherup, R. D. 1999. Apocalyptic Imagery in the Book of Ezekiel. *TBT* 37:10–17.
Wolff, H. W. 1934. Die Begründungen der prophetischen Heils- und Unheilssprüche. *ZAW* 52:1–22. Reprinted as pages 9–35 in Wolff 1964.
———. 1951. Das Thema "Umkehr" in der alttestamentlichen Prophetie. *ZThK* 48:129–48. Reprinted as pages 130–50 of Wolff 1964.
———. 1978. Prophecy from the Eighth through the Fifth Century. *Interpretation* 32:17–30.
Wong, K. L. 2001b. A Note on Ezekiel viii 6. *VT* 51:396–400.
———. 2003. Profanation/Sanctification and the Past, Present and Future of Israel in the Book of Ezekiel. *JSOT* 28:210–39.
Wright, B. G. 1998. Talking with God and Losing His Head: Extrabiblical Traditions About the Prophet Ezekiel. Pages 290–315 in Stone and Bergren 1998.
Wright, J. E. 1997. Hebrews 11:37 and the Death of the Prophet Ezekiel. Pages 147–58 in *The Echoes of Many Texts: Reflections on Jewish and Christian Traditions: Essays in Honor of Lou H. Silberman*. Edited by W. G. Dever and J. E. Wright. Atlanta: Scholars Press.
Yaron, K. 1964. The Dirge Over the King of Tyre. *ASTI* 3:28–57.
York, A. D. 1977. Ezekiel 1: Inaugural and Restoration Visions? *VT* 27:82–98.
Ziegler, J. 1945–48. Die Bedeutung des Chester Beatty-Scheide Papyrus 967 für die Textüberlieferung des Ezechiel-Septuaginta. *ZAW* 61:76–94. Reprinted as pages 321–39 in Ziegler 1971.
———. 1953. Zur Textgestaltung der Ezechiel-Septuaginta. *Bib* 34:435–455. Reprinted as pages 394–414 in Ziegler 1971.
Zimmerli, W. 1951. Das Gotteswort des Ezechiel. *ZTK* 48:249–62. Reprinted as pages 133–47 in Zimmerli 1963b. Eng. trans. The Word of God in the Book of Ezekiel. *Journal for Theology and the Church* 4 (1967):1–13. Reprinted as pages 96–106 in Zimmerli 2003.
———. 1953. Ich bin Yahweh. Pages 179–209 in *Geschichte und Altes Testament: A. Alt zum 70. Geburtstag dargebracht*. Edited by W. F. Albright. Beiträge zur historischen Theologie 16. Tübingen: J. C. B. Mohr (Paul Siebeck). Reprinted as pages 11–40 of Zimmerli 1963b. Eng. trans. I Am Yahweh. Pages 1–28 in Zimmerli 1982a.

———. 1954b. Die Eigenart der prophetischen Rede des Ezechiel. Ein Beitrag zum Problem an Hand von Ez. 14:1–11. *ZAW* 66:1–26. Reprinted as pages 148–77 in Zimmerli 1963b.

———. 1957a. Das Wort des göttlichen Selbsterweises (Erweiswort), eine prophetische Gattung. Pages 154–64 in *Mélanges Bibliques rédigés en l'honneur de André Robert*. Travaux de l'Institut Catholique de Paris 4. Paris: Bloud et Gay. Reprinted as pages 120–32 in Zimmerli 1963b. Eng. trans. The Word of Divine Self-Manifestation (Proof-Saying): A Prophetic Genre. Pages 99–110 of Zimmerli 1982a.

———. 1957b. "Leben" und "Tod" im Buche des Propheten Ezechiel. *ThZ* 13:494–508. Reprinted as pages 178–91 in Zimmerli 1963b.

———. 1958. Israel im Buche Ezechiel. *VT* 8:75–90.

———. 1960. Le nouvel "Exode" dans le message des deux grands prophètes de l'exil. Pages 216–27 in *Maqqél shâqédh: Hommage à Wilhelm Vischer*. Montpellier: Causse, Graille & Castelnau. German version in Zimmerli 1963b, 192–204.

———. 1963a. Der Wahrheitserweis Jahwes nach der Botschaft der beiden Exilspropheten. Pages 133–51 in Würthwein and Kaiser 1963. Reprinted as pages 192–212 in Zimmerli 1974b.

———. 1965. The Special Form- and Traditio-Historical Character of Ezekiel's Prophecy. *VT* 15:515–27. Reprinted as pages 11–23 in D. E. Orton, ed. *Prophecy in the Hebrew Bible*. Leiden: Brill, 2000. Reprinted as Form and Tradition in the Book of Ezekiel. Pages 107–17 in Zimmerli 2003.

———. 1967. Ezechieltempel und Salomostadt. Pages 389–414 in *Hebräische Wortforschung: Festschrift zum 80. Geburtstag von Walter Baumgartner*. VTSup 16. Leiden: Brill. Reprinted as pages 148–64 in Zimmerli 1974b.

———. 1968. Planungen für den Wiederaufbau nach der Katastrophe von 587. *VT* 18:229–55. Reprinted as pages 165–91 in Zimmerli 1974b. Eng. trans. Plans for Rebuilding After the Catastrophe of 587. Pages 111–33 in Zimmerli 1982a.

———. 1969b. The Message of the Prophet Ezekiel. *Interpretation* 23:131–57. Reprinted as pages 75–95 in Zimmerli 2003. = Die Botschaft des Propheten Ezechiel. Pages 104–34 in Zimmerli 1974b.

———. 1972b. Deutero-Ezechiel? *ZAW* 84:501–16.

———. 1974a. Das verhüllte Gesicht des Propheten Ezechiel. Pages 135–47 in Zimmerli 1974b.

———. 1979b. Vom Prophetenwort zum Prophetenbuch. *ThLZ* 104:cols 481–96. Eng. trans. From Prophetic Word to Prophetic Book. Reprinted as pages 419–42 in Gordon 1995. Reprinted as pages 22–42 in Zimmerli 2003.

———. 1980. Das Phänomen der "Fortschreibung" im Buche Ezechiel. Pages 174–91 in *Prophecy: Essays Presented to G. Fohrer*. Edited by J. A. Emerton. BZAW 150. Berlin: de Gruyter.

———. 1982b. Ezechiel/Ezechielbuch. *TRE* 10:766–81.

Zipor, M. A. 1991. Ezechiel 16.7. *ZAW* 103:99–100.

Zyl, A. H. van. 1961. Solidarity and Individualism in Ezekiel. *Ou-Testamentiese Werkgemeenskap van Suid-Afrika* 4:38–52.

Indexes

Index of References

47:7 237
47:8 237
47:9 237
47:10 237
47:11 237
47:12 237
47:13–48:35 234
47:13–23 62, 236, 239
47:13 237, 238
47:14 34, 237, 238
47:15–20 237, 238
47:15 239
47:17 239
47:18 238
47:19 240
47:21–23 232
47:21 238
47:22–23 124, 237, 238
47:23 238
48 234, 237, 238
48:1–29 62
48:1–7 237, 239
48:1 239
48:2–7 239
48:4–5 237, 239
48:7 240
48:8–22 239, 240
48:8–20 241
48:8 234, 239
48:10–12 239
48:10 239
48:11 219, 239
48:12 230, 240
48:13 239
48:15–20 240
48:15 239
48:21–22 212, 240
48:21 231
48:23–29 237, 239, 240
48:23 234
48:28 240
48:29 240
48:30–35 62
48:30–34 239, 240
48:35 43, 240

Daniel
1–6 125
4:7–9 Heb. 185
4:10–12 185
4:11 Heb. 186
4:14 186
6:10 114
7 53
7:13 73
8:5 94
8:8 94
8:12 191
8:13 191
8:17 76, 93
8:21 94
9:24 191
10 53
10:5 102
11:15 138
12:1 120
12:2 210
12:4 93

Hosea
1:2–3 167
1:11 210
3:5 214
4:13–14 131
5–6 210
5:4 115
6:6 226
8:4 137
8:9 132
9:8 81
10:1 129
11:1 149
13–14 210

Joel
1:15 94
2–3 53
2:2 214
2:10 187
2:13 115
2:17 100
2:23–24 199
2:28–29 103
2:28 115, 204
2:31 187
3:1 Heb. 115, 204
3:1–2 Heb. 103
3:2 216
3:12 216
3:18 236
4:2 Heb. 216
4:12 Heb. 216
4:18 Heb. 236

Amos
1–2 170–72, 216
2:6–8 172
2:8 132
3:3–8 129
3:12 128
4:1 217
5:18–20 93, 183, 184
5:18 94
5:20 94
5:21–25 226
7:3 189
7:6 189
8:2 93
8:9–10 94
9:7 130
9:13–14 199

Obadiah
12–15 173

Jonah
1:3 176

Micah
1:8 167
4:1–4 138, 154
4:3 216
6:6–8 226
7:11 120

Index of Authors